LINGUISTIC ORGANISATION AND NATIVE TITLE
THE WIK CASE, AUSTRALIA

The image used on the cover of this book shows Noel Peemuggina mapping Kuurn-engkech, a site in his own country (Estate 6, Wik-Ngathan language), with Morrison Wolmby, Kirke River, Cape York Peninsula, October 1977.

At the time Noel said, in Wik-Ngathan:

> The water birds, were here, Burdekin duck [minh kuurn], geese and others too. Those two [Peter Pumpkin Wolmby and Bob Peemuggina] used to hunt them. Whistle ducks, magpie geese, and tea tree and the poison tree [*yuk upen*] were here too. My two elder brothers, sons of those two men, used to go hunting Burdekin duck here.[1]
>
> The day-shade for this place is Thoeker, up on top there, a place for sitting down. They would return from here to [the base camps] Moekeyn and Pulthalpempang. They never spent wet seasons at Thoeker.[2] Only there at Moekeyn and Pulthalpempang [in this area] did they erect [wet season huts]. I also used to come here hunting, from there to Kuurn[-engkech], right back to Moekeyn and as far as Thoeker.[3]
>
> The bushfire meats [e.g. reptiles, mice, small macropods, hunted by organised burns] here belong to us exclusively. Your old grandfathers and fathers left this country [for us].[4]
>
> I have never taken someone else's country, no, only taking my own country – from father to son. Absolutely.[5]

---

1   Not in Sutton (1995a), *minh kuurn* was confirmed by Ron Yunkaporta (13 September 2019, pers. comm.) as the same as Wik-Mungkan *minh koon*, the Burdekin duck or shelduck *Radjah radjah* (Kilham et al. 1986:70; Barry Alpher supplied the updated Latin name, 13 September 2019, pers. comm.). *Engkech* means 'long, extended, tall': PS.
2   This brief account employs a traditional distinction between wet season base camps, day-shades or 'dinner camps', and the resource site in question (Kuurn-engkech). On Wik site use types see further Sutton (2010).
3   Noel grew up in bush bands and had little contact with Aurukun Mission until well into adulthood.
4   This is a reference to Peter Sutton having been taken as a son by Victor Wolmby, who was a son of Peter Pumpkin Wolmby. Sutton thus was a putative grandson to both Pumpkin and his brother Bob.
5   Translated by Peter Sutton.

LINGUISTIC ORGANISATION AND NATIVE TITLE
THE WIK CASE, AUSTRALIA

**PETER SUTTON
AND KEN HALE**

PRESS

ASIA-PACIFIC LINGUISTICS

Published by ANU Press
The Australian National University
Acton ACT 2601, Australia
Email: anupress@anu.edu.au

Available to download for free at press.anu.edu.au

ISBN (print): 9781760464462
ISBN (online): 9781760464479

WorldCat (print): 1257514000
WorldCat (online): 1257518525

DOI: 10.22459/LONT.2021

This title is published under a Creative Commons Attribution-NonCommercial-NoDerivatives 4.0 International (CC BY-NC-ND 4.0).

The full licence terms are available at
creativecommons.org/licenses/by-nc-nd/4.0/legalcode

Cover design and layout by ANU Press

Cover photograph: Noel Peemuggina mapping Kuurn-engkech, a site in his own country (Estate 6, Wik-Ngathan language), with Morrison Wolmby, Kirke River, Cape York Peninsula, 1977. Photograph by Peter Sutton.

This edition © 2021 ANU Press

Contents

List of figures	vii
List of maps	xi
List of tables	xiii
Linguistic conventions	xv
1. Introduction	1
2. Talking language: A tribute to Ken Hale	17
3. Linguistic and territorial organisation: The Wik classical system	25
4. Linguistic demography of the Wik Region	77
5. Languages of the Wik Native Title Claim Area	101
6. Wik Subgroup lexical history	133
7. Wik Subgroup grammatical history	177
8. Conclusion	221
Appendix 1: Wik clans	225
Appendix 2: Wik estates	391
References	463
Indexes	479

List of figures

Figure 6.1: Paman languages, lexical sharing and geographic distribution   146

Figure 6.2: Lexical sharing under fictitious Dyirbalngan intrusion into Middle Paman area   146

Figure A1.1: Victor Wolmby, Apelech ceremony leader, 1972   361

Figure A1.2: Estate 40 site: Malnyinyu (Pera Head), Barracuda and Bluefish Story Place, 1988   362

Figure A1.3: Estate 34 site: Yagalmungkan, red ochre source, 1988   362

Figure A1.4: Estate 34 site: aak penchiy (danger place) behind mangroves, Norman River, 1988   363

Figure A1.5: Estate 1 Thikel-aampeyn base camp and rich resource site, 1985   363

Figure A1.6: Estate 1 site: Waathem, with Cecil Walmbeng, 1985   364

Figure A1.7: Estate 3 Isobel Wolmby mapping site Thooerpenith, 1976   365

Figure A1.8: Estate 3 Johnny Ampeybegan mapping base camp site Wachnyathaw, 1976   365

Figure A1.9: Estate 3 mapping party at Wachnyathaw, 1976   366

Figure A1.10: Estate 3 Fred Chaney at Watha-nhiin (Peret) Outstation 1979   366

Figure A1.11: Estate 4 site: Uthuk Aweyn (Big Milky Way, aka 'Big Lake'), 1976   367

Figure A1.12: Estate 4 Johnny Ampeybegan at his birthplace site Yaal, Big Lake, 1976   367

Figure A1.13: Estate 5 Lomai Woolla at Kencherrang, Brown Snake Story Place, 1985 — 368

Figure A1.14: Estate 5 mapping Kencherrang area, David Martin with Raymond and Lomai Woolla, 1985 — 368

Figure A1.15: Estate 6 site: Aayk swamp, Estuarine Shark Story Place, 1977 — 369

Figure A1.16: Estate 6 site: Kuthenhthang cremation mound, 1977 — 369

Figure A1.17: Estate 6 mapping site: Wiip-aw (across river), shade camp, 1977 — 370

Figure A1.18: Estate 6 Noel Peemuggina at Waathanem-ompenh, wet season base camp, 1977 — 370

Figure A1.19: Estate 6 Silas and Caleb Wolmby digging Aayk well, 1977 — 370

Figure A1.20: Estate 7 site: Mithenthathenh cremation mound, 1977 — 371

Figure A1.21: Estate 11 site: Thew-en (Cape Keerweer), Woven Bag Story Place, 1977 — 371

Figure A1.22: Kirke River area aerial photo used in field mapping; pinpricks are site locations — 372

Figure A1.23: Estate 12 site: Um-thunth (Moving Stone, Story Place), 1977 — 373

Figure A1.24: Annie Kalkeeyorta, Estate and Clan 12, Aurukun, 1987 — 374

Figure A1.25: Mortuary ceremony, Aurukun, 2009 — 375

Figure A1.26: Estate 14 mapping party, Ti Tree area, 1990 — 375

Figure A1.27: Estate 14 Ti Tree Outstation, 1979 — 376

Figure A1.28: Estate 14 Francis Yunkaporta observes as Bob Massey introduces Fred Chaney to spirits at Wanke-nhiyeng (Ti Tree Lagoon), Two Girls and Moon Story Place, 1979 — 376

Figure A1.29: Estate 15 Rupert Gothachalkenin, Thaangkunh-nhiin well, wet season base camp and danger place, 1977 — 377

Figure A1.30: Estate 15 Thaangkunh-nhiin, inner camp site, 1977 — 377

LIST OF FIGURES

Figure A1.31: Estate 20 Mapping Kuu'eneng base camp,
    Knox River area, 1978   378

Figure A1.32: Estate 20 Mangk-puypeng, Dog Story Place,
    Knox River, 1977   379

Figure A1.33: Estate 20 Piithel, wet season base camp,
    with Jack Sleep and others, 1977   379

Figure A1.34: Estate 23 site: Thanmel, all-season base camp with
    cremation and fighting grounds close by, 1977   380

Figure A1.35: Estate 23 mapping site: Weten (Dish Yard),
    all-season base camp, 1977   380

Figure A1.36: Ron Yunkaporta, middle Archer River, 1990   381

Figure A1.37: Estate 49 John Koowarta, Clan 39, Archer River,
    1990   381

Figure A1.38: Inland forest mapping, Kendall River Holding, 1991   382

Figure A1.39: Aerial photo of Kendall River mouth with likely
    hunting fires, 1957   383

Figure A1.40: Estate 21 Sydney Wolmby and others at Ngaateng
    swamp, 2007   384

Figure A1.41: Estate 106 Empadha, South Kendall Outstation,
    1978   384

Figure A1.42: James Kalkeeyorta, Clan 109, Aurukun, 1982   385

Figure A1.43: Estate 123 Pu'an Outstation at Thuuk River, 1978   385

Figure A1.44: MacNaught Ngallametta, Clan 97, Aurukun 1987   386

Figure A1.45: Mapping Koepenth swamp, dry season camp site,
    Estate 3, with Paddy Yantumba, 1977   386

Figure A1.46: Ron Yunkaporta tape recording at the bora tree
    where he was an initiand in 1970, Aurukun, 2006   387

Figure A1.47: Apelech ritual during mortuary ceremony,
    Aurukun, 2006   388

Figure A1.48: Hula dancers, mortuary ceremony, Aurukun, 2009   388

Figure A1.49: Alan Wolmby (Clan & Estate 6) 'baptising'
    John von Sturmer near Aayk, 1971   389

ix

List of maps

Map 1.1: Location of the study area	1
Map 1.2: Cape York Peninsula	2
Map 1.3: Australian language density distribution	3
Map 3.1: WCYP language countries (McConnel)	52
Map 3.2: WCYP language countries (Sharp)	53
Map 3.3: WCYP language countries (Thomson)	54
Map 3.4: WCYP language countries (Tindale 1940)	55
Map 3.5: WCYP language countries (Tindale 1974)	56
Map 3.6: WCYP language countries (Walsh)	57
Map 3.7: WCYP language countries (Dixon)	58
Map A1.1: WCYP ceremonial groupings	228
Map A2.1: Clan estates and languages: Weipa sheet	392
Map A2.2: Clan estates and languages: York Downs sheet	393
Map A2.3: Clan estates and languages: Aurukun sheet	394
Map A2.4: Clan estates and languages: Wenlock sheet	395
Map A2.5: Clan estates and languages: Cape Keerweer sheet	396
Map A2.6: Clan estates and languages: Archer River sheet	397
Map A2.7: Clan estates and languages: Merapah sheet	398
Map A2.8: Clan estates and languages: Rokeby sheet	399
Map A2.9: Clan estates and languages: Holroyd sheet	400

Map A2.10: Clan estates and languages: Kendall River sheet   401
Map A2.11: Clan estates and languages: Strathburn sheet   402
Map A2.12: Clan estates and languages: Ebagoola sheet   403
Map A2.13: Clan estates and languages: Edward River sheet   404

List of tables

Table 3.1: Bush camp census data 1928 and 1931	32
Table 3.2: Shift in surnaming of babies, Aurukun 1960–87	70
Table 4.1: Wik-Way estates	79
Table 4.2: Northern coastal estates	81
Table 4.3: Northern pericoastal estates	82
Table 4.4: Southern estates	83
Table 4.5: Coastal and pericoastal named varieties	84
Table 4.6: Inland named varieties	84
Table 4.7: Coastal and pericoastal technically defined Wik Subgroup languages	85
Table 4.8: Inland technically defined languages	85
Table 4.9: Technically defined languages	86
Table 4.10: Reconstructed number of estates per language	87
Table 4.11: McConnel's estimates of those living in 1929	88
Table 4.12: Summary of McConnel's pre-European Wik population estimates	88
Table 4.13: Birdsell's estimate of tribal populations for 23 western cases	94
Table 5.1: Thomson's lists of Wik-Way language varieties	105
Table 5.2: Thomson's 'also' list of Wik-Way language varieties	105
Table 5.3: Gajdusek's list of Wik-Way language varieties	107
Table 5.4: Gajdusek's 'other' list of Wik-Way language varieties	107

Table 5.5: Gajdusek's north of Archer River Wik-Way language varieties	107
Table 5.6: Hale's list of Wik-Way language varieties	108
Table 5.7: McConnel's list of Wik-Way language varieties	109
Table 5.8: Tindale's list of 'Winduwinda' (Wik-Way) language varieties	110
Table 5.9: Wik Subgroup varieties schematically listed from north to south	128
Table 5.10: Estates and their language affiliations	130
Table 6.1: Proto-Paman lexical items (from 100-word test list) occurring in all modern Paman branches	137
Table 6.2: Wik languages and Middle Paman neighbours south and east	139
Table 6.3: Wik languages (+) and three Northern Paman languages	141
Table 6.4: Middle Paman and Northern Paman comparisons	142
Table 6.5: Wik languages (+) and three noncontiguous Paman languages south and east	143
Table 6.6: Middle and Southern Paman languages compared	144
Table 6.7: Average shared vocabulary, the Paman family of CYP	145
Table 6.8: Lexical percentages shared by the modern Apachean languages	155
Table A1.1: Modern surnames and their clan and estate affiliations up to c. 1978	351
Table A1.2: Estates and related surnames as at c. 1978	356

Linguistic conventions

1, 2, 3	first, second and third person
2	dual (hence 22s = second person dual subject, 22.NOM second person dual nominative; 12s = you and I subject
3	plural (hence 23s means second person plural subject, 13NOM means first person plural nominative)
~	alternates with
*	reconstruction
ACC	accusative case
ERG	ergative case
FUT	future tense
NOM	nominative case
Ñ	laminal nasal unspecified as to whether palatal or dental
O	object (hence 1O = first person object 'me')
Ø	zero marking
PST	past tense
S	subject
TH	laminal stop unspecified as to whether palatal or dental

Orthography

The neutral unstressed vowel schwa, written [ə] in phonetic script, is represented as /e/ in the sections of the book written or compiled by Peter Sutton, following the conventions published in Sutton (1995a), except when using the Wik-Mungkan script established by the Summer Institute of Linguistics (Kilham et al. 1986), in which schwa is represented as /a/.

In the chapters written by Ken Hale he uses [ə] in attestations from less analysed languages, and zero in the case of Wik languages (e.g. he writes [wuʔə̃ŋ̊] 'whistled' as wu'nh).

Schwa does need to be indicated in Wik languages because of the need to distinguish CC from CəC. The following examples illustrate the point:

CC	CəC
thalp	thalepal
yaalp	kaalep
kulp	ngalep
milng	ngaleng
ngalnh	pulenh
punyp	inyep
inm	punem
mayng	kuyeng
punng	nganeng

An unsolved mystery here is that in the Wik English of adults in the 1970s, schwa was rare or non-existent. 'Totem' was pronounced [tóutam] and 'people' as [pí:pal], for example. This evidence may reflect on the status of schwa in the Wik varieties.

Sutton renders initial and intervocalic /ñ/ as /ny/ and syllable and word-final /ñ/ as /yn/. Hence 'stone' in Wik-Ngathan, phonemically /kupiñm/, is spelled /kupiynm/, and 'big' in Wik-Ngathan, phonemically /awəñ/, is spelled /aweyn/ as in the place Uthuk Aweyn 'Big Lake'. R.M.W. Dixon (2002:xxxi) uses /nj/ for the palatal nasal.

Special phonetic symbols in Ken Hale's chapters and here come from the International Phonetic Association symbol inventory.[1]

---

1 www.internationalphoneticassociation.org/content/full-ipa-chart, accessed 13 September 2019.

Linguistic variety abbreviations

Ad	Adithinngithigh
Ag	Agu Tharrngele
Al	Wik-Alken
An	Andjingith
Ar	Arrithinngithigh
At	Alngith
Ay	Ayapathu
CC	China Camp Muluriji
Dw	Ndwa'ngith
El	Wik-Elken
Ep	Wik-Ep
Gi	Giramay
I/P	Iyanh/Pakanh
In	Wik-Iincheyn
It	Wik-Iit
Iy	Wik-Iiyanh aka Kug-Iyanh
Iyi	Wik-Iiyanyi
Iyn	Wik-Iiyeyn
Ja	Japukay
Ji	Jirrbal (dialect of Dyirbal)
Ka	Kaanju
Ke	Wik-Keyenganh
Kp	Koko Pera
Kr	Kungkara
La	Latumngith
Li	Linngithigh
Lu	Luthigh
Ma	Kugu Mangk
Mam	Mamngayth
Mb	Mbiywom

Me	Wik-Me'enh
Mh	Mungkanhu
Ml	Muluriji
Mm	Kugu Muminh
Mn	Wik-Mungkan
Mp	Mpalicanh
Mt	Mamangathi
Mu	Kugu Mu'inh
Na	Anathangayth
Nd	Ndra'ngith
Nk	Ngkoth
Nn	Wik-Ngathan
Nr	Wik-Ngatharr
Nrw	Ndrwa'ngayth
Og	Ogonjan
Pa	Wik-Paach
Pk	Pakanh
Rn	Ndrangith
Ta	Kuuk Thaayorre
Ti	Wik-Thint
Tr	Trotj
Ty	Thyanngayth
Ug	Kug-Ugbanh
Ur	Uradhi
Uw	Kug-Uwanh
Wa	Ngwangathi
Ya	Kuuku-Ya'u – Umpila
Yd	Yidiny
Yi	Kugu Yi'anh
Yin	Yinwum
Yl	Kuuk-Yala?
Ym	Kuku Yimijirr

1
Introduction

Peter Sutton

This book is for people who are interested in the linguistic anthropology and linguistic prehistory of Aboriginal Australia, and in how these bodies of scientific knowledge may play forensic roles in the resolution of Indigenous claims to native title over Australian lands and waters.[1] It is also a reference work that tabulates linguistic and anthropological details of a particular region of western Cape York Peninsula (CYP) (Map 1.1). In that respect it is also meant as a long-term historical and cultural resource for the descendant families of the region.

We focus here on the peoples and languages of the central-western part of Cape York Peninsula (CYP), between the Embley and Edward rivers. CYP is usually defined as the mainland of Far North Queensland north of the sixteenth parallel of latitude (Map 1.2).

Map 1.1: Location of the study area
Source: AIATSIS

---

1 An excellent introduction to the role of linguistics in native title cases is Henderson and Nash (2002).

LINGUISTIC ORGANISATION AND NATIVE TITLE

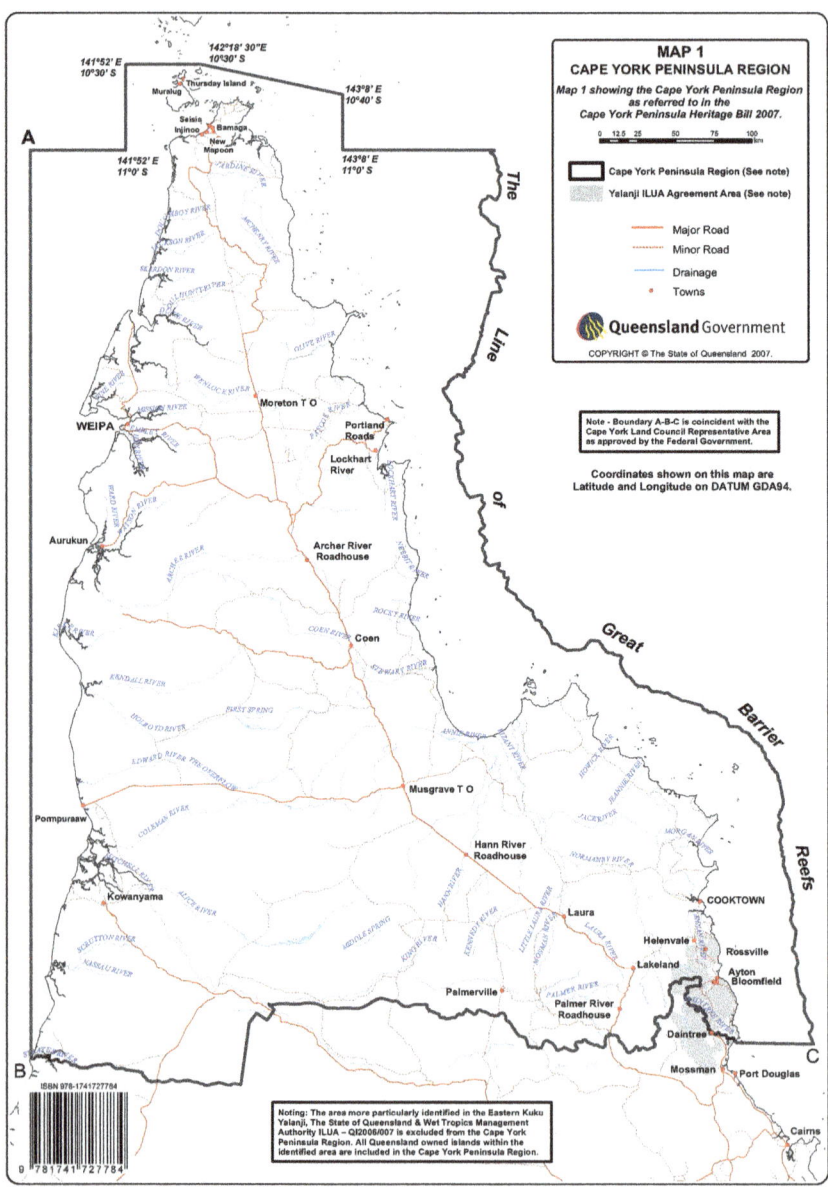

Map 1.2: Cape York Peninsula
Source: Queensland Government

1. INTRODUCTION

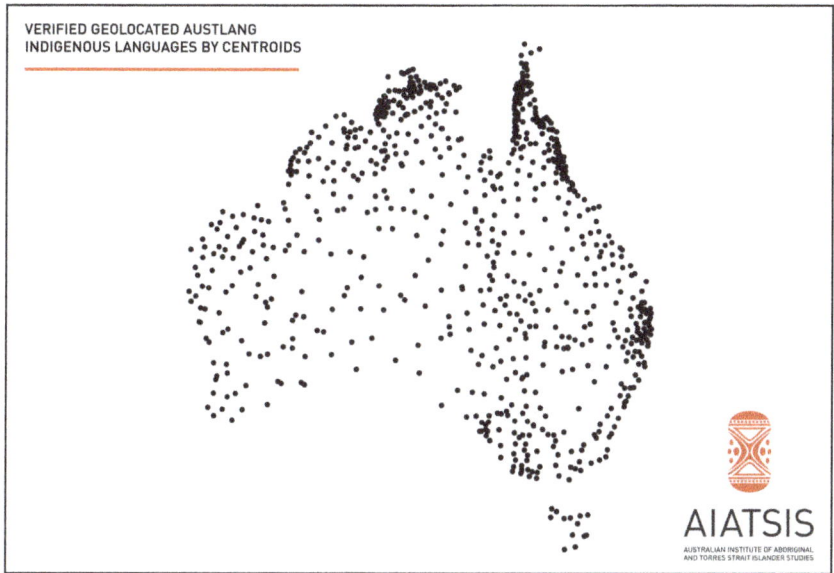

Map 1.3: Australian language density distribution
Source: AIATSIS

At the time of British colonisation, this peninsula of 288,804 square kilometres was the home of 43 distinct Indigenous languages made up of many scores of dialects.[2] Dialects are mutually intelligible varieties of a single language; distinct languages on the other hand are not mutually intelligible. This was one of the most densely varied linguistic landscapes in Australia (Map 1.3).

Since British imperial conquest, most of these languages have become moribund or are spoken only by very few people, but a small number continue to have fluent speakers. The most strongly surviving CYP language, Wik-Mungkan, comes within the purview of this study. While most of the language-owning groups of the classical (pre-colonial) period still have descendants, their speech has mostly undergone shift to a community-based language such as Wik-Mungkan (of Aurukun) or Guugu-Yimidhirr (of Hope Vale), or, as is the majority case, to English or Cape York Creole or both.

---

2   The figure of 43 is based on data in Dixon (2002:xxxi–xxxiii). By way of comparison with CYP, the United Kingdom has an area of 243,610 square kilometres.

The study area for this book lies between the towns of Weipa in the north, Coen in the east, and Pormpuraaw in the south (Map 1.2). We refer to this as the wider Wik Region. The wider Wik Region includes the traditional countries of peoples owning Northern Paman languages in the north, between Aurukun and Weipa, and those owning the Wik Subgroup languages in the south and inland, between Aurukun, Coen and Pormpuraaw (Wik and Kugu people).[3] Many of the Northern Paman languages covered here fall within the geopolitical identity of the Wik-Way people. The Kugu Ngancharra[4] varieties of the Wik Subgroup are dialects of the southern part of the Wik Region between Kendall River and Edward River. We unpack these various distinctions in some detail later in the book, especially in Chapter 5.

Language owners

Our focus here is on linguistic varieties and their geographical distribution in specific tracts of land, which has its basis in the linguistic identities of traditional clan countries, under sacred cultural traditions. These clan countries are usually called estates. Each estate has an inherent linguistic variety identity, which on the estate maps (Maps A2.1–A2.13) is shown by an abbreviation. The abbreviations are listed in the front matter to this volume. The geographical distribution of linguistic varieties we examine here has nothing to do with the residential locations of speakers of those varieties, as we explain below.

As in Australia generally, in the Wik Region those who own each traditional country (clan estate) own its particular dialect by a rule of descent from ancestors of the same clan. It remains the descendants' dialect whether they speak it or not. And being able to speak a particular variety does not grant one ownership of the dialect nor of its clan estate(s). In short, in the classical system prior to recent post-colonial developments, linguistic identity and traditional rights in country do not arise from behaviour (place of residence, speaking competence) but from descent-based identity (clan membership). The chief flaw in earlier conceptions of 'dialectal tribes', the predominant one being that of Norman Tindale (1974), was that they claimed language group membership was based on speaking

---

3   We use 'Wik Subgroup' in the same sense as does Dixon (2002:xxi).
4   I spell this dialect cluster cover term Kugu Ngancharra. In Chapters 6 and 7 here Ken Hale follows the Smith and Johnson (e.g. 2000) spelling of Kugu Nganhcara.

a language, and territorial identity was based on residence in or regular occupation of a bounded tract. This behaviour-based model is now in the past.

Each clan's linguistic identity was implanted in their estate by sacred mythical figures at the beginning of the world, in the Wik Region, as in so many others in Australia (Sutton 1997b). This is why, in classical Wik society, one might be a speaker of many linguistic varieties but only one, usually, was spiritually one's 'own language', and it was the dialect that belonged to one's estate-owning clan. In the study region, all clan dialects were named. A few clans had more than one linguistic variety as their own.[5]

The Aboriginal language owner/speaker distinction first entered the academic record in Sutton (1978:17, emphasis original), where I stated:

> In Aboriginal Australia, as far as I am aware, there is a *universal* distinction between the language one 'owns' by way of patrilineal descent,[6] and other languages. Language is ritual property. People can use each others' languages, as indeed they commonly do and on occasions must. A theory of linguistic communities which simply separates language knowers from language users will overlook in the Australian case a whole ideology—of great pragmatic importance—about language owners.

I repeated this distinction between language owners and language speakers in Sutton and Palmer (1980), which was the unrestricted anthropological report for a claim under the *Aboriginal Land Rights Act 1976* (Northern Territory). In that case, the Aboriginal Land Commissioner, Toohey J, accepted the evidence of conjoint succession to traditional ownership of all the estates of the Malak Malak–owning clans, whether unpopulated or extant, by a smallish group of surviving descendants of the same language group. The Malak Malak language group was thus recognised as a descent-based, language-based country group and as the Traditional Owners of the land, and this was published in Toohey J's report (Aboriginal Land Commissioner 1982). This group was not recruited on the basis of who spoke what but on the basis of who could claim filiative descent from owners of clan estates whose intrinsic linguistic identities were Malak Malak.

---

5 See Appendix 1: Clans 1, 2, 3, 13, 21, 28, 96, 140.
6 I would now add: 'or other intrinsic bases such as, in the post-classical era, cognatic descent, or, in the Western Desert, conception or birth place for earlier generations, and in many Western Desert post-classical settlements, identification with the local communalect'. On the post-classical shift to cognatic descent of language identities across Aboriginal Australia see Sutton (2003:206–221).

More widely published thereafter were the following. Using Sutton (1978) as her main source, Francesca Merlan came to the same view on the language owner/speaker distinction (Merlan 1981). I once more laid out descent-based factors for language group identity in Sutton (1991:53). In Sutton (1997b:240) I again expressed the view that Aboriginal languages 'are owned, not merely spoken. They are inherited property … Languages belong to specific places, and the people of those places'. I revisited the language ownership matter in Sutton (2003:76). In the meantime, Alan Rumsey published an identical view citing Sutton (1978) and Sutton and Palmer (1980) and other case material as his sources in his oft-cited paper on the subject (1993:199).

The *Aak* mapping report

Just before the native title era, which began in the legislative sense in 1993,[7] several colleagues and I put together a 1,000-page report on around 2,000 sites and about 100 clan countries in the Wik Region (Sutton et al. 1990). This volume is often referred to here as the *Aak* (= 'Country') volume after its short title. That database was the outcome of over 20 seasons of intensive field mapping, using specific sites as the starting point for understanding the larger entities they underpinned, namely clan estates, linguistic countries and sub-regional geopolitical groupings such as ceremonial, riverine or drainage-based alliances. The main field workers doing the Wik Region mapping 1969–89 had been, in chronological order, John von Sturmer and John Taylor, Athol Chase, Peter Sutton, David Martin, John Adams, Roger Cribb (plus archaeological sites) and Philip Hunter.[8] In the course of this work, our Wik instructors took us physically to well over 1,000 sites so that their map coordinates would be accurate, photographs and sketches could be taken, and knowledgeable people could record their stories for each place, usually on audio tape as well as in notes taken by the anthropologists.

---

7   *Native Title Act 1993 (Commonwealth)*.
8   Sutton (2016a) provides details of the history of the ethnographic mapping of Cape York Peninsula, including the wider Wik Region. For copies of broad-brush ethnographic maps of the Wik Region drawn up by earlier scholars see Sutton (1978, and in the present volume: Maps A2.5–A2.11). For a film showing a moment in the mapping of Wik countries during the 1977 season see David MacDougall's *Familiar Places* (1980).

The construction of the *Aak* volume during 1989–90 was in response to the request by the Wik people of Aurukun for support in their application for an emergency declaration by the Federal Minister for Aboriginal Affairs under the *Aboriginal and Torres Strait Islander Heritage Protection Act 1984*. They were seeking this declaration in order to protect their landscape from the proposed 1989 seismic survey program of the mining company Comalco. After copies of our report were submitted, Comalco deferred its proposed field program indefinitely.[9]

Within a few years the report had acquired a new purpose. It formed part of the detailed evidentiary base for the Wik native title case expert reports of 1997.[10] We carried out a substantial amount of further mapping field work 1989–97, and this resulted in a further site and estate record of over 230 pages, which supplemented the 1990 report.[11]

The *Wik* native title case

The *Wik* native title case, which ran for 20 years (1992–2012), was one of a small number of Indigenous land claims that played pivotal roles in the history of Australian property law.[12] Before *Wik* were the 1971 Gove case (*Milirrpum*), where a doctrine of native title was rejected, and *Mabo* (1992), where it was accepted.[13]

During the *Wik* saga, in 1996 the High Court of Australia found in favour of the Wik peoples' claim that native title rights could survive on pastoral leases,[14] titles that cover the vast area of 44 per cent of Australia.[15] (While most of the Wik claim area lay outside the pastoral lease zone, significant tracts in the eastern sector lay inside the zone.) This was the biggest legal break-through in favour of Australia's Indigenous peoples' rights in land and waters since *Mabo*.

---

9 More detail on these events is provided at Sutton et al. (1990:1).
10 Sutton (1997a).
11 Sutton et al. (1997).
12 The documentary film *Wik vs Queensland* (2018) gives an authoritative account of this saga.
13 *Milirrpum v Nabalco* (1971) 17 FLR 141; *Mabo v Queensland (No 2)* [1992] HCA 23, (1992) 175 CLR 1 (3 June 1992), High Court.
14 *Wik Peoples v The State of Queensland* [1996] HCA 40, (1996) 187 CLR 1 (23 December 1996), High Court.
15 www.austrade.gov.au/land-tenure/Land-tenure/pastoral-leases, accessed 27 September 2018.

The Wik peoples' claims finally came to an end in a series of five consent determinations, reached in 2000, 2004, 2009 and 2012, under which the Australian Federal Court accepted the Wik peoples' case for native title on the basis of the expert reports their counsel had submitted. This meant that litigation, and the stresses and huge expenses of adversarial legal action, were avoided. It also meant that examination and cross-examination of lay claimant witnesses and expert witnesses were rendered unnecessary. This book is in part based on the anthropological and linguistic evidence that was foundational to that case. Most of that evidence had been recorded before the native title era.

In the process of reaching these post-Gove landmark stages, and during the flood of native title applications, negotiations and litigations that flowed from them, Australian society itself changed. In particular, large numbers of Indigenous people gained at least partial recognition for what remained of their ancient pre-conquest property rights, and they increasingly became participants at the table rather than people who, if they were lucky, got to be consulted about land use from time to time.

The majority of Australian native title claims lodged since 1993 have been made by people identifying with particular named language groups and their language countries. The corporate bodies set up to manage the affairs of native title holders are typically identified as having as their members people from the same linguistic countries. In this sense, a large proportion of the ancient language groups of Australia, often called tribes, live on permanently—albeit transformed—as part of the fabric of contemporary Australian society.

Ken Hale

My co-author in this volume, American linguist Kenneth Locke Hale (1934–2001), who preferred to be called Ken, carried out field work on a very large number of languages, not just in Australia but internationally. He was a supremely gifted polyglot and also an academic linguist of distinction, who taught in the Linguistics Department of the Massachusetts Institute of Technology from 1967 to 1999.[16]

---

16   For book tributes to Ken's life work see Carnie (et al.) (2000), Kenstowicz (2001), and Simpson et al. (2001).

1. INTRODUCTION

In 1960 Ken did a linguistic survey of Cape York Peninsula, Queensland, and much of the comparative contents of his chapters in this book come from those recordings. In that time, he spent 1–17 August at Aurukun Presbyterian Mission, where he worked on five different Wik Subgroup and Northern Paman languages.[17]

After I was appointed principal expert witness for the Wik native title case by the Cape York Land Council (CYLC), I suggested to lawyer James Fitzgerald of the CYLC that he request from Ken a report on Wik linguistic prehistory. Amidst his manifold commitments, Ken found time to write a two-part report interrogating Wik linguistic history for evidence as to the length of time the Wik peoples had been territorially at their present locations.[18]

We needed something on this because, at that time in the evolution of native title case law, it was still considered necessary to provide evidence of continuity of traditional tenure by the same people in the same country since the establishment of British sovereignty, which in this case was understood to be 1788. Later it came to be accepted that continuity of law and custom from the period when *effective* sovereignty was established, until the present, would be all that could be and needed to be proven. This date varied widely from region to region because the control of the colonists expanded into different places at different times over more than a century after 1788.

Ken's reports played a key role in removing doubt about the since-sovereignty question from the negotiation agendas of the two main parties. These parties were the Wik peoples as represented by the Cape York Land Council, led by Noel Pearson, and Ebsworth Lawyers, and the Queensland Government's Crown Law department. The vital role of Ken's reports in the negotiations was facilitated by their assessment by a Queensland Government employee, Colin Sheehan, who had academic linguistic training. In fact, he was an ex-student of Dr Luise Hercus of The Australian National University, an eminent specialist in Aboriginal languages. In the early 1990s, Colin and I were in the same room in Brisbane when the parties' legal representatives discussed Ken's work. As Colin explained the significance of Ken's reports, one of the

---

17   See further Chapter 2.
18   Hale (1997b), here Chapters 6 and 7.

State's planks of resistance suddenly fell away.[19] Ken's work had shown that, in the case of the Wik Subgroup area, which was the lion's share of the claim area, territorial stability was essentially centuries old. This technical demonstration, following on the other evidence of Wik peoples' continuity of connection to their countries, was the beginning of the long road to a final consent determination of native title.

This book in part acknowledges Ken Hale's key role in that historic chain of events, but it also adds a further tribute to his life and work in its Australian phase.

In 1997, I wrote to Ken to suggest we combine our various Wik expert reports as a book and get it published.[20] Ken's reply was swift: 'I really like the idea!'[21] Sadly Ken passed away before we could weld the book together between us, and the present volume has had to be constructed by myself. I have left Ken's two chapters as they were in 1997, apart from correcting typos, renumbering tables, and adding a few footnotes. No doubt there have been many new developments in the world literature on linguistic generalisations since 1997. There have also been advancements in scholarship on Paman and Pama-Nyungan languages since 1997. However, the historical importance and enduring value of Ken's chapters justifies their being published at the present time.

I first met Ken Hale when he took part in a conference at The Australian National University in 1974, organised by the then Australian Institute of Aboriginal Studies (AIAS, now AIATSIS). Ken gave several papers, some of them in a symposium I convened on languages of Cape York Peninsula. These papers were published as *Languages of Cape York* (Sutton 1976) and four of the papers published there were by Ken (Hale 1976a, b, c, d).

Later that year we travelled to Darwin with fellow linguist Geoffrey O'Grady to attend a meeting with the Northern Territory Education Department for the purpose of discussing the introduction of a bilingual education program for Aboriginal school students. I was sent along by my

---

19   Sheehan later wrote a report where the role of the linguistic evidence, and Ken's submissions in particular, were described as clinching the question of Wik occupation of the claim area since before the establishment of British sovereignty (Sheehan 2002:24–25).
20   Sutton email to Hale, 10 October 1997.
21   Hale email to Sutton, 10 October 1997.

employer, the AIAS, and as a novice linguist I was fascinated to sit and listen to the two veterans and old colleagues during their exchanges over dinner at the Hotel Darwin.

Ken and I kept in touch over the years that followed, including when I sent Ken a copy of my PhD thesis (Sutton 1978). His response was encouraging:

> Dear Peter: Thank you so much for sending me your dissertation. It is excellent—I read the whole thing last night, and will probably read it again soon. I'm also pleased you mentioned my work—I really like to get mentioned.[22]

Peter Sutton

I began decades of working with Wik people in a short mapping trip in January 1976, with Athol Chase and John von Sturmer, while we were mapping sites and estates north of Aurukun. I had by then already spent cumulatively about 12 months doing linguistic field work elsewhere in Cape York Peninsula and Far North Queensland in the years 1970–75.

From 1976 I began living at times in Aurukun Presbyterian Mission, as it then was, but for most of my field work time, in the late 1970s, I was residing out in the bush based at Peret Outstation 60 kilometres to the south in the great wetlands of the Cape Keerweer[23] region, or in temporary bush camps. From those bases I worked with local people to develop an in-depth study of the roles played by language variation and political action in people's systems of relationships with their tribal countries, including land tenure and succession. The outcome of that work was Sutton (1978).

Authors of Appendices 1 and 2

Sutton (2016a) includes a history of the cultural mapping roles played by the authors of the two appendices here, namely Sutton, Martin, von Sturmer, Cribb, Chase, Taylor and McConnel, to which the reader is referred.

---

22 Hale letter to Sutton, 19 June 1979.
23 Cape Keerweer was mapped geographically and named by Willem Janszoon in 1606, during the earliest known European exploration of an Australian coast (Heeres 1899). See Figures A1.21 and A1.22.

Acknowledgements

Our first debt, as always, is to our Aboriginal mentors, whose energetic engagement with researchers over generations has resulted in the rich record that is partially reflected in this book. They are too many to name here in full—however, they are in Sutton et al. (1990) and Sutton et al. (1997)—but the following were key instructors for the site and country mapping, and the extensive genealogies and totemic information, that underpin Appendices 1 and 2 and Maps A2.1–A2.13:

> Sam Kerindun, Fred Kerindun, Uki Pamulkan, Mabel Taisman, Myrtle Chevathun, Jean George, Alice Mark, Ronnie John, Lenford Matthew, Violet Yunkaporta, Nellie Taisman, Cyril Owokran, Isobel Wolmby, George Sydney Yunkaporta, Clive Yunkaporta, Paulina Peemuggina, Francis Yunkaporta, Alan Wolmby, Morrison Wolmby, Ron Yunkaporta, Archiewald Otomorathin, Lomai Woolla, Rex Walmbeng, Cecil Walmbeng, Jack Spear Karntin, Johnny Lak Lak Ampeybegan, Denny Bowenda, Charles Taisman, Alfred Taisman, Arthur Pambegan, Geraldine Kawangka, Maud Yunkaporta, Noel Peemuggina, Mikompa Peemuggina, Peter Peemuggina, Jack Sleep Yunkaporta, Paddy Yantumba, Dan Gothachalkenin, Yukwainten Gothachalkenin, Koppa Yunkaporta, Bob Massey Pootchemunka, Small Eric Pootchemunka, Nigel Pootchemunka, John Kelly Pootchemunka, Marybelle Pamtoonda, Mary Walmbeng, Mulloch Wolmby, Stewart Korkaktain, Jackson Woolla, Roddy Shortjoe, Dawn Koondumbin, Wompey Keppel, Rosie Ahlers, Peret Arkwookerum, James Kalkeeyorta, Rodney Karyuka, Tommy Eileen, Abiu Holroyd, Duncan Holroyd, Jimmy Kendall, Dugal Tarpencha, Stingaree Barney, Mickey Edward, Ned Edward, Joe Ngallametta.

Ken Hale's main language teachers for this part of CYP were Sam Kerindun, Joe Marbendinar, Jim Henry, and Billy Ngakapoorgum (Aurukun), and Tictic, Frank Moreton, Andrew Mark, Willie, Robert Hall, Monty Motton, Arthur Dick, Hector, and Keepas (Weipa).

Specific factual data on Wik Region clans and estates, here listed in Appendices 1 and 2, have been drawn from the limited publication of Sutton et al. (1990) with additions from the follow-up report (Sutton et al. 1997). A draft of the 1990 report was taken to Aurukun in November 1989 where John von Sturmer and I conducted fact-checking and permissions discussions with 14 sets of families whose countries and

1. INTRODUCTION

clans were represented in the volume. Those consents are reflected here, although the great bulk of Sutton et al. (1990, 1997), namely the data on around 2,000 specific sites recorded in the field and elsewhere, is not contained in this book.

I must also acknowledge in particular Victor Wolmby (1905–76, Figure A1.1) who took me as a son in the months before his passing, and who was my first instructor in learning his clan dialect Wik-Ngathan, at Aurukun Presbyterian Mission in the 1975–76 wet season. He passed away in March 1976 before I began mapping field work a few months later, and his role as mentoring father was assumed by his clan brother Noel Peemuggina (1910–82, Figure A1.18). My principal Wik-Ngathan language teacher, and most indefatigable site and estate mapping instructor, was Victor's widow Isobel Wolmby née Gothachalkenin (1917–89, Figure A1.7).

Especially in those days, traditionally oriented remote Aboriginal people like the Wik peoples were most at home in dealing with people they classed as kin. Non-Aboriginal people were thus at times taken into their world and made relatives. In 1976 I was suddenly thrown into a network of what was then over 600 people, to each of whom I was then related as a specific kind of relative, and each of them to me. Victor's patrilineal clan estate (number 6 Aayk, near Cape Keerweer), his clan dialect (Wik-Ngathan), and his totems (Chiiyn-chiiyn 'Bush Rat', and many others, see Clan 6 Appendix 1), were spoken of as mine, as they were also of the rest of the Wolmby and Peemuggina descent group from the Aayk estate. Happily, this inclusion of one of the Wik native title case experts in one of the Wik claimant families was never raised as a problem during the long and strenuous legal negotiations.

By and large, the field records on which this book is based were made before and outside of the native title legal process, principally between 1969 and 1990, although some were generated in the period 1991–97. Earlier cultural and linguistic mapping from the period 1927–34, recorded by anthropologist Ursula McConnel (1886–1957), has also been included here, along with smaller contributions from other sources as acknowledged.

The fact that the Wik Region was already well-researched in terms of traditional country ownership was one of the main reasons it was chosen by Noel Pearson and the Cape York Land Council as the first Queensland mainland native title case in 1992.[24]

Specific consultations about publishing Appendices 1 and 2 were carried out in Aurukun by David Martin in 2019. Collective support for the publication of the Appendices was passed as a formal motion of the Wik, Wik Way[25] and Kugu traditional land owners body Aak Puul Ngantam ('Our Fathers' Fathers' Country') on 24 September 2019. In 1995 Napranum Aboriginal Corporation gave me access to Co-ordata (1994). All are to be thanked for their collaboration.

Where scholars have contributed to the contents, they are specifically acknowledged. However, in particular, I acknowledge the special contributions of David Fernandes Martin, John Richard von Sturmer, Roger Llewellyn Dunmore Cribb, Athol Kennedy Chase, John Charles Taylor and Ursula Hope McConnel. I also thank two anonymous manuscript referees for their most helpful suggestions, most of which have been adopted here.

The information on clans and estates of the Kugu Ngancharra region that has been compiled here has been extracted from von Sturmer's PhD thesis (1978), which is openly available electronically from the Library of the University of Queensland. Early clan estate maps for the area between the Archer and Kendall rivers appear in my own PhD thesis (Sutton 1978), which is also publicly downloadable from the same site.

On some of my mapping trips I worked collaboratively with anthropologists John von Sturmer, David Martin, Roger Cribb, Athol Chase and Marcia Langton. I also had the fine company and assistance of John Adams (Aurukun Mission staffer), Dermot Smyth (ecologist) and Philip Hunter (solicitor for the Wik case) on a series of mapping expeditions, and I thank them all here.

---

24 It was lodged in 1992 as a common law claim. It went on under the Native Title Act after that act was passed in 1993.
25 Note that we spell this in linguistic-anthropological contexts with a hyphen (Wik-Way), but the legal reports have Wik Way. The meanings are the same. We retain both depending on context.

Although Ken Hale gave his permission in 1997 for his *Wik* case reports to be published here (as Chapters 6 and 7), I also thank Ken's son Caleb Hale for his approval of the present publication.[26]

Funding for the field work and other research behind this book came from the Australian National Research Council (McConnel), The National Science Foundation (USA) and the Massachusetts Institute of Technology (USA) (Hale); and for the more recent scholars: the Australian Institute of Aboriginal and Torres Strait Islander Studies, the Australian Commonwealth Department of Education, University of Queensland Department of Anthropology and Sociology, Aurukun Shire Council, Aurukun Community Incorporated, Australian Department of Aboriginal Affairs, the Australian Heritage Commission, the South Australian Museum, the Australian Research Council, and the Cape York Land Council.

The clan estate maps (Maps A2.1–A2.13) were kindly prepared by Joyce Gehr for the Cape York Land Council and this publication.

Financial support for copyediting and indexing this book by Angela Terrill was provided by the Australian Research Council Centre of Excellence for the Dynamics of Language at The Australian National University.

This book was put together because of a suggestion by Nicholas Evans that I publish my 1978 PhD thesis on Wik linguistic anthropology. I thank him for this encouragement.

Peter Sutton
School of Biological Sciences, University of Adelaide
Division of Humanities, South Australian Museum
30 June 2021

---

26   Caleb Hale email to Peter Sutton, 8 March 2018.

2
Talking language: A tribute to Ken Hale

Peter Sutton

A little history[1]

In 1960 Ken Hale spent 1–17 August at Aurukun Presbyterian Mission, Cape York Peninsula, recording basic materials in five different languages. These included the northern Paman language Linngithigh, and the Wik Subgroup varieties Wik-Ep/Wik-Me'enh, Wik-Ngatharr, Wik-Mungkan, and Kugu Muminh, the latter being a variety of Kugu Ngancharra. His consultants included Sam Kerindun (Linngithigh), Joe Marbendinar (Wik-Ep/Wik-Me'enh, Wik-Ngatharr, Wik-Mungkan), Jim Henry (Wik-Mungkan), and Billy Ngakapoorgum (Kugu Muminh).[2] Given that Ken spent such a short time there, it is remarkable that Aurukun people have remembered him 'talking language' with them in a competent way, long after the event.[3]

In about 1976, Ken sent a taped message in one of the languages, Linngithigh, to Fred Kerindun, the son of Sam Kerindun, the latter having passed away by then. Sam had been one of Ken's main linguistic

---

1   An earlier version of this chapter appeared as Sutton (2001).
2   The dates of Ken's visit are derived from the Aurukun Mission Diary (MS2483, AIATSIS Library, Canberra). Information about Ken's consultants is from copies of his field notes (MS4114, AIATSIS Library, Canberra). Aurukun ceased being a mission, and became a local government area township, in 1978.
3   'All thought it a prodigious achievement', John von Sturmer (pers. comm.).

consultants at Aurukun. His was a phonologically difficult Northern Paman language with little overt resemblance to the Wik Subgroup languages Ken also studied in this instance.[4] The Aurukun people's perception that Ken's ability to absorb a language was extraordinary was no exaggeration.

The Aurukun Mission diary of the day, chiefly maintained by Superintendent Reverend William MacKenzie, was rather more offhand in its response to Ken's visit. Bill MacKenzie was, according to his own record, a 'cot case' with ill health for most of Ken's time at Aurukun, but his diary entries for this period were no different from the usual. Records such as 'grind valves and re-cut seats on kerosene engine' or 'repaired broken brake-line Ford Blitz' were common. It is of note that MacKenzie's entries moved from referring to 'Dr Hale' to 'Ken Hale' by late in Ken's visit, probably a sign of something positive in MacKenzie's reception of Ken. It was certainly in contrast with MacKenzie's use of the formal 'Mr McCarthy' all the way through the Aurukun diary entries covering Frederick McCarthy's ethnological visit to Aurukun 16–29 November 1962, for the AIAS. That visit was cut short when MacKenzie arranged for the manager of the nearby Weipa mine to fly McCarthy out before his expected field time had expired. Earlier MacKenzie had come into conflict with anthropologists then working in the area (Ursula McConnel in 1927, Donald Thomson in 1933). Both were banned from visiting Aurukun.

Aurukun mission diary entries about Ken Hale

Monday 1 August 1960:

> Watt Leggatt [Presbyterian Mission lugger, probably coming from Mornington Island Mission] arrived 5.30. Ted Butler, Dr Hale, Gully, Pompey, Prince, Larry & Dick.[5] Had good trip.

---

4   See Hale (1964, 1966, 1997a).
5   These men were probably: Ted (E.C.) Butler, missionary; Aboriginal men Gully Peters, Pompey Wilson, Prince Escott, Larry Lanley and Dick Roughsey, from Mornington Island. Ken Hale spent two months there between July and October 1960 (Ngakulmungan Kangka Leman 1997:3–6). The Aurukun and Weipa visits seem to have been interpolated into this more extensive field work.

Tuesday 2 August 1960:

> Dr Hale had Sam Kerindun to help him with Lengitie[6] language, also Polly [Blowhard].

Friday 12 August 1960:

> Dr Hale still working with Sam

Sunday 14 August 1960:

> Jack[7] & Ken Hale went to Wutan afternoon load girls to pick up coconuts.

Wednesday 17 August 1960:

> Reliance [Aurukun Mission boat] away 7.30. Ted Butler & Ken Hale went up [presumably to Weipa], also 3 Mornington men.

And that is it. Ken went on to Weipa. The people Ken worked with at Weipa, whose languages were all Northern Paman, included: Tictic (language: *Yinwum*), Frank Moreton (*Ngkoth*), Andrew Mark (*Arrithinngithigh*), Willie (*Mbiywom*), Robert Hall (*Ndrrwa'angith*), Monty Motton (*Ndrra'angith*), Arthur Dick (*Mamngayth*), Hector (*Ndrrwa'angayth*), and Keepas (*Alngith(igh)*).[8]

As in most other cases dealt with here, the main language consultant was usually both a full owner of the variety concerned, not merely a competent speaker of it, and a, if not the, politically pre-eminent member of his or her land-holding group. I take this to be an index of the cultural and political importance attached to acting in this language teaching role in that era. It is notable that many other scholars' linguistic and anthropological consultants have been local 'bosses'.

Meanwhile, back at Aurukun, there had been an intriguing mission diary entry about an outbreak of mild Bolshevism, which occurred just after Ken left for Weipa.

---

6   i.e. Linngithigh (lexicon published as Hale 1997a).
7   Jack was probably a mission staff member.
8   No dates or places are provided in the field notes that I have seen (MS4114, AIATSIS Library, Canberra). I have respelled personal names here to be as they were most often officially recorded, and have added surnames where I know who the people were from my own work in the area.

Saturday 20 August 1960:

> People wanted talk with Rev Sweet[9] & self. Some grievances over no work. Mostly of infantile nature. Denny B re store wages. Morrison re wages. Allan re child endowment. Paul[10] re people having children - repercussion from Mornington Islanders. Went on till 1.15. J.R.S. [Rev Sweet] explained shortage of money. Most of the men very loyal ... Sam [Kerindun] offered that people's Communion offering be devoted to money shortages. RS [Rev Sweet] very graciously thanked him but that would not be enough.

The MacKenzie regime was very autocratic, morally strict and at times dished out corporal punishments decided upon by the Superintendent. Ken was a left-of-centre modern. I can't help guessing there may have been a causal link between Ken's 16 days at Aurukun and the lodging of multiple grievances three days later.

Cultural implications of 'talking language'

One day in about 1976 a Wik man, Peter Peemuggina, asked me if I knew a 'Doctor Keneyl', and, if so, how and where was he? I replied to Peter that I did indeed know Ken, who was often at home in America.

This was not the last time Wik people inquired after Ken or brought his name up in conversation, the most recent to my knowledge being in 1999.[11] He clearly made a significant impact on them. They also spoke of the anthropologists Ursula McConnel and Donald Thomson, who had spent many months living among Wik people in the 1920s and 1930s. It was understandable that these two long-stayers would be remembered. Stories about them were told and retold by fires on the long evenings of quieter days, by those who had known them personally. In terms of the time he had spent there, Ken was just another short-term visitor whose name and identity would normally have been forgotten like all the others, but this was not how people saw it at all.

---

9   The Reverend James R. Sweet.
10 i.e. Denny Bowenda, Morrison Wolmby, Alan Wolmby and Paul Peemuggina, all 'Cape Keerweer' (lower Kirke River system) men.
11 Amanda Reynolds (pers. comm.). Peter Peemuggina was still alive at the time of writing, i.e. 2021.

What made the difference, as I understand it, was Ken's ability to speak local languages, at least to an extent and well, in a phenomenally short time. No doubt another factor would have been Ken's capacity to relate to the people from whom he was learning. The very act of approaching their languages with seriousness, and taking the trouble to study them carefully, combined with what was probably a rather startling ability to sound like he was born there, would all have smoothed the way to being memorable.

I doubt, though, that even this feat alone would perpetuate such memories of a brief visit four decades later. I think a deeper and specifically Aboriginal cultural factor is also at work here.

In a small-scale society it is possible, and in fact in Cape York Peninsula it was highly likely under classical cultural conditions, that an adult would personally know and be genealogically related to everyone else who shared a common primary language affiliation, especially at the level of the named language variety.[12] In the Wik Region this was the case whether the affiliation was at the level of the small patrifilial clan groups, which averaged around 20 or so members, which are dialect-holding entities, or at the level of the proper-named linguistic varieties shared by a number of different clan groups, or even at the level of linguistic macro-groupings, which are based on a recognition of degrees of grammatical and lexical similarities between sets of separately named varieties.

In addition, in the Wik Region, as in so many other parts of Aboriginal Australia, the mere fact that someone can speak the same language as oneself is usually taken to imply that the other person must be kin, related to ego somehow or another, in either an actual or a classificatory sense. In the absence of disputation the default relationship to one's kin is one of underlying amity. There is also a common view that linguistic competence in an Aboriginal language by a non-Aboriginal person must imply not only cultural competence and understanding, but also an acceptance of the worth of Aboriginal culture itself and thus of its peoples.

When a non-Indigenous person is heard speaking an Aboriginal language—a situation still rare in Australia outside the Western Desert— Aboriginal people are usually quickly of the view that this person has

---

12   Actually, not all Cape York Peninsula language varieties had names, but in those cases known to me the different varieties could still be identified by salient linguistic characteristics (e.g. different words for 'no'), or by references to the main totem of a clan owning the variety, or by a 'big country name' for an area the language belonged to.

in some significant way entered into their world of values, their web of relationships, their patchwork of country identities, and furthermore that this is someone who does not look down on them, who is not 'stuck up'.

People who can 'talk language', as it is so often put in Aboriginal English, speak what the ancestors spoke. The ritualised process of talking to the spirits of the 'Old People' when visiting particular places is itself often referred to in English simply as 'talking language'—because the ancient ancestors did not know English.[13] To 'talk language' is not merely to make evident one's linguistic education, but in a sense it is also to reproduce the characteristic voice of the Old People who were ancestral to some particular network of kin.

A common shorthand Aboriginal expression of this recognition of outsider skills in insider matters is to say of the person that he or she 'knows'. In classical Aboriginal thought there is more to this 'knowing' than mere grammatical competence or cultural familiarity. In the Wik area, as has been documented over much of Australia, languages are held by their Aboriginal owners to have been implanted in specific countries at the foundation of the world, by heroic ancestral figures or, as they are known in Cape York Peninsula, 'Stories'.[14] A small clan of anywhere between one and a few score people, in Wik thought, is itself considered a micro-linguistic group with its own unique variety of speech,[15] a variety that is typically specified by naming a principal totem of the clan, as explained in more detail later in this book. Language is, in this sense, at once both spiritual and political.

---

13 That is, 'talking language' is sometimes a shorthand idiomatic way of referring to the addressing of ancestral spirits—'We go to place X, we talk language', i.e. 'When we go to place X, we will address the spirits in an appropriate local language'. In my experience, spirits are only rarely addressed using English.
14 One legendary account of the creation of Wik Subgroup languages is provided by Noel Peemuggina in Sutton (1997b). In that legend the named varieties are implanted estate by estate as the two culture heroes, the Pungk-Apelech (Clearwater Knees) Brothers, move across the landscape establishing totemic centres in each clan's estate. In a number of other accounts referred to in that paper, drawn from other parts of Australia, Dreaming (Story) beings implant or recognise specific languages across whole linguistic territories, typically beginning to speak a new language as each linguistic territory is entered and switching to another on departure from it.
15 Sutton (1978:138), von Sturmer (1978:325–26), Smith and Johnson (2000:366–67).

The first people spoke these respective varieties when the world was young, and their descendants ideally speak the same way today, or at least used to.[16] The highly emotional and spiritual links between one's principal ancestral language variety and the deepest reaches of local identity were made clear when naming that variety by means of the primary totemic symbol of each descent group. This, as well as the intrinsic connection between that variety and a passionately held clan country or homeland, meant that choice of speech variety was no casual matter in this society. To choose any Aboriginal speech variety, especially one other than a *lingua franca* (in this case Wik-Mungkan), was to immediately implicate specific areas of country and to demonstrate links to their particular people.[17]

In 1960, into this intense world where speech varieties resonated daily not only with the people's geopolitics but also with their cosmogony and ontology, stepped a young American who almost overnight began to speak and sound like one of their own. This was a unique experience for the Wik people of Aurukun, as it no doubt was for others elsewhere. Those who were old enough to appreciate the import of it at the time continued for decades to regard Ken Hale with enduring interest and respect, and not a little awe.

---

16   While a number of Wik varieties such as Wik-Me'enh and Wik-Ep are moribund, and Wik-Ngathan and Wik-Elkenh/Wik-Ngatharr have only adult fluent speakers, Wik-Mungkan is the first language of most children at Aurukun, and some Kugu Ngancharra varieties persist reasonably well, especially at Pormpuraaw. Wik-Way varieties seem now to have only senior adult speakers of even modest competence.

17   Conversely, to mainly employ a *lingua franca* and abandon use of one's own speech variety also has its motivations, although in many community situations it is hard to separate motivation from necessity in this domain.

3

Linguistic and territorial organisation: The Wik classical system

Peter Sutton

Totemic clans

In somewhat simplified terms, the Wik patrilineal descent group is the elemental linguistic and country-holding unit of classical times and on into at least the 1970s. It is a set of people formed on a principle of shared genealogical origins. Until recent decades, the descent principle was simply patrilineal.[1] That is, a person at birth acquired a primary landed estate, its named dialect, a set of clan totems, a set of clan totemic names (differing according to gender), plus a set of totemic names that they may use for their own dogs (again differing by gender). The default rule was that these came to a newborn child through its father and father's father. A catalogue of Wik totemic clans including their dialects and totemic names is provided in Appendix 1. A catalogue of their estates is provided as Appendix 2.

In most cases, this clan identity was also that of a person's father's father, and his father, and their siblings both female and male, back through time to the earliest memories, although there have been some principled exceptions to this pattern, which are discussed in Appendix 1: Clan list.

---

1   The shift to a principle of cognatic descent is discussed later.

Not only is this patrilineal pattern what people specify from their memory, but it can also be attested in many cases from the written record. A comparison of the ethnographies of the 1970s–90s with that of Ursula McConnel in 1927–28, on the relationship between clan identities and the location of estates held by those clans, is available from Appendix 1. This material, as well as the field notes of Donald Thomson made in the region in 1933, provides ample evidence of relative stability in the system of relationships between particular patriclans, particular named dialects, particular totems, and particular estates.[2]

This kind of patrilineal continuity is not merely the consequence of what anthropologists call serial patrifiliation—that is, the cumulative result of an ascending series of one-off filiations to fathers. Wik culture actually conceives of the pattern as continuous, and symbolises the nature of this descent, for example, by the use of the term for 'father's father' (*puul*) as the basis for the term meaning 'patrilineal totem' in several of the languages distinctive to the region, including the *lingua franca* Wik-Mungkan. The common Wik-Way term for patrilineal totem is *olay*, which in Linngithigh, at least, literally also means 'father's father' (Hale 1997a). In Wik-Mungkan, one's *aak puul* is one's patrilineal estate (Kilham et al. 1986:5), *puul-way*[3] is 'patrilineal totem' (ibid.:195; McConnel 1930a:181–205; Thomson 1946), and both are based historically on the ancient proto-Paman root **puula* 'father's father' (Hale 1976c:58), which does not often occur alone in Wik languages but is embedded in the Wik-Mungkan compound *puul-wuut* 'father's father', *wuut* literally meaning 'old man' and in *aak puul* 'father's father country'. In southern Wik languages the equivalent of *puul-way* is *kam-waya* (von Sturmer 1978: Chapter 10). This *kam* is most likely to derive from proto-Paman **kami* 'parallel grandparent, i.e. father's father and mother's mother'.[4]

---

2   For some of the more obvious evidence of such continuity see Appendix 1, Clans 31, 33, 34, 36 and 39 for a sample of matches between McConnel's 1929 data and our own dating from the 1970s to the 1990s.
3   In the upper Archer dialect of Clan 75 the equivalent is *puul-ay*. The evidence thus suggests that Wik-Way *olay* 'totem' may be etymologically the same compound, hence *ol-ay* would derive historically from something like **puul-way*. The pronunciation *pulway* has also been recorded in Wik-Mungkan.
4   While *kam* means 'mother's mother' in contemporary Kugu Nganccharra, von Sturmer (1978:321) argues, successfully in my view, that its historical derivation is from a term meaning 'parallel grandparent' (i.e. both MM and FF), here the reference being to FF (father's father). Note also that *kami* means 'parallel grandparent' (FF/MM) in Cape York Peninsula languages Yintyingka, Guugu-Yimidhirr, and Kuku-Yalanji. Cognates *kame* and *kemiy* have the same FF/MM meaning in CYP languages Pakanh and Wik-Ngathan respectively.

In Wik-Ngathan the term for 'totem' is *kooenhiy*, literally 'sibling'. An animal totem is *minh kooenhiy* 'meat sibling', and an edible plant totem is *may kooenhiy* 'vegetable sibling'. This use of the sibling term presumably reflects the widespread Aboriginal emphasis on the structural equivalence of grandkin and siblings, although it may also be a reference to the father's father's father's father (FFFF) and his brothers (and probably sisters), who in these and many other Aboriginal languages are classified as one's siblings.

While a classical Wik clan principally recruits by descent, not all of its members in every case will know of or claim common descent from a single remembered apical ancestor. Some of the clans do consist of people descended from a single remembered common ancestor, but many do not. As elsewhere in Australia, this does not of itself compromise the definition of the clan as a group recruiting essentially on a principle of descent.

It is thus quite common for a clan to consist of two or more genealogical segments. While there is a high degree of agreement between the relevant group members as to the relationships of genealogical connection between living or recently deceased people, the further back in time one goes, the more likely one is to find that memories of upper generation links between individuals differ. Some may say, for example, that two long deceased members of the same clan were full siblings, while others may say they were only parallel cousins. Incorporation of a foreign patriline into a clan has occurred in modern times.[5]

Clan segments may be ranked, such that the relative seniority of their founding members is recognised. This is a pattern reported for the southern Wik area, among the Kugu Ngancharra (von Sturmer 1978: 337–39). The ranking is made manifest, in particular, by the selection of different 'Big Names' (based on clan totems) for different siblings. It is also possible that different segments within a clan, descended from different siblings, may identify more with one of the clan's totems than another and thus differentiate themselves while holding the same estate. There is not much evidence for this in the northern Wik area, although some fragmentary material supports the likelihood that it occurs there to some

---

5   In the case of Estate 3 (see Appendix 2), there was in the early twentieth century a formal incorporation of the Bowenda patriline into Clan 3. The Bowendas had come to Aurukun from the Doomadgee region, far away, headed by King Bowenda. When he died, his widow Lily married Moses Ampeybegan of Clan 3, and her children with Bowenda were taken by Moses as his children also and thus became members of Clan 3.

extent: descendants of the Wikmunea branch of Clan 6 are known as *Nguungk Piith* ('Grassbird Clan Dialect'), while members of the Pumpkin segment of the same clan are known as *Nguungk Chiiynchiiyn* ('Bushrat Clan Dialect').[6]

These dialect identifiers, like a large number of others, use a principal totem of the clan (sometimes, a clan segment) as the base of the dialect names (here, Grassbird and Bushrat). In Wik ideology, each patriclan has its own dialect, given to it at the beginning of the world.[7] However, several clans also share a different kind of dialect name, based not on a totem but on one of its distinctive lexical features, such as the names that translate as 'Language Go' (Wik-Me'enh, Kugu Mu'inh, Wik-Iiyanh and so on) and 'Language Eat' (Wik-Mungkan). These are the collective linguistic identities commonly referred to as 'tribes', 'dialectal tribes', or 'language groups', in the Australian anthropological literature. More detail on this topic is given in Chapter 5, along with a catalogue of linguistic varieties of the Wik Region.

Not only clans but particular clan segments may emphasise as major totems some phenomenon with which another clan group also identifies. Different groups may use this symbolic sharing on occasion to express a sense of unity among themselves, as when members of a Brolga-associated clan from the Wik area emphasise their amity with another Brolga clan from the Thaayorre language area south of Edward River. People of the same totem, regardless of clan membership, may use those endearing forms of mutual address that stress the quality of 'having the same name' (e.g. *ngalamp* 'namesake', from *ngal* 'we two' and *nhamp* 'name'). In general, however, merely having the same totem as another person does not of itself reach into the heart of how political relationships between groups are conducted.

In summary, a classical Wik clan is a small-scale structural (descent-based) country-holding unit, a unit of totemic identity, and the primary dialectal unit. It is not a residential unit, a household, a camp, or any other kind of economic or physically aggregating set. Nor is it the *exclusive* province within which rights and interests in country are generated and transmitted, although it is the primary domain and entry point for enjoying country

---

6   David Martin, pers. comm., 1997.
7   A detailed account of an example of the mythological genesis of Wik languages, provided by Noel Peemuggina (Clan 6), is in Sutton (1997b).

rights in the classical system. Its members typically have rightful interests in the estates of clans other than their own, such as those of their non-patrilineal forebears (mother's father's patriline especially) and their affines (in simple terms, their spouses and in-laws).

Households, camps, and bands

A bush camp or band, by contrast,[8] was an on-the-ground residential, hunting or other action group. Camps had no formal names, but could be referred to, using the name of the dominant member of the camp, as 'So-and-so's mob'.

As far as we can tell, classical Wik bands, like others well documented elsewhere, were in the past made up usually of individual members drawn from several or even many clans at any one time, and were thus also polyglot groups. Clans were, as they mostly are now, normally out-marrying, so even at the core level of the married couple, at least two clans would normally be represented in any camp in which there was such a couple. A widowed mother present in the camp or household of her married son or daughter—a rather typical arrangement—would frequently be from a third clan. Where the camp had as its core two sisters and their husbands, the husbands would often be from two different clans also. This means that members of a single clan would normally be found scattered through a number of bands at any one time. Conversely, a camp of 10 or 20 people would typically contain people drawn from between several and perhaps a dozen different clans.[9] Wik people do not attribute proprietorial interests in land and waters to bands, or their modern equivalents of households, holiday camps, carloads, outstations, hunting parties and so on.

Band sizes are hard to reconstruct for the period prior to the gradual settlement of Wik Region people at missions, towns and pastoral stations. They would have varied widely from the small, atomised pattern of the

---

8   Since the debate between L.R. Hiatt (1962, 1966) and W.E.H. Stanner (1965) over Aboriginal local organisation, the use of the earlier term 'horde' for an Aboriginal residential group has all but disappeared. This term, as used by A.R. Radcliffe-Brown (1930–31), tended to conflate the descent-based land-holding group with the land-utilising camp group. Anthropological terminology has basically settled for naming the former the 'clan' and the latter the 'band'. A critique of the term 'clan' by Ian Keen (1994, 1995, 1997), particularly as it has been applied in north-east Arnhem Land, has not persuaded us to abandon its use in the Wik context.
9   This can be seen in the lists of names of those present at specific events in the bush recorded during site mapping (see Sutton et al. 1990), and, for more recent times, in the compositions of outstations, hunting parties, households in townships, and so on.

wet season, when people were isolated in small groups, and more or less immobilised and dwelling in waterproof shelters, to the large ceremonial congregations of the late dry season.[10] One tends to think of bands as small foraging groups, averaging, say, 25 people, but larger semi-nomadic camps have been recorded elsewhere, at least, and have been called 'communities' by some anthropologists (see section below, this chapter, Communities). Not only did bands change size, they also changed composition, certainly seasonally, probably from week to week, and probably on occasion from day to day.

1928.10.03 Report on Aurukun mission:
Particulars of native camps:
- Aurukun mission – 56 men, 53 women, 28 boys, 24 girls
- Mouth of Love River, 20m south of Archer River – 25 men, 13 women, 2 boys, 1 girl
- Ootuk [Uthuk Aweyn, Big Lake], big swamp on way to Kendall River – 5 men, 5 women, 1 boy
- Yonko [Yu'engk] district [Cape Keerweer area] between Ootuk and Kendall – 43 men, 19 women, 3 boys, 5 girls
- Knox Creek district north of Kendall – 8 men, 19 women, 9 boys, 6 girls
- Mymungkum [Maymangkem] people inland from Yonko [Maymangkem probably refers to Kencherrang area in this case] – 13 men, 5 women, 5 boys, 2 girls
- Ornyawa [Oony-aw] people behind Mymungkum [north-east Kirke system] – 8 men, 12 women, children in mission
- Ti-tree people south of Mymungkum down to Kendall – 4 men, 4 women, 3 girls
- Warkum [Waakemem] people inland around Love River – 5 men, 4 women, 2 boys, 2 girls
- Wik-ngartona [Wik-Ngathan] people Kendall mouth – 19 men, 12 women, 7 boys, 5 girls
- Wik-ngenchera [i.e. Kugu Ngancharra] people from Kendall mouth to Holroyd mouth – 25 men, 33 women 8 boys, 9 girls
- Patchim [Pechem, 'From Savannah Woodland'] people inland from Kendall to Holroyd – 12 men, 17 women, 2 boys 4 girls

TOTAL: 232 men, 195 women, 67 boys, 61 girls[11]

---

10   For details of seasonal site use by Wik bands, see Thomson (1939), and Sutton (2010).
11   These last figures total 555. However, MacKenzie's details above indicate 161 at Aurukun plus 386 in the bush = 547.

3. LINGUISTIC AND TERRITORIAL ORGANISATION

It is fortunate that in the Wik case there are some demographic details available for people who had not as yet settled at Aurukun Mission. William MacKenzie, then superintendent of Aurukun, recorded the following figures for certain sets of people occupying the bush south of the mission in 1928, while he was on an overland field visit to the Holroyd River from Aurukun:

> These numbers, with the exception of the mission figures, are based on the numbers counted while on patrol this year down to the Holroyd River. These numbers are not complete, for we did not see some of the old people nor all the children, especially down near the Holroyd, where the people were very shy.

Three years later MacKenzie reported:

> NATIVE CAMPS: North and south of the Archer the people live mainly in the Mission, only going out camping at intervals … There are native camps at each of the following places, Yonko [*Yu'engk*, Cape Keerweer], Errimunka [*Eeremangk* = Knox River], Kendall River, King Creek and Holroyd River on the coast, while inland the Mymunkum[12] [eastern Kirke River area], Ornyawa [north-east Kirke system], Ti-tree, and Patchim [upper Holroyd] tribes have their camps. None of these camps are in a fixed locality, nor are the numbers always the same; the people sometimes come into large camps more especially when there is a good food supply and plenty of water, and again splitting up into family groups as the large swamps with the lilies and panjees [edible roots of a swamp grass] get eaten out. Approximate numbers as follows:
>
> YONKO: 20 males, 18 females, 5 children
>
> ERRIMUNKA: 15 males, 14 females, 2 children
>
> KENDALL: 25 males, 30 females, 10 children
>
> HOLROYD: 30 males, 35 females, 15 children
>
> MYMUNKYUM: 15 males, 13 females, 3 children
>
> ORNYAWA: 2 males, 3 females
>
> TI-TREE: 15 males, 12 females, 4 children

---

12   Our informants in the 1970s referred to Maymangkem as an environmental 'nickname' for people from the Ti-Tree area, i.e. the eastern tributaries of the Kirke system. Roughly translated it means 'From Plentiful Food Area' and is not a linguistic title. Since the figures here for 'Mymunkum' and 'Ti-tree' are practically identical, MacKenzie may have taken the same figures twice under different names. On the other hand, the earlier report suggests Maymangkem, in MacKenzie's usage, referred to people concentrated about the Kencherrang area on the middle Kirke, downstream from Ti-tree. In 1960, MacKenzie gave Tindale the term 'Mimungkum' for the Ti-Tree group (Tindale 1974:181).

PATCHIM: 10 males, 8 females, 3 children

CONDITIONS: means of subsistence, native food, game fish, and roots, wild honey. There was no distress from lack of food.

[William MacKenzie, Aurukun, to Chief Protector of Aboriginals, 1931.]

Naturally these numbers are overall well down compared with what they might have been a century earlier, due to the experience of epidemics of the kind described by elder Jack Spear Karntin in the film *Familiar Places* (1980). Unlike so many other Aboriginal peoples and some inland Wik people from the pastoral frontier, these particular groups referred to by MacKenzie did not suffer massacres by colonists and native police. The number of children in the more northerly camps in MacKenzie's reports would have been further reduced by the 1930s because of the influence of the mission, which by this time had reached down to about the Knox ('Errimunka') in its gradual southward extension. As mission influence spread, increasing numbers of bush children were taken to Aurukun where they lived in dormitories, leaving the bush camps with few children. In general, the closer to Aurukun, the smaller the numbers in these inter-War residential aggregates. Overall figures are: children 45, women 133, men 132 (total 310). The sub-regional aggregates of bush people recorded in these two instances by MacKenzie here had an average size of 38.75 persons, but the actual camp sizes within this domain set were variable, according to MacKenzie: 'None of these camps are in a fixed locality, nor are the numbers always the same'.

If each of these entries by MacKenzie were descriptions of single aggregated camps, the band figures for bush camps south of Aurukun in the dry seasons of 1928 and 1931 would be as set out in Table 3.1.

Table 3.1: Bush camp census data 1928 and 1931

District	Head count 1928	Head count 1931
Lower Love River	41	not listed
Ootuk	11	not listed
Yonko	70	43
Knox Creek	42	31
Mymungkum	25	31
Ornyawa	20	5
Ti-tree	11	31

District	Head count 1928	Head count 1931
Warkum	13	not listed
Kendall mouth	43	43
Wik-ngenchera	75	80
Patchim	35	21
TOTALS	**386**	**285**

These figures, while valuable and useful, are based on group labels that are not fully comparable. That is, some of these area names refer in English to river systems (e.g. Kendall River, Holroyd River), some to lower river systems called after a main site near their mouths (Yonko, Errimunka), some to major focal inland sites (Warkum, Ootuk, Ornyawa, Ti-tree), some to a language or set of similar languages (Wik-ngartona, Wik-ngenchera), and some to a social 'nickname' based on the environmental type of country in the clan estates of prominent group residential members (Mymunkum, Patchim). Even if such problems could be erased, however, could such aggregates have been, in the past, the nearest equivalent to 'native title holders'?

It is clear that small bands, larger sub-regional residential aggregates, or their modern equivalents (households, outstations, townships) would be inappropriate 'units' for the process of recognition of native title rights and interests. Households or bands (camps, foraging groups) are notably labile, people being added to them or removed from them at frequent intervals through visiting. Not infrequent cases of conflict also lead to camps or households splitting up for a time. Clans, by contrast, are traditionally viewed by the Wik as enduring corporate entities. They have memberships that change only slowly as births, adoptions and deaths add and remove individual members. The ideal target of the stable corporation is not always met, as in any other society. Clan composition is from time to time disputed. Sets of people (branches, sub-clans) are sometimes added through incorporations and amalgamations, or deleted through clan fission. More importantly, in this context, Wik people conceive of primary rights and interests in country as arising in a privileged way from an essential relationship of identity with, and descent from, one's ancestors, and thus from a higher law than mere human whim. In essence their tenurial system is understood to be not voluntaristic but law-governed. The presence of a person in a land-using residential group is, by contrast, very much a matter of daily decision-making by individuals and families, and reflects the changing states of interpersonal and inter-kin-group politics.

The nature of residence on Wik lands has changed historically far more than the nature of Wik land tenure, since the arrival of pastoral stations in the inland in the late nineteenth century, and the arrival of the Moravian (later Presbyterian) Mission at Aurukun on the coast in 1904. The nearest thing to a pre-settlement band in the present-day Wik case is an outstation camp,[13] a weekend fishing and hunting party, or a township household, although such households, unlike bush camps, are spatially arranged in rows on streets.[14] David Martin has made detailed analyses of Aurukun household composition in terms of clan memberships, rates of mobility between houses, and age and sex breakdowns, from the 1980s (Martin 1993: Chapter 6). Sutton collected some detailed statistics on clans represented at Wik outstations in the 1970s (Sutton 1978:103; Map 13). In *Aak* (Sutton et al. 1990) and the more recent mapping data there are details of remembered camp compositions of the distant past. There seem to be no radical differences between the composition of these various residential aggregates, apart from the relative fixity of the housing being used, the largely post-1970s addition of spouses or partners from other communities (e.g. from Weipa, Pormpuraaw, Groote Eylandt or Bentinck Island) with whom contact has been comparatively recent, and the additions of some non-Aboriginal people as permanent members of the community.

There has always been a stronger emphasis on bands in north American native title cases and legislation than in Australia. But such changeable sets of people, with annual foraging patterns that would vary considerably depending on inter-group relations and annual variations in rainfall, for example, would not be suitable for translation into a form of legal recognition of customary tenure in the Australian case. Apart from the fact that they no longer exist in the same form as they did before settlement, bands, it should be remembered, did not have 'estates' of the highly well-defined and durable sort one finds in the case of the Wik clan estates and larger entities such as the riverine groupings, and had considerably variable compositions over any period of weeks or months. Bands did,

---

13   See Martin and Martin (2016) and Sutton (2016b) for histories of Wik outstations.
14   I have, however, seen a few bush camps set up by bush-reared people where each couple's sleeping place was separated from the next by a small fire, forming a neat row of parallel swags.

however, have regular ranges of travel and foraging (Stanner 1965), and their members also made occasional very long journeys beyond their usual ranges in order to take part in ceremonies with distant groups.

Bands did not confer primary landed identity on their members, while clans do. (Clans have outlived the semi-nomadic foraging bands of the past.) Bands did not have formal names, although, like the outstations and households of today, they could be referred to by expressions based on the name or other identity of the leading person in the band ('So-and-so's mob'), or by using the clan-cluster nickname that typified the core area in which definitive band members had their estates, or by using the name of some geographic focal point frequented by band members. There is no fixed notion of a band's range, although older Wik people in the 1970s could roughly specify how far they would travel in the bush when young (Chase and Sutton 1981:1838).

Core and dominant members of bands certainly seem to have had more or less regular haunts amounting to what Stanner (1965) termed a 'range'. The usufructuary rights of bands are ultimately grounded in clan tenurial rights in estates, however. A band, as such, did not itself have land-use rights as distinct from those of its members individually. Band membership of itself would not confer usufructuary rights in land or waters. Indeed, the word 'membership' is perhaps too corporate-sounding a term for the phenomenon of living with others.

From the data available it is clear that the typical annual range of a man and his wife or wives and various of their children, with or without other relatives, could greatly exceed the size of any one of the sub-regions named in the MacKenzie census lists for 1928 and 1931. Annual events such as cremation ceremonies, for example, attracted people from widespread parts of the Wik Region to single points (Sutton 1978:149, Sutton et al. 1990).

Clan estates, by contrast, offer specifiable sets of sites that define each estate with some stability, and as structural devices clans themselves offer a relatively well-bounded and commonly stable set of core land holders who share not only an estate but a set of totems, totemic names, a ritual group membership, a dialect affiliation, and so on, which are forms of identity and affiliation that resist instant or cavalier realignments. Among their many other functions, the number and complexity of Wik clan totems, and their often convoluted and archaic expression in names and other locutions (see Appendix 1), appear to form a highly conservative and successful barrier against any casual reworking of the tenurial landscape.

A clan's estate and a band's range are also of different epistemological orders, something that is easily obscured when they are paired so habitually. But the former term suggests the corporate and the customary-legal, while the latter is more like behavioural description. Furthermore, the kinds of 'rights and interests' that are focused on matters of landed identity and the proprietary relationship to country are typically those most often associated in many peoples' minds with collective clan (or tribal etc.) membership, while specific rights to use country, such as to catch fish or pick fruit, are typically associated with individual actions. The 'right to forage' is a different kind of right from the right to use possessive first-person pronouns when naming countries, although these rights are intertwined (see section below, this chapter, Households, camps, and bands).

But it is a false dichotomy to pit totemic estate-holding clans against wider categories such as riverine groups or ritual groups[15] in order to find only one of them to be the 'true locus' of land tenure, as if one had to make an exclusive choice between the two. In the Wik case, however, it was, in the classical system, the clan that held a privileged position in Aboriginal discourse about rights in land, although such rights were not confined to the clan. This places the emphasis on recognition of the persistence of the regional tenure system, within which any particular localised proprietary interests are 'carved out'. The regional tenure system is maintained by the regional Wik population, not estate by estate separately.

Earlier accounts

The earlier anthropologists' writings are basically compatible with this approach, although they present a simpler picture and concentrate very heavily on the most local level of tenure. Of the Wik people, Donald Thomson wrote (1939:211–12):

---

15   These terms are explored in more detail below.

> The [patrilineal] clan is the land-owning group; all the members of the clan have hunting rights over the territory of the clan into which they were born. Others, members of the horde[16] who enter the group by marriage or adoption, never acquire ownership of the territory, but secondarily, the right to hunt over it as members of the occupational group. An individual may be permitted, by the recognition of certain bonds of relationship, i.e. by kinship ties, to hunt in the territories of other clans, for example a man is invariably permitted to hunt in the clan territory of his mother.

Ursula McConnel (1957:xv) said of the Wik people: 'Each ground is owned by a clan, members taking their names from the personal characteristics of the pulwaiya [totemic ancestors] over whose auwa (abode) they preside and perform the required ritual'. As McConnel herself realised, however, this is not strictly true of coastal clans whose members' totemic names refer to totems that in a number of cases do *not* have corresponding totemic centres ('auwa' sites) in their own estates, but may occur in others' estates or in no known estate at all. In a letter written at Kendall River to A. R. Radcliffe-Brown in 1928 she said:

> The totems are all localised & it is recognised that certain are 'brother' grounds ^ ie. 'same company' & others not—marriages take place between the grounds lying nearest to one another, not so often between grounds at a distance. Down here on the sandbeach however, there are names & totems not localised on these grounds, but on Munkan grounds & I think this is due to displacement owing to intrusion of people from outside for the physical type here is quite noticeably different from that of the Munkans. (Elkin Papers, University of Sydney Archives, 4/1/57, letter of 3 October 1928)

She published this comment in a revised and expanded form two years later when she again referred to her speculation that 'there may have been a displacement in the coastal region owing to the intrusion of an alien element' (1930a:183 fn.). There is no evidence of any specific 'alien element' of a recent or dramatic kind that would account for such differences, however. Furthermore, two of the coastal clans have estates affiliated with the predominantly inland language Wik-Mungkan (see Estates 12, 20 in Appendix 2) and appear to have been long in situ. The fact that inland

---

16 'Horde' here refers to the band or camp.

clan totems were also to be found as the Beings of sites in their estates, while on the coast there was no such regular correspondence, has all the marks of ancient and entrenched practice.

The language of Wik land tenure

In the Wik languages and in English, people of the Aurukun region will commonly express a possessive relationship between people and particular places or whole land areas by employing the normal genitive/dative ('oblique') pronouns; hence, in Wik-Ngathan, *aak ngathunm* 'my country', *aak thanent* 'their place', *nhath ngampunent* 'our homeland' and so on. A possessive suffix on nouns conveys a similar relationship of possession (*Johnny-ntam aak* 'Johnny's country'). The fact that traditional country is not conceived of as a chattel, however, is in part reflected in the fact that kin terms are uninflected for possession in cases such as *aak puul* (Wik-Mungkan, 'father's father land' [and, usually, by implication, one's own land]), *aak kaath-kaal* (Wik-Ngathan, 'mother and mothers' brother land'), and *aak pepiy* (Wik-Ngathan, 'mother's father country').

Places possessed in this sense are also places of origin, whether or not the people concerned were born or had an early phase of residence at the places concerned. This is expressed by the use of ablative suffixes in Wik languages (such as *-m*) and the preposition 'from' in English, e.g. *Than Eeremangkem* (Wik-Ngathan, 'They are from Knox River'), '*Ngampel Yu'engkem*' (Wik-Ngathan: 'We are all from the *Yu'engk* [lower Kirke River] area'); *Than Oony-awam* (Wik-Mungkan, 'They are from Ornyawa Lagoons country') and so on. The same expressions can, however, also be used of current places of residence ('We are from Aurukun') without any firm implication of customary rights of possession. It is usually recognised that the town site of Aurukun, for example, belongs at the finest-grained level to Estate 29 (see Appendix 2).

People who hold responsibility for country under traditional Aboriginal law are said to be 'looking after' it (*kooepeyn*, in Wik-Ngathan). This verb has two senses: an intransitive usage, 'to wait', and a transitive usage, 'to be custodian of, look after, supervise'. The Wik-Mungkan verb *kuupan* has these same two usages (Kilham et al. 1986:80).

In Cape York Peninsula English, the term 'tribal land' is in common currency as referring to land affiliations based, not purely on residential history, but on inheritance through various principles of Aboriginal customary law. The communal rather than individual emphasis of this notion is partly suggested by the choice of the term 'tribal'. In recent decades the term 'clan' has also come into vogue at Aurukun and is often used to refer to the five rather large ceremonial groupings that have geographic groupings at their base (see section above, this chapter, Regional ceremonial groups, and Map A1.1), and occasionally to outstation groups, or to what I and other anthropologists would call a 'clan' in the technical sense (an estate-holding descent group). Context will usually make it clear in what sense the phrase is intended.

These English words may be interpreted as various translations of indigenous terms such as X-*punchan* (Wik-Mungkan) or X-*poencheyn* (Wik-Ngathan, Wik-Elken), which are adjectives meaning 'belonging to place X, usually under Aboriginal customary law'. These expressions appear to be based on gerunds derived from intransitive verb stems, which in each case have a root meaning of 'to descend, to go down into' (see Kilham et al. 1986:191; Sutton 1995a:82). This is probably a reference to the fact that the totemic and heroic ancestral Beings who created the landscape's clan estates and their sacred totemic places (*aw*, Wik-Mungkan; *eemoeth*, Wik-Ngathan, Wik-Elken etc.; *awu* in the inland and southern Wik Subgroup languages), thus allocating people to territory, 'went down' into the earth at the site of the totemic centres. Increase rites performed at such places are referred to as 'throwing' (*thee'an*, most Wik languages) the phenomenon. This is the standard idiom used for digging a hole in the ground such as when unearthing tubers, or for cleaning out an existing well.

In Wik-Ngathan the phrase X-*weykanh* means 'to belong to X [place]', 'to have X [area] as one's lawful run' (Sutton 1995a:124). Older people's Wik-Mungkan also has the cognate idiom *aakan wakan*, literally 'to follow a country', meaning 'to come from [place X]' (Kilham et al. 1986:2). In the southern Wik languages *pama* X-*wakanh* means literally 'people who frequent X', the latter verb carrying the primary suggestion of legal occupiers rather than mere inhabitants (von Sturmer 1978:270–71).

Other local terms expressing relations of belonging between people and land are often translated into English as 'countryman', 'owner of the land' or 'boss for the land', and 'full country', 'own country', 'really country', 'company land', and so on. The first set stresses the bond between a set of two or more people or groups of people based on common relations to land, and the second set stresses various levels of exclusivity and sharing in possessive relations with land.

The first term, 'countryman', is matched in Wik-Mungkan by *aak-kunch* ('owner(s) or boss(es) of a certain territory', Kilham et al. 1986:3,76) and in Wik-Ngathan by *aak-koenth* ('members of clans with adjacent or nearby estates who share country and knowledge and who engage in joint activities such as cremations', Sutton 1978:128).

As explained by von Sturmer (1978:274–78), the English expression 'full country' in the southern Wik Subgroup region translates *agu kunyji* or 'heartland'. *Kunyji* in varieties of Kugu Ngancharra is cognate with the expressions *kuunch* and *kooenhiy* in other Wik languages, and all three refer to siblings. (These are not the same as *kunch* and *koenth*.) *Agu kunyji* is non-company land normally inherited from the father. Company land, rights in which are also normally inherited from the father, are referred to in Kugu Ngancharra as *agu ngalagun*. Both company and non-company land in the south are *agu pibinam*, 'country from father'. In Wik-Mungkan the expression *aak puul* ('father's father country') is the usual term for country inherited from father/father's father, and is often translated as 'real country' or 'proper country'. These expressions reflect the traditional privileging of patrilineal descent as a primary pathway to membership of land-holding groups in the Wik Region. As explained elsewhere in this book, a post-classical tendency of choosing between any immediate ancestors as sources of country identity has been emerging.

The southern term *agu ngalagun* has an equivalent in Wik-Ngathan in *aak thaa' mayng* (respect form: *aak thaanth math*), literally 'country mouth together'. The Wik-Mungkan equivalent is *aak thaa' karrp* (same translation). This refers to company land, land held in common between two or more identifiable land-associated groups. Dative pronouns, commonly used for possessive constructions, are frequent in the use of such expressions, e.g. *aak ngampunt mayng* ('our [plural inclusive] joint land', Wik-Ngathan). Places held in common between two or more clans are in this company category in its narrowest or strictest sense, but conjoint interests in land extend outwards from this most local sense to the arena of the cluster of a number of adjacent estates and even to the wider riverine groupings of many estates (see next section).

There was in the past, and to a far lesser extent in recent decades, a correlation between the geographic closeness of clan estates and the genealogical closeness of their traditional owners. Close relations (Wik-Ngathan *uu'eth*) are classically associated with a particular local district, known as *aak uu'eth*, 'home country' (Sutton 1995a:114), more specifically 'area of one's blood relations and close family'. This may be larger than a single clan estate but is smaller than a large region such as the Archer-Kendall area, although it is the sort of term that would have variable scope of reference depending on social context.

Small estate clusters

In a number of cases, two clan estates are very closely linked and on occasion spoken of, and perhaps at times strongly conceived of, as being 'one'. Estates 14 and 27, for example, are contiguous and lie on tributaries of the same river system, the upper Kirke River. At times in the past they have been presented to ethnographers as two distinct but closely linked estates, each held by minimally distinct clans—that is, the clans in each case have all totems in common except one, and this one difference is reflected in the major surnames now associated with each clan (Pootchemunka and Ngakyunkwokka; see Appendix 1: Clans 14 and 35; Appendix 2: Estates 14 and 27). By the 1990s, however, the two estates had essentially merged to become one.

The two clans retained their distinct identities as sets of surnamed descent groups and indeed experienced a marriage between two of their respective members. In any one generation their members are not 'brothers and sisters' but 'cousins', so marriage between their members is certainly not prohibited by traditional incest prohibitions on marriages between (real or) classificatory siblings. So, in an exceptional case having 'one estate' is not of itself a bar to intermarriage. Nor is the possession of some or even many of the same totems a bar to marriage. The key bar to marriage or the forming of a recognised liaison among Wik people, aside from local political factors, is being in a kinship relationship deemed unacceptable, either by closeness of blood, or by reason of being in the wrong category (such as classificatory 'father/daughter', 'sister/brother' or 'mother-in-law/son-in-law').

In another case it is clear from a comparison of McConnel's 1929 data (McConnel 1930b) and our own that two closely linked estates have been, at least for some long time, merged into one in the area of Running Creek, which flows west to the Archer River, and the adjacent head of a tributary running south-west into the Kendall River. That is, in 1929 McConnel's 'local groups' IX(a) and IX(b) had estates that together are now identified as Estate 49 (*Ku'-aw*), belonging to Clan 39 (Koowartas). In 1929 the members of McConnel's group IX(a), antecedents of the present Koowartas and with an estate on Running Creek, numbered eight to 10 people, while group IX(b) (whose estate was on a Kendall tributary) contained only one surviving member, who was female. The extinction of the patriline for the latter group must have occurred not long afterwards, as by the 1990s any distinction between the two estates appeared to have lapsed. This cannot be taken to be the end of the story, though. The fact that the Running Creek drainage is into the Archer River system, while that of old estate IX(b) is into the Kendall system, remains obvious and may well form the basis of the re-emergence of two estates here in the future, especially given current population increases among Wik people.

In a different case, that of Estates 3 and 4 (Small Lake and Big Lake respectively), the very close linkages between the two estates, which are contiguous and on the same drainage system flowing south to the Kirke River, have allowed them to almost become one. These two areas are known in local languages as *Uthuk Eelen* ('Small Lake') and *Uthuk Aweyn* ('Big Lake'), or *Weenem Eelen* and *Weenem Aweyn* (Wik-Ngathan), or *Uthuk Mayn* and *Uthuk Pi'an*, or *Weenem Mayn* and *Weenem Pi'an* (Wik-Mungkan), respectively. These two lake names are references to stellar constellations (*uthuk*, 'Milky Way', *weenem*, 'Southern Cross'), possibly also to lawyer cane (*weenem*). They are qualified by the adjectives *eelen* (Nn) = *mayn* (Mn) 'small', and *aweyn* (Nn) = *pi'an* (Mn) 'big'. Their English names, unpoetic as they are, are used here as they are more widely known.

In the pre–World War II period, Clan 3 and Clan 4 had been of common language, Wik-Elken, and shared at least their major totem (Magpie Goose), but their members had intermarried. By the mid-1970s Estate 3 (Small Lake) had long been without clear successors after its former owning clan (Clan 3) had become extinct. At that time a series of succession negotiations was entered into between parties with interests in the estate. A few people of Clan 6 had had a father's mother from Clan 3 and they sought succession on this basis. One man from the adjacent Estate 28 (Clan 31) claimed long association with the area from babyhood. Members of Clan 4, with the abutting Estate 4 and a past history of close intermarriage with erstwhile members of Clan 3, maintained an interest also.

The arguments of the person who claimed long if intermittent physical presence on the estate were widely dismissed as insufficient. The descent-based claims were treated with considerable respect. By the early 1990s the succession had been effectively resolved in favour of members of Clan 4 (two branches: Ampeybegans and Bowendas, the latter being in the first rank in relation to Estate 3 and therefore now given a distinct Clan number, 59). Whether Bowendas could maintain central roles in the affairs of both estates (3 and 4) for very long was not clear. Members of Clan 4 could claim an exceptional combination of ancestral connections, immediate estate proximity, same dialect as that of Clan 3, a shared principal totem *Minh Kalpay* (Magpie Goose), and a history of presence on the estate under negotiation, on top of which they had a vigorous and prominent spokesman, Denny Bowenda (1932–2008). It is my view, however, that the original close structural linkage between the two estates also mitigated against their becoming further 'separated' through a succession involving people from south of the Kirke (from Estate 6) who were making an attempted succession to Estate 3 on the basis of ancestry.

In the area of the lower Embley River there are estates held by a set of clans whose totems are almost all the same (Clan 67/Estate 46, Clan 68/Estate 47, Clan 70/Estate 39, Clan 80/Estate 146, Clan 84/Estate 149). Two of these, however, are of the Alngith language (Clans 67, 80), two are of Linngithigh language (Clans 68, 84) and one is of Mamangathi language (Clan 70). There are contexts in which estates 46 (lower Embley south side) and 146 (Weipa Peninsula) are regarded as 'one', because of three main factors: the estates are contiguous, the relevant clans share most or all totems, and they also share a common language affiliation. It is clear, however, that at the most localised level a distinction between the two clans and estates was recognised by senior members of both. For most younger people, however, such finer points are today of less importance as they lean more towards an areal approach, still identifying with focal ancestral sites ('main places') but also with an area composed of several classical estates.

Where a person identifies with a broad Wik sub-area (e.g. 'Bottom Kendall', i.e. the lower Kendall River area), but is unable to be precise about clan estate boundaries, for example, it remains true that their identification with the broader area is historically rooted in their origins as a descendant of a clan that holds a definable estate within it. Such people may refer to older or more knowledgeable individuals if they need to obtain more precise territorial information about themselves. In some cases, the location of estate boundaries is no longer an issue: several clans may have become extinct, leaving a number of estates in an area without proximate title holders[17] for the time being, and conjoint succession to such estates may be occurring.

In conjoint succession, clans holding neighbouring estates collectively act as custodians of estates whose clans have become extinct. This is true for the Wik-Way area, although in that case there is a distinction (not a very hard and fast one) between the surviving northern and southern Wik-Way, the southern Wik-Way having particular responsibility for the area south of about Beagle Camp. This particular form of 'clustering' is a response to rapid depopulation, which early in the twentieth century seems to have affected the Wik-Way area more than other parts of the Wik Region.

Roth (1905) suggested this depopulation north of the Archer was caused by aggression from the east and south by other Aboriginal people. There is no other evidence in support of this. The population density between the Archer and just south of the Embley was much lower than at Albatross Bay or south of the Archer, to start with, as the zone lacks substantial wetlands and has no rivers. Infertility and disease appear to have been the main causes of depopulation among the Wik-Way, judging from the death records and genealogical data available.[18]

In the area of the Thuuk River and middle lower Holroyd (in their local usages) there are two estates, numbers 123 (near the coast) and 130 (inland). A single *Kug-Uthu* or 'Dead Body Language' clan group is associated with both, although Estate 123 is particularly associated with two clan segments (A: Ngallametta/Ngallapoorgum/Ngakapoorgum, B: Wunchum) and Estate 130 with a third (C: Mimpanja/Yantumba).

---

17   See Sutton (1996) for the distinction between proximate and underlying customary Aboriginal titles.
18   In Sutton (2017) I have tabulated the Aurukun records on age at death and cause of death for those people known to the Mission, or known to the Aurukun Shire that succeeded it in 1978.

3. LINGUISTIC AND TERRITORIAL ORGANISATION

In spite of their relative unity, segments A and B have the coastal language Kug-Uwanh, while segment C has the inland language Wik-Iiyanh.[19] Homogeneity of language is clearly not a pre-requisite for co-membership of such a group, just as in the lower Embley case examined above. In order to distinguish such clusters of clans and estates, they might be described as 'macro-clans' and 'macro-estates'.

Ursula McConnel thought that such cases of close linkage or possible merging of estates and their clans were the result of recent depopulation in the 1920s. She said:

> Owing to the disintegrated state of the clans and their depleted numbers it is sometimes difficult to ascertain where one clan ends and another begins. In cases of uncertainty I have grouped as sections of one clan, totemic groups which may form separate clans (McConnel 1930a:81fn.).

While the frequency of occurrence of such cases might have been accelerated by the loss of population in the region in the early part of the twentieth century, the mechanisms involved seem too consistent and widespread to be described as new developments as such. They seem to rest on classical structural principles.

There are several other kinds of small localised clustering of Wik clan estates. Those dealt with below are 'nickname' groupings, spirit-image centre groupings, cremation countrymen groupings, localised totemic cult groups, and outstation groupings.

Clans with adjacent estates often share what is locally referred to in English as a 'nickname' based on a local environmental typifier or a major placename (see Sutton 1978:126–28). Thus *Kuuchenm*, for example, is the nickname for several clans with estates characterised by the lancewood tree (*yuk kuuchen*, *Thryptomene oligandra*, Sutton 1995a:30) that grows on the sandridges in the lower Kirke River area. (For a listing and map of several such clusters in the area Love River to Kendall River, see Sutton 1978:127, Map 9.)[20]

Clans who send the spirit-images (*koetheth maayn*) of their recent dead to a common spirit image-centre also make up small clusters of groups with adjacent estates. Some of these spirit-sending centres (*aak pam-kaawkeyn*

---

19 John von Sturmer, pers. comm., 1997. See Appendix 1: Clan list.
20 Where recorded, these nicknames are provided for each clan in Appendix 1.

in Wik-Ngathan, *aak kaa'-kuchan* in Wik-Mungkan) are used uniquely for the deceased of a single clan, while others may be common to several clans whose estates are clustered together in the same area. For two such sets of estates see Sutton (1978:Map 12). Human spirit-images are normally sent to their homeland areas at night and shortly after the death. The practice was widespread among Wik peoples until recently. It was a form of continuity in the maintenance of connection with country, which an outsider might describe as 'cultural' or 'spiritual' but which for those engaged in the practice involves the sending of an aspect of a person's actual substance to their traditional country.

Sets of clans whose members were cremated in common cremation grounds, prior to the introduction of burial as a result of mission influence, constitute sets of 'countrymen' (in Wik-Ngathan, *aak-koenth*) at a certain localised level. In the 1970s older people could list the clans whose members were cremated at such single points. Such clusters were probably in general made up of just a few clans whose estates were adjacent (see Sutton 1978:128, Map 12).

There are also small clusters of estates whose primary holders share a localised totemic cult affiliation, such as Shark in the lower Kirke River area (Estates 4, 5, 6, 7, 8), and Dog in the lower Knox River area (Estates 15, 16, 18, 20). For further examples of these particular types of clusters see Sutton (1978:140).

The clans holding the estates closest to, and including, a particular outstation also form clusters for whom the name of the outstation may function as a common badge of identity. In some cases, tee-shirts carrying the name of the outstation may be purchased and worn by members of clans from such clusters, especially at special events such as mortuary ceremonies. The name of an outstation has become a legitimate, if only middlingly precise, form in which people may answer questions about where their traditional country lies. (For examples of four outstation clan estate clusters studied in the 1970s see Sutton 1978:Map 13.)

Riverine identity groups

Clans with estates on the same riverine drainage system are typically significant allies who for a long time past have closely intermarried and who identify with each other, both in times of conflict and at other times, by reference to their common river of origin. Before the advent of English, the riverine group names appear in the main to have been based on an extension of the scope of the name of a principal site close to the mouth of the river, except where the relevant grouping was based on just the upper reaches of a large river system. The Love River people were formerly known as the people from *Thoekel* (known in another dialect as *Thukali*, the 'Tokalie River' of old maps), the name of a base camp site near the river's mouth. The 'Cape Keerweer' (lower Kirke River) people were formerly known as the people from *Yu'engk* (the missionaries' 'Yonka River'), a site near the Kirke mouth. The 'Knox River' people were formerly known as the people from *Eeremangk* (the missionaries' 'Errimangk'), a site at the mouth of that river. And so on. Rivers as wholes were not named. Creeks were named 'X-arm' where X was a site name, as in *Punth Iincheng* 'Iincheng Creek'.

Between the Archer and Embley rivers, depopulation earlier in the twentieth century may have reduced the effectiveness or relevance of identity groupings based on the lower Archer, Ward and Watson rivers, but it is also notable that no major river system enters the sea between the Archer and the Embley, so the geography does not lend itself easily to riverine groupings in the way that the area south of Archer River does.

The area from the lower Archer to the Embley is often referred to collectively as 'Wik-Way', but there is still a distinction made, at times, between the lower Archer/Ward River/Norman River area and the zone between there and the Embley, the latter being the northern Wik-Way area. The Watson River area is not usually identified as Wik-Way and is often conjoined with the adjacent Tompaten Creek area. The latter is locally known as Small Archer and the relevant riverine identity is also described as 'Small Archer' (see Appendix 2).

By the 1970s, the main and active riverine group terms were:

- 'Archer River' (subdivided into 'Small Archer' (Tompaten Creek) and 'Main Archer', the latter again subdivided into 'Top Archer', 'Bottom Archer' and 'Archer Bend')
- 'Love River' (subdivided into 'Bottom Love' and 'Top Love')
- on the Kirke River system: 'Cape Keerweer' (lower Kirke River system), 'Kencherrang' (middle Kirke River, an outstation name), 'Oony-aw' (upper northern Kirke tributary, a site and estate name), 'Ti Tree' (upper eastern Kirke River tributaries)

- 'Knox River' (the Knox Creek of official maps)
- 'Kendall River' (subdivided into 'Top Kendall', 'Bottom Kendall' and 'South Kendall', the latter being the 'Holroyd River' of official maps)
- 'Thuuk (Snake) River' (the Hersey Creek of official maps)
- 'Christmas Creek' (the Balurga Creek of official maps)
- 'Holroyd River' (the Christmas Creek of official maps, subdivided into 'Top Holroyd' and 'Bottom Holroyd').

Note also that the lower Edward River is in local Kugu Ngancharra usage referred to as 'Breakfast Creek'.

Relationship patterns after the mid-1970s show a gradual trend away from tight-knit marriage clusters or connubia within these riverine groups (Martin 1993:Chapter 2, cf. Sutton 1978:106–17), but as forms of identity based on country of origin the broadly inclusive riverine groupings, and Wik-Way as a different kind of sub-regional designation, continued to have great salience for Wik people.

Regional ceremonial groups

Large sets of clans with estates in a particular sub-region, typically one larger than any of the cluster areas described above, make up the five ceremonial groupings Shivirri, Apelech, Winchanam, Puch and Wanam, locally referred to at Aurukun as 'the five clan groups' (Map A1.1).

The Shivirri (also known as Shivri, Chivirri, Saarra) ceremonial group is more or less co-extensive with the category of Wik-Way, and relates to the sub-region from the Archer to the Embley River.

Winchanam, being the northern inland Wik ceremonial group, includes the majority of the 'topside' people within the Wik universe. The relevant sub-region is basically the middle and upper Archer system and Small Archer (Tompaten Creek), south via the heads of the major watercourses to the upper Kendall–Holroyd area. The late John Koowarta belonged to this ritual group, and its name has thus entered legal history.[21] Although now principally identified with a particular inland ceremonial content

---

21 *Koowarta v Bjelke-Petersen* (1982) 153 CLR 168.

and style (dance, myth, song, paint), Winchanam was also the name of the second stage of male initiation across the whole Wik Region south of Archer River, a ceremony that was last held in 1970.

The 'bottomside' (coastal) Wik people, i.e. people whose ancestral clan estates are on and near the coast or coastal floodplains south of the Archer River, belong to either Apelech, Puch or Wanam ceremonial groups. Apelech group members have estates on the upper and lower Love, lower and middle Kirke, and lower Knox rivers. South of there, Puch (also known as Key-elp) estates are on the lower Kendall and Thuuk rivers. Further south again, Wanam estates are on the Holroyd River and Christmas Creek (as named in in local usage). Clearly, the entry point to membership of these five ritual groups is via one's clan of birth.

These ritual groups have unambiguous core memberships, but some of their core members' estates border on those of neighbours whose inclusion in the same ceremonial group is less definite or central, or who have dual identification with adjoining ceremonial groups. For example, the lower Knox River estates (15, 18, 19, 20) are Apelech, like those to their north as far as Love River. The middle Knox River people of Estate 16 'come in with' Apelech and 'give them a hand', and are described as 'mixed [with] Apelech' but are not widely regarded as Apelech pure and simple. Their own immediate inland neighbours, on the head of Knox River, are Winchanam (see Appendix 2: Estate 17) like most of the other northern inland Wik groups.

Thus, between the coast proper and inland proper there are sometimes estates and estate-holders, who are intermediate between the two in terms of certain aspects of cultural identity and alliance patterns.

These ceremonial group identities remain of importance for Wik people. Performances of their distinctive dramas are a regular part of house-opening ceremonies for deceased Wik individuals (see the film *House-Opening* [1980]). The heroic legendary figures of such ceremonial forms are held to have allocated the estates of each particular sub-region to the various totemic clans at the foundation of the world (Sutton 1997b).

The coast/hinterland distinction

The broadest and most powerful internal geopolitical distinction among the Wik peoples is the coast/hinterland division, often referred to locally as 'bottomside' and 'topside' people, or the equivalent 'saltwater' and 'freshwater' people. This was so in the past, when the population was far more decentralised, but it remains highly significant in spite of the fact that most Wik people now spend most of each year close to the coast at Aurukun.

This is clearly because the relevant terms refer not to residential arrangements but to the location of the clan estates of the relevant people, regardless of where those people reside. Many of the estates of Wik people are far distant from settlements such as Napranum, Aurukun or Pormpuraaw. Not all are near outstations. Thus the distinction is ultimately one between people as land-holders, made on the coast/hinterland axis, not one based on population distributions. One is an inlander or a coastal person, a freshwater or saltwater person, for life.

At Aurukun there has long been a decreasing correlation between where people are housed in the village and the orientation of their estates of origin, but many inlanders still live at the eastern (inland) end of Aurukun and many coastal people still live at the western end—the 'topside' people of the village are concentrated at the upper or inland end, and the 'bottomside' are concentrated at the lower or Gulf end. This reflects the universal tendency of classical Aboriginal groups to reside on the side of a residential site that reflects their territorial origins.

Communities

This term is used in three main ways in writings on Aboriginal people. One refers to what Barry Smith (1989) has called the 'geographic community', basically the population of Aboriginal people at a settlement such as Aurukun, Napranum or Pormpuraaw, regardless of how socially integrated such a collectivity may or may not be. Another sense of 'community' refers to an Aboriginal social field within the wider context in which it is embedded, such as the Aboriginal community of Cairns, or the Aboriginal community of Australia.

The third sense is one confined to anthropological writings such as those of Meggitt (1962) and Hiatt (1965). In these cases, one from the fringe Western Desert (Meggitt) and one from north-central Arnhem Land (Hiatt), clusters of local land-holding groups were named and these authors also implied that these named groups were land-occupying groups as well. From a detailed examination of their data (Sutton 2003:98–107), I have concluded that if these 'community' names were used in this latter sense, it was by extension or in some other way distinguishable from their primary function as titles for clusters of tenurial units.

Such a dual function also seems to be characteristic of Wik names that refer primarily to localised clusters of estates and their relevant clans. Thus riverine terms such as 'Kendall River mob' might on occasion refer not only to people whose ancestral country lies on the Kendall drainage system, but by extension to such people together with their spouses and others living with them at a certain time.

Tribes and language groups

A common language affiliation may be shared by clans that have contiguous estates, but it may also be shared by clans with non-contiguous estates. In the latter case, these clans may belong to different sub-regional political groupings such as different riverine alliances and regional ritual groups. The distribution of any one language can be mosaic-like, cropping up here and there across the landscape, separated by estates belonging to other languages.[22] Earlier ethnographers did not know enough about the details of land relationships and language affiliation to know this, and produced a 'one language per area' model on maps (Maps 3.1–3.7).[23] Specific Wik languages are not typically coterminous with the salient geo-political classical groupings of the region.

---

22 See Map 2.3 in Sutton (1991:63).
23 Maps 3.1–3.7 are details of those published by McConnel (1957:xviii), Sharp (1939:440), Thomson (1972:vi), Tindale (1940, 1974 [including maps]), Walsh (1981–83), and Dixon (2002:xxviii). These are the principal linguistic maps of the study area based on independent research other than those presented in Maps A2.1–2.13.

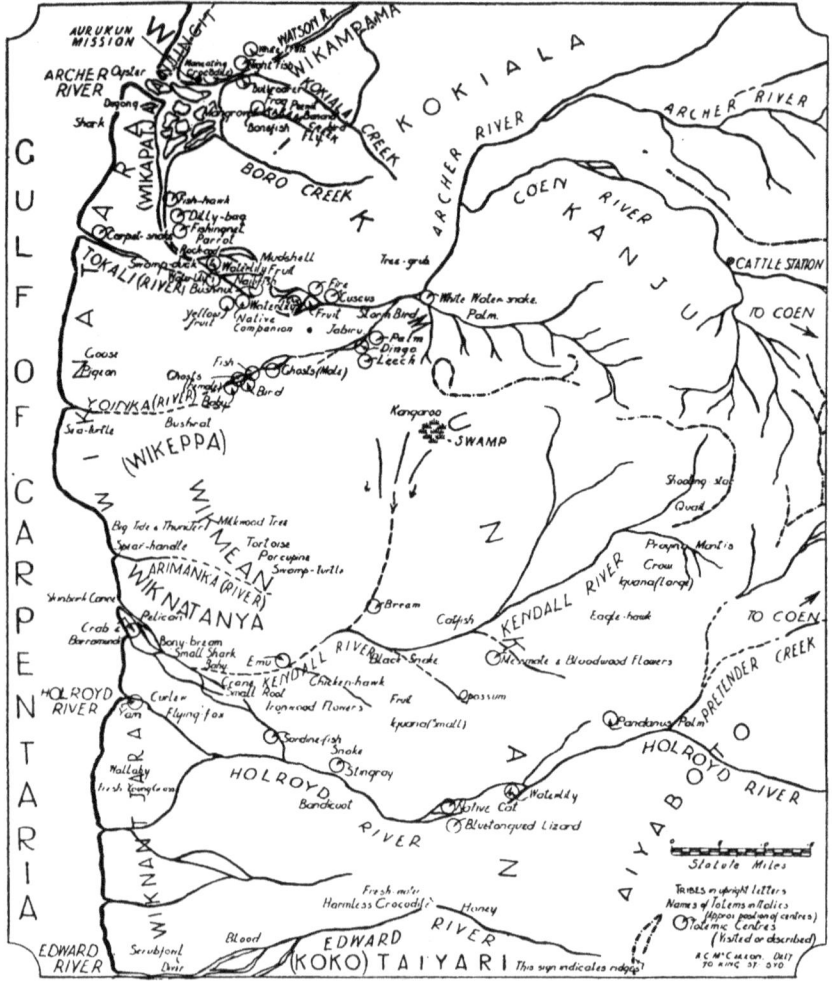

Map 3.1: WCYP language countries (McConnel)
Source: McConnel (1930a)

3. LINGUISTIC AND TERRITORIAL ORGANISATION

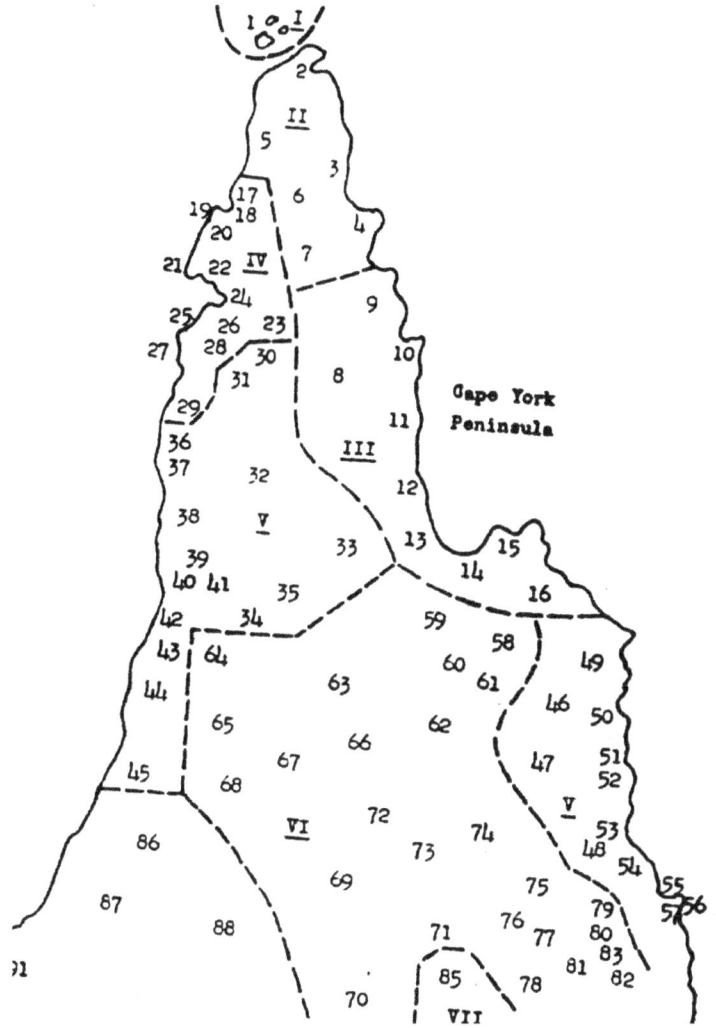

Map 3.2: WCYP language countries (Sharp)

IV[24] Tjongandji type: 17 Ngathokadi; 18 Tepethiki; 19 Tjongandji; 20 Yop'ngadi; or Ngerikadi; 21 Wimarango; 22 Ngwatangeti; 23 'Kauwala'; 24 Lenngeti; 25 Mamangeti; 26 Latangeti; 27 Anda'angeti; 28 Aditinngeti; 29 Wik Alkina or Wik Natera.

Extinct tribe: Wik Tinda and perhaps others.

V Yir Yoront type (western sector only):

30 Kok Mbewam; 31 Kok Iala; 32 Wik Munkan and Wik Ianyi; 33 Aiabado; 34 Aiakampana; 35 Aiabakan; 36 Wik Me'ana; 37 Wik Natanya; 38 Wik Ngantjera; 39 Ngantja; 40 Ngentjin; 41 Taior; 42 Yir Yoront; 43 Yir Mel; 44 Koko Pera; 45 Koko Papung and Koko Paperum.

Source: Sharp (1939)

---

24 Sharp's Roman numerals here refer to types of totemic systems.

53

LINGUISTIC ORGANISATION AND NATIVE TITLE

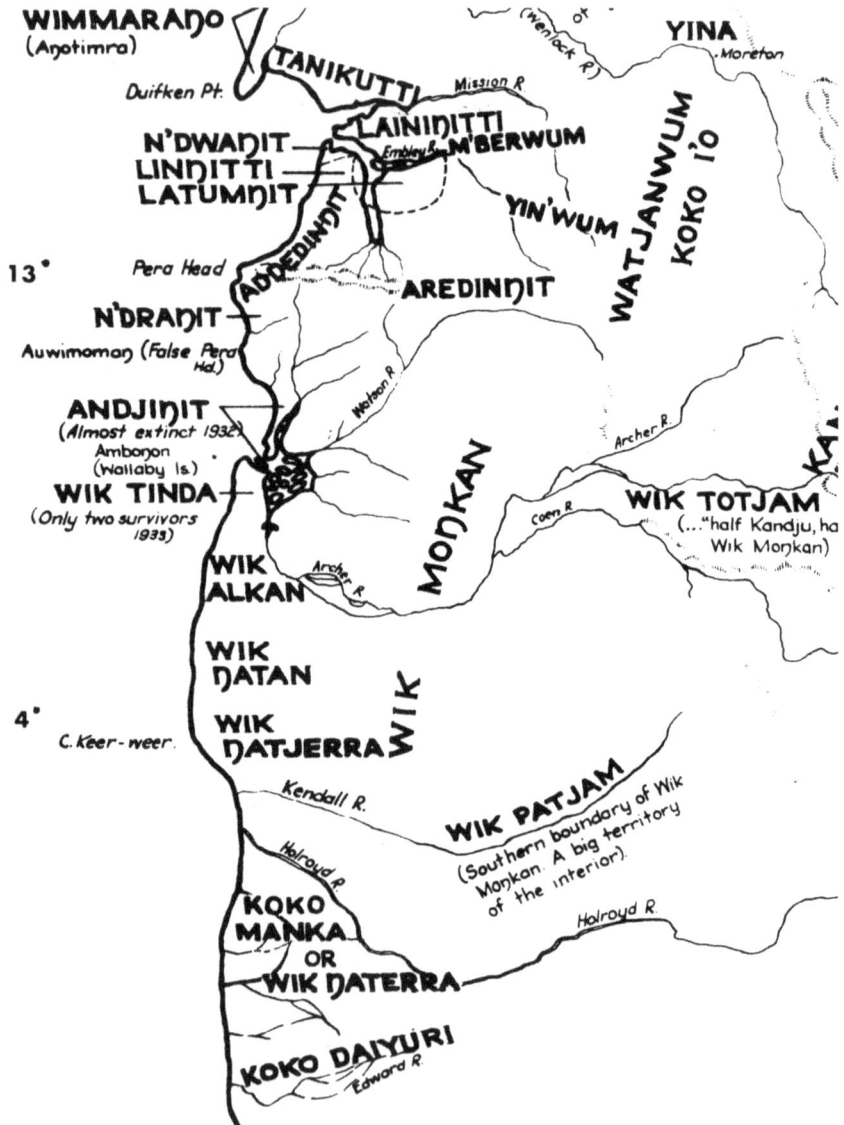

Map 3.3: WCYP language countries (Thomson)
Source: Thomson (1972)

3. LINGUISTIC AND TERRITORIAL ORGANISATION

Map 3.4: WCYP language countries (Tindale 1940)
Source: Tindale (1940)

LINGUISTIC ORGANISATION AND NATIVE TITLE

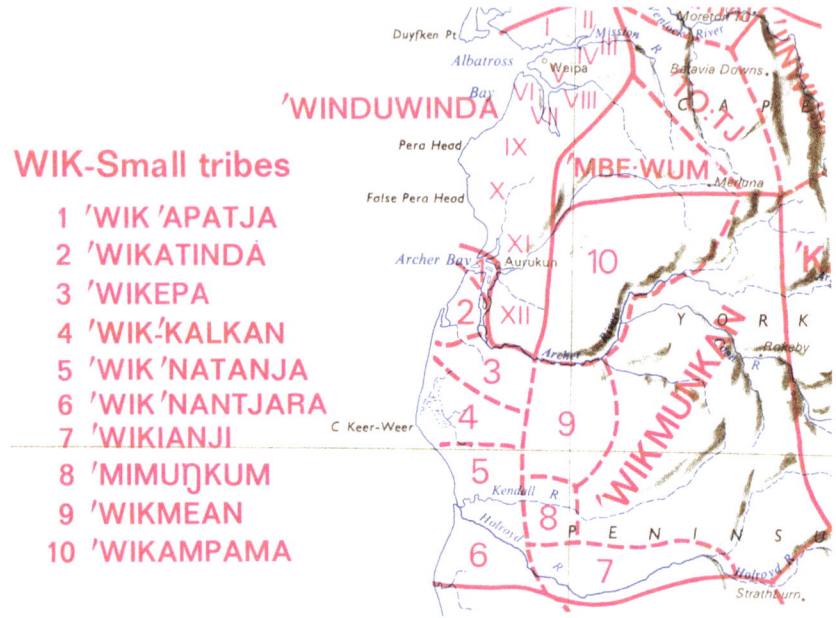

Map 3.5: WCYP language countries (Tindale 1974)
I Tanikuit [Thanikwith], (Tannikutti, Dainiguid, Tannagootee)
II Ndruangit [Ndrwa'ngith]
III Ndwangit [Ndwa'ngith], (Ndwongit)
IV Ngawangati (Ngawateingeti, Ungauwangati)
V Alingit (Lengiti, Lenngiti, Alngid, Limretti [?typographical error])[25]
VI Mamangit [Mamangith], (Mamangiti, Mamngaid)
VII Latamngit (Lätamngit)
VIII Nggot (Gott)
IX Aretinget [Arrithinngith]
X Ndraangit
XI Leningiti
XII Andjingit
Source: Tindale (1974)

---

25 Tindale's suggestion.

3. LINGUISTIC AND TERRITORIAL ORGANISATION

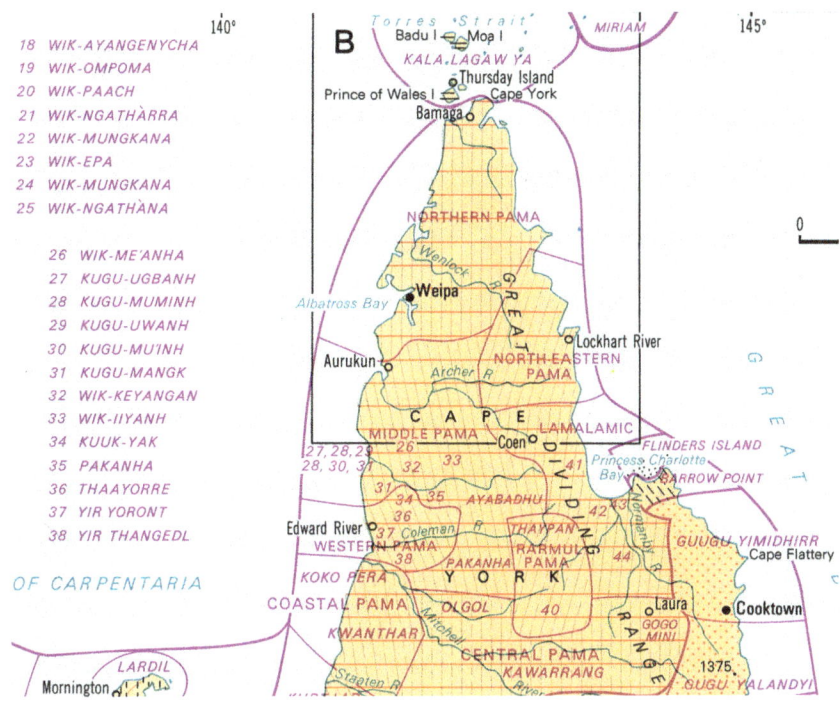

Map 3.6: WCYP language countries (Walsh)
Source: Walsh (1981–83)

In Wik tradition, several clans may have a common language, with a single shared name such as Andjingith, Mbiywom, Wik-Ngathan, Wik-Me'enh, Wik-Mungkan, Kugu Uwanh or Kugu Muminh. The languages may have different names depending on the variety being used. Hence, self-named Andjingith is known as Wik-Ayangench in Wik-Ngathan, self-named Mbiywom is known as Wik-Ompom in Wik-Mungkan, self-named Kugu Muminh is known as Wik-Muminh in Wik-Mungkan, and so on.[26] These names are generally based on distinctive items of vocabulary. For example, *muminh* means 'go, walk', and *mungkan* means 'eat', and *ngathan* is a rarely encountered oblique first person pronoun 'mine'.

---

26   For a catalogue of such alternate language names see Chapter 5.

LINGUISTIC ORGANISATION AND NATIVE TITLE

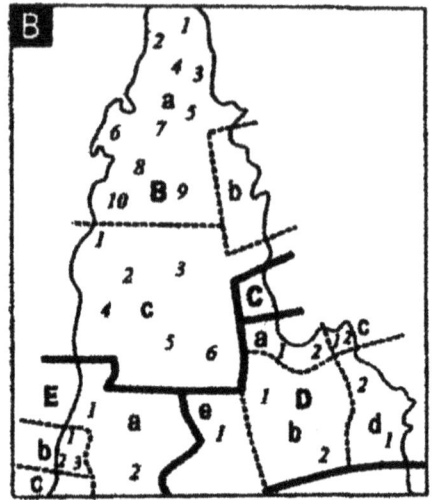

Map 3.7: WCYP language countries (Dixon)

Ba Northern Paman subgroup

Ba1 Gudang (other dialect: Djagaraga)

Ba2 Uradhi (other dialects Angkamuthi, Yadheykenu, Atampaya)

Ba3 Wuthati

Ba4 Luthigh (other dialect Mpalitjanh)

Ba5 Yinwum (probable other dialect Njuwadhai)

Ba6 Anguthimri (other dialects Nggerikudi or Yupungati, Tjungundji, Mpoakwithi, Awngthim (with subdialects Mamngayt, Ntrwa'ngayth, Thyanngayth), Ntra'ngith, Alngith, Linngithigh)

Ba7 Ngkoth (other dialects Tootj[27] (or Kauwala), Ngaawangati or Ungauwangati)

Ba8 Aritinngithigh (or Aritinngayth) (other dialect Latamngit)

Ba9 Mbiywom

Ba10 Andjingith

Bb Umpila (other dialects Kuuku Yani, Uutaalnganu, Kuuku Ya'u, Kaantju)

Bc Wik subgroup[28]

Bc1 Wik-Ngathan (= Wik Iinjtjenj) (other dialect Wik-Ngatharr (= Wik-Alken = Wik-Elken)

Bc2 Wik-Me'nh (other dialects Wik-Ep (= Wik-Iit), Wik-Keyenganh)

Bc3 Wik-Mungknh (Wik-Munkan) (other dialects Wik-Iiyanh (= Wik-Iiyenj = Wik-Iiyanji = Mungkanhu)

Bc4 Kugu Muminh (Wik-Muminh) (or Kugu/Wik-Nganhcara) (other dialects Wik/Kugu + Mu'inh, Uwanh, Ugbanh, Yi'anh, Mangk, Iyanh)

Bc5 Bakanha (or Ayabakan(u))

Bc6 Ayabadhu

Source: Dixon (2002)

---

27 I think this is a typo for Trotj: PS.
28 Dixon also published a specific map called 'Languages of the Wik subgroup, Bc' (Dixon 2002:387).

Wik clans, according to local traditions, acquired their languages during the founding legendary period when heroic figures implanted local dialects along with sacred sites, culture, and customary law in the landscape (Sutton 1997b). Languages are an important form of symbolic property, and one's own 'real language' is thus something normatively acquired by patrilineal descent, in the classical system. Merely being fluent in such a language does not confer proprietary rights in it, nor does the inability to speak one's clan's language deny one the right to claim it as one's own.

While on occasion the fact of sharing the same language may be adduced as evidence of some form of unity of identity with someone else, this is far less common here than in most parts of Aboriginal Australia. In short, the Wik show little commitment to the notion of the 'language group' as a geopolitical unit of much salience, and do not normally use these language names as names of land-based identities with proprietorial significance, although they always have sub-regional connotations. It is true that cover terms such as Wik-Way (an exonym 'Language-Bad' referring to a variety of languages between the Archer and Embley rivers) and Wik-Ngencherr (an exonym referring to the self-named Kugu Ngancharra, the southern Wik peoples whose language names begin with *Kugu*), do have geopolitical substance in the region, and refer to sets of languages, even if these sets are not uniquely and highly bounded. Non-Wik people, such as Thaayorre people at Pormpuraaw, have long recognised the people from between the Archer and Edward rivers as having a certain unity, one that they mark by calling them 'Mungkan' or 'Mungkan-side' people, as is the case at Pormpuraaw (Taylor 1984) and at Coen and Port Stewart (Sutton et al. 1993). This again is an exonym not usually used by Wik people themselves. It is a case where a lingua franca dialect name has become adopted as the outsiders' collective term for the polyglot nation hosting that lingua franca. Exonyms typically simplify things.

At a finer-grained level, however, there is indeed a 'language group' model of land tenure among Wik people but this arises from their classical view that each clan has (or had) a distinctive dialect, one associated with their estate and their clan or clan segment's principal totem (Sutton 1991; von Sturmer 1978:325).[29] The phenomenon was widespread in classical

---

29 For further elaboration of Wik traditional dialectology see Sutton (1991:55–59).

Australia. The Wik Regional clan dialects are sociologically largely the same as the 'patrilects' described by David Nash (1990) for the north-central Northern Territory.

Thus, for example, northern Yunkaportas (Clan 12) may be referred to as Wik Korr', '[Those with] Brolga Language', and the largest segment of the Wolmbys (Clan 6) as Wik Chiiynchiiyn, or Nguungk Chiiynchiiyn '[Those with] Bushrat Language'.[30] However, clans that share a principal totem, and thus are said to have 'the same Story' and thus the same totemic dialect name, may also recognise dialectal or even deep linguistic differences between their speech varieties. For example, Clan 123 has Kugu Uthu 'Dead Body' as principal totem, as also does Clan 130, but the dialect of Clan 123 is Kugu Uwanh while that of Clan 130 is Wik-Iiyanh.

Society, nation

The anthropological use of the term 'society' would not normally apply to the Wik, or to Aurukun, or to any of the smaller groupings I have discussed, but might apply to, say, the Aboriginal people of Cape York Peninsula or indeed of mainland Australia as a connected whole.

The term 'nation' could apply to the Wik peoples as a whole. Elsewhere I have discussed such entities on a continent-wide basis (Sutton 1990, 2003:90–2, 97–8).

In view of what I have suggested above, the model that seemed most appropriate for asserting native title in the Wik case was one of the clans, not separately and severally but collectively, articulating with each other in a complex way to form higher-level groupings of varying scopes, within the broad rubric of the Wik (including the Wik Way[31]) nation. The consent determinations in favour of their claim repeatedly referred to the successful applicants as 'the Wik and Wik Way peoples'.[32]

---

30 Note that *wik* and *nguungk* are equivalent in meaning, but the latter is the respect form, and both may be encountered in this context.
31 Wik Way, with no hyphen, in this book refers to legal usage; Wik-Way is my anthropological usage, based on primary word stress on /wik/.
32 *Wik Peoples v State of Queensland* [2000] FCA 1443; *Wik Peoples v State of Queensland* [2004] FCA 1306; *Wik and Wik Way Native Title Claim Group v Queensland* [2009] FCA 789.

3. LINGUISTIC AND TERRITORIAL ORGANISATION

Membership in any of the higher level country-based Wik groupings above the clan level depends critically on one's clan membership in the first instance. Socially recognised descent is the cornerstone of clanship. Riverine group, ritual group and nation memberships flow ultimately from the most local of affiliations to clan and estate. It is these latter ancestral ties that link individual Wik people back to the countries their forebears held and occupied before their residential arrangements were significantly altered in the last century, mainly through centralisation and the new economy.

It is important, in the present context, that the various Wik peoples share a common set of principles governing both tenure and use of land and waters. The system of 'traditional laws and customs'[33] under which individuals hold their rights and interests in country in the Wik Region is not an individual creation, or a clan creation. It is the creature of the Wik nation and the wider society of other Aboriginal nations to which the Wik belong. Wik customary tenure law does not have a hard and fast geographical or social boundary, beyond which all or most aspects of customary tenure law are different. The Wik share much with their neighbours to the south, east and north.

One reason why the Wik native title application was made by the Wik and Wik Way peoples collectively, rather than by separate clans, or separate riverine groups, for example, was not merely for reasons of convenience and economy, but more importantly because it is only at the wider societal level that the self-sustaining nature of the tenure system becomes fully functional.[34] It is also at this wider level that the relative coherence of the Wik tenure system, as played out in any given location, becomes adequately apparent to the observer. This is made most plain when one considers the nature of succession to estates whose clans' patrilines have died out. There are many examples of kinds of succession in Appendices 1 and 2. Briefly, such cases show that succession to estates whose clans have

---

33 This is the antique language of Section 223 of the *Native Title Act 1993*. McConnel (1957:168) used the expressions 'native law', 'tribal law', and 'native laws' in relation to the Wik. In that context she was writing in particular about social control and conflict resolution, but her detailed accounts of land tenure in the region may also be defined as accounts of customary laws regarding proprietorial interests in country.

34 On the general problem of 'slicing the pie'—determining the most appropriate level of inclusiveness at which native title applicant groups should be defined—see Sutton (1995c).

died out is not an arbitrary matter, or a matter for resolution by brute force. While bases of competing succession arguments may differ, the Wik recognise only certain kinds of arguments as legitimate.[35]

The Wik

The Wik peoples are a regional Aboriginal cultural group. Like other regional groups of similar type, which are often called 'nations' or 'confederacies', this one consists of a number of subgroups as outlined above. The Wik subgroups share cultural heritage, exercise a mainly common system of custom and law in relation to land, and engage in a set of active interrelationships that mark them as distinctive, although they have until recently had no autogenous collective name for this relative regional unity.

It is common for regional macro-groupings of this type to have no autogenous name for themselves. In eastern Cape York Peninsula, the 'nation' names Lamalama, Yiithuwarra and Kuku-Warra are all derived from the usages of those belonging to areas near to, but outside, those of the nations concerned. Kuku-Warra, interestingly, means 'Language-Bad/ Difficult' as does Wik-Way. In the case of the Lamalama and Yiithuwarra, as in that of the Wik-Way and now the Wik generally, the outsiders' title for them has recently become internalised.

The anthropological literature introduced the terms 'Wik-speaking peoples'[36] (Thomson 1936:374) and 'Wik tribes' (McConnel 1936:455). McConnel in several publications referred to all these 'Wik tribes' on occasion as 'the Wikmunkan' or 'the Wikmunkan and allied tribes', a rather misleading usage. While Wik-Mungkan is the regional lingua franca, only a minority of Wik people identify with the Wik-Mungkan language as being their own ancestral tongue.

Scholars of the 1970s used the term 'the Wik' to refer to the same people (von Sturmer 1978; Sutton 1978; von Sturmer 1980; Martin 1993). The scope of this expression was then limited to those people affiliated with languages of the Wik genetic linguistic group (Wik Subgroup), from

---

35 See further below under 'Principles of succession'.
36 Strictly speaking, 'Wik-speaking' is not literally what Thomson or others meant by this phrase, as there are people not formally affiliated with or identifying with Wik languages who have nevertheless learned them and speak them well. 'Wik-owning' would have been more appropriate.

between the Archer and Edward rivers, and thus did not include the Wik-Way people or their original languages, which belong to the Northern Paman genetic linguistic group (Hale 1964).

The Wik peoples, on a number of cultural and social criteria, may be distinguished, but they are not isolated. No Aboriginal group is an island. Such groups typically have a solidly recognisable core membership and a less well-bounded periphery. The integrity of the gentle gradients between Wik and non-Wik in certain areas, such as that in the area of Rokeby, is not violated by recognising broad unities such as the Wik. On the south the Wik have in the past been far more highly bounded by their meeting with the Thaayorre people, though this is changing through co-residence at Pormpuraaw.

The Wik-Way

From Albatross Bay to just south of Archer River, along a narrow coastal strip, are the estates of the Wik-Way people (in the modern sense—see next paragraph), whose clans own a set of closely related languages that are radically different from those to the south of them but middlingly related to those of the Mapoon area to the north. Some of these people formed the core of the Weipa Mission[37] and others formed part of the core of Aurukun Mission as they were established in 1898 and 1904 respectively. On the eastern or inland side of the Wik-Way estates, on the upper Watson River, Kokialah Creek and north to the middle Embley and Myall Creek areas, were the estates of clans whose members are not identified as Wik-Way in the modern sense, but whose languages were most closely related to those of the Wik-Way grouping, as all were Northern Paman varieties (Hale 1964). In earlier times it seems clear that 'Wik-Way' was a term applied, from a south-of-Archer perspective, to any language to the north, including the inland ones such as Mbiywom and Nggoth.

The modern senses of this term are narrower. The most usual one has the Wik-Way area running from the Aurukun Airstrip (north side) via Ikeleth and the Ward River, north to Embley River, excluding the Watson River system and the Jackin Creek area.

---

37 Weipa Mission was originally established on the middle Embley River by Moravian missionaries. In 1932–33 it was moved downstream to the coast at Jessica Point and was known as Weipa South. In 1990 it became the Aboriginal Shire of Napranum.

During the early and middle parts of the twentieth century, many members of clans whose estates lay between the Archer and Embley rivers became based at Aurukun and gradually came under strong cultural influence from the Wik Subgroup peoples, their southern neighbours. Those based at Aurukun shifted their first language of daily use from a Wik-Way-type language to Wik-Mungkan, the Aurukun mission lingua franca. In doing so, they did not abandon their own languages of affiliation, and their descendants continue to identify with those languages, even though they no longer speak them. Wik-Way people have also abandoned a prescriptive marriage rule that was formerly a mark of significant differences between themselves and the Wik Subgroup peoples from the south.

In a number of cases, however, Wik-Way estates clustered about the abutment area of the Northern Paman and Wik linguistic subgroups—the lower Archer River and Love River areas in particular, and on the upper Kirke River—underwent language shifts from a Northern Paman variety to a Wik Subgroup variety during the late nineteenth and early twentieth centuries. Details of each case are provided in Appendix 2.

Wik-Way people who did not settle at Aurukun became based at Weipa and elsewhere, and there has thus been some cultural divergence within descendants of members of this grouping over several generations. Many of its members may be regarded as culturally 'Wik people', while some others may not, but their country is still regarded, particularly from an Aurukun perspective, as Wik-Way country. There is also some inconsistency in the way 'Wik-Way' identity is ascribed to people at the present time.

Furthermore, the term Wik-Way ('Language-Bad/Difficult'), which is part of local usage especially at Aurukun, is from a Wik Subgroup language, not from a Wik-Way or Northern Paman type of language.[38] (The term is parallel to *les Anglais* as a term for the English.) The Wik-Way languages do not have *wik* for 'language' or *way* for 'bad/difficult'. The Wik-Way languages are difficult languages from a Wik Subgroup perspective (or indeed almost any perspective) because of their sound systems, even though their grammar is fairly typical of Cape York languages generally. The Wik Subgroup phonologies and phonotactic systems are much more straightforward. I do not know whether or not there was once an indigenous Wik-Way equivalent of Wik-Way, although Winda-Winda may have been an approximation (see further discussion, Chapter 5).

---

38   On the definition of Wik-type and Northern Paman–type languages, see Chapter 5.

Although some degree of integration between Wik Subgroup and Wik-Way people has long been the case around the Archer River region, and older people from there were in the past systematically bilingual in both Wik Subgroup and Wik-Way types of language, the distinction has some continuing reality in people's minds. This is in spite of the fact that residential bases for some Wik-Way have been at Aurukun while others settled at Weipa or elsewhere, and the Aurukun-based Wik-Way people have lost all but a few fragments of their old languages (such as Andjingith, Linngithigh, and Alngith) and have adopted Wik-Mungkan as their first language of daily use. Some older Wik-Way people are competent speakers of other Wik languages also, such as Wik-Ngathan.

Principles of succession

Where an estate-owning clan has become extinct—an occurrence that is always a significant likelihood in a small-scale society where clans average about 25–35 members—it is normal for succession to the vacant estate to be activated by those with various pre-existing legitimate interests. Resolution of any particular case may take some years, perhaps decades, where it is contested. High on the list of pre-existing interests are having had a mother in the extinct patriclan group, especially if this structural factor is combined with other qualifications such as having a long history of personal association with the country in question, and knowledge of its place-names, stories, and resources.

Also high on the list, but of less power in debate, are connections to more distant antecedent holders of the estate (such as father's mother, or mother's mother), or the mere proximity of one's father's estate to the one falling vacant. Having a different language from that of the extinct clan appears to have been no barrier to succession, but any form of real distance—geographically, socially, genealogically—would pose great problems for anyone pretending to succeed to such an estate. Birthplaces and places of cremation or burial occasionally figure in arguments about the legitimacy of people's claims to land. However, these are site-specific forms of connection rather than estate-based ones, and they usually obtain just for the relevant person and their lifetime, and may not be transmitted to a succeeding generation.

I observed over some decades an attempt by Alan Wolmby (Clan 6, Estate 6) to extend his personal connection to Ikeleth, a key site in an untenanted estate north-west of Aurukun where he was born in 1930, into a primary custodial relationship with the estate itself. In those days, a newborn was spiritually connected to a particular tree close to their birthplace by the afterbirth being customarily buried beneath that tree. Alan's attempt was not very successful, in spite of his community prominence and political acumen. In a later attempt, after Alan's death, his son Rexie Wolmby tried to use his father's birthplace as leverage for his own expression of interest in the Ikeleth estate (Estate 57, Lower Ward River). Lifetime individual rights in a site did not translate licitly into descent group succession to a whole estate, and Rexie's attempt failed.

When I first visited the area of Thoekel (Lower Love River, Estate 1) in 1974, the last patriclan members (Clan 1) had passed away and the estate was up for succession. The main contenders were the Peinkinna branch of the upper Love River (Estate 2, Clan 2), and the offspring of Carlippe, one of the last Thoekel patriclan members. The Peinkinna argument was based primarily on immediate proximity of estates on the same drainage—they were 'all one river'. The Walmbeng siblings for whom Thoekel was mother's and mother's father's country (also that of their MZ and MB and MFZ and MFB) had their own patriclan country (Estate 8, Warpang) quite a distance away and just inland from Cape Keerweer, so their case was based on immediate descent and not on proximity of patri-estate. Over roughly two decades, the succession was debated and disputed, until eventually it was settled in favour of the Walmbengs. Blood, alongside Rex Walmbeng's force of character, eloquence, and political dexterity, had won out over proximity, drainage, and persistence.

Adoption and incorporation

Adoptions of individuals may result in a child having two paternal ties to country, one to that of the 'real father' and one to that of the adoptive or 'step-father'. It seems that the individual's life-history, and the choices they may make when older, may affect which of the two gradually becomes dominant.

There are two cases of incorporation of families, rather than adoption of individuals, into clans among the Wik. In one case,[39] a family that originated in the Nicholson River region in the NT/Queensland border area became integrated into Wik society beginning in 1941, after being brought there by missionaries who were also bringing some Bentinck Island people to Aurukun (MacKenzie 1981:94), and they were granted customary land rights in the area of Uthuk Aweyn and Uthuk Eelen, also known as Watha-nhiin (Estates 4 and 3). They have retained an interest in their ancestral Nicholson River land, at least among the upper generations, and were successful claimants in the Nicholson River land claim in the early 1980s.[40]

A small number of non-Aboriginal individuals, including myself, have also been incorporated as kin into particular Wik families and are locally regarded as clan members with estate rights similar to those of their fellow clans-people, possessing the same totems and the same clan dialect, but none of them were native title applicants in the Wik case. Had they been so, they probably would have been legally excluded from recognition on the grounds of race.

Shifts in the mode of reckoning descent of tenurial interests

The descent system, as far as country affiliations go, has been modified since the 1970s in a slow process of transformation, so as to be open to cognatic rather than purely unilineal descent.[41] Cognatic descent recognises descent group membership where the entry point is filiation to either parent, not just the father or just the mother.

In the 1990s, recruitment to country groups by patrifiliation, the classical ideal, was still strong among the Wik peoples, but a post-colonial pattern had by then also emerged.

---

39 For the other case see Appendix 2: Estate 5.
40 See Aboriginal Land Commissioner (1984:42–3); Denny Bowenda of Aurukun was listed there as Danny King, as his father was King Bowenda, and he was known by either surname, depending on location.
41 For discussion of this type of transformation, which in many parts of Australia is more advanced than it is in the Wik Region, see Sutton (2003:206–31).

At that time a small but increasing number of children were taking their primary country affiliation from their mothers, at times, under the aegis of a powerful mother's father or mother's mother who was able to prevent the primary identification of their descendants shifting outside their own group.

The relationship between official surnames and country became more complicated. In the preceding decades of mission history there was a simple rule for the assignment of surnames: children took the surname of their father, and he was normally legally married to the mother, who herself also took her husband's surname upon marriage. In those decades there was a consistent relationship between the surnames recorded by mission staff and the patrilineal clan groups and therefore countries.

The system of surname allocation appears to have begun to apply to people reaching marriageable age, and their offspring, after about 1930. This is consistent with the extreme likelihood that it was a system devised and imposed by Rev. William MacKenzie 1897–1972 (Wharton 2000). MacKenzie ran Aurukun Presbyterian Mission from 1923 to 1965 as superintendent, with his wife Geraldine MacKenzie as matron and school teacher (Cruikshank and Grimshaw 2015). When the MacKenzies arrived, people often had both 'bush names' (i.e. totemic names,[42] also nicknames) and English ones (including words for animals such as Cockroach, Bandicoot, and Cockatoo, or descriptors like Wildfellow and Shortfellow and 'Left-hand' pronounced 'Lapan'), but had not as yet adopted a European first name/surname system.

What became Wik surnames during the 1920s and 1930s were largely a rendering by mission staff of one of the pre-existing totemic names of male members of particular clans.[43] These totemic names were typically oblique and poetic references to totems held by the clan. Since men in the same clan shared more than one such name, there were sometimes several different surnames recorded, more or less by accident, for members of a single clan, including siblings. This added further complications. For example, the Landises (with a European-derived surname) were of the same clan (Clan 15) as Gothachalkenins and Eundatumweakins. Actual siblings in this clan included people with different surnames, such as the brothers

---

42   Those recorded are listed under each clan in Appendix 1.
43   Thomson (1946) gave a pioneering account of the Wik Subgroup naming system for people and dogs. In Appendix 1, the clan totemic names recorded for women, men, male dogs, and female dogs are listed.

Billy Landis, Rupert Gothachalkenin and Bob-Wallace Eundatumweakin, all sons of Billy Wildfellow and his wives. In classical terms, all Landis men, like all Gothachalkenin and all Eundatumweakin men, shared the names Ku'-thaach-elkenh ('Dog + Rising Breakers', 'Gothachalkenin' in mission records) and Ooentetham-weykenh ('Goes about on its belly', 'Eundatumweakin' in mission records), among others. These came from the fact that among their clan's many totems were *Thaach* ('Breakers') and *Ngamel* ('Flat-tailed Stingray'), a bottom-dwelling elasmobranch.

Billy Landis probably acquired his English surname at the government-run Palm Island penal Aboriginal settlement off the coast of Queensland near Townsville. Names derived from non-Aboriginal people (e.g. Mittaboy ('Mr Boyd'), Mitherropsen ('Mr Robertson'), and Mithedaya ('Mr Dyer')) were not a large proportion of Wik names, and were used as first names in these instances, or as surnames in the cases of Lawrence, Kepple, Parker, and Day. Wik surnames derived from river names include Kendall, Holroyd, and Edward. Sometimes a forebear's first name would become the surname for his descendants, as in the case of the George, Fruit, Blowhard, Jingle, John, Matthew, and Shortjoe families.

Occasionally a clan's men shared a totemic name with men of a different clan and, as a result, in the mission period there developed pairs of clans sharing the same surname but holding different estates and, in most cases, being affiliated to separate languages. These include the pairs Yunkaporta (Clans 12 and 20), Pootchemunka (Clans 9 and 14), Owokran (Clans 60 and 82), Peemuggina (Clans 6 and 19), Koonutta (Clans 10 and 90), Woolla (Clans 22 and 31), and Yantumba (Clans 28 and 130). There are also, for example, four distinct Wik clans sharing the English settler name Kepple (see Clans 69, 75, 116, and 117), and two sharing the river name Edward (Clans 129 and 144).

Some people, when travelling outside the Wik world, would alter their names, perhaps to make it easier for others to pronounce them. For example, Francis Yunkaporta called himself 'Frank Porter' when 'outside' (*an yoon*, Wik-Mungkan), and Eembinpawn Gothachalkenin called herself 'Betty' when in Cairns Base Hospital. Mrs Geraldine Kawangka sometimes called herself 'Miss Geraldine' when in the city of Cairns.

Women of a particular clan also shared a set of traditional female names that were different from the male names. In classical times, women kept their own names for life and did not change them upon marriage. During the mission period, women's names, but not men's, were sometimes reduced to key letters, such as 'K.O.' for Kornamnayuh, or 'M.K.' for Mikompa.

By the 1960s, the MacKenzie-era surnaming system had been stable for several decades, and the relationship between surname and clan country had been stable for the same period. From the late 1960s onwards, however, the surname/clan relationship began to destabilise.

Table 3.2 summarises the surname system shift between 1960 and 1987 of those born at Aurukun. This table is derived from data in Sutton (2017). The figures in parentheses are the number of non-Aboriginal fathers in the sum. There were no non-Aboriginal birth mothers in the data. In two cases children were given surnames of both parents; these were both cases of a European father and Wik mother who were in a stable relationship.

Table 3.2: Shift in surnaming of babies, Aurukun 1960–87

Birth year	Child takes F surname	Child takes M surname
1960	11	0
1961	26	0
1962	15	0
1963	20	0
1964	19	0
1965	18	1 (1)
1966	24	0
1967	20	2
1968	28	4
1969	23	1
1970	19	5
1971	19	7
1972	23	15
1973	16	11 (2)
1974	10	11 (1)
1975	12	9
1976	7	24
1977	8	10 (1)
1978	10	15 (2)

Birth year	Child takes F surname	Child takes M surname
1979	8	18 (2)
1980	3	11
1981	10	17 (2)
1982	1	22
1983	5 (1)	14
1984	0	6
1985	1	24
1986	1 (1)	20 (1)
1987	3 (1)	22 (1)

It follows from this table that in the years 1960–64 (as for some decades previously) no child had a surname other than its father's. By 1976, surnames for children derived from their mothers had become the predominant pattern. From being patrilineal, surnames had become matrilineal, in a remarkable transformation of practice by members of a younger generation. Estate assignment for children did not become matrilineal but cognatic in base and increasingly optative (choosing which parent or grandparent to follow for country identity). In the years 1967–72, mothers giving their babies their own surname were aged between 17 and 24 and having their first child. Married couples who had been having offspring before the departure of MacKenzie in 1965 continued to surname new children after their fathers, well into the new era (Sutton 2017).

What caused this dramatic shift? Here I am concerned to deepen the causal analysis I made in Sutton (1997a). At that time I considered the triggers for these changes to have been the decrease in stable marriages, and in fact the virtually complete disappearance of any new formal marriages once the MacKenzie era ended;[44] an increase in the number of different men fathering the children of any one woman; men also having children with multiple partners; the emergence of children fathered by non-Aboriginal men; and the increased financial independence of mothers. While generally I retain this analysis now, in fact, as Table 3.2 shows, the number of children fathered by non-Aboriginal men was only ever a tiny proportion between 1965 and 1987. Mother-surnamed children conceived with Aboriginal fathers totally outstripped in number

---

44   David Martin (1993:321–27) provides figures on the collapse of formal marriages at Aurukun.

those conceived with non-Aboriginal fathers from 1967 to 1987. Non-Aboriginal paternities were not, as it happens, a primary driver of change in the allocation of surnames.

To those factors I would now add specifically the introduction of the single-parent pension, which occurred in 1973 and gave women more independence; the decline of the power of Wik patriarchy; the decline and fall of the mission patriarchy; and the increasing liberation of women, including their newly independent travel to the public towns of Weipa, Coen, and Cairns. The major shift in Wik surnaming practices occurred between the end of the 42-year MacKenzie domination regime in 1965 and the arrival of full-blown mission liberalism in about 1974.

Here I examine some of the fine-grained record that sheds some light on the initial change period, which can be fairly precisely located in the five years 1968–73. I have anonymised references to individuals but their names are in my unpublished records.

During the MacKenzie era and shortly afterwards, extramaritally conceived children with Indigenous fathers presented the surname allocation issue to people and it was dealt with in several ways. Recognition of the status of such children was not new. 'Steal-piccaninnies' and 'outside blanket' babies were long recognised by Wik people and there are cases on the record going back well past the MacKenzie surname era to bush times. Openly acknowledged extramarital paternity and actual versus social fatherhood were embedded in traditional practice and language. For example, Wik languages distinguish 'begetter' from 'upbringer', as in Wik-Ngathan *wunypenh* and Wik-Mungkan *wunpan* ('begetter'), as distinct from Wik-Ngathan *thawan* and Wik-Mungkan *emathan* ('upbringer').[45]

Cases of births resulting from extramarital relationships during the MacKenzie era and just afterwards include the following. In 1955 a W-surnamed woman had a son by a Yam Islander and the boy was given the mother's married surname (i.e. her husband's). In 1956 a W-surnamed young woman (unmarried) gave birth to a son by a married Wik man, but the child was assigned the surname of the man its mother soon married,

---

45 Thomson (1936) presented cogent evidence gathered in the field in 1933 that Wik tradition recognised the biological role of the genitor in reproduction.

not that of the publicly acknowledged genitor. The child continued to be identified at least as much with his genitor's country as with his pater's but always bore his pater's surname.

In 1967 a P-surnamed unmarried woman gave birth to a child she had to a married Wik man, and the child was assigned her surname not the father's. In 1968 a K-surnamed woman had a son by a married Wik man, and again the boy was given his mother's surname not his father's. In 1972 a P-surnamed unmarried woman had a daughter by a married man and again the daughter received her mother's surname not the father's.

Non-Aboriginal fathering of Wik children basically began in the late 1960s, although there were rare instances before then. For example, in about 1915, YG (c. 1899–1982) gave birth to her first child, a daughter conceived with a European man. She told me this in 1976. The baby did not survive long.

The next child born to a Wik mother and non-Aboriginal father, in my records (Sutton 2017; there may have been others), was LG, the first of her mother's children, who was born in 1965. She was given the surname of her mother. Next in the records was the first child of SO, born in 1970. She was to have four children born 1970–78. Apart from the case of her first child, the genitors were all non-Aboriginal and she never named any of them on the birth records, and all four offspring were allocated her own surname.

In 1972 a T-surnamed woman had a son by an unrecorded non-Aboriginal man and the boy was given his mother's married surname, i.e. her husband's. In the same year, a W-surnamed unmarried woman had a son by an unrecorded non-Aboriginal man and the son took her own surname. She had three further children by non-Aboriginal fathers; these also took her surname but one was known by his father's as well as his mother's.

These two women were among the elite intelligentsia of Aurukun, highly astute, literate, excellent speakers of English in addition to their Aboriginal languages, and very assertive. A C-named woman, who was also in the same elite-intelligentsia group of young women of that era, had children with non-Aboriginal men in the 1980s, one child taking her surname and another taking the father's.

The years 1970–72 were a crunch point in social and cultural change in Wik society, though the pattern started to change by the mid-'60s. It was only after MacKenzie left in December 1965 that people were free to visit towns like Cairns as individuals, of their own volition. This journey to what locally is called 'the outside' represented sophistication and liberation as well. It is no surprise that it was culturally mobile, talented and assertive young women who made the break, and that in many cases they conceived with non-Aboriginal men while in Cairns.

The year 1965 was also the last of MacKenzie controlling lives at Aurukun with an iron fist. In the early 1960s, he and his wife Geraldine defied the order of the Presbyterian Board to close the Aurukun dormitories, and teenage girls and boys continued to live in separate dormitories controlled by the mission staff until immediately after the end of the MacKenzie regime (MacKenzie 1981:202). As a rule, girls transited rapidly from dormitory to wedding, under the MacKenzie regime's apparatus for preventing sexual misbehaviour.

The Presbyterian Church (from 1977 the Uniting Church) liberals who replaced MacKenzie and immediately closed down the dormitories were soon trying to devolve decision-making power to the people. And the new regime did not control people's marriages nor their movements in and out of Aurukun as their predecessors had done.

The aeroplane was as much a game changer for Aurukun-based Wik people as the camel had been for the Yankunytjatjara of Central Australia. Aurukun in the MacKenzie years was terribly inaccessible in the dry season and only accessible by air or boat in the long wet and post-wet flooding seasons. And MacKenzie kept it socially isolated too, by expelling unwanted visitors and being reluctant to allow Aurukun inmates to travel to any other centres except when on contract work approved of and usually arranged by the mission.

The first aircraft to land at Aurukun did so on 28 January 1941 (MacKenzie 1981:91–2). Regular mail plane visits to Aurukun from Cairns, operated by bush pilots, seem to have begun in 1962.[46] As late as early 1967 these flights occurred only twice a month. In August 1967 the frequency was doubled to weekly.[47] From the late 1960s on, the archival sources include names of Wik passengers in increasingly substantial numbers.

---

46   AIATSIS MS1525/4, item #80, 'Bush Pilots 1962–1975'.
47   AIATSIS MS1525/1, item #15. 'Aircraft movements, landings 1966–1975'.

Without this kind of fine detail, one is justifiably wary of broad-brush statements about social change and its causality. Here one can, with the aid of the daily records meticulously kept by the mission, piece together a complex process as it unfolded in incremental stages. In short, the shift away from patriliny was happening in the late 1960s along with a (minor) shift to non-Aboriginal paternity but not because of it.

The end of the MacKenzie regime was also the effective end of newly contracted formal marriages at Aurukun, although I think I have seen photos of weddings from as late as maybe 1972. Apart from a momentary revival in 1976 (when a kind Reverend unwittingly married an underage girl from Groote Eylandy to a local Wik man, an attempt by the Groote family to do a dynastic manganese royalty-retaining marriage), as far as I know there were no formal marriages until perhaps the early 2000s when somebody revived the custom in the form of a church wedding. On a visit to Aurukun at that time I was taken to be introduced to the groom because he was such a curiosity, and regarded as almost a freak.

The end of formal marriage meant not only no wedding ceremony but a departure from the old cross-cousin partnering rules by many, an explosion of promiscuity, and serial cohabitation—'just living' as they said—but also many stable de facto partnerships. Under MacKenzie, sexual behaviour was carefully monitored and misdemeanours noted in the mission diary and punishment delivered, sometimes in ways now quite illegal. These included shaving a woman's head and chaining her to a public tree.

While William MacKenzie was Superintendent of Aurukun 1923–65 he ruled with severe control. He knew that marital and extramarital relationships were the most common focus of conflict in Wik social life and its most common daily cause. He required proposed marriages to be discussed with him and he required the relatives of the couple to make formal agreement with the union before it could take place. In most cases the relatives signed the written agreement or, when illiterate, put an X identified as their mark, with Bill MacKenzie usually signing off himself so as to make the agreement fully formal. These were not marriage certificates—those were separate, typewritten statements or printed forms that were filled in at the time of the wedding and were held in a different mission file.

By the time of his retirement in 1965, MacKenzie had significantly broken the formerly massive powers of the Wik gerontocracy, through quelling spear fighting, physically challenging and fighting or thrashing men who resisted him, incorporating men into the mission hierarchy, and countless other measures, documentary evidence for which is plentiful. Paralleling the decline of Wik male authoritarianism was the decline of male authoritarianism in the Presbyterian Church. After MacKenzie, the new guard in the church were leaning over backwards to be kind and nice, a great contrast to the man who fitted the model of the 'policeman-missionary, with a gun in one hand and a Bible in the other' (Chaseling 1957:22). MacKenzie's kindness was sternly paternal, effective in saving lives but at the expense of Wik autonomy. At times he was very brutal.

I do not wish to imply that these changes only occurred because MacKenzie's rule ended and women were becoming economically independent. A shift away from formal marriage and the bestowal of fathers' names on children, towards de facto and other relationships in which children were increasingly bestowed with their mothers' surnames, was happening at the same time in Australian and Western society generally. The shifts I describe here were in part a result of the end of Aurukun's extreme isolation, both physically and culturally.

4

Linguistic demography of the Wik Region

Peter Sutton

In this chapter I focus on the number of clan estates per linguistic variety, beginning in the north of the region, and proceeding south. Further information about the same linguistic varieties may be found especially in Chapter 5.

The main reason for focusing on number of estates per variety is to arrive at estimates of dialect-owning populations in the proto-colonial period. This is on surer ground than an attempt to estimate numbers of speakers of those varieties. In the 1970s, after a period of population loss, residential concentration and sedentisation, older people were still multilingual but often asymmetrically so. For example, while all owners of Wik-Me'enh also spoke Wik-Mungkan, most speakers of Wik-Mungkan did not speak Wik-Me'enh. Older Wik-Me'enh people also spoke Wik-Ngathan, but only some Wik-Ngathan people spoke Wik-Me'enh. This seems to have been a reflection of relative population numbers.

Wik-Way

The Wik-Way linguistic varieties are a geopolitically defined subset of the Northern Paman subgroup of Paman languages. The Wik-Way area is between the Archer River and the Weipa Peninsula to its north. There are other Northern Paman languages further north beyond Weipa to the tip of Cape York Peninsula, but they are not discussed here. Here I examine just the subset of Northern Paman speech varieties whose owners were part of the Wik native title claim.

Regarding the varieties listed here, and particularly considering their sharing of phonological developments and lexicon, Ken Hale (1966:163ff.) has presented evidence that they may be subgrouped as follows (some would say as five technically defined languages):

1. Alngith/ Linngithigh
2. Mamangathi /Thyanngayth/ Ndrrwa'ngayth/ Ndrra'ngith
3. Ngkoth /Trotj
4. Arraythinngith
5. Mbiywom.

However, the first two subgroups appear to belong to a dialect chain (Hale 1966:175) such that each shares at least 80 per cent of basic lexicon with at least one of the other varieties, but at the opposite extreme two of the chain's members, Thyanngayth and Linngithigh, share only 54 per cent.

Here I list language varieties under their self-name, but they also had a variety of other names in different languages. Arraythinngith, for example, was known as Arrithinngithigh in Linngithigh, and as Arrithinngayth in Ndrrwa'ngayth (Hale 1966:166), and I can add that it was also known as Arraythinngith, possibly in Ndrra'ngith, and as Arreythinwum, probably in Yinwum. It probably had several other names as well—one expects there to have been a Wik version something like *Wik-Arrithangathiy, for example, but it has not been recorded.

Given that Adithinngithigh and Arrithinngithigh seem to have been identified with only one estate each and the names are so similar, it might be tempting to consider their distinct spellings mere artefacts of the recording process, but the names are indeed distinct and moreover the relevant estates are non-contiguous and owned by different people (my own field work). Basically, McConnel's rough map (1939–40:55) seems to have been the first to get it right, showing 'Adetingiti' separate from 'Aritingiti' (in spite of demurrings by Sharp 1939:265fn.). Similarly, Ndrra'ngith and Ndrrangith estates are non-contiguously located and have distinct custodians. (The dialect names here differ only by the presence of the glottal stop /'/ in the first.) Separate again are Ndwa'ngith and Ndrrwa'angathi, the countries connected with the latter two lying too far north to come within the purview of the mapping research referred to here. In short, unravelling the complexity of language variety nomenclature in the Wik-Way sub-region has had to rely heavily on accurately heard phonetic renderings of the names.

According to Ken Hale, Mamngayth (Mamangathi) is one of three virtually identical dialects subsumed under the title Awngthim (Hale 1966:165). According to Crowley, Mamangathi is referred to as one of several 'groups' speaking the Awngthim language, and the implication is that these were exogamous clan-groups rather than dialect groups per se (see Crowley 1981:150). The data I have suggest that the name Mamangathi (Mamngayth, Mamangithigh, etc. depending on the language in which it is being named) functioned as the name of a linguistic variety, and was not just a clan name. I am not aware of clans being formally named in the region.

Table 4.1: Wik-Way estates

Named variety	No. of estates c. 1900
Adithinngithigh	1
Alngith	2
Anathangayth	1
Andjingith	8 (+ two possibles)
Arraythinngith	1
Latumngith	1
Linngithigh	4
Mamangathi	1
Mbiywom	4 (+ two possibles)
Ndrra'ngith	2
Ndrrangith	1
Ngkoth	1
Paach (Wik Paach)	4[1]
Total	31 (35) (average 2.38 (2.69))

---

1 Of these estates, two were also probably affiliated with Andjingith. They are also included under Andjingith above as 'possibles'.

Wik Subgroup

Here I give clan estate figures for the varieties of the Wik Subgroup of the Middle Paman group of languages whose countries fell within the Wik native title case claim boundaries. I omit south-eastern Wik varieties Ayapathu and Pakanh(u) (also known as Aya-Pathu, Aya-Pakanh, etc.). They mainly fall outside the study area in this case.[2] Very closely related to each other as dialects of a single technically defined language, they are also very similar to Wik-Iyanh and Wik-Mungkan but given their geographical coverage one expects local varieties to be more divergent the further apart they are. There are two estates affiliated to each of Ayapathu and Pakanh in our data from the hinterland of western Cape York Peninsula. There were in the past at least five more Ayapathu estates on and inland from the western shores of Princess Charlotte Bay on the east coast of the Peninsula. These have passed to the Mumpithamu clan (of the Uuku Umpithamu language, not a Wik variety) and in fact to the whole modern Lama Lama tribe.

Coastal and pericoastal varieties of the Wik Subgroup

In Chapter 5, I present a schematic listing of Wik Subgroup linguistic varieties classified into coastal, pericoastal and inland environments.

By 'coastal' speech, I generally mean varieties whose clan estates include areas somewhere between the sea and the flood plains that lie between the Holocene and Pleistocene dune systems of western Cape York Peninsula. The Holocene systems lie commonly just behind the beach. The Pleistocene dune systems lie commonly about 10–20 kilometres east of them, abutting, on their east, the vast messmate forests of the interior. The dune systems carry Indo-Malaysian dune thickets that are very rich in resources. Between the Archer and Edward rivers there is an abrupt transition from coastal environments to the great messmate forests of the inland in the region. Note also that the same forest environment runs right to the beach strip north of the Archer River in the Wik-Way area.

---

2   See Verstraete and Rigsby (2015:1–17) for details regarding these two varieties and their countries. I also acknowledge Ayapathu/Mumpithamu data from Bruce Rigsby, pers. comm., and Ayapathu/Pakanh data from Bruce Rigsby and Philip Hamilton, pers. comm.

By 'pericoastal' dialects, I mean varieties whose clan estates include areas somewhere between the Holocene dune system and the dry sclerophyll forests that dominate the inland east of the Pleistocene system and have no frontage on the Gulf of Carpentaria coastline. This zone is neither true coast nor true inland: it includes tidal reaches and flood plains, but also dry sclerophyll forest. This two-way liminality is reflected culturally and politically in a number of ways. Linguistically, however, the pericoastal varieties leaned more strongly to the inland dialect types, and were predominantly called Wik-Mungkan in the north and Wik-Iyanh in the south.

By 'inland' varieties, I generally mean varieties whose clan estates include areas running east of the Pleistocene dune system up to the Great Dividing Range far to the east. This is country dominated by forests of *Eucalyptus tetrodonta* (Darwin stringybark, messmate) and other hardwoods, a far less rich environment than the coastal and pericoastal zones, and a zone with vastly larger clan estates and vastly lower linguistic diversity.

Northern coastal

Varieties here are arranged very roughly north to south, but they tend to occur in a patchwork arrangement not in single-variety blocs.

Table 4.2: Northern coastal estates

Named variety	No. of estates c. 1900
Wik-Alken/Wik-Elkenh[3]	5
Wik-Ngatharr	3
Wik-Ngathan[4]	7
Total	**15** (average 5.0)

These three varieties are dialects of a single technical language, although Wik-Ngathan is clearly distinct from the others in a number of morphosyntactic and lexical ways and unlike the other varieties does not

---

3 Some say this is the same as Wik-Ngatharr and others say it is not, but, in any case, they are very similar or virtually identical varieties. Wik-Ngatharr appears to be originally the Wik-Mungkan name for the variety self-named Wik-Elkenh, but has become widely adopted.
4 One Wik-Ngathan variety was renamed Wik-Iincheyn in the late 1970s but has since reverted. This name is also said to occur further south but I have no precise details to hand (John von Sturmer, pers. comm.).

engage in synchronic initial-dropping and certain other complexities that reduce the appearance of similarity that one gains from inspecting lexical cognates. 'Mutual intelligibility' is especially problematic here. Wik-Alken/Wik-Elkenh and Wik-Ngatharr are different names for what is as far as I know the same dialect.

Also on the coast are two Wik-Mungkan estates (12 and 20, Appendix 2), not contiguous with each other or with any other Wik-Mungkan estate, and thus surrounded by estates affiliated with other languages (in both the named sense and the technical sense). For the purposes of this table they are located further below with the other Wik-Mungkan estates, the great majority of which are in the inland. There was, however, no particular close interaction in the past between coastal and inland Wik-Mungkan people, the coastal people intermarrying and living with other coastal people and being multilingual, not showing any preference for spouses of the same language.

Northern pericoastal

Table 4.3: Northern pericoastal estates

Named variety	No. of estates c. 1900
Wik-Ep/Wik-Iit	4
Wik-Me'enh	4[5] [+ 1 possible]
Wik-Keyenganh	1
Total	9 (10) (average 3.0 (3.3))

These varieties of a single language form a north–south cluster of estates running along the pericoastal plains between just south of the Kirke River and just south of the Kendall River.

Southern (coastal, pericoastal, inland)

These varieties are dialects of a single (technical) language, the Kugu Nganhcarra described in the work of Smith and Johnson (e.g. 2000). I prefer the practical spelling Kugu Ngancharra. (It is known as

---

5   One estate's language was known as *both* Wik-Ep and Wik-Me'enh, unlike others north of it known as Wik-Ep and others south of it known as Wik-Me'enh. This dual naming may or may not reflect an empirically midway variety.

Wik-Ngencherr in northern Wik Subgroup languages.) Of these Kugu Ngancharra varieties, Wik-Iyanh is closest to Wik-Mungkan and like most of the Wik-Mungkan countries it also belongs to the inland region. Lexically it reflects a sustained relationship with Wik-Mungkan but it is structurally closer to other Kugu Ngancharra languages (Smith and Johnson 2000). Varieties are here arranged roughly north to south, but apart from Wik-Iyanh they occur in something of a patchwork pattern, as also do those north of them along the coast.

Table 4.4: Southern estates

Named variety	No. of estates c. 1900
Wik-Iyanh[6]	16
Wik-Iyanyi[7]	1
Kug Ugbanh	3
Kugu Muminh	7
Kug Uwanh	3
Kugu Mu'inh	6
Kugu Yi'anh	1
Kugu Mangk	2[8]
Total	**39** (average 4.8)
(Mostly) inland[9]	
Wik-Mungkan	8 [+ 1 possible]
Wik-Iyeyn[10]	2
Mungkanhu	1 [some doubt]
Total	**10 (12)** (average 3.6 [possibly 4.0])

---

6   Under this term this I include the self-named dialect Wik-Iyanh Tharr-tharrn, known in Wik-Ngathan as Wik-Iyanh Yaarrk, a name translated into English as 'half Wik-Iyanh' (see Sutton 1978:183–84).
7   Here I tentatively include Wik-Iyanyi, a variety from the top of Kendall River and probably west of Coleman Creek, but am not sure that this is a self-name. It may be similar to, or an alternative name for, Pakanh.
8   Smith and Johnson (2000:358) consider Kugu Mangk likely to be an alternative name to Kugu Yi'anh, while some say they are distinct (von Sturmer 1978:171).
9   As stated above, two Wik-Mungkan estates that are coastal 'outliers' have been included here as their patrilects are demonstrably much the same as inland Wik-Mungkan, although there are differences. The identification of Wik-Iyeyn and Mungkanhu as varieties of the same language as Wik-Mungkan is tentative. They may belong with Wik-Iyanh in the Kugu Ngancharra set, as they fall south of the Wik-Mungkan estates proper, but data that would solve the question are not to hand.
10   Technically Wik-Iyeñ.

If we rearrange the data on estates per named variety so as to isolate the inland estates from the coastal and pericoastal we get the following:

Table 4.5: Coastal and pericoastal named varieties

Named variety	No. of estates c. 1900
Wik-Alken/Wik-Elkenh	5
Wik-Ngatharr	3
Wik-Ngathan	7
Wik-Mungkan	2
Wik-Ep/Wik-Iit	4
Wik-Me'enh	4 [+ 1 possible]
Wik-Keyenganh	1
Kugu Mangk	2
Kugu Muminh	7
Kugu Mu'inh	6
Kug Ugbanh	3
Kug Uwanh	3
Kugu Yi'anh	1
Total	**52 (+1) (average 3.7)**

Table 4.6: Inland named varieties

Named variety	No. of estates c. 1900
Wik-Mungkan	8 [+ 1 possible]
Wik-Iyeyn	2
Mungkanhu	1 [some doubt][11]
Wik-Iyanyi	1
Wik-Iyanh	16
Total	**27 (29) (average 5.4 (5.8))**

---

11   The doubt in this case is whether Mungkanhu is another name for a variety more often known as e.g. Wik-Iyanh. For this reason I place Mungkanhu among the 'possibles' in the total here.

However, if we rearrange the data so as to suppress dialect differences and treat each technically defined language as a single unit, but restrict the estate figures just to each of the inland/non-inland halves,[12] we find the following:

Table 4.7: Coastal and pericoastal technically defined Wik Subgroup languages

Named variety	No. of estates c. 1900
1. (Ngathan, Ngatharr, Elkenh/Alken)	15
2. (Ep/lit, Me'enh, Keyenganh)	9 (10)
3. (Mungkan, Mungkanhu, Iyeyn)	2
4. (Kugu Ngancharra varieties)	22
Total	48 (49) (average 12.0 (12.25))

If we exclude the two Wik-Mungkan coastal outliers, however—and the evidence[13] suggests these probably derived from an inland or pericoastal clan by succession and fission at some point in the last two or three centuries—this latter average would rise to 15.3 (15.7).

Table 4.8: Inland technically defined languages

Named variety	No. of estates c. 1900
3. (Mungkan, Mungkanhu, Iyeyn)	10 [+2 possibles]
4. (Kugu Ngancharra varieties)	17
Total	27 (29) (average 13.5 (14.5))

Thus, in terms of technically defined languages, the inland ones are not significantly larger in terms of reconstructible populations than are the coastal ones.

---

12 A broad inland/coastal division is probably the most profound of the classical lines of social cleavage within the Wik Region as in so many others. The people from pericoastal estates, although in many ways occupying an intermediate position between the sandbeach and the inland forests, can be appropriately combined with the sandbeach people at this level of a gross distinction between the inlanders and the rest.

13 Apart from a shared dialect, they shared six of a possible 12 totems for which the data may be compared, and all four totemic personal names (three male, one female) for which data may be compared. Their totem species are characteristic of pericoastal and inland country rather than of the ocean.

Disregarding distribution and arranging the languages in order of numbers of estates, we arrive at the following:

Table 4.9: Technically defined languages

Named variety	No. of estates c. 1900
4. (Kugu Ngancharra varieties)	39
1. (Ngathan, Ngatharr, Elkenh/Alken)	15
3. (Mungkan, Mungkanhu, Iyeyn)	10 (12)
2. (Ep/lit, Me'enh, Keyenganh)	9 (10)
Total	**73 (76)** **(average 18.25 (19.0))**

Reconstructing populations

If we estimate that these Wik estates were held by groups averaging somewhere in the range of 15–25 clan members prior to the effects of European contact, the number of owners of a technically defined language would have averaged in the range 275–475.

The average clan membership could conceivably have been higher, perhaps as much as 30, but as can be seen below, my estimated maximum of 2,000 for the study area prior to colonial impacts divided by an estimated 80 clans gives an average figure of exactly 25, a figure only calculated at the very end of all the others. Remarkably, this is also the 'magic number' for the average small land-owning 'horde' in Joseph Birdsell's scheme of things (see section below, this chapter, Language group size and the 'magic number' of 500).

In 1976, the average size of the 18 extant clans whose estates lay between the Love and Kendall rivers along the coast was 21 persons. The sample was 377 people (Sutton 1978:104). The average here is comparable with similar figures from other parts of north Australia (see Peterson and Long 1986:69) where Peterson's 11 non-Wik northern examples yield a patrilineal group average size of 22.7. If the extinct clans are rated as having zero members and added to the calculations, the Wik sample average of 1976 is lower (14.5), but still within the normal range for north Australia. The latter, on the basis of nine non-Wik northern non-desert examples (Peterson and Long 1986:69), ran from a depleted 11.1

(Yir Yoront) to a somewhat exceptional 45.3 (Yolngu), all calculated by a more complex method than my own crude averages but with not very dissimilar results. If we also omit the somewhat distinctive Yolngu from that list, the average for eight northern samples drops to 19.8 with a range of 11.1–28.8.

However, the degree of Wik depopulation well prior to 1976 had been substantial and followed the introduction of exotic diseases to the region in the late nineteenth and early twentieth centuries. Clans with estates closest to river mouths seem often to have had fewer survivors than others. Just how far the Wik clans were along the road to population recovery by 1976 is unclear but I think they still had a way to go. In order to get a longer-term picture, I have estimated that in c. 1900 Wik patrilineal estate groups would *on average* fall within the range of 15–25 persons. Individually, they would have ranged between none and probably a few dozen.

The range of reconstructible populations owning each technically defined language as at about the year 1900, using the 15–25 persons range and multiplying it by the number of estates per language, is as follows:

Table 4.10: Reconstructed number of estates per language

4. (Kugu Ngancharra varieties)	585–975
1. (Ngathan, Ngatharr, Elkenh/Alken)	225–375
3. (Mungkan, Mungkanhu, Iyeyn)	150–300
2. (Ep/lit, Me'enh, Keyenganh)	135–250
Totals	**1,095–1,900**

Assuming we have missed at least some estates in our research, it would be safe to say there were at least 80 estates associated with languages of the Wik Subgroup between the Archer and Edward rivers and inland to about Rokeby and the upper Edward River in c. 1900. On the same clan-size assumptions made immediately above, the immediate pre-European population of the area would thus have been roughly of the order of 1,200–2,000 people.

Ursula McConnel's rough estimates of those living in 1929, based on far less specific data, are as follows:

Table 4.11: McConnel's estimates of those living in 1929

Archer River Wik-Mungkan	50–100
Holroyd, Kendall, Edward rivers	200 approximately
Coastal [Wik] tribes	200–300
Totals	**450–600**

Source: McConnel (1930a:99)

She added: 'According to report the population was once [i.e. before the development of coastal trade] three or four times as great' (McConnel 1930a:99).

Most of the Wik peoples were coming into regular contact with missionaries at the same time as immunisations and other kinds of modern practice were becoming standard, from the 1920s onwards. In their case, a large number of these immunisations were recorded by date and individual's name on the back of personal data cards kept by the mission staff. Apart from some of the earlier-contacted groups, which appear to have lost most or all of their members in several cases, the Wik Region generally is unlikely to have lost over 90 per cent of its people within the first 60 years in the way the Lake Eyre region did (Tindale 1941:73). On both McConnel's figures and mine (see above), at most the loss of Wik population is likely to have been about 75 per cent, to when it reached its lowest point, probably less than a decade before McConnel's first visit in 1927. From a population estimated above to have been of the order of 465–875, the Wik-Way from between the Archer and the Embley seem to have declined much more significantly, to perhaps even less than 10 per cent of their original numbers, although the details have not been worked out as yet.

McConnel's pre-European Wik population estimates may be summarised as:

Table 4.12: Summary of McConnel's pre-European Wik population estimates

	lower estimate	upper estimate
In 1929	450	600
Before: if 3 times as many	135	1,800
Before: if 4 times as many	1,800	2,400

Shortly afterwards, however, McConnel wrote:

> The Wik-munkan tribe[14] is composed of approximately thirty such local clans, of which a few are practically extinct, the majority have from one to five members, a few from five to ten members, whilst others … have from ten to twenty members … one clan has at least forty or fifty members. As all these clans were probably at one time equally large, it may be assumed that the Wik-munkan tribe must have originally numbered from fifteen hundred to two thousand people (McConnel 1930a:181).

This method of reconstructing populations by extrapolating backwards from surviving knowledge of clan estates was probably that of McConnel's supervisor, A.R. Radcliffe-Brown. In the same year he published his 'Former numbers and distribution of the Australian Aborigines' (Radcliffe-Brown 1930), which made the point that 'Any accurate estimate of the numbers of aborigines in any district requires a knowledge of the extent (i.e., area occupied) and the volume (i.e., number of persons) of the horde and the number of hordes in the tribe' (Radcliffe-Brown 1930:688; in this context his 'hordes' = my 'clans'). For the area now known as the Pilbara (Western Australia), he concluded from his own field work that 'the normal or average horde in former times [in the region] cannot have numbered less than 30 persons, men, women and children' (1930:688). He came to a similar conclusion using his own work in northern NSW (1930:694).

I regard McConnel's reconstructed figures here as being somewhat unreliable, given that the number of clans or local groups affiliated with Wik-Mungkan has been inflated by the incorporation into McConnel's listing of many non-Wik-Mungkan estates, including those whose language is actually Wik-Iyanh and some that are, for example, Mbiywom (exogenously 'Wik-Ompom'). While Wik-Iyanh is closely related to Wik-Mungkan, Mbiywom is Northern Paman and Wik-Mungkan is Middle Paman and the two are thus only distantly related and are mutually unintelligible.

These include, for example, McConnel's Wik-Mungkan local groups I and VI, which in the 1970s were still remembered as having been Mbiywom but had transitioned to Wik-Mungkan. Her XI(a) had been Andjingith but was in transition to Wik-Mungkan in the 1970s. Her Wik-Mungkan

---

14 McConnel here used 'Wik-munkan' as a cover term for all the Wik tribes.

groups XIII(c), XIV(a), XVII, XVIII, XXI were recorded in the 1970s as still having the language identity of Wik-Iiyanh. Her Wik-Mungkan group XXIV was Wik-Iiyanh and Pakanh. Her XVI we recorded as Wik-Iiyanh (formerly?) and Wik-Mungkanh. Her group XIII(d) is very possibly the Wik-Iyanh Clan 113 in Appendix 1. Her XI(b) is Clan 2, identified in the 1970s as Andjingith, Wik-Mungkan, and Wik Paach, but transitioning to Wik-Mungkan-only. It seems that McConnel was adopting the term 'Wik-Mungkan' as a cover term for many of the Wik Subgroup inland peoples, and people with Northern Paman languages who were undergoing language identity shift to the lingua franca Wik-Mungkan, even if their own variety was not Wik-Mungkan in classical times. It may have been the case that McConnel's Wik-I(i)yanh informants tended to identify as Wik-Mungkan in the Aurukun Mission context, thus giving rise to her broad usage of the term.

McConnel (1930a:204–5) tabulated 25 'local groups of the Wik-Munkan tribe' between the Archer and Edward rivers, with surviving population estimates for 1929, but this yields a total population estimate of only 132–167 and it seems to omit a large number of Wik estates, especially coastal ones. On the basis of detailed accounts of estates in Sutton et al. (1990), northern Wik Subgroup estates numbered 43, southern Wik Subgroup estates numbered 53, yielding a total of 96. The rest of the Wik native title claim area—the Wik Way and Watson River areas north of Archer River—totalled 26 estates. The all-up total for the present study area is 122 clan estates.

McConnel shows only one extinct clan, which is most surprising. Even if possible sub-clans (e.g. McConnel's IX(a), IX(b), etc.) are separated out, the maximum number of deducible estates in her Wik-Mungkan list only rises to 36.

Second, 30 clans in a population of 2,000 would yield an average reconstructed figure of 67 people per clan, which is way above the approximate average sizes for the north Australian literature. In the absence of any specialised regional social organisational complexity of the kind that may account for the figure of 55 per clan for the Yolngu in 1976,[15] it is extremely unlikely the pre-European Wik would have reached an average clan size of anything like 67.

An estimate of 1,200–2,000 people affiliated to varieties of four technically defined languages (see Chapter 5), using fine-grained mapping data, clearly matches quite well with McConnel's estimated total for the same region based on a rather different method. The fine-grained method also yields a range of estimated owner populations per language (as technically defined) of 135–975, which is an enormous span and one that shows how the use of a rule of thumb of '500 people per language' can be quite remote from the local facts. If instead we examine the reconstructible population ranges for proper-named linguistic varieties in the Wik case, it extends from a low of 15–25 (e.g. Wik-Keyenganh with one estate) to 240–400 (Wik-Iyanh with 16 estates). Most of the 18 named Wik varieties considered here fall well below these latter figures, in fact 16 of them fall below Wik-Mungkan which had eight or nine estates (120–225 people).[16]

Turning again to the northern area between the Archer and the Embley, an estimate based on 15–25 people per clan multiplied by 31–35 clans comes to a rough population estimate of 465–875 people. Given there are 13 named language varieties in this case, that comes to about 35–60 persons per named variety. Even if we were to assume an average of 35 persons for each of 35 clans, that would still result in an average of only 94 persons per named variety in this area. These were very tiny linguistic country units.

In terms of technically defined languages (i.e. sets of mutually intelligible dialects), I am unable to conclude exactly how many there were in this small area, but a figure of six or more seems not unreasonable, given the comparative data already published by Ken Hale.[17] At a figure of six such 'technical' languages the estimate of how many people there were on average per language comes to a range of 77.5 to 145.8 using 15–25 as the

---

15   The range is cited by Keen (1978:21) as 4–230, so his approximate average figure of 55 is an average for extant clans only. Adding those with zero persons to the calculations, the average comes down to 48.63 (1070 ÷ 22). In 1928–29, W.L. Warner, who worked in a similar part of the region, found Yolngu clans averaged 40 or 50 individuals (1937:16).
16   Even if pre-colonial clans averaged 35 members instead, this figure would rise only to 280–315. All of which leads to the fascinating question as to why it is that Wik-Mungkan has become not only the Indigenous lingua franca of Aurukun and parts of its wider region, but has also predominantly replaced a large number of other varieties formerly spoken in the region.
17   Especially Hale (1966:163–76).

clan average. Assuming 35 as the clan average, the average reconstructible population for each technically defined language would still be only 204 persons. In world terms these are stupendously small numbers.[18]

Language group size and the 'magic number' of 500

These are extremely modest figures, and fall well below the rule of thumb figure of about 500 people per Australian 'tribe' that has at times been used.

For example, R.M.W. Dixon's major textbook on Australian languages said 'There were around 600 distinct tribes in Australia … It is thought that each tribe had something of the order of 500 members on average' (1980:18). This latter figure, which was not repeated in Dixon (2002), may derive from the work of Joseph Birdsell[19] or perhaps from that of A.P. Elkin (see below, this section).

However, as Birdsell himself pointed out, Krzywicki (1934) had derived a mean value of Australian tribal populations 'as approximating 500 persons on the basis of data collected from the literature' (Birdsell 1973:339). Even earlier, A.R. Radcliffe-Brown (1930:693) had used the figure of 500 in order to make tribal estimates in at least one case. While reconstructing Victorian populations he said, 'If we allow only 500 persons for a tribe or language and only 100 to 120 for a dialect' (1930:693), thus prefiguring Birdsell's 'magic number' of 500 by over 20 years.

The source for Elkin's figures is not clear. In his general introductory work on Aborigines he said that 'the membership of a tribe varied from about 100 to 1,500, and averaged about 500 or 600' (1938:10).[20] In turn, R.M. and C.H. Berndt, in their own introductory work, cited Elkin's figures without dissent, although they added that 'Tindale speaks of 500 as the average, but adds that this may be too high' (1988:33–4). Tindale's considered view was that the mean was about 450 (1974:110).

---

18   I offer analysis and continent-wide data on the subject of Australian language group sizes in Sutton (2019).
19   e.g. Birdsell (1953; 1957:53; 1958:196; 1968:230; 1973:339; 1979:136; 1987:10, 1993:34).
20   See also Elkin's pers. comm. to Radcliffe-Brown (1930:689).

The figure of 500 persists in works such as the archaeological text by Harry Lourandos, who cites Birdsell as authority for stating that 'tribes' 'tended to average … around five hundred' (1997:15). There Lourandos notes, however, that L.R. Hiatt questioned the 'magic number' estimates of Birdsell, who had stated that 'the size of the dialectical [sic: dialectal] tribe statistically tended toward a constant value which was estimated as approaching 500 persons' (Birdsell 1968:230). Hiatt (1968:245) responded that Elkin's estimated tribal size range was

> about 100 to 1,500 or 2,000. I recorded numbers in nine tribes near the Liverpool River of Arnhem Land. The largest of these … is about 300. There was a good deal of intermarriage, particularly around the edges of this largest tribe.

Birdsell demurred at times from Norman Tindale's conclusion that pre-contact Aboriginal dialectal tribes approximated '400 to 600 persons with a mean of around 450' (1974:8). Birdsell considered the 'magic number' of 500 people per tribe to be a statistical abstraction that was approximated when such groups reached a relatively constant size under conditions of equilibrium, but the empirical data

> in fact represents [sic] a fairly wide range of values, and indicate that serious disturbances of the balanced condition may not be compensated for until tribal population actually falls below 200 individuals or exceeds 800 individuals. (Birdsell 1958:196)

Birdsell's technique for estimating contact-period tribal sizes was primarily based on a single case of population decline published by Tindale (1941:73).[21] On this basis, Birdsell made the working assumption that all Aboriginal populations declined by 50 per cent every 25 years after contact, thus suppressing the variation between misfortunes experienced by groups in different regions. He also made no allowance for the resurgence of populations after they reached their lowest point, which for many groups appears to have been around the time of the Spanish influenza pandemic of 1919. To reconstruct a tribal population, one made an estimate of living numbers and added to it 50 per cent for each period of 25 years since contact. Applying this doubtful method to 18 Western Australian tribes 'examined' in 1952–54, and adding five

---

21   The case was the Lake Eyre District.

further reconstructions drawn from the work of others, Birdsell presented a list of 23 reconstructed tribal sizes for the western half of the continent (1993:33–4).

From this list Birdsell (1993:10) concluded that

> the tribes are larger than average for the continent. Of the 23 tribes, only six fell into the normal range of 400–599 ... The pattern in ecological space was not consistent, for desert tribes included both very large ones and very small ones.

The list defined each reconstructed tribe as 'Large', 'Medium' or 'Small', and the ranges involved are as follows:

Table 4.13: Birdsell's estimate of tribal populations for 23 western cases

Size	Number	Range
Large	9	750–1976
Medium	8	448–618
Small	6	192–324
Total	**23**	**Average 648**

Source: Birdsell (1993:33) (Note that the smallest figure is elsewhere (p. 34) given as 142.)

Not only did just six of these tribes fall into what Birdsell regarded as the 'normal' range of 400–599, but even on internal grounds this set, which ranges from the Kimberley coast in Western Australia south-east to the Mann Ranges in South Australia and east to the Tanami Desert (Northern Territory), contained almost twice as many non-medium cases as medium ones. In what sense then is an average of 648 a productive figure here? And in what sense is 500 an 'optimum figure' (Birdsell 1973:348) or a 'normal optimum size' (p. 349) for a pre-contact Aboriginal linguistic group when there are so many that may be reconstructed as having been well above or below it numerically?

Unfortunately, Birdsell's figures are based on named linguistic groupings only, and do not take into account the degrees of similarity and difference between their speech varieties. He generally makes an assumption that having a distinctly named language variety implies a high degree of social closure from those with other varieties, an assumption that cannot be generally sustained, whether or not neighbouring varieties were highly similar or profoundly different. Linguistic exogamy was variable but commonly substantial.[22]

---

22 For hard data see e.g. Sutton (1978:107–12; 2013a; 2013b).

Linguistic groups large and small

Birdsell did attempt to deal with cases such as the reconstructed populations for Kamilaroi[23] (6,000–7,000), Wongaibon (some thousands), Wiradjuri (3,000) and Barkendji (3,000), all from western New South Wales, and concluded that 'this deviant pattern' was not ecologically driven but probably resulted from the absence of strict patrilineality in assigning territorial interests. The emphasis of such groups on bilaterally derived rights and interests would have extended social networks beyond those of individuals in more strictly patrilineal tribes. He made no suggestion, however, that these exceptions were merely recorded midway through a particular phase of waxing and waning about an optimum figure of 500 persons in each case. Presumably this might have entailed a further hypothesis of an oscillation between patrilineality and bilaterality in reckoning the descent of land rights in western New South Wales, which would be even less likely.

On the other hand, Birdsell was prepared to refer to regions of small tribes as 'areas of apparent tribal fragmentation'. These 'primarily centred around the Boulia region in Queensland, the Daly River area on the western coast of Arnhem Land, and the so-called Murngin area of northeast Arnhem Land' (Birdsell 1973:341). His main hypothesis for explaining these exceptions was some form of fragmentation that occurred in the wake of the spread of initiatory rituals involving circumcision and subincision respectively (Birdsell 1973:341–6). The fact that the Daly River area had no such rituals in the relevant period was not addressed. In any case, there are so many 'exceptions' now demonstrable, including the many 'small tribes' of Cape York Peninsula—another region where there is no record of circumcision or subincision ever having been practised—that this argument is quite unconvincing as an Australia-wide generalisation.

Norman Tindale, in a chapter entitled 'Tribes large and small', attempted to explain why some tribes such as the Wiradjuri, Kamilaroi, Warlpiri, and Wadjari numbered in the low thousands, many others numbered 450 to 500, and yet others were significantly smaller (1974:110–17). His approach here was to fall back on economic determinism. The large tribes, he argued, tended to depend on grain-harvesting for their subsistence, while the smaller ones were relatively sedentary groups using rich and reliable

---

23   I retain the author's spelling of language names in this context.

food environments, mainly coastal and estuarine environments intensively exploited for marine resources, or rainforest areas where the canopy yielded a constant food supply and rainfall was almost year-long. Like Birdsell, he also cited the Daly River as an exceptional example of 'small tribes of sedentary type', although in that case many were not on the coast per se but exploited wetlands areas nearby (1974:113). The others, one might conclude, were the non-coastal, non-rainforest, non-wetland, non-grain-dependent language groups with sizes frequently approximating 450–600 people. No such pattern is clearly evident from the data (Sutton 2020).

Among several examples of 'small tribes', Tindale cited the Wik area and what in this book has been referred to as that part of the Wik-Way area immediately to its north (1974:112–13). The smaller the area covered by a language variety name, the more Tindale seems to have been inclined to regard it as a 'sub-tribe', more or less on principle. In his catalogue of tribes he listed the Wik Subgroup language names as separate tribes, but from the Archer River to just north of the Embley he listed the names of 12 language varieties as 'hordes or incipient small tribes' under the 'valid embracing name' of '*Winduwinda*' (Winda-Winda) (1974:188–90; see Map 3.5 above). It seems likely that the origin of the term Winda-Winda is essentially geographical, centred on the 'Winda Winda Creek' area and covering groups with lands between the Archer and Mission rivers.[24] But there are 'valid embracing names' for many congeries of language groups and Tindale's preference for entering the Wik-Way languages under *Winduwinda* seems unmotivated, except perhaps as a means of dealing with exceptional regions that fell outside his figures for average tribal sizes. In any case, he decided not to be too dogmatic about this particular arrangement: 'Those who feel inclined to regard the Winduwinda and Jupangati [Mapoon area] assemblages as having full tribal status may add a further dozen or more to the number of Australian tribes, bringing the total to over 600 tribes' (Tindale 1974:113). Writing about his field work on the same area, Lauriston Sharp said: 'Again in this area of small tribes it is not easy to distinguish local groupings, clans, or slightly differentiated linguistic groupings from tribes' (Sharp 1939:264; see Map 3.2 above).

---

24   See also W.E. Roth (1910:96 & Pl.XXXI, more detail in the MS version 1900:2–4), McConnel (1939–40:62), and Hale (1966:176), on Winduwinda/Windawinda (Winda-Winda). The term has become archaic.

Patterns of diversity in the wider Wik Region

Especially in the coastal and pericoastal areas, it is clear that in the wider Wik and Wik-Way region linguistic diversity was both real at a technical level and also highly valued and marked culturally. Even near-identical dialects could have distinct autochthonous names.

Just over half the 13 named Wik-Way varieties for which reasonably good mapping is available are intrinsically associated with just one estate each. This is within an area approximately 100 kilometres north–south by 75 kilometres east–west. In the past this concentrated Babel represented a challenging prospect for any newcomer, in spite of the regional tradition of highly skilled multilingualism. Although there were some marriages between Wik-Way and northern Wik Subgroup people prior to the effects of colonisation, a reason given to me for the difficulty of arranging such marriages was that Wik Subgroup people from south of the Archer were daunted by the difficulty of the languages to their north. Certainly the Wik-Way languages are phonologically much more complex than Wik Subgroup ones, but their sheer number and diversity would also have been a problem for those not brought up there, given the necessity to be a polyglot in order to survive socially, and to treat one's kin with respect, in this part of the world.

In the nineteenth and twentieth centuries, and probably earlier for one or two cases, language shift from Wik-Way-type languages to Wik Subgroup languages was occurring between the Archer and Kirke rivers. These events took place at the clan estate level, as can be seen in the detailed data in Appendix 1. This description is to be preferred to 'tribal expansion' given that population replacement by linguistic groups as a whole was not the norm.

This cultural transformation moved northwards along the coast and westwards towards the coast. It was probably accelerated by the impact of colonisation, as the Wik-Way lost much population and owners of Wik Subgroup varieties moved in to Aurukun on the north side of the Archer from the south, thus being better able to pursue succession to depopulated estates near the Archer and Love rivers to which they had connections. The emergent mission culture of Aurukun, after an initial period in which

Wik-Way languages held sway,[25] developed Wik-Mungkan as the town lingua franca and as the first language of most children regardless of their families' linguistic backgrounds.

The owners of the farthest inland Wik Subgroup varieties seem to have interacted closely with central peninsula people such as Kaantju. That is, genetic linguistic relationships here as in so many cases are not always aligned with social relationships. At the southern end of the Wik Region, where the Kugu Ngancharra varieties met Kuuk Thaayorre, social closure for the Wik was at its greatest (John von Sturmer, pers. comm.). Thaayorre is middlingly related to the Wik varieties but is not of the same subgroup, and at least superficially resembles Wik languages more than Wik-Way ones do—yet it seems there were more marriages between Wik and Wik-Way than between Wik and Thaayorre in the early twentieth century, even though there were not a great many. This relatively light social integration with coastal neighbours until several decades ago is possibly a reflection of the general northward and westward thrust of estate succession and ensuing linguistic and other cultural expansion by the Wik Subgroup people in protohistoric times. There may, however, be other explanations.[26]

The area just south of the lower Archer River represented a break-point between two regional *Sprachbünde*, one (Wik-Way) demanding greater multilingual competence than the other. To return to the figures above, linguistic diversity in the region is not so great in the inland as on the coast, an exception possibly being the Wik-Way area north of Archer River in which there is really not the same coast/hinterland distinction as obtains in a quite profound way south of Archer River. The geomorphology north of the Archer is clearly very different. North of the Archer to the Embley there is no pericoastal flood plain, and no Holocene and Pleistocene dune systems and sclerophyll forests extend virtually to the beach in most areas. The flood plains and Pleistocene dune systems south of Archer River hosted a great concentration of people, and thus also of estates. For this Wik Subgroup region (Archer-Edward rivers), proportionately more inland estates than coastal estates are identified with fewer proper-

---

25   In 1910, at the opening of the Aurukun church on 22 September, 'Mamus held the morning service in the Winda-Winda (Weipa language) which is understood by most northerners in Aurukun' (Richter 1910). Aurukun began in 1904.
26   The dynamics of classical period regionalism within Cape York Peninsula are as yet little explored, but there is enough data on which to develop models.

named linguistic varieties, most notably in the cases of Wik-Iyanh and Wik-Mungkan. Furthermore, the historical-linguistic genetic diversity of the coastal Wik varieties is far greater than that of the inland.[27]

Thus, from both a nomenclature perspective as well as a technical comparative one, this means the inland Wik Region is comparatively uniform linguistically, being dominated by the closely related varieties Wik-Mungkan and Wik-Iyanh. A comparison of basic lexicons (Sutton 1978:178) showed Wik-Mungkan sharing 75 per cent with Wik-Iyanh and 77 per cent with Kugu Mu'inh, which would usually suggest reasonable mutual intelligibility, but in terms of phonological developments, morphology and morphophonology Wik-Iyanh belongs more with the Kugu Ngancharra subgroup than the one to which Wik-Mungkan belongs (Smith and Johnson 2000:364). Furthermore, while coastal varieties can be non-contiguously distributed in terms of their estates, both at the level of vernacular proper-named varieties and even that of technically defined languages,[28] the inland ones appear thus far to be the opposite and we have no evidence that they occur other than in single geographical blocs.

If we ignore the way the people themselves assign different names to varieties and look just at technical similarities and differences, the inland Wik varieties constitute only two (technical) languages divided among about 30 estates, while the coastal and pericoastal varieties constitute five technically defined languages divided among over 40 estates. The most genetically distant varieties of the Wik Subgroup, Wik-Ngathan/Wik-Ngatharr/Wik-Elkenh, do not have estates in the inland.

These observations are consonant with the general tendency for the cultural life of the coastal people, and not merely their demographic distribution, to show greater intensity and diversity than that of inlanders. For example, while the coastal Wik groups surveyed here fall into four sub-regionally distinct ritual groups, known in Aurukun English as 'clans' or 'tribes', inlanders from between the Archer and Kendall rivers all share a single ritual identity across an area that greatly exceeds that of the coastal and pericoastal groups combined. Ceremonial diversity, along with linguistic diversity, is thus proportionately much lower in the inland than it is on the coast.

---

27 See Hale, this volume, Chapters 6 and 7, and Sutton (1991:60, 63).
28 See e.g. the map in Sutton (1991:65) and maps A2.1–A2.13 below.

5

Languages of the Wik Native Title Claim Area

Peter Sutton

Regional macro-groupings

Most of the ethnological literature sources on the area between the Mission and Edward rivers that predate the 1970s couch their maps and group descriptions in terms of relationships between languages and land areas.[1]

Above that level, the classical social and cultural macro-groupings along the coast in the region between what are now Old Mapoon and Pormpuraaw were basically three (here dealt with from north to south). Macro-groupings 2 and 3 belong to the Native Title Claim Area, and macro-grouping 1 does not.

Macro-grouping 1

From Port Musgrave to Albatross Bay about a dozen or so clans owned among them three or four distinct but closely related languages. No cover term for them is available but their general cohesiveness is clear from the literature (Roth 1900; Crowley 1981 particularly). After colonisation, these groups settled at Mapoon (begun 1891) and dominated its early

---

1   See Maps 16–22 in Sutton (1978) and Maps 3.1–3.7 above.

population. North of them and covering the whole tip of Cape York Peninsula the clans owned dialects of a single, but different, language that has been described by Crowley (1983) under the title of Uradhi.

Macro-grouping 2

From Albatross Bay to just south of Archer River,[2] along a narrow coastal strip, are the estates of the Wik-Way people, whose clans own a set of closely related languages, which are clearly different from those to the south of them but middlingly related to those of the Mapoon area (see 1 above). These people formed the core of the Weipa Mission and part of the core of Aurukun Mission as they were established, respectively, in 1895 and 1904. On the eastern or inland side of the Wik-Way estates, on the upper Watson River, Kokialah Creek, and north to the middle Embley and Myall Creek areas, are the estates of clans whose members are not identified as Wik-Way in the modern sense, but whose languages are most closely related to those of the Wik-Way grouping.

In earlier times it seems clear, from Ken Hale's and Norman Tindale's work in the 1960s for example, that 'Wik-Way' was a term applied, from a south-of-Archer (Wik Subgroup) perspective, to any language to the north, including the inland ones such as Mbiywom and Ngkoth of the upper Watson and Hey rivers respectively.

The current senses of this term are narrower. One, for example, has the Wik-Way area running from the Aurukun Airstrip (north side) via Ikeleth and the Ward River, north to Embley River, excluding the Watson River system and Oyenten. This is the predominant sense of the term among those to whom it applies at Aurukun.

Macro-grouping 3

From about Love River south to Moonkan Creek and inland to about Rokeby, Meripah, and the upper Holroyd, and from there in a narrow band east to Princess Charlotte Bay, are the estates of the clans owning languages that are members of what is called here the 'Wik Subgroup' of languages. These five distinct languages and their many named dialects form a distinct genetic subgroup within the Cape York Peninsula (Paman) language family.

---

2   See Wik-Paach estates 43 and 44, Map A2.3 this volume.

Philip Hamilton has established that Pakanh and Ayapathu, languages associated with the uplands and Great Dividing Range between the upper Holroyd River system and the coast at Princess Charlotte Bay, are genetically part of the Wik Subgroup and are close dialects of a single language.[3] It appears, however, that only those affiliates of Pakanh and Ayapathu with estates close to the Wik heartland are socially and culturally integrated with the Wik peoples. This is why the country of such people was included in the Wik native title application.[4]

A number of the relevant historical and anthropological records identify people of this south-eastern interior area, the upper Kendall and Holroyd River systems, not by estate totemic centres or by language but by a geographically broad environmental typifier, Pechem (Wik-Mungkan), Pachem (Wik-Ngathan), meaning 'those from open country' (cf. 'Wik Patjam' in Thomson 1972:vi). *Pech* (Mn) and *pachel* (Nn) are adjectives meaning 'clear, open, white'. They are used to denote savannah landscapes.

It is typical of Aboriginal Australia that the Wik bloc should be relatively clearly defined at the coast, but is less rigidly defined in the less resource-rich inland: the greater the scarcity, the more mobile the original population would have been and the more outward-looking their approach to inter-group relations (Sutton and Rigsby 1982). It is also typical that people whose countries lie along the upper watersheds should have affiliations and associations with those downstream from them on more than one side of their uplands. Thus, while a number of Ayapathu people, for example, have links to mainstream Wik people and indeed have a Wik-Subgroup-type language, in the past some of them had estates at Princess Charlotte Bay in the area of Running Creek. Succession to these estates has been by the Port Stewart Lamalama (Rigsby and Hafner 1994). From a west coast perspective, however, the Wik *cultural* bloc may be seen quite properly to fade out on the upper Holroyd system in the south-east, and not to extend right to the east coast.

---

3   Philip Hamilton, pers. comm., 29 March 1997.
4   For details of Ayapathu people with countries close to or part of the Wik Region see Chase et al. (1998:79–95).

Land/language affiliations between the Archer and Mission rivers: Wik-Way-type languages

Here I discuss the area covered by Macro-grouping 2 above, proceeding to survey the literature on each language running approximately from north to south. Before doing so, I discuss in more detail the content of the broad geopolitical categories 'Wik-Way' and 'Winda-Winda'.

Languages covered by the term Wik-Way

As is often the case in Aboriginal Australia, where regional macro-group terminology is concerned, and as noted above, the term Wik-Way was originally an outsider's term. It means 'Language-Bad/Difficult' in several of the languages of the Wik Subgroup, e.g. in Wik-Mungkan, Wik-Ngathan, and others. It has now become a self-designation at least among those Wik-Way who live in the Aurukun Shire and many who live at Napranum.

It is a term with more than one legitimate meaning. It seems to have long had at least two ranges of reference, a narrow sense and an extended sense, although the narrow sense may now be dominant (the 'modern sense', see Chapter 3: The Wik-Way). I now examine all available lists of languages coming under these ranges of reference. Note that here I transliterate the ethnographers' spellings into a 'Standard' spelling that is not only for the most part linguistically more accurate but also provides language names in the form used within the relevant language. This accounts for some systematic differences between the two (e.g. the self-named Ndrwa'ngathi is called Ndrwa'ngith in some other languages whose comitative suffix is different, and for the same reason Arrithinngithigh appears to have been called Arrithingwom in Mbiywom).

Thomson

In 1933 Donald Thomson (1933:File no. 276, undated), presumably at Aurukun, recorded two lists of languages known collectively as 'Wik-Way' by people speaking Wik-Mungkan, and in each case the lists were subdivided into a primary list and a secondary list. The latter was introduced in his notes by the word 'Also…' in one case, and bracketed below the main list in the second. The added languages may represent afterthoughts

5. LANGUAGES OF THE WIK NATIVE TITLE CLAIM AREA

by his informants. With two exceptions (Thomson's 'N'got'tungit', which is Ngkoth as pronounced in another language probably as Ngkothngith; and 'Tan'ngat', which is Thanikwithi as pronounced in another language, probably as Thyanngayth), the primary list in each case refers to languages from between the Archer and Watson rivers in the south and the Mission and Wenlock rivers in the north. The secondary or additional languages specified belong to the next macro-grouping north of there between Albatross Bay and Port Musgrave.

Table 5.1: Thomson's lists of Wik-Way language varieties

THOMSON LIST 1	THOMSON LIST 2	STANDARD
Additin'ngitti	Adedingit	Aditinngithigh
Lin'ngitti	Lin'ngitti	Linngithigh
N'dwangit (gerri'gerri) [listed under Lin'ngitti & bracketed as 'Same']	N'drangit	Ndrwa'ngathi
Latum'ngit	Latum'ngit	Latumngith
Andjingitti	Andjingit	Andjingith
Alingit	Alingit	Alngith
Aredin'ngit	Aredinngit	Arrithinngithigh
Mberwum	M'berwun	Mbiywom
N'dra'ngit	N'drangit	Ndra'ngith
–	Lin'ngit	?Laynngith [= Alngith]
–	Ngernbudi	–
[On edge of page:] Tjong'ndji, Tjongandji	[Bracketed:] Tjungundji	Tjungundji

Table 5.2: Thomson's 'also' list of Wik-Way language varieties

THOMSON'S 'ALSO' LIST	STANDARD
Yangit [Yangith?]	Yangathimri[5]
Yin'wum	Yinwum
Tiep'the [Tyaepthi?]	Taepadhighi
M'bawsan	Mbaatjan
O'ngit	[cf. Alngith]

---

5 Cf. AnguThimri (Crowley 1981).

THOMSON'S 'ALSO' LIST	STANDARD
Watjanwum	_6
Tan'ngat [Thyanngayth]	Thanikwithi
O'natangit [Anathangith]	Anathangayth
N'got'tungit [Ngkothngith]	Ngkoth
Otak	–

McConnel

Ursula McConnel expanded her knowledge of groups north of the Archer River during her 1934 field work at Aurukun, Weipa and Mapoon (1936:69; 1939–40:59).

In her writings she does not mention the term Wik-Way, but her discussions of language-related groups and their land associations (especially 1939–40:57–64) suggest some subgroupings that are relevant here. For example, she devotes a single paragraph to a discussion of nine languages (listed below, see discussion of Winda-Winda) whose owners had land between the Embley River and Wallaby Island in the mouth of the Archer. It is of interest that she does not include Mbiywom in this list, but discusses it in the context of inland groups having the languages Yinwum, Trotj, and (inland) Kaantju. Trotj, however—which was very close linguistically to Ngkoth (Hale 1966:165)—is also discussed (along with Ngkoth) as part of her list of nine languages between the Embley and Archer rivers. She placed Mbiywom in a 'northern group' in terms of social organisation, a group described as those from 'north of the Watson River' (1939–40:64).

McConnel (1939–40:60) referred to at least a number of these languages as those that had names suffixed with '-Niti' or '-Nati'—that is, names of their languages tended to end in the comitative suffix *-ngthi, -ngithigh*, or *-ngathi*. Note that these would be appropriate suffixes in which to name the languages from within only a few of them, such as Linngithigh in the case of *-thigh*, or *-ngathi* in the case of Mamangathi. In other languages the same languages may be named using distinct but mostly related and semantically equivalent suffixes, e.g. *-ngith, -ngayth, -wom*.

---

6   On *-wum*, cf. Mbiywom, Yinwum, Arrithingwom, see this chapter, Code L12.

Gajdusek

In 1956, Daniel Carleton Gajdusek, a genetics researcher, visited Weipa and recorded a list of 'small tribes which the Wik-Mungken [sic] refer to as the Wik-Waiya (meaning "speech bad"), clustered about Albatross Bay at the mouths of the Mission, Hey, and Embley Rivers' who had been centralised at Weipa (Simmons et al. 1958:64–5):

Table 5.3: Gajdusek's list of Wik-Way language varieties

GAJDUSEK	STANDARD
Wimmarango	Wimaranga
Tanikutti	Thanikwithi
Lainingitti [Laynngithi]	Alngith
M-Berwum (Bywoom)	Mbiywom
N-Dwangit (Dragnite) [Ndrwa'ngayth]	Ndrwa'angathi
Linngitti	Linngithigh
Aredinngit [Aritinngith], (Aritchenite [Aritinngayth])	Arrithinngithigh
Latumngit	Latumngith

(Apart from Wimaranga, which is from the coast just north of Albatross Bay [Capell 1963: Y–25], and a language of macro-grouping 1 described above, the others are all of macro-grouping 2.)

Gajdusek then listed 'other tribal names of the region' as:

Table 5.4: Gajdusek's 'other' list of Wik-Way language varieties

GAJDUSEK	STANDARD
Yeemwoom	Yinwum
Teepani	[?Taepadhighi]
Gott	Ngkoth

He located two further languages (usually included in Wik-Way) north of the Archer on the coast:

Table 5.5: Gajdusek's north of Archer River Wik-Way language varieties

GAJDUSEK	STANDARD
Andjingit	Andjingith
N'drangit	Ndra'ngith

Hale

In 1960 Ken Hale recorded the term Wik-Way as referring to all the languages north of the Watson River, a north-side tributary of the Archer River, as far as the tip of Cape York, all of which share aberrant sound systems and whose vocabularies are very different from those south of the Archer and Watson rivers (and indeed they vary a great deal among themselves) (Hale 1964:248). Thus in Hale's terms (1966:162), Wik-Way is equivalent to his Northern Paman linguistic subgroup of the Paman family. He sampled 13 Northern Paman languages and published a technical comparison of them along with a sketch grammar of one, Linngithigh (1966).

Hale listed those of which he had knowledge from north to south as follows (spellings here have been transliterated from phonemic symbols to keyboard characters, and only a few need to be standardised; standard forms are only supplied here where they differ, as self-designations, from the other-dialectal form recorded by Hale, or where Hale uses /Nt-/ and I use /Nd-/):

Table 5.6: Hale's list of Wik-Way language varieties

HALE	STANDARD
Uradhi	
Mpalitjanh	
Luthigh	
Yinwum	
Linngithigh	
Alngith	
Thyanngayth	Thanikwithi
Mamngayth	Mamangathi
Ntrwa'ngayth	Ndrwa'angathi
The three above are collectively known as: Awngthim	
Ntra'ngith	Ndra'ngith
Ngkoth	
Aritinngithigh	Arrithinngithigh
Mbiywom	

Apart from the first four, Hale located these languages between Albatross Bay and the Ward and Watson rivers and they are within macro-grouping 2, as described above.

Languages covered by the term Winda-Winda

Roth

W.E. Roth (1910:96 and Plate XXXI)[7] listed groups from the area between Port Musgrave and Pera Head and indicated their homelands on a map. South of the Embley these included the Gautundi (lower Hey R., coastal, standard spelling uncertain, possibly Ngkoth) and Winda-Winda 'who speak Marma-ngati' (i.e. Mamangathi) but who were identified rather expansively as 'around coast from Pera Head to the Mission River'. It is clear from later work that Mamangathi is indeed the language of the southern side of the mouth of the Embley but also that Winda-Winda is a broad cover term that includes Mamangathi but also many other linguistic varieties. Roth did not record the term Wik-Way, but he did his work at Mapoon and Weipa (at its old site on the middle Embley) before the establishment of Aurukun, so there is no reason why he should have come across the term 'Wik-Way'.

McConnel

McConnel (1939–40:62) said Roth's 'Windawinda' (sic), which she claimed meant 'windward',[8] was a local name for 'some of the tribes recorded here', and in the same paragraph discussed the following languages associated respectively with these areas: between the Embley and Hey Inlet, up-river on Myall and Cox Creeks (Mission R.), False Pera Head, Hey Inlet, the lower Embley across to the then new location of Weipa Mission, Pera Head, south to the Archer River, both sides of the Ward River, and Wallaby Island in the Archer River mouth:

Table 5.7: McConnel's list of Wik-Way language varieties

MCCONNEL	STANDARD
Nggot	Ngkoth
To.tj	Trotj
Ndra'angit	Ndra'ngith
Aritingiti	Arrithinngithigh
Latamngit	Latumngith
Alingit	Alngith
Adetingiti	Aditinngithigh
Leini-ngiti	Linngithigh
Andyingit	Andjingith

---

7   There is more detail in the manuscript version Roth (1900:2–4).
8   I suspect this is a false etymology. For most of the year the area concerned is on the leeward side not the windward side. In any case, the word 'windward' in Cape York Creole is [windəd] not [windəwində].

In an earlier publication McConnel (1936:Part I:464) had recounted a myth from the 'Windawinda Creek' area and current official maps still have a 'Winda Winda Creek' between the Hey River and the coast. Hale (1966:176) referred to 'the Winduwinda area'. It seems likely that the origin of the term Winda-Winda is essentially geographical, centred on the Winda Winda Creek area, but loosely covering the groups with lands between the Archer and Mission rivers.

In that sense, as Tindale suggested (1974:190 and see below), we may take Winda-Winda to refer essentially to the same groups as the term Wik-Way in its narrower (and now more customary) sense.

Tindale

Norman Tindale (1963; 1974:189–90 and map) interviewed a man from the upper Hey River at Mornington Island in 1963. The informant's own language he recorded as A'retinget, but Tindale added in parentheses language variety names in more than one variety and from various literature sources. Tindale listed 12 'hordes or incipient small tribes' (1974:189 and map; Map 3.5 in this volume) under the broad designation Winduwinda (cf. Winda-Winda), providing locations for each (locations and associated people are listed later in this chapter in the summary of sources):

Table 5.8: Tindale's list of 'Winduwinda' (Wik-Way) language varieties

TINDALE	STANDARD
I Tanikuit [Thanikwith], (Tannikutti, Dainiguid, Tannagootee)	Thanikwithi
II Ndruangit [Ndrwa'ngith]	Ndrwa'angathi
III Ndwangit [Ndwa'ngith], (Ndwongit)	?Ndwa'angathi
IV Ngawangati (Ngawateingeti, Ungauwangati)	?Ngawangathi
V Alingit (Lengiti, Lenngiti, Alngid, Limretti [?typographical error][9]	Alngith
VI Mamangit [Mamangith], (Mamangiti, Mamngaid)	Mamangathi
VII Latamngit (Lätamngit)	Latumngith
VIII Nggot (Gott)	Ngkoth
IX Aretinget [Arrithinngith]	Arrithinngithigh
X Ndraangit	Ndra'ngith
XI Leningiti	Linngithigh
XII Andjingit	Andjingith

9   Tindale's suggestion.

This is fairly precisely a listing of languages that belong to the same subgroup and are distinct at the subgroup level from both their northern neighbours (Anguthimri and related languages) and their southern neighbours of the Wik Subgroup.

They are all shown on Tindale's map as belonging to specific parts of the area between the Archer River and the north side of the Mission River. Tindale provides as an alternate name for this grouping 'Wikwija (sic; 'bad speech'—name given by Wik-munkan)' (Tindale 1974:190)—i.e. Wik-Way (Tindale uses /j/ for /y/). A comparison shows that the list is very close to Thomson's core list of Wik-Way languages. Note, however, that Tindale's informant did not include Mbiywom (Tindale's Mbewum) in Winda-Winda. The status of Mbiywom in relation to the Wik-Way category is still somewhat unclear, as befits its intermediate location on the margins of both coastal and hinterland Aboriginal systems. The status of Wik-Ompom is perhaps unclear (see Code: L19 below). Wik-Ompom and Mbiywom are as far as I know just different names for the same dialect.

Tindale's reluctance to call these entities 'tribes' is revealing. Their crime, as it were, was that they were so small as to look like stark contradictions of Tindale's (and Birdsell's) dialectal tribe model in which language groups usually had a few hundred people. On his 1974 map, Tindale noted the coastal Wik Subgroup language names under the heading 'Small Tribes', as if they just squeaked in as tribes. Inconsistently, he showed equally small language countries south-west of Darwin (Daly River to Port Keats) and at the mouth of the Murray River simply as 'tribes'.

Summary of sources on land/language affiliations between the Mission and Archer rivers

The literature sources given below are much abbreviated, usually shown here only by a surname. Unless dates are specified, these citations refer as follows:

- Aak = Sutton et al. (1990)
- Bos = Bos (1973–74)
- Capell = Capell (1963) unless specified otherwise
- Crowley = Crowley (1981)
- Gajdusek = Simmons et al. (1958)
- Hale = Hale (1966)
- Hinton: Hinton (1963)
- Martin = Martin (n.d.)
- Mathews = Mathews (1900)
- McConnel '28 = McConnel (1928)
- McConnel = McConnel (1939–40)
- Roth = Roth (1900; 1910)
- Sharp = Sharp (1939)
- Sommer = Co-ordata Research (1994)
- Sutton = Sutton (1976–93, field book 136)
- Thomson = Thomson (1933; (map) = 1972)
- Tindale = Tindale (1974)

Note that the tilde (~) means 'alternating with'.

Languages are listed here approximately from north to south, from Mission River to Archer River. In two cases the survey extends south to the Love and Kirke rivers, where it can be shown that Wik-Way-type languages were the primary languages of affiliation at a remote time, having been gradually superseded by a Wik-type language in perhaps the late nineteenth century in one case, and the early twentieth in another.

Code: L1

Standard name: Thanikwithi

Source spellings: Mathews (from Hey): Tannagootee; Roth: tai-ni kudi, te-ana-ngada; possibly also den-ya kudi; Thomson: Tan'ngat (1933), Tanikutti (map); McConnel: Tainikuit; Gajdusek: Tanikutti; Capell: Tainukwiti (1955) Dainiguid (1963); Hale: Thyanngayth; Tindale: Tanikuit; Bos: Taieningit, Thainikwit, Tainikwite, T(h)ainikwit(h); Crowley: Thanikwithi; Sommer: Thainikuith.

Source locations: Mathews: [on CYP, no detail]. Roth: 'Stretching between the Pennefather and Pine Rivers' (tai-ni kudi); 'living low down on the south side of the Batavia River' (de-nya kudi); Thomson: (map) On the coast between the Pine and Mission rivers; McConnel: (1939–40: map) Andoom area, coast at Andoomajettie Point; Capell: 'North coast of Albatross Bay, near Weipa'; Hale: 'lower Mission River'. Crowley: 'the mangrove area north of the Mission River' (+ map); Bos: N of Mission River, including Ndheerang (swamp), Mbootjeth [cf. map Bochet Creek], Ndhun-ndhun-ing-dja ~ Ndhunndhuningdhya; Andoom, Ndherrang (swamp); Lwreeng, Luuth, Tji(ng)-tji(ng), Paingga, Treeng, ?Thumubwon; Sommer: Luenh, Mbuining, Ndhumdjith, Prunang, Ughindhing, Wanggath.

People: Bos: Cyril Hall, Kitty Dick, Eva York, Eric Paul, Joyce Hall, Mildred Barkley, Hilda Jingle, Gloria Fletcher; Sommer: Halls.

Comments: Roth: tai-ni kudi = 'mangrove'; They speak ang-a dimi (the 1st pers. pronoun) [i.e. Awngthim as said in Anguthimri?]; den-ya kudi = 'bush'. Roth also gives te-ana-ngada (te-ana = '1st. pers. pronoun') as the language of the O-amro=koro ('around the lower reaches of the Mission River'), a term not so far identified. Hale: from thyanh 'spearthrower', hence possibly Thyanhngayth. Crowley: Called Thyanngayth by the Linngithigh, language is Awngthim.

Code: L2

Standard name: Ndrwa'angathi

Source spellings: McConnel: Ndru'angit; Tindale: Ndruangit; Hale: Ntrwa'ngayth; Crowley: Drwa'angathi [Crowley's /Dr/ = my /Ndr/]; Bos: NdRwanget; Sommer's Ndrrua'ngaith ~ Nrrua'ngaith ~ Ndrua'ngaith anomalously relates to sites which fall within the area of L3 below.

Source locations: McConnel: (map) Andoom area between Pine and Mission rivers; Hale: 'lower Mission River'. Tindale: 'North side of Mission River' + map (map has it between Pine and Mission rivers). Crowley: 'in the Mission River area' map: north side of lower Mission River.

People: [information not available]

Comments: Hale: they speak Awngthim; Crowley: called Draw'ngayth [i.e. Ndraw'ngayth in our orthography] by the Linngithigh.

Code: L3

Standard name: Ndrrangith

Source spellings: Sutton (Book 83:133): Ndrrangith; Possibly Hinton: Ndrangit; Sommer: Ndrrua'ngaith ~ Nrrua'ngaith ~ Ndrua'ngaith (anomalous).

Source locations: Sutton: north side of lower Embley River at Wathayn. Sommer: Brumby Hole, Kuamther, Mandjunggar, Waram Thain.

People: Sutton: language of Clan 83 (Coconut); cf. Hinton: Norman Paul, Samualas.

Code: L4

Standard name: Ndwa'ngith

Source spellings: Thomson: N'dwangit (gerri-gerri); McConnel: Ndwangit; Gajdusek: N-Dwangit (Dragnite); Tindale: Ndwangit (Ndwongit).

Source locations: Thomson: (map) Urquhart Point area; McConnel: 'middle Mission River, north & south sides' + map (map has it north side at least); Tindale: 'North side of Mission River' + map (map has it straddling lower Mission River).

People: Thomson: [connection with Linngithigh unclear:] Billy Blowhard, Blink Jack, Tankappi, Anang'gan.

Comments: Thomson's location is odd; the balance of sources suggests Mission River.

Code: L5

Standard name: Ngwathangathi

Source spellings: Sharp: Ngwatangeti; McConnel: Ungauwangati; Capell (1963) mentions Ngwataingeti 'used by D. Moore as an alternative [to 'Windawinda'], but on unstated authority'; Tindale: Ngawangati.

Source locations: Sharp: (map) lower Mission River; McConnel: 'on the south side of the Mission River' + map; Tindale: 'lower Mission River' (+ map, which has them on south side of mouth of Mission River).

People: [information not available]

Comments: Compare the basis of the name of Ngkoth (from ngko 'this') ~ Ngkoth-ngith, and Capell's recording of Ngkoth as Nggwat.

Code: L6

Standard name: Anathangayth

Source spellings: Thomson: O'natangit; Hinton (1964 map): Onnatangnit Sutton: Anathangayth; Sommer: Anhathangaith.

Source locations: Hinton (1964 map): upper Hey River; Sutton: 20-mile (old Weipa Mission) and upstream along Myall Creek etc. (Estate 68); Sommer: Billy Lagoon, Kurrico Creek, Myall Creek (place mayal [site name]) Cox Creek and so on, Waipa (old mission site), Bingay, Jabiru Scrub, Nonda Spring, Yipatjiku [Kaantju name].

People: Sutton: Alice Mark and siblings, her father and siblings, her FF Okolkon.

Code: L7

Standard name: Alngith

Source spellings: Roth: Laini-ngadi (see Hale below); Thomson: map: Lainingitti (see Hale below), MS: Alingith (and cf. MS: O'ngit); McConnel: Alingit; Sharp: Lenngeti; Gajdusek: Lainingitti; Hinton: Arangit (1963), Alang yit (1964); Tindale: Alingit; Capell: Alngid; Hale: Alngith (= Laynngith); Bos: Lainingit, Lainngit, Laininget, Lainingt,

Liiningeth, Alnget, Alngeth, Alngaite; Martin: Alangithiy [Wik-Mungkan version]; Sommer; Alngith; Sutton: Alngith (Jean George, Chevathuns et al.), Laynngith (Johns, Maduas et al.).

Source locations: Roth: 'between the Pine and Mission Rivers (coastal blacks)' (map is the same); Thomson: (map) Weipa and east, between Mission and Embley rivers; McConnel: 'from the south side across the Embley River to where Weipa Mission is now situated' + map; Sharp: (map) Weipa area; Tindale: 'Weipa and east' + map; Hinton (1964 map): Weipa Peninsula; Bos: Uunanganam ~ Unanganam Ck, Beening Ck, Gonbung ~ Gonbang, Trunding ~ TRandhing, Lorim [Point], KamRindje [Kumrunja Beach] Rocky [Point], Awonga (~ Oogwang), Bridge, Tchwembit, 'all [Weipa] town', Napranum, shell hill, Baang Point, Wallaby Island, across to Hey Point, Ndhrrilkiatj ~ Ndhrilkiiatj Ck, Trrailak ~ Thrailak (swamp) [see map: Triluck Creek + marine swamp near mouth], as far as Coxy Point, Liithing ~ Liidhing [see map: Leithen Creek, Leithen Point], Anyiiyam ~ Anyiam Ck, Nggorainam. Martin: (map) about Weipa airstrip, Jessica Point, south to about Cyclone Island; Sommer; Mbining, Mbuin Wuth (Cool Pool).

People: Thomson (Alingit): Old Dick, adding: 'all at Weipa'. Hinton: Eddie John. Bos: *Liiningeth:* Albert Chevathun, Andrew Chevathun, Jean George, Richard Kelinda, Betty Bowenda, Gideon Chevathun, Norma Chevathun, Christina Chevathun, Julie Chevathun, Joseph Chevathun, Trevor Chevathun, Roy Chevathun, descendants of Matthew Fruit; *Alngeth*: Eddie John, Ronnie John, Matilda John, Colleen John, Ron Nicholas, Aileen Heinemann, Susie Madua; 'Note: Liininget[h] may also claim country [of Alngeth].' Elsewhere: 'Richard [Kelinda] can claim here too. If Eddie [John] goes > [then] Ronnie & Richard to back up'. [recorded at Napranum]. Martin: Kelindas, Chevathuns (Gideon, Norma et al.), Jean George; this branch of Chevathuns is in fact Kelindas; Sommer: Johns.

Comments: Alngith and Laynngith are alternative names for one language (Hale). Old sources indicate Laynngith was also called Layningathi and Layningithi, presumably in different dialects. In Alice Mark's language (Anathangayth) the Johns' language is called Alangayth (PS Book 83:112). This is not inconsistent with Bos's phrase 'lainingt or alngaite' [sic] and the heading 'Alnget/Lininget' followed by 'Same people'. Kitty Dick told Bos that Jean George's language and the John family's language was, in ideal practice, the same. Bos also notes, however, that 'liningati—diff >

[from] alnget' and 'alnget lininget different'. These references are probably to Linngithigh not Laynngith, especially since 'Fred' (Kerindun, see L15), whose language was Linngithigh, is here associated in Bos's notes with 'liningati' and 'Jean' (George) with 'alnget'. Alngith and Linngithigh are distinct but close dialects of a single language with no more than half a dozen good speakers remaining at Aurukun and Weipa in the 1960s (Hale).

Code: L8

Standard name: Mamangathi

Source spellings: Roth: marma-ngati; Sharp: Mamangeti; McConnel: Mamangiti, Ma.mangiti; Capell: Mamangidigh, Mamngaid; Hinton (1963): Mamangnit, Hinton (1964): Mamangit; Hale: Mamngayth; Tindale: Mamangit; Crowley: Mamangathi (called Mamngayth by the Linngithigh); Bos: Mamngaith, Mamngaitj, Mamnget; Sommer: Mamangaith.

Source locations: Roth: [referring to Winda-Winda, see Comments below] 'around coast from Pera Head to the Mission River' but map shows them only from Pera Head to the east side of the lower Hey; Sharp: (map) coast south of Albatross Bay; McConnel: (map) coast south of Albatross Bay; Hale: 'on Urquhart Point'; Tindale: 'South side of Albatross Bay' + map; Hinton (1964 map): Urquhart Point; Crowley: (map) Urquhart Point and south along coast; Bos: S of Embley, Baang –> Thiitj lagoon + timber country, ?Lwemdjin lagoon, Urquhart Point; Sommer: Mangrove Creek, Aniyam, Mbang (Urquhart Point), Ndhandjiprin, Ndrrilkiyatj, Nggoray(thim), Prendjim, Trailak, Wul Ndrran.

People: Hinton: Arthur Dick, Stanley Coconut Snr.; Bos: Yorks, Georgy, Bobby, Dick, Esther, Henry; Sommer: Dicks.

Comments: Roth: marma-ngati = first person pronoun, language of 'Winda Winda' people (see elsewhere); Hale: Mamngayth speak Awngthim. Clearly Mamangathi, Mamngayth, Mamangithigh are names for the same language, but as pronounced in different languages. The fact that the informants of various scholars had different language affiliations probably determines most of this variation in the record. One informant (Jean George) told PS that the Dicks' language was Nda'ngith, and that most others called it Ndrra'ngith (but it was the same language). This view is unusual.

Code: L9

Standard name: Latumngith

Source spellings: Thomson: Latum'ngit; Sharp: Latangeti; McConnel: Latamngit; Gajdusek: Latumngit; Capell: Ladamngid; Tindale: Latamngit; Sommer: Lathumngith ~ Latumngith ~ Latamngith; Sutton: Two main pronunciations, probably in different languages, have been recorded: Latumngith and Latamngith.

Source locations: Thomson: (map) between the middle Embley and the Hey; Sharp (map): about Hey River; McConnel: 'on Hey Inlet', (map) west side of Hey River; Tindale: 'West bank of Hay (sic) River' + map (map has it straddling the middle Hey River inlet); Sommer: Idholdja, Kokanin, Maingum (contested), Meunyam, Poghadhim, Thitj, possibly Pimpim; Sutton: Estate 53, west side of the middle Hey River.

People: Thomson: Doughboy, Saul; Sutton: Clan 52 (Blowhards, Ida Paul [mother of Joyce Hall and Thancoupie]).

Comments: Doughboy was mother's father to Joyce Hall, Thancoupie and others. [Inclusion of this land in the Wik-Way area by others is not accepted by Joyce Hall—or is it that she rejects the appellation 'Wik-Way' on the basis that, while a custodian of this estate, she herself is not Wik-Way because her primary identification is with her father's area further to the north?].

Code: L10

Standard name: Ngkoth

Source spellings: Thomson: N'got'tungit; McConnel: Nggot; Capell: Nggwat (1955), Nggod (1963); Hale: Ngkoth; Hinton (1963): Ngotsh, (1964): Ngot; Bos: Nggoth; Sommer: Nggoth; Sutton: Ngkoth, Chaa'-ngkooth ('language + ngkoth').

Source locations: McConnel: 'between the Embley River and the Hey inlet'; Capell: 'South side of Embley River near Weipa'; Hale: 'between the Embley and Hey Rivers south of their junction. The original site of Weipa Mission is said to have been in Ngkoth country.' Hinton (1964 map): east side of lower Hey River. Bos: Hey River, Hey and Embley rivers; Sommer: Akakan, Imbiorr, Kikelcha, Kuakanam, Mburrip, Ombon, Undrrang; Sutton: Estate 51: the south-eastern half, roughly, of the upper drainage system of the Hey River.

People: Hinton: Monty Motton, Frank Motton, Ruth Motton, Samuel Harry. Bos: Samuel; mother of ?Cyril Hall; Sutton: Clan 50 (Motton).

Comments: Hale: The name is from ngko 'this'. 'Informants state that Ngkoth and the presumably extinct Trotj are closely related dialects.' Compare Roth's unidentified 'Gautundi' of the lower Hey.

Code: L11

Standard name: Trotj

Source spellings: Sharp: [may be same as his 'Kauwala']; McConnel: To.tj; Wikalaṭa; Capell: Do:dj; Hale: Trotj; Tindale: Totj, To:tj; Bos: Trootj, Trrotj; Sommer: Trotj.

Source locations: [Sharp: (map) inland south-east of Albatross Bay]; McConnel: To.tj: 'on Myall Creek (upper Mission R.) and Cox Creek (upper Batavia R.)' (map has name between Myall and Cox Creeks); Tindale: Upper Mission River and Cox Creek (middle Batavia River); at York Downs; south to near Merluna; McConnel '28: Wikalaṭa: 'There is another Wik tribe too which I did not record which is further north again, the Wikalaṭa, which is at York Downs station & links up probably with the Wik ampamas on the Watson River'; Bos: 'Merluna Way, Pitch Lagoon (< dog c pitchy)', '20m –> York Down'; 'trotj baiwum (York Downs)'; Sommer: Waipa, Bingay, Jabiru Scrub, Yipatjiku (Billy Lagoon), Nonda Spring.

People: Bos: Alice and her sister Topsy (latter married Peter Costello's stepfather George).

Comments: Hale: very close linguistically to Ngkoth, and 'presumably extinct'. Jean George told Bos that Trootj spoke Baiwum (see L20). Bos pairs languages Trrotj and Yaath in the York Downs area.

Code: L12

Standard name: Arrithinngithigh

Source spellings: Thomson: Aredinngit; McConnel: Aritingiti; Capell: Aritingiti (MS), Aratingiti (1962), Aridingidigh (1963); Gajdusek: Aredinngit (Arichenite); Hinton (1963): Aretangnit, (1964): Aritenwum;

Hale: Aritinngithigh, Aritinngayth; Tindale: Aretingit; Bos: Arraithingwum; Sommer: Araythingwum ~ Araythingum; Sutton: Arraythinngith, Arrithinngithigh, Arreythinwum depending on language used.

Source locations: Thomson: (map) upper Hey River, south-east area; McConnel: 'on Hey Inlet' (map has it covering all the drainage into Hey River inlet); Capell: 'South of the Hey River', (map) about the upper Hey River; Hale: 'around the head of the Hey River'; Tindale: 'Upper Hay (sic) River and across to Pera Head' (map has it midway between the two); Bos: immediately to the south of Nggoth (see L10); Sommer: Hey River salt creeks, saltpans, swamps and lagoons, including Anhanggun, Atakun, Poghadhim; Sutton: Estate 52, Onhánggun area, i.e. The south-western creeks and associated drainage area of the upper Hey River system.

People: Thomson: Andrew, Luke, Bosun, Kallappi, Old Charlie Fish, Daniel (schoolboy); McConnel: Ch. Fish, Andrew; Hinton: Daisy Brodie, Gibson Jankai, Mark Andrew; Sutton: Clan 51 (surnames: Mark, Kangaroo, Daisy Brodie).

Comments: Tindale appears to have conflated Arrithinngithigh with Aditinngithigh. Called Arrithinngithigh in Linngithigh, and Arritinngayth in Ndrwa'ngayth; named after the Arrithinngithigh verb *arri-* 'to go'; Linngithigh, by contrast, has *li-* (Hale). The version Araythingwum appears to be in a neighbouring language having *-wum* as the comitative suffix (cf. Yinwum).

Code: L13

Standard name: Adithinngithigh

Source spellings: Sharp: Aditinngeti; Thomson: Additin'ngitti, Addedin'ngitti, Addenin'ngit (MS), Addedinngit (map); McConnel: Adetingiti; Capell: Adidingidigh; Tindale [see L12]; Sutton: Adithangath.

Source locations: Sharp: (map) inland from Pera Head; Thomson: (map) along coast from Pera Head to about Winda Winda Creek; McConnel: 'of Pera Head vicinity' (map has it at Pera Head and north-east along coast adjoining her Mamangiti); Capell: 'Mouth of Embley River'; Tindale: [see L12]; Sutton 83:36: at Pera Head, Estate 40.

5. LANGUAGES OF THE WIK NATIVE TITLE CLAIM AREA

People: Thomson: Violet, Colin, Mabel, Harry (sent to Palm Island—father of Mabel); Sutton: Animbi, Maggie Animbi, Harry Lifu (Luipo). Sutton: Formerly Clan 66 (that of Mabel [née Taisman] Pamulkan), now extinct.

Code: L14

Standard name: Ndra'ngith

Source spellings: Sharp: Anda'angeti; Thomson: N'dra'ngit (MS), N'drangit (map); McConnel: Ndra'angit (text), Ndraangit (map); Capell: Ndra?angid; Hale: Ntra'ngith; Tindale: Ndraangit; Sommer: Ndrra'ngith.

Source locations: Sharp: (map) coast south of Pera Head; Thomson: (map) coast south of Pera Head; McConnel: 'of False Pera Head vicinity' + map; Hale: 'around False Pera Head and the Norman River'; Tindale: 'Coast near False Pera Head' + map; Sommer: Akakan, Amban, Ikalath, Imbiorr, ?Ivikin, Kikelcha, Kuakanam, Mburrip, Nombon ~ Nombuan, Pimpim, Pirri (Pera Head) (disputed with Linngithigh), Undrrang.

People: Thomson: Goodman, Albert, Kerring'gan; Blind Captain, Yg. Jack, Norman. Capell (1963): '3 possible [linguistic] informants are at Aurukun: Sam and Angus Kerindun and Jimmy Clark'.

Comments: Although separated from Awngthim language-speaking groups (see L1, L2, L8) by Linngithigh and Arrithinngithigh, it was more closely related to Awngthim than to the intervening forms of speech; the name comes from *ntra* 'this' (Hale).

Code: L15

Standard name: Linngithigh

Source spellings: Thomson: Lin'ngitti; McConnel: Leningiti (map and 1940 text), Leini-ngiti (1939 text); Capell: Leningiti (MS, 1962), Lenngidigh (1963); Gajdusek: Linngitti; Hinton: Linginiti; Hale: Linngithigh; Tindale: Leningiti; Bos: Liningati, Lininget; Martin: Liinangithiy [Wik-Mungkan version]; Sommer: Liningith.

Source locations: Thomson: [does not appear on map]; McConnel: 'extend southwards to the Archer River'; map has it extending from Aurukun two thirds of the way north to the head of Hey River inlet;

McConnel: the inland side of the Ward River (+ map); Hale: 'south-west of the Embley River and west of the Hey in the area called Winduwinda' as located by his informants in 1960 but considers McConnel's location further south to be perhaps more accurate; Capell: (map) just south of Hey River, but 1963: 'Near Duifken [sic] Point and Weipa Mission Station' [appears to refer to Laynighithi = Alngith, see L5]; Tindale: 'West of lower Watson River and at Aurukun' + map. Hinton (1964 map): north of Aurukun. Martin: (map) west and south of Hey Point, False Pera Head area south-east of Norman river; Sommer: Aniyam, Mangrove Creek, Ivikin, Kokanin (Coxy Point and environs), possibly Lidhing, Maingum (contested with Latamngith), possibly Meunyam, Ndrrilkiyatj, Nggoray(thim), Pirri (Pera Head, disputed with Ndrra'ngith), Prendjim, Thitj.

People: Thomson: Violet's mother, Dick, Barry—son Joseph, Sam, Angus, Maggie, Jimmy Clarke, [then follows a list given as 'Same {N'dwangit (gerri'gerri) (Some at Weipa and Mapoon)', being: Billy Blowhard, Blink Jack, Tankappi, Anang'gan} the Lin'ngitti list continues:] Myrtle, Frederik (sic). McConnel: Anthony, Louie, Angus, Myrtle [on published genealogies]. Hinton: Lawrence Matthew, Maria Matthew, Minnie Matthew, Betty Robinson. Hale: Sam Kerindun. Martin: Myrtle Chevathun, Keriduns; Norman Go'olfrey, his country marked on map as Liiningathiy but 'claimed by all Wik Way people as joint area' (but see Ndra'ngith); Sommer: Matthews.

Comments: McConnel erroneously identifies Roth's Laini-ngadi (and Sharp's Lenngeti?) as Linngithigh, but see L7 Alngith). Capell (1963) gives 'Ndorndorin' as the name of a language 'Not accurately located but in area covered by Aurukun Mission'; this is a male personal name. Capell said a speaker of it was Jimmy Clark who lived at Aurukun; *Ndorndorin* was Jimmy Clark's Big Name (Aurukun Mission records). Tindale (1974:190) erroneously gives 'Ndorndorin (a horde name)' under 'Winduwinda'.

Code: L16

Standard name: Andjingith

Source spellings: Thomson: Andjingit (map), Andjingitti (MS); McConnel: Andyingit; Gajdusek: Andjingit; Capell: Andjingid; Tindale: Anjingit; Sutton: Andjingith, Wik-Ayangench (Wik-Mungkan version); Martin: Wik Ayangenych, Anychangithiy; Aak: Wik-Ay.ngenych.

Source locations: Thomson: (map) Wallaby Island (in Archer River) north along coast to just south of Norman River; McConnel: coastal side of the Ward River south to Wallaby Island (+ map); Gajdusek: 'On the coast north of the Archer River'; Tindale: 'Coast just north of Archer River' + map (map excludes Wallaby Island and Wuthan); Sutton: Estates 34, 35, 36, 43 and 57, probably 56, and formerly also estates 1, 2, 3 and 4, i.e.: from the south side of Norman River at Ichetang south via Waterfall and Ikeleth to the north side of the lower Archer at Wuthan and probably Yagalmungkan, south to the Yaaneng area on the other bank, up the Ward River to Paydan; formerly also upper Love River, now changed to Wik-Mungkan, formerly also lower Love River, now by succession Wik-Elken, formerly also Small Lake (Peret/Watha-nhiin Outstation area), now by succession Wik-Ngathan, and south again to Big Lake and the northern shores of the Kirke estuary (now only Wik-Ngatharr, by loss of Andjingith). Martin: (map) north side of mouth of Archer River, upper Ward River, east side of Ward River at e.g. Cowplace Survey Camp, Kampchin. Aak: Lower Archer, Bottom Love River (formerly), Top Love River (formerly), Small Lake (formerly), Big Lake (formerly).

People: Thomson: Mukkurrutt (female), Yukai, Robert; Sutton: William and his sons Jack and Norman Williams, from Wuthan area, also Myrtle (a refused promise of Colin Wolmby), and possibly Jacob Wolmby's mother's father Charlie William); Old Stephen Owokran and his brother Gilbert, whose daughter Barbara Owokran was Alison Woolla's mother, Old Murray and Cockatoo, and Cockatoo's half sister Thaankup, of lower Love River; Tharreway (male), Colin and Murray and their sister Kaalep ('Carlippe'), Rex Walmbeng's mother; Old Coconut of Small Lake and his brother Johnny and sister 'Wikatukkin' (Wik-thakenh, Chaalemnganh), and probably old Arraman of Big Lake. Martin: Wuthan area: Mokarathan et al., Geraldine Kawangka's MM?, claimed by Fred Kerindun, disputed estate on north side Archer mouth; Alan Wolmby (his birthplace area of Ikelath), interests in Ikelath being pursued by his son Rex; east side of Ward River: Cyril Owokran, Alma Moon (Morn. Is.), Jimmy and Gibson Clark, Alison Woolla's MM. Aak: Clan 1 (Old Murray, Cockatoo), Clan 2/29 (Peinkinnas, Taismans, formerly), Clan 60 (Owokran A.), Clan 82 (Old Stephen Owokran).

Comments: Known as Wik-Ayangench in Wik-Mungkan, Wik-Ngathan and other Wik languages.

LINGUISTIC ORGANISATION AND NATIVE TITLE

Code: L17

Standard name: Wik-Thint

Source spellings: Thomson: Wik Tinda; McConnel: Wikatinda; Gajdusek: Wik-Tinda; Capell: Adinda; Tindale: Wikatinda.

Source locations: Thomson: (map) on coast south of Archer River mouth; McConnel: 'the coastal strip from the mouth of the Archer River at Ya.nung to the Tokali [Love] River, eight miles to the south' (1939 + map) but her 1957:xvii map has 'Wik-Kalkan' [i.e. Wik-Alken] extending to here from Cape Keerweer, and no trace of Wik-Thint or Wik-Paach; Tindale: 'on the coast from Archer River south for about 8 miles (13 km.)'; Sutton: [no record of Wik-Thint, but dialect from here named totemically as Wik-Thum ('Fire Language') and area associated with Andjingith and Wik-Paach languages].

People: [information not available]

Comments: Thomson did not include them in his Wik-Way list, and McConnel specifically numbered them among the Wik 'tribes', as did Gajdusek (the 'Wik-coastal tribes'). Tindale essentially reproduces McConnel's data. From the little information available, however, the language of the area, however named, appears to have been more like the other Wik-Way languages to the north.

Code: L18

Standard name: Wik-Paach

Source spellings: McConnel: Wikapatya (map), Wika-pa.tya, Wikapatya (text); Tindale: 'Wik'apatja; Sutton: Wik-Paach, and probably the language variety also known as Wik-Ngaangungker (by Cape Keerweer people); Aak: Wik-Paach.

Source locations: McConnel: 'the mangrove-clad islands and southern banks of the wide-mouthed Archer River' + map; Tindale: 'centred on the mangrove islands of Archer River delta' + map (map shows it including Wallaby Island, assigned by McConnel to L16 Andjingith); Sutton: formerly south of Archer River, including Bamboo Station and Yaaneng areas, lower Love River area (now Wik-Elken by succession), and upper Love River (now changed to Wik-Mungkan); Aak: Bottom Love River (formerly), Lower Archer, Yaaneng.

People: McConnel: Mukana (female); Sutton: Maraya (?Maria) who was Ian Peinkinna's mother's mother (?Bamboo area, as Piinth-Eempel was their nickname in Wik-Ngathan), Old Murray (Maarriy) and Cockatoo (see also Andjingith), Stephen Owokran of Yaaneng; formerly also Peinkinnas and Taismans (now Wik-Mungkan). Aak: (Clan 1) Old Murray, Cockatoo; (Clan 2) Peinkinnas (formerly); (Clan 82) Old Stephen Owokran.

Comments: McConnel: 'known as the "mangrove people"'.

McConnel specifically numbered them among the Wik 'tribes'. Tindale essentially reproduces McConnel's data. From the little information available, however, the language appears to have been more like the other Wik-Way languages to the north.

Code: L19

Standard name: Kuuk-Yala (?)

Source spellings: Mathews: Kookeealla; McConnel: Kokiala; Sharp: Kok Iala.

Source locations: Mathews: [CYP]; Sharp: (map) east of lower Archer; McConnel '28: Kokiala: 'on Kokialo Creek ^ near to mouth of the Archer^ & which apparently spread along the N. bank of the Archer to the middle of the Peninsula. The other, Koki awa, tribe is on Sefton Creek, the head of the Batavia & runs down towards the Kokialas on the Archer … There is another Wik tribe too which I did not record which is further north again, the Wikalatha [see Trotj above], which is at York Downs station & links up probably with the Wik ampamas on the Watson River.'

People: Kokialah Creek is currently under the custodianship of Clan 33 and described as part of their estate, although their estate (31) centres on Mukiy and the Small Archer (Tompaten Creek) system to the south. This may be a case of succession by amalgamation, assuming Kokialah Creek was formerly the country of a clan now extinct.

Comments: The Matthews, McConnel and Sharp records may represent Kuuku-Yala or possibly Kuuk-Iiyala ('language-go'?), which would be a possible Kaantju name for a Wik language but one not recorded as such. The Kokialah Creek name has been recorded as Kok-yal(a) by von Sturmer and Sutton, but this may have come into Wik via English, losing the long first vowel. So far, I am not aware of any record of the language so it is hard to know where it belongs in terms of linguistic subgroups, but I was told it was similar to Wik-Mungkan.

Code: L20

Standard name: Mbiywom

Source spellings: Thomson: M'berwum (map), Mberwum (MS); Sharp: Kok Mbewam; McConnel: Mbeiwum (map), (M)beiwum (text); McConnel: Wik-ampama, Wikampama; Capell: Mbeiwum, Ambama; Hale: Mbiywom; Hinton: Mbywum; Tindale: Mbewum, Mbe:wum (map), Wikampama; Bos: Baiwum (language of Trotj); Sutton: Mbiywum, Mbeywom, Wik-Ompom, also known as Orrkel; Martin: Wik Ompam; Aak: Wik-Ompoma.

Source locations: Thomson: (map) middle Embley River; Sharp: (map) upper Watson system; McConnel: Mbeiwum: 'on the Watson River' (map has it on the upper Watson); McConnel '28: Wikalatha: 'There is another Wik tribe too which I did not record which is further north again, the Wikalatha, which is at York Downs station & links up probably with the Wik ampamas on the Watson River'; Wik-ampama: 'the middle Archer River and its tributary, Piccaninny Creek', 'on the upper Watson River and Piccaninny Creek' + map (map has it ranging between Kokialah Creek and Piccaninny Creek); Tindale: 'Middle Archer River; north to Watson River'; Sutton: Watson River area; Martin: upper Watson River, Moonlight Creek, Watson Crossing, Maanychawanh, Kilpatrick Station Landing, south to Merkunga Creek at e.g. Otwalanyin, Parrp-aw. Aak: Watson River. Gajdusek: M-Berwum (Bywoom); Hale: 'on the middle and upper Watson River and, more recently, on Myall Creek. York Downs and Merluna cattle stations are regarded by informants as being in Mbiywom country'; Tindale: 'Upper Watson River; at Merluna. Parry-Okeden has a name like Kokimoh (partly illegible on his map) in the area occupied by this tribe' [cf. Mathews 'Kokinno', Thomson (map) Koko I'o and its neighbour Yina]; Bos: 'trotj baiwum (York Downs)', Merluna way, Pitch

Lagoon; Sutton: Estates 29, 30, 33, 65 i.e. lower Watson River, middle Watson River, Oyonton/Watson Crossing area, east to Green Swamp/Layngay area on the upper Archer River.

People: Thomson: Annie, Hope, Dan (and 'plenty at Weipa'). Hinton: Willy George, Theresa Motton, Martha Dick; Bos: Alice and her sister Topsy (latter married Peter Costello's stepfather George)—and these Georges? Sutton: George family, Parkers and Days (all Clan 48), also late Koo'ekkas of Watson River (Clan 36), and Dan and Hope, Connie Clark (mother of Bessie Savo) and Polly Fruit (mother of Matthew and Lawrence Fruit) of extinct Clan 46, and Clan 75 (descendants of Charlie Kepple); Martin: Roy George, Willy George, Benny George et al; Eddie John's (Saul's) M country; Andrew Golpendun, Daisy Brodie et al. Aak: Clan 36 Koo'ekkas, Clan 48 Georges.

Comments: Thomson's location agrees with none of the others and is clearly too far north. The name Mbiywom probably comes from its word *mbiy* 'camp' (Hale). Bos records the unusual view that Mbiywom is the language of Trotj people. The evidence so far points to this being the same language as the one named Wik-Ompom in Wik languages. The latter is how its naming is understood by current members of relevant families.

McConnel regarded the 'Wikampama' as being one of the Wik 'tribes', partly on the grounds of the nature of their kinship classification system. They do not, however, claim a language of the Wik linguistic type (some still know parts of the language), as Mbiywom is quite different. The Mbiywom people, however, now mostly speak Wik-Mungkan as their main Aboriginal language.

Alice Mark said the language of Victoria, mother of Ronnie John, was Thaatj, and that Victoria was from a place called in her own language (Anathangayth) Eyvye [ejvjə], which is between Watson River and Green Swamp on the upper Archer. This would put this language at the location of Estate 65 and thus Thaatj may be another outsider-name for Mbiywom.

Wik Subgroup languages

Prior to the present research project, the state of academic knowledge of the names and locations of Wik-Way-type languages was in some disarray owing to the large number of language names recorded and the fact that some of them were so similar as to be easily confused with each other (e.g. Arrithinngithigh, Adithinngithigh, and Ndrra'ngith, Ndrrwa'ngith). For this reason, those languages have here been dealt with above in considerable detail.

For the Wik Subgroup languages the situation is less confusing, since the PhD theses of Sutton and von Sturmer already provide surveys of literature sources on these language names (Sutton 1978:36–41, Maps 7 and 8; von Sturmer 1978:572–79, Map 3). The nature of interrelationships among Wik Subgroup languages, and between them and others, is explored in some technical detail in Ken Hale's chapters here on the question of the time-depth and geographical stability of the Wik Subgroup languages. A graphic illustration of a preliminary statement of genetic relationships among Wik Subgroup languages is provided in Sutton (1991:60).

In Tables A1.1 and A1.2 below, I provide a numerically ordered list of such estates and their relevant languages, with an alphabetised reversal. Here I list them very approximately from north to south, starting at the lower Archer River and proceeding south via the drainage systems of Love River, the middle and upper Archer River, the Kirke River, Knox River, Kendall River, Hersey Creek, Holroyd River, and Edward River.

Table 5.9: Wik Subgroup varieties schematically listed from north to south

COASTAL	PERICOASTAL	INLAND
	Wik-Mungkan	
Wik-Elken	Wik-Alken	Wik-Mungkan
Wik-Ngatharr	Wik-Ep (aka Wik-Iit)	Wik-Mungkan
Wik-Ngatharr	Wik-Me'enh	Wik-Mungkan
Wik-Mungkan	Wik-Ngathan, Wik-Ngatharr	Wik-Mungkan
Wik-Ngathan (for a time: Wik-Iincheyn)	Wik-Ngatharr	Wik-Mungkan
Wik-Ngatharr	Wik-Keyenganh	Wik-Mungkan
Wik-Mungkan	Wik-Keyenganh	Wik-Mungkan
Wik-Ngathan	Wik-Ngathan	Wik-Iiyeyn
Kug-Ugbanh		
Kugu Muminh	Wik-Iiyanh	Mungkanhu
Kug-Uwanh		
Kugu Muminh		
Kug-Uwanh	Kug-Iiyanh	Wik-Iiyanyi
Kugu Mangk		
Kug-Ugbanh		

COASTAL	PERICOASTAL	INLAND
Kugu Mu'inh		
Kugu Muminh		
Kugu Mu'inh		
Kugu Mangk		Pakanh
Kugu Mu'inh		
Kugu Mangk		
Kugu Muminh	Iyanh/Pakanh	
Kugu Mu'inh		
Kugu Mangk	Kugu-Yi'anh	Ayapathu

A few of these names are more or less equivalents and represent usages in different local speech varieties. These are:

Wik-Alken = Wik-Elken = Wik-Ngatharr
Wik-Iiyeyn = Wik-Iiyanh = Wik-Iiyanyi = Mungkanhu
Wik-Ngathan = Wik-Iinycheyn

Thus far I have generally referred to any distinctively named speech variety in this context as a 'language' or a 'language variety'. Various subsets of the varieties listed immediately above, however, are mutually intelligible, sharing most of their grammars and lexicons. These sets of close varieties thus constitute what linguists—not the Wik people themselves in general—would call dialects of single languages. As a preliminary statement, those sets are as follows:[10]

1. (a) Wik-Alken = Wik-Elken = Wik-Ngatharr; (b) Wik-Ngathan = Wik-Iinycheyn
2. (a) Wik-Mungkan; (b) Wik-Iiyeyn = Wik-Iiyanh = Wik-Iiyanyi = Mungkanhu
3. (a) Pakanh; (b) Ayapathu
4. (a) Wik-Ep = Wik-Iit; (b) Wik-Me'enh; (c) Wik-Keyenganh
5. (a) Kug-Ugbanh; (b) Kugu Muminh; (c) Kug-Uwanh; (d) Kugu Mangk; (e) Kugu Mu'inh; (f) Kugu Yi'anh

---

10   It is possible that southern inland varieties of language 2 form a dialect chain continuous with language 3; further work is required on this.

LINGUISTIC ORGANISATION AND NATIVE TITLE

Estates and their linguistic varieties

Table 5.10: Estates and their language affiliations

ESTATE	LANGUAGE	ESTATE	LANGUAGE
1	An	21	Nn
1	Pa	22	Nn
1	El	23?	Me
2	An	23?	In
2	Pa	24	Nn
2	Mn	25	Uw
3	An	26	?
3	Nr	27	Ep
3	Nn	27	Mn
4	An	28	Mn
4	Nr	29	Mb
5	Ep	29	Mn
5	Al	30	Mb
6	Nn	31	Mn
7	Nr	32	Mb?
8	El	33	Mb
9	El	34	An
10	It	35	An
10	Ep	36	An
11	Nr	37?	Mn?
12	Mn	38	Nd
13	Ep	39	Mt
13	Me	40	Ad
14	Me	41	Nd
14	Mn	42	Mn
15	In	43	Pa
15	Nn	43	An
16	Me	44	Pa
17	Mn	45	Li
18	El	46	At
19	Nn	47	Li
20	Mn	48	Iyn
21	El	49	Iyn

5. LANGUAGES OF THE WIK NATIVE TITLE CLAIM AREA

ESTATE	LANGUAGE
51	Nk
52	Ar
53	La
55	Mb?
56	An?
57	An?
58	Mn
59	Iy
60	Iy?
62	Iy
63	Iy
64	Ay
65	Mb
66	Mn
67	Iyi
68	Rn
69	Na
105	Me
105	Nn
106	Ug
107	Mm
108	Mm
109	Mm
110	Uw
111	Iy
112	Iy
113	Iy
114	Iy
115	Mh?
115	Iy
116	Iy
117	Iy
118	Iy
119	Iy
120	Ay
121	Mm

ESTATE	LANGUAGE
122	Iy
123	Uw
124	Ug
125	Ug
126	Mu
127	Mm
128	?
129	Mm
130	Iy
131	Mu
132	Yi
133	Mu
134	Mu
135	Mu
136	Ma
137	Mm
138	Iy
139	Ma
140	Pk
141	Pk
142	?
143	Mu
144	?
145	?
146	At
147	Iy
148	Li
149	Li

6

Wik Subgroup[1] lexical history

Ken Hale[2]

Abstract

Patterns of lexical replacement (or vocabulary change) in the Paman languages of Cape York Peninsula provide evidence in support of the proposition that the Wik languages, and the Wik-speaking peoples, have been associated with the geographic area with which they are presently associated for a period greatly in excess of that separating 1788 from the present. Detailed evidence will be presented in support of the following two statements, which, in turn, support the general proposition. The first statement (i) deals with the relationship between the Wik languages and the larger linguistic entities to which they belong—namely, Middle Paman, and the much larger grouping termed Paman, to which most, if not all, Cape York languages belong. The second (ii) deals with the internal relationships within the Middle Paman branch, to which the Wik languages most immediately belong, and then with relations internal to the Wik group itself. Each statement includes an assessment (the most conservative estimate) of the time period that must be attributed to Wik residence in the region at issue.

---

1   Note: in this chapter and the next, Ken's use of the term 'Wik group' or 'Wik languages' refers to members of what elsewhere here I refer to as members of the Wik Subgroup: PS.
2   This chapter was written in 1997: PS.

i. The Wik languages are related to their Paman neighbours in a consistent manner. As a group, they show a stable and consistent pattern of lexical sharing with their fellow Middle Paman languages, with Northern Paman, and with the south. The stability of this relationship is of a character that could only exist if the ancestors of the Wik-speaking peoples developed their present linguistic traditions, with its own internal diversity, in situ, in a region corresponding essentially to that which they occupy at present.[3] They represent a piece in the linguistic mosaic of Cape York Peninsula that has developed over a period greatly exceeding a millennium. The Wik linguistic tradition, as an integral part of this mosaic, cannot in any linguistically understandable sense, be viewed as an intrusion of outsiders at any point within the millennium we now occupy.

ii. The lexical diversity of the Wik sub-branch of Middle Paman reveals two levels of linguistic differentiation the least of which is extensive enough to require at least 300 years to achieve; the greater of the two levels of differentiation, that which distinguishes the pair Nr-Nn (Wik-Ngatharr and Wik-Ngathan) from its Wik relatives, represents a degree of lexical differentiation requiring a period of time approaching a millennium. On the reasonable assumption that simplicity is to be preferred over complexity in hypotheses about migration, the internal diversity of the Wik language group must have developed in the area where the Wik-speaking peoples are now residing. Their residence in that region must exceed 300 years, at the very least.

Introduction

In this essay, linguistic evidence will be presented in support of the proposition that the Wik-speaking peoples of Cape York Peninsula have resided in their present location for a period of time greatly exceeding that separating the present from the year 1788. I will take the Wik group to consist of the clans and communities so identified in Sutton (1978) and in references cited there. For the purposes of the present discussion, I will make use of linguistic material from a representative sample of the Wik languages, including the following:

---

3 This statement by Ken is not vitiated by the fact that, as Appendices 1 and 2 at the end of this book reveal, there have been some language shifts by some clans in recent centuries. See Clans 4, 29, 33, 35, 36, 76 and 105: PS.

Mn: Wik-Mungkan(h)
Me: Wik Me'nh, Wik Ep
Mm: Kugu Muminh
Nr: Wik-Ngatharr, Wik A(a)lkan(h)
Nn: Wik-Ngathan(h)

The abbreviations given here follow the usage of Sutton (1978). As the list indicates, members of the Wik group, properly conceived, differ in their use of the Paman terms for 'language', and accordingly in the name given to the speech-form with which they are associated—some use the term derived from *wika*, others use that derived from *kuuku*. Both are legitimate forms descending from a Paman ancestor language and, as such, are genuine elements of the Cape York Peninsula linguistic heritage. For the sake of simplicity, we will refer to the groups that are of interest here as Wik, following established tradition in the anthropological and linguistic literature.

The five speech-forms listed above have been chosen because they represent reasonably well the extent of linguistic diversity within the Wik group as a whole; and, to some extent, they represent as well the linguistic characteristics of three discernible Wik subgroups: (i) Mn-Me, (ii) Nr-Nn, and (iii) the Kugu Nganhcarra subgroup (Smith and Johnson 1985, 1986; Smith 1986) represented here by Mm. In addition to linguistic materials from these Wik groups, we will make reference to materials from other members of the Middle Paman branch of the Paman (or Pama-Maric) language family, and to materials from Paman languages outside the Middle Paman branch. All of this is relevant to the question of the long-term residence of the Wik peoples in Western Cape York Peninsula.

The Wik languages belong to the Middle Paman branch of Paman (cf. Hale 1976c). Other Middle Paman languages include Kuuk Thaayorre (Ta) to the south and the Kaanju-Ya'u-Umpila (Ka, Ya) language to the east.[4] Material from these languages will be involved in our discussions, to some

---

4   One of the manuscript readers for our publisher considers this inclusion of Thaayorre in Middle Paman to be wrong: '(a) the phylogenetic affinity of Kuuk Thaayorre is not with Wik but rather with languages to the south: Yir Yoront, Koko Pera, Uw-Oykangand & Uw-Olkol ("Kunjen"), and languages down the coast to Normanton: Alpher 1972, on the basis of grammatical correspondences; Alpher and Nash 1999). (b) importantly, this fact does not interfere with Hale's argument, since it is the rank ordering of the shared vocabulary figures that matters here': PS.

extent, as will material from Pakanh (Pa), a southern extension of Wik. Linguistic data from Middle Paman languages are taken from sources indicated below:

Wik

Mn: Hale notes (1960); Kilham et al. (1986).
Me: Hale notes (1960).
Mm: Hale notes (1960); Johnson (English-Nganhcara glossary, 1989, received 1995); Smith and Johnson (1985, 1986); Smith (1986).
Nr: Hale notes (1960).
Nn: Sutton (1995a).
Pa: Hamilton and Yam (1994).

Non-Wik (South)

Ta: Hale notes (1960).

Non-Wik (East)

Ka: Hale notes (1960).
Ya: Harris and O'Grady (1976); Thompson (1976).

The lexical data that will be referred to in this discussion are given in Appendix A within this chapter. That collection includes not only material from the Wik and other Middle Paman languages, but also material from Paman languages outside the Middle Paman branch; specifically, it includes lexical data from 13 Northern Paman languages (cf. Hale 1976a) and from some dozen languages spoken south of the Middle Paman region—these latter will be referred to informally as Southern Paman, though, unlike Northern Paman, they do not constitute a single branch within the Paman family. Northern and Southern Paman are important here, as they help to locate Middle Paman and the Wik languages in the overall Cape York linguistic picture.

Appendix A of this chapter consists of 100 lexical items from the areas of vocabulary generally considered 'basic' and therefore most resistant to replacement, i.e. most conservative. The use of basic vocabulary here is in keeping with a long and established tradition in the study of linguistic diversity and language groupings. Though there are notable exceptions (e.g. Bergsland and Vogt 1962), replacement of basic vocabulary is in general slow and quite trustworthy in determining relative time-depth in the development of observed linguistic diversity among the members of language families and stocks.

The construction of a reliable list of basic items is not a simple matter, since the determination of what is basic and what is not basic is never clear. The list given in Appendix A attempts to represent vocabulary that is not culturally or regionally dependent (hence, avoiding kinship terms, material culture, and local zoological terminology). It includes 25 body parts, 1 bodily condition, 23 verbs, 10 adjectives, 9 determiners (pronouns, demonstratives, etc.), 2 terms referring to humans, 4 animal-related terms, 3 plant-related terms, 2 time adverbs, 3 quantifiers, 8 location terms, 11 natural features. Although no list is entirely successful, some measure of the conservative nature of this list can be gained by considering the percentage of Proto-Paman lexical items, which remain today in at least one language of each of the modern Paman branches. The following table lists (by number assigned in Appendix A of this chapter) the Proto-Paman reconstructions of items occurring in all modern Paman branches:

Table 6.1: Proto-Paman lexical items (from 100-word test list) occurring in all modern Paman branches

6 *pina 'ear'; 7 *THaa'a 'mouth'; 12 *THulpi 'stomach'
16 *ma'a 'hand'; 18 *pungku 'knee'; 20 *THaru 'foot'
26 *maaTHin 'hungry'; 33 *THana- 'stand'; 34 *Ñina- 'sit'
40 *wanta- 'leave'; 44 *paTHa- 'bite'; 48 *THarngka- 'laugh'
49 *mini 'good'; 50 *warra 'bad'; 51 *pama 'person'
65 *panTHi- 'burn'; 66 miÑa 'meat'; 69 *kuta(ka) 'dog'
70 *yuku 'tree'; 72 *mayi 'veg-food'; 73 *kaaway 'east'
76 *yiiparr 'south'; 78 *pakay 'down'; 80 *ngula 'bye and bye'
82 *kuuTHima 'two'; 89 *Cuungku 'long'; 93 *ngaani 'what'
94 *waari 'who'; 95 *wantu 'where'; 96 *ngayu~ 'I'
97 *Ñuntu~ 'you'; 98 *Ñulu~ 'he'; 99 ngali '1incl'
100 Ñupula~ '2du'

This is testimony, so to speak, to the longevity of these items in Paman and, correspondingly, a measure of the general conservative quality of the list from which they are drawn. These items represent descendent forms that, resisting replacement, have persisted in all of the modern Paman branches since the time of the Paman ancestral language. The time of ancestral Paman is clearly in the distant past, judging from the diversity of the Paman languages now spoken on Cape York Peninsula. Since this persistent vocabulary represents a third of the test list, we can be relatively certain that the list as a whole functions properly as basic in the required sense. A list of comparable length drawn from non-basic vocabulary would have few items traceable to Proto-Paman.

In Appendix A of this chapter, the lexical material is arranged so as to reveal the cognation judgements that have been made. Each item is given a number and an English gloss. The modern Paman forms are then listed by language. Each language is assigned a number, as indicated in the paragraph preceding the list. Where modern forms are shared by more than one language, they are grouped into 'cognate sets', each assigned a letter (a, b, c, etc.); where a modern form is not shared by another language, it is placed in a list labelled UR (for 'unrelated').

The linguistic position of Wik in Cape York Peninsula[5]

The Wik languages belong squarely and solidly to the linguistic legacy of Cape York Peninsula. They are members of the Middle Paman branch of Paman, and as such they share a number of linguistic features with their close neighbours to the south (Ta) and east (Ka, Ya), also members of the Middle Paman branch. Table 6.2 sets out the percentages of cognates shared by five Wik languages, with one another and with their Middle Paman neighbours, including Pa (Pakanh), a southern extension of Wik:

---

5   Recall that this refers to the Wik Subgroup only: PS.

Table 6.2: Wik languages and Middle Paman neighbours south and east

	Me	Mm	Nr	Nn	Pa	Ta	Ka	Ya
Mn	69	63	40	45	69	41	41	39
Me		59	49	48	56	40	36	34
Mm			41	40	59	42	36	37
Nr				86	40	32	29	31
Nn					43	33	32	34
Pa						40	46	(46)
Ta							26	25
Ka								70

It is obvious from Table 6.2 that the relationships within the Middle Paman branch vary in relation to the amount of cognate vocabulary shared. For example, Nr and Nn are extremely close, almost identical, lexically speaking, showing a figure of 86 per cent. By contrast, when these are compared to other Middle Paman languages, they show (jointly) a much lower percentage, an average slightly in excess of only 38 per cent; when these two are compared with other Wik languages, however, the figure rises to an average of 44, unsurprisingly, given the relative linguistic integrity of the Wik group. It is customary to use the terms 'dialect' and 'language' to characterise the relative distance among linguistic relationships within a linguistic branch or family. These terms have no precise scientific validity. They are nonetheless traditional, and no harm is done, surely, in declaring that Nr and Nn are a single language. Apart from this, however, the designation 'one language' is somewhat arbitrary in the Middle Paman situation. We might, for example, set the language boundary at 70 per cent plus/minus two or so (a figure somewhat lower than that suggested, for example, in the literature on glottochronology, cf. Gudschinsky [1956] and Swadesh [1954]). That would define Mn and Me as dialects of one language, and it would make Mn and Pa one language as well. The relation between Pa and Me in this triangle is paradoxical, of course, since these two share a much lower percentage of cognates (according to my count, at least). This situation is quite representative of efforts to use comparative materials to determine exact linguistic groupings. In general, however, it is possible to see the relevant features of the relationships within a linguistic branch such as this.

The picture that emerges here is the following, for the five core Wik languages: (i) Nr and Nn are clearly a unit, justifiably termed a single language;[6] (ii) Mn, Me, and Pa form a somewhat looser unit, greater than a single language, but a recognisable unit nonetheless; (iii) Mm belongs to another recognised unit, Kugu Nganhcarra, closely related to, and probably part of the sub-group containing Mn-Me-Pa—in any event, Mm is more distantly related to Nr-Nn. This agrees in the essential respects with the Wik-internal relationships delineated in Sutton (1978:176–81), though further research will be needed eventually to determine the details of the relationships between the Nganhcarra languages as a group (represented here by Mm, but see also below within this chapter Appendix B.5–6) and Mn on the one hand and Me on the other. Our purpose here is not to settle that issue, however, but rather to gain an appreciation of the relative degrees of separation among the Wik languages and their fellow Middle Paman cousins. From the perspective of shared lexicon, it is reasonably clear that there are at least three degrees of separation within the Wik group. The closest relationships are the dialect-level relationship between Nr and Nn (with 86 per cent of the test list shared between them) and the similarly close relationship internal to Nganhcarra (see Appendix B.5–6; Smith and Johnson 1986; Sutton 1978). The next closest relationship is that between Mn, Me, and Mm (sharing an average of 64 per cent); and the most distant relationship is that holding between the pair Nr–Nn and the rest of the Wik group (at an average of 44 per cent shared items).

Setting aside the extremely close Nr–Nn relationship, the Wik family can be said to reflect a reasonable amount of lexical diversity. The figures 44 per cent and 64 per cent are not high. They are the figures that are to be expected of languages whose genetic relationship is obvious by inspection; but they are figures that show, nonetheless, that the languages are not extremely close either. These figures are those of a language family whose members began to differentiate at a time relatively remote from the present. We will return presently to the question of how long ago this time must have been. Now, however, I will turn to the relationship between Wik (or Middle Paman generally) and its linguistic relatives to the north and south, with the purpose of revealing the integrity of the Paman family as a whole and of the linguistic position of Middle Paman within it. This will constitute part of the evidence for long-term residence of the Wik peoples in the area with which they are presently identified.

---

6   This relative unity underlies the single study of demonstratives in Wik-Ngathan and Wik-Alken (aka Wik-Ngatharr) by Louise Ashmore (2017): PS.

The languages to the north of the Wik Region are evidently related to the Wik languages, though the relationship is initially obscured by the radical sound changes that characterise Northern Paman (cf. Hale 1976a). Once these changes are understood, it is possible to recognise with considerable precision the lexical items that are shared between Northern and Middle Paman. In the following table, five Wik languages (plus two other Middle Paman languages) are compared with three selected Northern Paman languages: Li (Linngithig[h]), Ur (Uradhi), and Ar (Arritinngithig[h]).

Table 6.3: Wik languages (+) and three Northern Paman languages

	Li	Ur	Ar
Mn	29	28	30
Me	27	25	28
Mm	29	28	29
Nr	25	25	27
Nn	27	26	30
Ta	21	23	23
Ka	29	28	33

As expected, the figures here are lower than those internal to the Wik group, and they are on the average lower than the figures obtained for comparisons internal to Middle Paman in general. This simply reflects the evident fact that Middle and Northern Paman constitute distinct branches, or subfamilies, within the larger Paman linguistic family. The most important property that these figures have, however, is their consistency. With one minor exception, they fall within the range between 20 and 30 per cent. This is remarkable, particularly in relation to the comparisons involving the Wik group itself—in general, what is true of one Wik language is true of the others; the differences are minor and of no real significance, giving testimony to the integrity both of Wik and of Northern Paman. While only three Northern Paman are involved in the comparisons tabulated in Table 6.3, the picture remains the same when all 13 Northern Paman languages represented in Appendix A of this chapter are involved. In Table 6.4, I give the average shared by each of six Middle Paman languages with the Northern Paman languages jointly (figures rounded), and then the average shared by the Middle Paman languages (as a group) with Northern Paman (as a group):

Table 6.4: Middle Paman and Northern Paman comparisons

(a)	Average %, six Middle Paman languages compared (individually) to 13 Northern Paman languages: Mn 29; Me 27; Mm 29; Nr 26; Ta 22; Ka 26.
(b)	Average of averages, six Middle Paman (MP) and 13 Northern Paman (NP): MP–NP 26.

These figures reaffirm the range noted above, being between 20 and 30, with the general average, 26, approximately in the middle of the range.

I appeal to averages here in order to mitigate the effects of two antagonistic factors that must be recognised in using shared vocabulary to determine relative distance between groups of related languages: (i) geographic proximity and (ii) the natural process of lexical replacement. In general, in situations like that found in Cape York Peninsula, where the members of small linguistically related groups regularly interact with their close neighbours, geographic proximity is reflected in the density of shared vocabulary, even between groups belonging to distinct (though related) linguistic branches. The observable effect of this is that geographically contiguous, or nearly contiguous, linguistic groups will share items not found in more distant communities—as a result, of course, of the linguistic contact, often entailing bi- or multilingualism. This has the effect of raising the figure obtained in using a test list (like that in Appendix A) to assess linguistic relationships. Conversely, relatively greater geographic distance between linguistic communities (resulting in little or no contact) will be reflected in relatively more depressed test-list figures. Thus, geographic proximity, and the attendant rate of social contact, has a distorting effect on the normal process of vocabulary change and replacement. So, for example, if Ta (Thaayorre) is indeed a Middle Paman language, and if, as appears to be the case, it constitutes its own sub-branch within Middle Paman, then it should (*a priori*) share that same amount of vocabulary with each of the other Middle Paman languages. But it does not, as is clear from a superficial glance at Table 6.2. It shares much more with Mm (Muminh) than it does with Ka-Ya (Kaanju and Ya'u-Umpila), a reflection of the difference in geographic separation. Similarly, were it not for the distorting effect under discussion, Ta would be expected to share the same average percentage of test-list vocabulary with Northern Paman as do the other Middle Paman languages. Again, this is not the case; its more removed southern location is reflected in its relatively depressed average of 22 per cent shared test-list vocabulary in relation to the Northern Paman block—compared, for example, to the average of 26 for Middle and Northern Paman generally.

The upshot of the preceding discussion is that geography (in particular, sociocultural geography reflecting greater or lesser social interaction among peoples occupying a region) must be taken into consideration when assessing linguistic relationships. Cognation figures cannot be understood in complete isolation from geography in this sense, a fact that was well understood in the earliest work on Indo-European and has informed work of this sort throughout the history of comparative linguistics. Let us now look at relationships between Middle Paman and communities to the south and south-east, an area of considerably more internal diversity than that represented by Northern Paman. Table 6.5 gives the figures for Wik (plus two other Middle Paman) comparisons with Kp (Koko Pera, a southern neighbour of Ta and Yir-Yoront), Ym (Guugu Yimidhirr, the language of Cooktown and adjacent coast and inland regions north of Cooktown), and Og (Ogo-Njan, Ogonjan, an 'initial-dropping language' spoken south of the Mitchell River).

Table 6.5: Wik languages (+) and three noncontiguous Paman languages south and east

	Kp	Ym	Og
Mn	24	20	22
Me	23	17	20
Mm	24	22	22
Nr	25	14	20
Nn	24	14	19
Ta	30	21	20
Ka	20	18	18

Here again, the figures are in general lower than for comparisons internal to Wik or internal to Middle Paman as a whole. They are similar to the figures obtained in the comparison of Middle Paman to Northern Paman (cf. Table 6.4)—they are, however, somewhat lower on the average, reflecting, perhaps, the fact that two of the languages belong to quite distinct Southern Paman groups at some geographic remove from the Middle Paman region. The effect of geographic proximity and contact is clearly evident here in the relatively higher figures for Kp (Koko Pera). The averages (rounded) are set out in Table 6.6:

Table 6.6: Middle and Southern Paman languages compared

(a)	Average %, six Middle Paman languages compared (individually) to nine Southern Paman languages: Mn 19; Me 18; Mm 20; Nr 15; Ta 21; Ka 15.
(b)	Average of averages, six Middle Paman (MP) compared with nine Southern Paman (SP): MP-SP 18.

Although the MP–SP comparisons reveal somewhat lower averages of shared test-list vocabulary than do the MP–NP comparisons, there is an important similarity. They are relatively consistent, reinforcing the impression of stability in the relationships within the Cape York Peninsula region as a whole. In these more distant relationships, there are no erratic deviations suggesting recent major movements of populations.

To complete the picture of wider Cape York Peninsula linguistic relations, as reflected in shared vocabulary, let us now consider figures for Northern Paman in relation to Southern Paman. Average percentages are as follows (see Appendix A of this chapter for abbreviations):

- Average per cent, 13 Northern Paman languages compared (individually) to nine Southern Paman languages: Ur–SP 18; Mp–SP 16; Lu–SP 15; Yi–SP 16; Ty–SP 16; Ma–SP 16; Nrw–SP 16; Nd–SP 17; Al–SP 15; Li–SP 15; Ngg–SP 15; Ar–SP 15; Mb–SP 13.
- Average of averages, 13 Northern Paman (MP) and nine Southern Paman (SP): NP–SP 16.

These figures show the same consistency as that found in the other intergroup comparisons. In general, for all of these comparisons, no language deviates greatly from the shared average of the group to which it belongs. The average is generally close to the middle of the range, reflecting stability for the region. Individual extremes are not great, but they are interesting. Ta shows a low average figure in Table 6.4 but a high individual figure in Table 6.5. These are probably related phenomena; its contacts to the south can be expected to result in higher figures locally and, assuming that these contacts are important and strong, they will tend to lower the figures for the north—the more test-list items shared to the south, the fewer will be shared to the north, assuming that the southern items are distinct from the corresponding northern ones. This is not always true, however, since geographically separated languages can, of course, independently retain a relatively large inventory of the common lexical heritage, particularly in the absence of strong and persistent external influences (cf. the Icelandic-Old Norse example of Bergsland and

Vogt 1962). It is possible, for example, that the slightly higher figure for Ur (Uradhig) above reflects a circumstance of this sort. However, these deviations are minor and of little or no significance for the problem at hand; the overall picture is one of great consistency and stability.

The averages shared by Northern Paman, Middle Paman, and Southern Paman are reassembled in Table 6.7:

Table 6.7: Average shared vocabulary, the Paman family of CYP

	MP	SP
NP	26	16
SP	18	

As expected, given the geographic separation, the NP–SP comparison shows a figure that is lower, albeit only slightly lower, than that for NP–MP. Interestingly, however, the pair NP–MP evidently forms a block in relation to our nine-language SP sample—NP and MP agree in sharing a figure with SP that is 8 to 10 per cent lower than that shared by NP and MP with each other. This might, ultimately, permit us to group NP and MP into a single 'Upper Paman' subfamily, as opposed to the southern languages. But such a move is premature at this time, since our sample of southern languages is too meagre and scattered to reflect accurately the full and true genetic subgrouping of them.

Within NP, the average shared test-list vocabulary is 46 per cent, an average that is 20 per cent higher than the closest relationship outside NP, i.e. that with MP. Within MP, the average is 41 (or 44 if close, intra-language, percentages are included, raising the figure artificially); and the percentage within the Wik group itself is 48 (raising by almost 10 per cent, artificially, if close intra-language percentages are included). Within SP, as represented by the nine samples included in Appendix A, the figure is a low 22 per cent, an unsurprising reflection of the internal diversity and scattered nature of the sample.

The overall lexical and geographic integrity of the Paman family is rather clear, in outline at least, from the figures that we now have. In Figure 6.1, the linguistic groups are arrayed from north to south. For each group, the average percentage of shared test-list vocabulary is given, following the colon, and each group is connected to the others by a line indicating the average percentage shared by the pair.

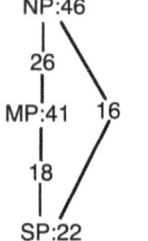
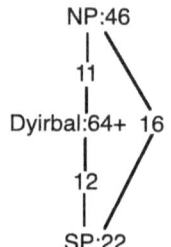

Figure 6.1: Paman languages, lexical sharing and geographic distribution

Figure 6.2: Lexical sharing under fictitious Dyirbalngan[7] intrusion into Middle Paman area

This pattern of sharing and geographic distribution suggests extraordinary stability; a typical pattern among related language groups, developing over a long period of time. From south to north, or north to south, there is a cline—the greater the remove, the greater the lexical separation, and, conversely, adjacent groups share more than separated groups. Northern Paman and Middle Paman reveal their integrity as groups by showing a higher average of shared test-list vocabulary internally than externally.

There is no indication of any significant recent migration into the Wik and general Middle Paman areas. If the Wik peoples did indeed represent an intrusion into the area, this would necessarily have been an intrusion in concert with the people constituting the Middle Paman group as a whole, and it would be so far in the past as to be virtually impossible to separate from the very earliest movements into the area.

A true and recent intrusion into the Wik and general Middle Paman region would be obvious. Suppose, for example, that speakers of the Dyirbal dialects—represented in Appendix A by Ji (Jirrbal) and Gi (Giramay)—had moved from their rainforest homeland some two or three centuries ago and settled in the present Middle Paman region, displacing the people now there. The lexical figures would reflect this clearly, and the relationships to the north and south would be different from what appears in example (8) in Chapter 7. On the average, these Dyirbal dialects share 11 per cent of test-list items with the 13 NP languages sampled, and they share 12 per cent with the nine languages of our SP sample. Figure 6.2 depicts the north–south pattern of lexical sharing in this imagined scenario, assuming absence of the present-day Middle Paman people.

---

7   Dyirbalngan are the people who own the Dyirbal language (Dixon 1972:23): PS.

The hypothetical Dyirbal intrusion produces a dip in lexical sharing proceeding from NP to SP, so that the extremes, NP and SP, share more than either does with the intrusive tradition. It is clear that the Wik peoples and their Middle Paman cousins do not fit this pattern. If the Middle Paman groups had been represented here, and, say, the imagined Dyirbal intrusion had split the MP-speaking population into two groups, the dip in lexical sharing would have been more dramatic, since sharing across the divide would, naturally, be greater than in Figure 6.2; the same would be true, though to a somewhat lesser degree, if the intrusion were to the north or south of present-day MP, separating it geographically from NP or SP. In any event, the pattern of sharing would not be as it in fact is. The facts evidently support Figure 6.1, not Figure 6.2, suggesting that Wik cannot be an intrusive group.

A final point in relation to the question of intrusion from outside the area. If speakers of Dyirbal dialects moved to the Middle Paman region, they would almost certainly leave a residual population behind in the homeland, this being the usual pattern in migration (in the absence of extreme conditions requiring wholesale migration). And they would therefore be most closely related linguistically to those who stayed behind. If the Wik peoples were an intrusive population, we would expect them to have relatives outside the area, relatives linguistically *closer* to them than their recently acquired neighbours. In fact, however, the Wik languages are closer to their neighbours, including both their Middle Paman relatives and their more distant Northern Paman relatives, than they are to any known linguistic group outside the area. That is to say, there is no plausible location outside the area that can be identified as a homeland from which an intrusive Wik-speaking people could have come. To be sure, the Wik languages are related to languages all over Australia, but their *closest* relatives are near at hand.

It is relevant to our general theme here to consider the question of 'time-depth' in relation to the patterns of lexical sharing observed in the Paman family of Cape York Peninsula—as represented schematically in Figure 6.1 and, in somewhat finer detail, in the various comparisons cited in the text leading to the conclusions summarised in Figure 6.1. Assuming that the observed patterns represent a relatively stable situation, how long has it taken for that situation to develop? That is to say, taking it for granted that the Paman languages are all related and therefore descend from a common ancestor, how long has it taken for the single common ancestor (i) to subdivide as it has into the present branches and sub-branches and (ii) to achieve its present distribution in Cape York Peninsula.

To address this question, we must entertain the widely accepted proposition articulated by Sapir in his renowned 'time perspectives' monograph to the effect that 'the greater the degree of linguistic differentiation within a stock the greater the period of time that must be assumed for the development of such differentiation' (Sapir 1916). We assume here that lexical replacement represents one kind of linguistic differentiation and that, like other kinds, it takes time—the greater the replacement, the greater the time involved.

It is possible to gain some appreciation of the time-depth involved in the Paman family (and in subregions of the Paman area) by comparing the patterns of lexical sharing observed there with those observed in other areas of the world that are to some extent comparable and where we have some reasonable estimate of the dates of separation.

The Northern Athabaskan[8] communities of western Canada and interior Alaska exhibit a relatively stable relationship to the lands they occupy, and they have differentiated over time into a number of recognisable branches (called substocks by Hoijer 1956). Although linguistic differentiation within Athabaskan is certainly less than what we have observed for Paman, it is nonetheless instructive to compare the two families—their situations are not altogether dissimilar. It is reasonably certain that the maximum time-depth in Northern Athabaskan is around a millennium. The time-depth for the family as a whole is somewhat more than this if the geographically separate Southern and Pacific Athabaskan languages are taken into consideration. Within the northern group, the comparison showing the lowest percentage of shared lexical items is that between Kutchin and Sarcee, at 63 per cent (based on a 100-word lexicostatistic test list; Hoijer 1956). In general, Sarcee and Galice (both somewhat separate geographically from the other northern languages) show the lowest percentages (both languages averaging 71 in comparisons with the other six Northern Athabaskan languages examined by Hoijer). These percentages are, of course, much higher than the lowest observed within Paman; and they are higher than the lowest figures within each of NP, MP, and SP as well.

---

8   One of our publisher's manuscript readers pointed out that there have been significant developments in research on Athabaskan since 1997: PS.

If the lexical figures for Athabaskan correspond to a maximum time-depth of a thousand years, then, if this is a comparable situation in any sense, the time-depth within Paman is much greater. To what extent is it comparable? First, the time-depth of a millennium is generally accepted on independent grounds as corresponding to the time when Athabaskan peoples began to move south, eventually settling in the region occupied by the present-day Apacheans (D. Gunnerson 1974; J. Gunnerson 1979; Gunnerson and Gunnerson 1971). The Apachean–Northern Athabaskan lexical comparisons yield percentages that are comparable to those for Sarcee and Galice in relation to the rest of the north. Thus, we have a correlation between shared lexicon and known time-depth.

But, to what extent can we use this to assess time-depth in Cape York Peninsula? We know that lexical comparisons between individual languages do not yield percentages that can be relied on to estimate anything like the 'date of separation'. The rate of lexical replacement in a language is simply not regular or constant, a fact that is dramatically brought out in the work of Bergsland and Vogt (1962). However, this has not, and should not, entirely discourage the use of the lexicon in reaching some estimation of time-depth through comparison with like situations in which the *actual* time-depth is known.

An individual language may, and usually does, show irregular and even erratic rates of vocabulary replacement at different times in its history, being subject to a range of varying pressures, influences and forces. But two languages will seldom be subject to the same pressures and influences at the same time; three even less, and so on (see Lees 1953, for some discussion of the 'independence assumption' in lexical decay). Accordingly, separate languages should not be expected to, nor do they, replace all the same items. This is why one observes that paradoxical comparisons 'wash out', so to speak, when the set of comparisons is enlarged. The Mn–Me–Pa comparison is paradoxical (Mn–Me 69; Mn–Pa 69; Me–Pa 56), but the relation of each of these languages to the rest of Middle Paman is unproblematic (with averages, including close relationships in the tally, as follows: Mn 51, Me 49, Pa 50).

It should be pointed out, of course, that in some areas of the world, including Australia, lexical replacement is institutionalised, typically in relation to mourning observances and respect relationships. This can, to some extent, elevate the rate of replacement above the ordinary, as illustrated, for example, in the rather spectacular lexical relationships observed by Bergsland for West Greenlandic and East Greenlandic (Bergsland and Vogt 1962). But here again, the use of a larger sample of languages—in the Eskimo case addition of Inuit materials from Canada and Alaska, and Yupik materials from Alaska and Siberia—would rather quickly correct the picture (were it not already obvious, as it was to Bergsland in the Greenlandic case). It is, nonetheless, worth considering the possibility that institutionalised lexical change could be accommodated in devising measures of lexical diversity for language groups. Of course, *recognised* institutionalised lexical replacements (as in the East Greenlandic case) must be taken into account; but for the most part, it is not possible to identify such replacements with certainty, just as it is not always possible to recognise borrowings (part of the 'geographic proximity factor'), especially when closely related languages are involved. To cite a concrete example, is the Middle Paman word *kooter* 'head'—recorded by Sutton for Nn and by Kilham et al. for Mn—a true shared retention in Mn and Nn? I assumed not, and rather that it was basically Nn, but I cannot be absolutely certain—work of this sort is fraught with questions of this kind. In the absence of direct and absolute identification of institutionalised replacements and spurious resemblances due to borrowing, the most one can do is refrain from taking particular shared-vocabulary figures too literally—i.e. to have in mind instead a range of flexibility, much in the spirit of the correctives discussed in the literature on lexicostatistics (reviewed, for example, in Hymes 1960, and explicated in detail in Gudschinsky 1956). In any event, it is not at all clear that a general corrective formula can be devised for use here, and I will assume that the best that can be done is to work with the gross figures obtained and to bear in mind that some flexibility must be allowed in interpreting them.

Taking all of this into consideration, I believe that it is legitimate to compare the Athabaskan and Paman situations and to maintain that the generally low figures internal to Paman reflect far greater time-depth for Paman than for Athabaskan. And, therefore, given the reasonably certain time period involved in Athabaskan, the time-depth represented by Paman is far in excess of a millennium, perhaps several millennia.

This conclusion is reinforced by a number of established correlations between time-depth and lexical replacement, including the following from Lees (1953), in which the percentages represent the test-list vocabulary retained by the modern language from an early sample associated with a date that is reasonably well-attested historiographically: (1) Old English of

900–1000 / Modern English: 76.6; (2) Plautine Latin of 200 BCE / Early Modern Spanish of 1600: 62.5; (3) Plautine Latin / Molière's French of 1650: 62.5; (4) Old High German of 800–900 / Modern German: 84.2; (5) Middle Egyptian of 2100–1700 BCE / Coptic of 300 BCE: 53.0; (6) Koine Greek of 250 BCE / Modern Athenian Greek: 69.0; (7) Koine Greek / Modern Cypriote: 67.8; (8) Ancient Classical Chinese of 950 CE / Modern Mandarin: 79.6; (9) Old Norse of 800–1050 CE / Modern Swedish: 85.0; (10) Classical Latin of 200 BCE / Modern Tuscan: 68.6; (11) Classical Latin / Modern Portuguese: 62.9; (12) Classical Latin / Modern Rumanian: 56.0; (13) Classical Latin / Modern Catalan: 60.6. To these can be added Hattori's per-millennium figures for Japanese, from Old Japanese of the eighth century: Kyoto 78.4; Kameyama 79.0; Tokyo 80.4 (Hattori 1953), and Satterthwaite's figures for Qoranic Arabic [645–650 CE] and Modern Meccan Arabic: 82.3 (Satterthwaite 1960). The percentages here are not directly comparable to those we have considered heretofore, since they correspond to the figures obtained when comparing an ancestral language. Since, to a degree (cf. Lees 1953), individual languages proceed independently in the matter of vocabulary replacement, the vocabulary retained in common by two related languages will, in general, be lower than that retained by either one of them from their common ancestor.

While a single language may retain from its ancestor 80 out of 100 test-list items over a period of a millennium, two languages descending from that ancestor may share only 65, or so, of those items after that same period of time. Thus, distorting influences aside, figures for shared retentions are lower than those of a single language in relation to its ancestor. Taking this into consideration, the figures for lexical sharing within Paman and, in particular, the relatively stable NP–MP 'block', includes figures well below many of those seen in the 15 comparisons just cited, for which a time-depth can be asserted with relative certainty. Again, it is clear that the Paman family shows respectable time-depth, even if very liberal error-factors are admitted in the calculations given. The maximum time-depth greatly exceeds a millennium as does that in the NP–MP region.

The conclusion, in relation to the Wik peoples, seems to me to be the following:

The Wik languages are related to their Paman neighbours in a consistent manner. As a group, they show a stable and consistent pattern of lexical sharing with their fellow Middle Paman languages, with Northern Paman, and with the south. The stability of this relationship is of a character that could only exist if the ancestors of the Wik-speaking peoples developed their present linguistic traditions, with its own internal diversity, in situ, in a region corresponding essentially to that which they occupy at present. They represent a piece in the linguistic mosaic of Cape York Peninsula, which has developed over a period greatly exceeding a millennium. The Wik linguistic tradition, as an integral part of this mosaic, cannot in any linguistically understandable sense, be viewed as an intrusion of outsiders at any point within the millennium we now occupy.

The internal relations of the Wik language group

The Wik languages form an integral part of the Middle Paman branch within the Paman family and, as such, share with other languages of that branch lexical material that is more or less exclusive to it. Some items of this tradition are given in reconstruction below, in which numbers correspond to those used to identify items in the test-list of Appendix A (items numbered above 100 are from an extension of that list):[9]

> 5 *kaa'a 'nose'; *14 *punTHa 'upper arm'; 9 *THalpi 'tongue'; 19 *yangkar 'shin'; 24 *parin 'skin'(?); 30 *nga(a)THi- 'hear'; 41 *THaa'i- 'throw'; 45 *umpi- 'cut'; 56 *punga 'sun'; 60 *ngaka 'water'; 62 *THuma 'fire'; 81 *thono- 'one'; 91 *THarran 'hard'; 114 *piña 'FaSi'; 118 wuñi- 'frightened'; 119 *nhaaNHi 'fly'; 133 *wuynpa- 'put'; 136 *wiipa 'shade'; 140 *NHuuma-~ 'smell'; 144 *THuli 'spearthrower'; 145 *puunha 'soft'; 162 *kacin 'yamstick'. [22 reconstructions]

These items represent part of a distinctive Middle Paman lexical heritage, of which the Wik languages partake, identifying them with a particular sub-tradition within the Paman family as a whole.

The percentages of test-list items shared by the Middle Paman languages are presented in Table 6.2, and some discussion of those figures is given there in the associated text. Our interest now is in the Wik group itself.

---

9   As an indication that these items are 'more or less exclusive' to Middle Paman, I must point out that 9 *THalpi 'tongue' has reflexes elsewhere, e.g. Djabugay jalbarr 'flame', Yalarnnga thalpirri 'beard', and 60 *ngaka 'water' has the reflex ngaka 'water' in Wangkumada and Pirriya, languages of south-west Queensland: PS.

We can see that, while Wik is closely related to the southernmost (Ta) and easternmost (Ka, Ya) Middle Paman languages, on an average, the Wik languages appear to form a group slightly separate from them. Thus, while the general average of shared test-list material is 41 per cent for Middle Paman as a whole, this figure rises to 48 when the Wik languages alone are considered. (These are the averages obtained when especially close intra-language percentages are eliminated; when these close relationships are included in the averages, the figures are 44 and 57, respectively. These higher figures are, however, artificial.)

Assuming that the Wik languages are in fact a genuine subgroup within the Middle Paman branch, is it possible to say anything about its internal structure? We have in fact suggested that there is a Wik-internal classification of languages (cf. Sutton 1978, and our discussion in the early paragraphs of Chapter 7 this volume), specifically, one that identifies the pair Nr–Nn as representing the greatest degree of separation within the group. These languages share an average of 43 or 44 per cent with the other Wik languages, while Mn–Me–Pa–Mm share an average of 50 or slightly more with other Wik languages, and an average of 62 among these four alone, excluding Nr and Nn. This asymmetry is also reflected concretely in the fact that there is a body of test-list vocabulary shared by these four languages, to the exclusion of Nr–Nn. These items are listed as follows:

> 2 *ngulV 'forehead'; 6 *kona 'ear'; 11 *yuwVn 'armpit'; 17 *kuman 'thigh'; 27 *mungka- 'eat'; 32 *THawa- 'speak; 39 *ma- 'take'; 43 * pii(yi)ku- 'hit'; 55 *raaku 'ground';[10] 63 *THoko 'smoke';[11] 74 *kuwa 'west'; 77 *kani 'up'; 87 *kaci 'far'; 88 *THinTHu 'near'; 92 *i- 'this'; *104 *paapa 'breast';[12] *105 *wuña 'OBro'; 116 *ma'a^eka 'fingernail'; 117 *pupi 'firestick'; 134 *engkV^thaa'a 'rib'; 139 *yapa 'OSi'; 147 *atu 'sugarbag'; 154 *pangku 'wallaby'. [23 reconstructions]

In short, the greatest lexical diversity within the Wik sub-branch is that represented by the separation of Nr–Nn from its fellow Wik languages, at an average somewhere between 43 and 44 per cent.

---

10 Hale's Nr Informant had given *nhath* for 'ground', but that dialect, as does Nn, also has *aak* <*raaku for 'place, ground, country etc.': PS.
11 Note that Wik-Ngatharr does have *thok* 'bushfire': PS.
12 Nn does have *peepeth* 'female' (*-th* is a comitative suffix) presumably from *paapa + comitative; Nn also has *paap* 'two-stick frame for weaving bags'; in Nn the bottom corners of the bags, which begin on the tops of the sticks, are *yuunh kuyeng* 'bag breasts': PS.

Assuming the usual simplicity metric in postulating migrations, in the absence of strong counter-evidence, we will maintain that any significant linguistic division, resulting in distinct languages or subfamilies, represents a *local* development; any other assumption would require separate migrations into the area in which the linguistic diversity is found. Accordingly, in the absence of counter-evidence, we must assume that the internal diversity of the Wik group developed in the region where the Wik languages are now found. If we can estimate a time-depth for this diversity, then we will have an estimate of the minimum period of residence of Wik-speaking peoples in the area.

The figures we have are 44 per cent, or so, for the greatest division within the sub-branch, and 62, or so, for the next major division. These figures, on the face of it, and assuming the Old World comparisons are appropriate, already suggest an antiquity for the Wik sub-branch approaching a millennium and, certainly, exceeding half a millennium (cf. Lees 1953). If Wik differentiation began in situ, as the simplicity-of-migrations argument would suggest, then the Wik languages have been in their present location from a time long before 1788.

Before concluding this discussion, I would like to consider the question from the viewpoint of the more recent period, directly relevant to the issue at hand, looking back to a time between 200 and 300 years ago (i.e. the seventeenth century, approximately). How much lexical diversity can we expect to have developed within that period? To address this question, I will again compare situations that are, to some extent, similar—in this case, situations involving indigenous languages recorded or cited in the colonial period. Where forms of speech known in the colonial period to be dialects of a single language are now spoken by distinct and separate populations, the question will be, how much lexical replacement (as represented by shared cognate percentages) has taken place since unity? In some cases, the data have to do rather with replacement within one tradition over time. The cases are presented below.

Case I

Arizona Tewa and Río Grande Tewa. The Arizona Tewa moved to the Hopi community in 1695 to escape Spanish oppression (Dozier 1966). Percentage of shared test-list items, based on vocabularies in Dozier and Hale (1965) and O'Grady (1961): 92, 98 (with variation reflecting uncertainty in judgements).

Case II

(a) Southern Sumu (Ulwa) and Northern Sumu (Panamahka). These groups were as territorially distinct though related entities in 1600; Sumu unity and territorial contiguity was effectively destroyed during the Miskitu raids of the eighteenth century (Helms 1971). Shared cognates from 100-word list in modern Ulwa and Panamahka: 62 per cent to 72 per cent (the latter when compounds are admitted, one part of which is cognate, from Hale and Lacayo 1988). (b) Modern Twahka and Panamahka, closely related dialects of Northern Sumu and so recognised in 1600; now living in separate villages in interior Eastern Nicaragua. Percentage shared cognates: 90 (based on material assembled by Hale and Melendez 1994).

Case III

Pima of Ónavas, of Sonora, Mexico, and O'odham (Pima-Papago) of Northern Sonora and Southern Arizona. These were recognised as parts of a contiguous dialect chain in 1647, when Padre Baltasar de Loaysa was assigned as Jesuit priest to Ónavas, where, quite possibly, he wrote the Névome grammar (of Ónavas Pima) attributed to him; the linguistic integrity of the Pimería Alta was disrupted in the nineteenth century. Percentage of shared cognates: 96 (based on materials in Hale, Cox, et al. 1977, and Saxton et al. 1983).

Case IV

Apachean (Southern Athabaskan). Fray Alonso de Benavides's comment in 1630 that, although the 'huge Apache nation' had one language, which 'since it is so extensive it does not fail to vary somewhat in some bands (rancherías), but not such that it cannot be very well understood'. The percentages shared by the modern Apachean languages are set out in Table 6.8 (based on Hoijer 1956); the abbreviations are for Chiricahua, Navajo, San Carlos, Jicarilla, and Lipan:

Table 6.8: Lexical percentages shared by the modern Apachean languages

	Nav	Chir	SC	Jic
Chir	94			
SC	89	91		
Jic	89	92	87	
Lip	87	91	84	91

Case V

Modern Carib and the ancestral Dominican Carib of 1650 CE. Cognates remaining amount to 93.5 per cent (cited in Lees 1953).

Case VI

Yucatec Mayan. Modern Yucatec retains 95.8 per cent of 212 lexical items recorded by missionaries in 1540–1700 (Lees 1953).

These examples demonstrate repeatedly that the extent of lexical replacement occurring since the seventeenth century is extremely small. The percentages are high, only that for the Ulwa–Panamahka comparison (which really does not belong here) reaches a respectably low point, equalling the lower average of 62 of the Wik-internal comparisons. This relatively low percentage is certainly due to the circumstance that Ulwa (Southern Sumu) has been distinct from Twahka-Panamahka (Northern Sumu) for a long time, a fact that is reflected in certain rather dramatic morphological changes as well. Setting this figure aside, the percentages involved in the 'case studies' I–VI above represent a range to which the *closest* Wik-internal relationship belongs—i.e. that of Nr and Nn.

Assuming that it is appropriate to employ these cases in assessing Wik time-depth, their implication is clear. The lexical diversity that exists within the Wik sub-branch is much in excess of that which has occurred in the comparison cases I–VI, representing lexical change occurring at least since the seventeenth century. Putting aside the closest Wik-internal relationships, there are two primary levels of lexical differentiation, the greater being represented by the average of 41 per cent shared test-list vocabulary, the lesser by the average of 62 per cent. Even the higher average is significantly lower than the percentages involved in cases I–VI. Assuming the validity of the comparison, the conclusion is almost unavoidable that Wik-internal linguistic differentiation, as represented by lexical change, is greater than that which could have taken place in the past 300 years.

In summary, the lexical diversity of the Wik sub-branch of Middle Paman reveals two levels of linguistic differentiation, the least of which is extensive enough to require at least 300 years to achieve; the greater of the two levels of differentiation, that which distinguishes the pair Nr–Nn (Wik-Ngatharr and Wik-Ngathan) from its Wik relatives, represents a degree of lexical differentiation requiring a period of time approaching a millennium. On the assumption that simplicity is to be preferred over complexity in hypotheses about migration, the internal diversity of the Wik language group must have developed in the area where the Wik-speaking peoples are now residing. Their residence in that region must exceed 300 years.

Appendix A: Comparative Paman Vocabularies[13]

1. Language abbreviations

(1) Ur: Uradhi; (2) Mp: Mpalicanh; (3) Lu: Luthigh; (4) Yin: Yinwum; (5) Ty: Thyanhngayth; (6) Mam: Mamngayth; (7) Nrw: Ndrwa'angayth; (8) Nd: Ndra'angith; (9) Al: Alngith; (10) Li: Linngithigh; (11) Nk: Nggoth; (12) Ar: Arrithinngithigh; (13) Mb: Mbaywom; (14) Mn: Wik Mungkanh; (15) Me: Wik Me'anh, Wik 'Ep; (16) Mm: Wik (properly Kugu) Muminh; (17) Nr: Wik Ngatharr, Wik Alkanh; (17') Nn: Wik-Ngathan; (18) Ta: Kuuk Thaayorre; (19) Kp: Koko Pera; (20) Kr: Kungkara; (21) Og: Ogonjan; (22) Ag: Agu Tharrnggele; (23) Ym: Kuku Yimijirr; (24) Ml: Muluriji; (25) CC: China Camp Muluruji; (26) Ja: Japukay; (27) Yd: Yidin; (28) Ji: Jirrbal (dialect of Dyirbal); (29) Gi: Giramay (dialect of Dyirbal); (30) Ka: Kaanju; (30') Ya: Kuuku Ya'u-Umpila.[14]

2. Vocabularies and cognation judgements

Numbers followed by a period represent the items of the test-list; numbers without period correspond to the numbers assigned to the languages listed above; assumed cognates are collected in sets assigned a letter of the alphabet:

1. head: (a) 2, 3 walap; 4 welap. (b) 5, 6 trwak. (c) 7–10 aran. (d) 15 kölp; 17 kolp; 17' kulp. UR: 1 wapʉn; 11 yan; 12 irwa; 13 with; 14 kùcek; 16 pìntheka; 17' kooter, puun; 18 paant; 19 cekóont; 20 gathal; 21 olkol; 22 əlkiwrə; 23 ngapay; 24 tangu; 25 tukul; 26 pata; 27 tunku; 28 tingkal; 29 mukal; 30 mumpalu.

---

13   As these vocabularies were typically collected during short-term one-off field work there are bound to be minor errors here and there. I have left Ken's text intact: PS.
14   17 and 17' (17 prime) are sister dialects of the same language.

2. <u>forehead</u>: (a) 2 nggala; 3 nggay; 4 nggal. (b) 5, 7, 9, 11 pay. (c) 6, 8 pathan. (d) 10, 12 with. (e) 14, 16 ngul-ngangka; 15 ngula; 24, 26 ngulu. (f) 17 uka, 17' uuk. UR: 1 yapi; 13 onto; 18 kòrirkr; 19 cilkokóorr; 20 lirrpirr; 21 iNjər; 22 əkwəənə; 23 piti; 25 muncu; 27 ngumparr; 28 puyin; 29 nguun; 30 yangku.

3. <u>nape</u>: (a) 1 wukan; 2 kwana; 3, 5–7 kwan; 8 kan; 9 kwan. (b) 17 in; 17' inm. (c) 21 oroolng; 22 ərəwlngə. (d) 24, 25 cakay. (e) 26 tukul; 27 cukul. (f) 28, 29 tara. UR: 4 mbut-ngkuun; 10 mbru'um; 11 thwandək; 12 ndyac; 13 notok; 14 monkən-taa'a; 15 mìcaa'a; 16 muci-dhaa; 19 man-kuur; 20 mpuwic; 23 currcurr; 30 kuyka.

4. <u>eye</u>: (a) 2 ndyaga; 3 ndyag. (b) 5–7, 12 ndhwa; 8 ndha; 9 thwa; 10 tha. (c) 14, 15 mee'a; 18 meer. (d) 16 thantha-dhuka; 17 thanth, 17' thant. (e) 19 ceel; 20 iil; 26, 27 cili. (f) 23, 25 miyil. (g) 28, 29 kayka. UR: 1 ipan; 4 awunj; 11 nggwi; 13 müü; 21 iMən; 22 əlpiyələ; 24 ngayma; 30 mii'i (< 14–15), ku'un, tuntu.

5. <u>nose</u>: (a) 2 kwakanha; 3, 5, 11 kwakanh. (b) 4 iyi; 6–10, 13 iri; 30 nhiiyi. (c) 14, 15 kaa'a; 16 kaa'-guthu; 17–17' kaa'. (d) 18 koow; 19 kow; 20 uuw; 26, 28 kuwu. (e) 23 puciil; 24, 25 pucil. UR: 1 mugnhu; 12 pwanj; 21 ilNgər; 22 muu; 27 tikir; 29 wutu; 30 kaanci.

6. <u>ear</u>: (a) 2 maminhu; 3 maminh; 4 map. (b) 5–7, 9 wa'. (c) 8, 10 iwug. (d) 12 alo; 18 kaal; 30 kaalu. (e) 14, 15 kona; 16 kon-mangka, (f) 17–17' pin; 19 pin-thakéel; 21 iNa-ngəl; 22 ənyə; 26, 27 pina. (g) 23–25 milka. UR: 1 ukʉci; 11 inheminh; 13 anta; 20 ringkarr; 28 manga, walu; 29 karupa; 30 yampa.

7. <u>mouth</u>: (a) 1 nangga; 2 angka; 3 aka; 5–8 ngga; 9–10 ka. (b) 4 lin; 11 lyan. (c) 14–15, 17–17' thaa'; 16 thaa'-'aku; 30 tha'a. (d) 18–19 thaaw; 20 aag. (e) 28–29 ngangku. UR: 12 ari; 17' thaanth; 21 ekənh; 22 əbi-tənə; 23 parkaa; 24 canga; 25 ñumpul, ngantal; 26 piñi; wari.

8. <u>tooth</u>: (a) 1 ngambu; 2 ampu; 3 apu; 5–7 mbaw; 17–17' ngamp. (b) 8, 10 lidh; 9 lwidh; 22 liyə; 23 muliir. (c) 11 udhapuñ; 13 adhapunh. (d) 14–15 koonh. (e) 24–29 tirra. UR: 4 inañ; 12 thiyig; 16 kanu; 18 kiin; 19 kulng; 20 yaak; 21 anggul; 30 kanca.

9. <u>tongue</u>: (a) 1 lalan; 3 əlan; 5–10, 12 lan; (b) 4 lin-atra; 11 lyan. (c) 14 thaa'-nganth; 16 thaa'-ngantha; 20 nciir; 21 endhaawər; 23 ngancaar. (d) 15 thaʉp; 17–17' thalp; 18 man-theepər; 30 thaapi. (e) 19 nheelper; 22 əlpiinhə. (f) 24–25 ñapil; 26 ñawil. (g) 28–29 calngkulay. UR: 2 pundhanhu; 13 lip.

10. shoulder: (a) 2 anggala; 3 anggay; 28 pangkal. (b) 5–12 thol. (c) 15 'ingk; 16, 30 'ingki. (d) 17 milpir; 17' milpər; 18 meper. (e) 20 rrakil; 21 arraagəl. (f) 24–26 pinta. UR: 1 agaw; 4 ithag; 12 kwunduń; 13 both; 14 pìcem; 19 rrapakóow; 22 əkwilə; 23 ngaku; 27 wukul; 29 tikil.

11. armpit: (a) 1 adhərrəmbinhu; 2 ntharrambinha. (b)3 amog; 5–7 mawg; 8, 10–12 amog; 9 mog; 17–17' ngam; 21 amur; 28–29 ngaamur. (c) 1 wadhu; 4, 12–13 athu; 30 waathu. (d) 14–15 yuwən; 16 yuwən-anci. (e) 18 kaap; 24–25 kapari. (f) 19 ngaméerr; 20 maarrg. (g) 26–27 kancarr. UR: 22 maawnə; 23 kaamurr; 30 maapu.

12. liver: (a) 1 lipa; 2 ipa; 4 pya; 12 pa; 13 pe; 18 thiip; 20 yiib; 23–26 cipa; 28–29 kipa; 30 yipa. (b) 3 thandak; 6, 8 tharrak; 9–20 thandrag. (c) 5 kuyc; 7 kuc. (d) 14–15 woongkəń. (e) 17–17' maak; (f) 21 eethə; 22 əthu. UR: 16 wanha; 17' kookem; 19 pokóol; 24 culpi (? cf. stomach); 25 kuńu, wapa; 26 kalmpara; 27 kumpukara.

13. stomach: (a) 1 lɯtpi; 14 thip; 15 thüp; 17 thilp; 17' thölp; 24–25 culpi; 30 yul'i. (b) 2 abidha; 3 abidh. (c) 4, 13 amay. (d) 3 arya; 5–10 ara. (e) 11 pya; 24 cipa. (f) 16 kuna-waya; 18 kun-thir. UR: 12 othin; 19 kumaarrp; 20 wuurrg; 21 orəl; 22 ərəwmə; 23 kampur; 26 palku; 27 tupurr; 28 pampa; 29 cucu; 30 ngangka.

14. upper arm: (a) 1 winda; 2–3 indya; 5–7 ndrya; 8–10 ndræ; 11 ndya. (b) 14–15, 17–17', 18 punth; 16, 30 puntha. (c) 24–25 wakuy. (d) 19 theerr; 26–27 cirri. (e) 28–29 karakal. UR: 4 irranh; 12 kwunduń; 13 ütük; 17 miy'; 20 malwur; 21 orrəl; 22 aarru; 23 ngakuur; 26 kungka.

15. elbow: (a) 1 yutu; 24–27 curru. (b) 3 igugurr; 13 ogorr. (c) 4 pat; 6–7, 9 pa'y. (d) 5 'awndh; 10 'ondh. (e) 8 'aran; 10 a'aran. (f) 14 yuungk; 30 yuungka. (g) 15, 17–17' kucənt. (h) 16 punti; 18 punt. (i) 28–29 puru. UR: 2 kuthińu; 11 pay (borrowed from 6–7, 9); 12 thambrog; 19 punth; 20 puul; 21 əteekər; 22 ərəwlə; 23 yurngkal.

16. hand: (a) 1 mata; 2 atya; 3, 8, 10 a'a; 4 ntra; 5–7, 9 'a; 11 tra' 12–13 ta; 14–15, 17' ma'; 16, 30 ma'a; 17 ma'-pungk; 19–20 maar; 21 aarə; 22 əri; 24–26 mara, (b) 28–29 mala. UR: 12 abinjin; 18 yuur; 23 mangal; 25 carkumu; 27 manti.

17. thigh: (a) 1–2 ithina; 3, 5–11 thin. (b) 12 mwan; 13 muun; 14–15, 18 kumən; 16 kumən-'ucənda; 21 uMon; 23, 30 kuman. (c) 19 cərriic; 20 dhaarr; 26–28 carra. (d) 24–25 malpin. (e) 17–17' thatəl. UR: 4 nggoy; 22 ngurry-anəwngə; 29 ngaka.

18. knee: (a) 1 wunggu; 2 unggu; 3, 11 nggu; 4, 8, 10 nggo; 5–7, 9 nggwu; 12 nggwung; 13 ngguu; 14–15, 17–17', 18 pungk; 16 pungku-bindha; 20 ngkuyil; 23–30 pungku. (b) 21 ilndəl; 22 pay-ndələ. UR: 19 pekəcíic.

19. shin: (a) 2 untyuugu; 3 u'ug; 4 ontro; 13 ontok. (b) 5–7, 9 thu'; 8, 10 tho'; 11–12 thot. (c) 14–15, 17 yangk; 16 yengka; 18 yangkar. (d) 24–25 ngarri. UR: 1 acpaw; 17' yoompənh; 19 thuur; 20 muuk; 21 akəl; 22 amaadhə; 23 pipaar; 26 pala; 27 wulu; 28 wurrmpurr; 29 wayal; 30 thumpa.

20. foot: (a) 1 nukaw; 3, 9 kway; 5–7 kwe; 8 ke; 10 kay. (b) 2 atyuu; 4, 12 tyu; 11 tro; 13 twi; 14–15, 17–17' tha'; 16, 30 tha'u. (c) 18 thaamər; 19 thəméel; 21 iMəl; 22 maalə; 23 camal. (d) 24–29 cina. UR: 20 niimp.

21. blood: (a) 2 kucaka; 3 kucak. (b) 4 kumpali; 13 kumpli. (c) 5–7 trelim; 8 tralim. (d) 9 kumbwinh; 10 kombwinh. (e) 16 kamu; 18 kam; 30 kamu. (f) 17 köy'; 17' köö;[15] (g) 24–25 mula. UR: 1 ṭicṭic; 11 piwirr; 12 ipwur; 14 caapəra; 15 wukəlpa, ngoolpənga; 19 purrméen; 20 gaanh; 21 olñil; 22 əgwiləm; 23 karrmpi; 26 kalpal; 27 kawarr; 28 wakuli; 29 wirrañ.

22. fat: (a) 2 aniyarra; 3–4 aniyarr. (b) 5, 7–10 ki'. (c) 11, 13 lewinj; (d) 15 piintəñ; 17' piinth(h)əyn. (e) 24–25 wantul. (f) 26–27 kilmparr. (g) 28–29 cami. UR: 1 ukətanganhu; 6 mbawlwamanh; 12 anhon; 14 thanth; 15 pinəm; 16 yi'i; 17 nguyin; 18 rithərr; 19 piirr; 20 dhaamp; 21 ungə; 22 nuwədə; 23 mampa; 30 ku'i.

23. bone: (a) 2 akwuyu; 3 akwuy. (b) 1 apṭdha; 4 piiy; 5–8 pwi; 9–12 puy. (c) 15 'eengk; 16 'angge. (d) 17–17' minc. (e) 23 paciipay; 24–25 pacipay. (f) 26–27 tatakal. (g) 28–29 wurrmpurr. UR: 13 ilkuth; 14 kaanca; 18 piinth; 19 thuur; 20 muuk; 21 errndin; 22 əkə; 30 yinkin.

24. skin: (a) 1 akṭic; 2 akugu; 3 akug; 4 kuw; 5–7 kawg; 8–9, 12 kog; 16 'aku. (b) 11–12 awanmanh. (c) 14–15, 17' pe'ən; 18 peetn; 22 ətiinə. (d) 21 anggər; 24 pangkarr. (e) 24–25 yulpan. (f) 28–29 kuka. UR: 10 iwin; 13 awu; 17 'uwal; 19 picéelngk; 20 muurrg; 23 ngarraa; 26 tumpul; 27 wurra; 30 pi'i.

---

15   This should be köö': P.S.

25. headhair: (a) 2 undhandha; 3 ndhandh; 4, 11 ndhwandh. (b) 5, 7, 9 'ya; 8 i'ya; 10 in'a; 12 itya. (c) 6, 11, 13 nga. (d) 14 yangəna; 16 yengan; 18 yaangən; 30 yangan. (e) 15, 17–17' muyən. (f) 21 alən; 22 lanə. (g) 24–25 mungka. (h) 27, 29 murray. UR: 1 ampinhambi; 19 cəkóorr-məngóorr; 20 iic; 23 muuri; 26 kulmpi, cipi; 28 wumpu.

26. hungry: (a) 2 andhima; 3 andhim; 5–7 adhaymr; 8, 10 adhim; 9 adhaym; 14–15, 17–17' meec; 16 maayin (?). (b) 11–13 iwam. (c) 24–25 takuy. (d) 26 taliir; 27 talii. (e) 28 ngamir; 29 ngamirpin. UR: 1 wʊrama; 4 imbyum; 18 punkurtharr; 19 thakathaali; 20 ilpiingincin; 21 orrmbir; 22 ərəwm-əlbüürə; 23 tingkacirr; 30 uuli.

27. to eat: (a) 2–3 kwa-; 5–7 nggwa-; 8 ngga-; 14–15 mungk-; 16 mungka-; 18 mungk. (b) 4 atha- ~. (c) 9–10 cim (FUT) ~. (d) 11 lya-; 12 la- ~. (e) 17–17' thic-. (f) 24–25 nuka-. (g) 26–27 puka-. UR: 1 tɨña–; 13 twe-; 20 -ilk (FUT) ~; 21 unja-; 23 puta-; 28 cangka-; 29 nanpa-; 30 yangku-.

28. to die: (a) 1 alga-; 22 əlkəy-. (b) 4 adha-; 11 andha-' 12–13 adha- . (c) 5–7 bwi-; 8 obi-; 21 elbi-. (d) 9 igö-; 10 igo-. (e) 14 'uthəm-; 16 'uthəma-. (f) 17 wayingk-; 17' wayngkan-. (g) 24–27 wula-. (h) 28–29 kuyipi-. UR: 2 mpama-; 3 aya-; 15 mula (N); 18 wonpər; 19 pumáa-; 20 ruci-; 23 piini-; 30 maka-.

29. to see: (a) 1 aci-; 2–3, 5–11 ci-; 4 nci-; 16 nhaawa-; 18 nhaa-; 19 nhaakal, nhacerr; 20 a- ~; 23 ńaa-; 24 ñaci-; 25 ña- ~ ñaci-. (b) 14–15 thath-; 30 yathu-. (c) 17 ngaac-; 17' ngeyc-. (d) 21 ata-; 22 əta-. (e) 28–29 pura-. UR: 12 olwa-; 13 we-; 26 ngunta-; 27 wawa-.

30. to hear: (a) 1–2 ami-; 3 mi-; 5–7, 9 may-; 8 mi-; 30 ngami-. (b) 4, 11–13 pwa-. (c) 14 ngey-; 15 ngeyy-; 16 ngêe-; 17 ngeec-; 17' ngeeth-; 18 ngayarr (C). (d) 19 pinəngk-nháakal; 21 aNa-ata-; 26 pina-ngunta-; 27 pinaa-. (e) 20 a-; 25 ña- ~ ñaci-. (f) 23 milkaa-ña-; 24 milka-cana-. (g) 28–29 ngampa-. UR: 10 ngaña-; 22 rəy-.

31. black: (a) 2 unggu; 3 ngguu; 4 ngge; 10 nggo-dhro; 30 thuungku ~ thungkuthungku. (b) 5–7 arow; 8 aro; 9 aru. (c) 11 ngul; 13 nguul. (d) 14–15, 18 ngotn. (e) 17–17' mak; (f) 19 ngolthóorr; 20 lthuurg. (g) 21 ocər; 22 əlcuurə. (h) 24 ngumpu; 25 ngumpunngumpun. (i) 26–27 pukal. UR: 1 unma; 12 ithiyin; 16 ngunca; 23 muñi; 28 kucu; 29 kinkin; 30 wumpi.

32. to speak: (a) 1 əca- ~ ica-; 2–4, 8, 10–12 ca-; 5–7, 9 cᴜa-; 13 cii-. (b) 14–15 thaw-; 16 thawa-. (c) 17 wiik-; 17' wiiyk-; 18 yiik; 19 yikyá-. (d) 21 og-irrka-; 22 ərkyə-; 23 yirrka-; 5 kuku-yirrka-. (e) 28–29 wurrpa-. UR: 20 ku- 24 palkawa-; 26 puwalpuka-; 27 ñangkaci-; 30 inga-.

33. to stand: (a) 1 anja (PRES) ~ anyi-; 2 njapa ~ ña-; 3 ña-; 4 njir ~ ngiri (IM); 8 nja ~ ni-; 9 njar ~ niri-; 10 njay ~ ni-; 12 ñag ~ ña-; 30 yaañi-. (b) 5–6 nhalam ~ nhalma-. (c) 14–15, 17 can-; 16, 18, 24–29 cana-; 17' than-; 22 əNaay-. UR: 7 mbawm ~ mbamu-; 11 ngang ~ nganga-; 13 nithdha- ; 19 thərré-; 20 nan (FUT); 21 erni-; 23 yuuli-.

34. to sit: (a) 1 inja (PRES) ~ ina-; 2 ingkapa ~ ina-; 3, 13, 20 ina-; 4 nggal ~ ina-; 5–7 nggewr ~ (e)ne-; 8 ngga ~ ina-; 9 kya ~ ina-; 10 nggay ~ ina-; 11 nya-; 12 inja ~ ina-; 14 ñin- ~ ñiin-; 15, 17–17' nhiin-; 16, 30 nhiina-; 18 nhini-; 19 ñiné-; 26–29 ñina-. (b) 21 in.gya-; 22 ən.gya-; 23 ñinka- [NOTE: (b) is probably cognate with (a), ultimately]. (c) 24–25 punta-. UR: 30 pa'aka-.

35. to go: (a) 1 ana-; 2–3 nya (PRES); 18 yaan; 22 nəy; 28 yana-; 29 yanu-. (b) 4 lini (PRES) ~; 8, 10 li-; 9 lay-; 19 kalé-; 21 eli-; 26–27 kali-. (c) 5–7 ang (PRES) ~ angi-. (d) 13 me-; 16 mumi-. (e) 17–17' iinc-. (f) 24–25 tunga-. UR: 11 mbi-; 12 arring ~ arri-; 14 iy-; 15 me'-; 20 -ip ~ -ik; 23 cata-; 30 waatha- ~ yuta-.

36. to run: (a) 1 wili-; 2–3. 9–10 lili-; 4 lyand (PRES). (b) 5–8 ca'aci-. (c) 17–17' maawk-; (d) 24–25 (± cinpal-)warri-. (e) 26–27 (± cinpal-)cungka-. (f) 24–27 cinpal. UR: 11 mbimb (PRES); 12 arritik (PRES); 13 mele-; 14 mo'-; 15 nhünp-; 16 nhunka-; 18 riricər-; 19 kunce-; 20 wura-; 21 arrnggori-; 22 mbilərəy-; 23 tuta-; 28 cingkali-; 29 puyici-; 30 yiiyimpi-.

37. to fall: (a) 1 alga-; 4 akii-; 12 ika-; 13 alka-; 14 keek-; 22 əlkyə-. (b) 2 unjii-; 3, 11 njii-; 5–7 njü-; 8–10 nji-. (c) 15 'enc-; 16 'ance-. (d) 17 uulnt-; 17' ulntan-. (e) 18 wontər; 19 wantáa-' 26–27 wanta-. (f) 28–29 paci-. UR: 20 wulpa-; 21 intha-; 23 puli-; 24 kungkuci-; 25 tara-; 30 alngki-.

38. to climb: (a) 1 anbəñi-; 2–3, 5–10 mbani-; 4, 11 mbaa-; 12–13 mba-. (b) 14 mat-; 16, 23 mata-. (c) 17–17' wump-. (d) 18 thaangk; 19 thakangk (FUT). (e) 24–25 taka-. (f) 26 maka-; 27 maki-. (g) 28–29 wayinci-. UR: 15 waangk-; 20 nci-; 21 alti-; 22 əray-; 30 piyingka-.

39. to take: (a) 1 apə-; 3 pya-; 5–7 pra-; 8 præ-; 9–10 ræ-. (b) 2 inja-; 12 anja-. (c) 14 mam-, maay-; 15 maay-; 16 maa-; 20 ma- ~; 23 ma-; 25 mani-. (d) 17–17' kaar-; 18 kal. (e) 26–27 tuka-. (f) 28–29 puti-. UR: 4 one; 11 mbe-; 13 mu-; 19 wicirr-; 21 ingka-; 22 ərrmba-; 24 wunti; 30 yawa.

40. to leave it be: (a) 1 andə-; 2–3 ndya-; 4–11 ndra-; 12–13 nda-; 14–15, 17–17' want-; 16 wanta-; 18 want (?); 19 waa- ~ want (PAST); 30 wana. (b) 21 onggi-; 22 nggwi. (c) 24–25 pawa. (d) 28–29 kalka. UR: 20 gi-; 23 tupi-; 26 wampa-, paraa-; 27 paca.

41. to throw: (a) 2 apu; 3, 5–7 pu-; 8–10 po-; 13 polpo-. (b) 4 mbyambi-; 11 mbya-; 12 mba-; 23 campa-; 30 yampa. (c) 14–15, 17–17' thee'-; 16 thîi-. (d) 21 eembi; 22 mbwi-. (e) 28–29 mata-. UR: 1 rathi-; 18 thunp; 19 reenga; 20 ra-; 24 wanta- 25 yilpa-; 26 tapa-; 27 kilpi.

42. to give: (a) 1 uthi (IM), ukaw (PAST) ~; 20 wukələ-; 21 uka- ~ uko; 23 wu- ~ wuci-; 28–29 wuka-. (b) 2–3 aya-; 6–7 ya-. (c) 5 pu-; 8–10, 13 po-. (d) 4 mbii-; 11 mbya-; 12 mba-. (e) 15 pal-wunp-; 17 wuñp-. (f) 14, 17' thee'-. (g) 16 waa(wa)-; 19 wa-; 26 waa-. (h) 24 taci-; 25 taya-. UR: 17' nhiinang-; 18 rek; 22 nggwi-; 27 wiwi-; 30 ngungka-.

43. to hit: (a) 2, 4 ngka-; 11 ka-; 12 nja-. (b) 9–10 ca-. (c) 5–7 irringi-; 8 irringa-. (d) 14 piiyək-; 15 peyyək-; 16 piigu-. (e) 17 pal(k)-; 17' palk-; 28–29 palka-. (f) 13 ne-; 19 ku- ~ kunt (PAST); 23 kunta-; 24–25 kuni-. (g) 21 ito- ~ ita-; 22 ətɥə-. UR: 1 arʉ-; 3 thæ-; 18 theerng; 20 riga-; 26 tuka- ~ tuu-; 27 punca-; 30 kanci-.

44. to bite: (a) 1 watha-; 2–13 tha-; 14–15, 17–17', 18 path-; 16, 30 patha-; 19 pəthé-; 21 eethə-; 22 thəy-; 26 paya-; 27–29 paca-. (b) 24–25 payka-. UR: 20 lidha-; 21 errca-; 23 cinta-.

45. to cut: (a) 1 utə-; 2 utwa-; 3 u'a-; 5–7 'wa-; 8 o'a-. (b) 9–11 ndro-; 12 ndo-. (c) 14 ump-; 15, 17–17' ömp-; 16 umpi-. (d) 18 yak; 19 yəkée-; 21 eekə-; 22 əka-; 24–25 yaka-. (e) 26 kuni-; 27 kunta-. (f) 28–29 kunpa-. UR: 4 iror (IM); 13 katlo-; 20 ñi-; 23 waki-; 30 muunga-.

46. to spear: (a) 1 anggya-; 2 nggii-; 11 nggi-. (b) 2–3 igu-; 4 ige-; 5–7 gyu-. (c) 8–10 nji-. (d) 12 ndya-; 30 yina-. (e) 17 waarrp-; 17; warrp-. (f) 21 eema-; 22 əməy-; 23 taama-; 24-25 tama-. (g) 26–27 paka-. (h) 28–29 currka-. UR: 13 pee-; 14 pung-; 15 münhp-; 16 ye(n)ta-; 18 ko'orr; 19 thana-; 20 ri-.

47. to cry: (a) 1 rungga (PRES); 4 nggwa-; 12 nggwala-; 13 nggula-; 28–29 tungkarra-. (b) 2 pudhi-; 3 pugdhi-. (c) 5-7 gwimr-ne-. (d) 8, 10–12 imamca-. (e) 14–15 peey-; 18 pawarr; 19 perrə-. (f) 21 adhi-; 22 ədhii-; 23 paaci- ~ paca-. (g) 24–25 pati-; 26 parri-; 27 pati-. UR: 9 rulcwa-; 16 paabi-; 17 iik- ; 20 rula-; 17' ööth-; 30 uuci-.

48. to laugh: (a) 1 anggərri (PRES); 2 nggarrak-unjii-; 3 nggayk-unjii-; 4 nggitaw-adha-; 5–7 ngga'y-ma; 8 ngga'ak-owa-; 9 ngga'æ-go-; 10 ngga'ma-; 11 nggata-; 12–13 njat-dha-; 14 thengk-; 15 theyngk-; 16 thangkanggi-; 18 thangkar; 21 nggəra-. (b) 17 köp-kee'-; 17' köp- ~ köyp-. (c) 26–27 mangka-. (d) 28–29 miyanta-. UR: 19 mukónə-; 20 mpathirra-; 22 njalnggwu-; 23 tinga-; 24 puncay-warri-; 25 yacarri-; 30 ngaacilangka-.

49. good: (a) 2 uyungambithig; 11 oyongmbwith. (b) 3 cay; 5–7 nje; 8 njæ; 13 nja. (c) 4 ne; 12 ni; 14–15, 17–17', 18 min; 16, 30 mini. (d) 9–10 adhar. (e) 24–25 ngulkurr. (f) 26–27 kurri. (g) 28 cikil; 29 cikal. UR: 1 ikənma; 11 mææg; 19 watáarr; 20 wiingk; 21 almuy ~ alMuy; 22 nuwədə; 23 tapaar; 30 wanthi.

50. bad: (a) 2 mbwucaka; 3 mbyug; 4 mpyucek; 9 mbwug; 13 mbwinthrra. (b) nggarpr; 8 nggorpr. (c) 10, 12 bræ; 11 mbræ. (d) 14–15, 17–17' way; 16 waya; 18 warr; 19 wet; 23 warra; 26 warray. (e) 21 ee-ndhing; 22 ndhi. (f) 24–25 puyun. UR: 1 gatha, w¬cpu; 20 mukwarr; 27 cankan; 28 walkay; wiiki; 30 wii'u. (NOTE: There is a notation saying that 17 *way* is borrowed from 14–16. I don't recall the evidence for this.)

51. person: (a) 1–2 ama; 3–9, 11, 13 ma; 10, 12 m·a; 14–15, 17–17', 18 pam; 19 pam (?); 16, 23–27, 30 pama; 20 aam; 21 aaMə; 22 məy. (b) 28–29 yara.

52. woman: (a) 1 undawa; 5–7 ndrwarm; 8, 10 ndram; 9 ndrwam; 11 ndwa. (b) 2 upugu; 3 puug. (c) 17–17' pu'əth. (d) 24–25 calpu. UR: 4 mbemandh; 12 irrwa; 13 taca; 14 wanc; 15 köw; 16 kudhe; 18 paanth; 19 pakacáalu; 20 wacwac; 21 urrujal; 22 ndhiindhəmə; 23 ngaancu; 26 pancilcarray ~ pancil; 27 puuña; 28 yipi; 29 kumpul; 30 ukulngkumu.

53. to dig: (a) 1 angə-; 3, 5–7 nga-; 8 anga-. (b) 2 ti-; 4 te-; 9 'ay-; 10 i'i-; 11 tre-; 12 iti- ~ ti-; 13 tii-; 14 we'-; 16, 30 wa'i-. (c) 17–17' muc-. (d) 23–25 paka-. (e) 28–29 tiku-. UR: 15 thüüc-; 18 raw; 19 purəmpu-; 20 wupa-; 21 enu-; 22 aləɥ-.

54. stone: (a) 1 athambu (in ERG case) ~; 2 thambaga; 3 thambag. (b) 4, 12 kandkand; 5, 8–9 kandhak; 6–7 kanj; 11 kand. (c) 17 kupəñəm; 17' kupiynm. (d) 26–27 walpa. UR: 4 kupum; 10 præ'; 12 ipwa; 13 kalng; 14 muka; 15 ngaythəpinh; 16 pi'i; 18 therrep; 19 ngoliñ; 20 rriimp; 21 olcing; 22 əlguunhə; 23 nampal; 24 cangka; 25 kulci; 28 tipan; 29 nangkay; 30 kul'a.

55. ground: (a) 2 udhadha; 3 udhadh; 4 odhadh. (b) 5–6, 8–10 nja. (c) 14–15 'aak; 16 'agu; 18 raak; 21 agur; 22 əgaɥrə. (d) 17 nath; 17' nhath. (e) 23–25 pupu. (f) 28–29 cikay. UR: 1 nani; 7 mbri; 11 ngga; 12 abi; 13 ilpi; 19 paath; 20 lthuuw; 26 pulngan ~ purrngan; 28 capu; 30 ngaaci.

56. sun: (a) 1 wunga; 5–7, 11–12 ngwa; 8, 10 nga; 9 onga; 14–15, 17–17', 18 pung; 16 punga; 19 puung; 24, 26–27 pungan; 25 wungar. (b) 2 ntha-langgwanjig; 3 tha-mburrig; 4 ntha-wuy. (c) 28–29 karri. UR: 13 mbwa; 14 kinc; 20 ñaan; 21 errnding; 22 aathyə; 23 ngalan; 30 kampala.

57. moon: (a) 1 acana; 2 ncana; 3 acan; 9–10 canam. (b) 5–6 'andhik; 7 'ayndhik; 8 a'endhik. (c) 14 kep; 16 kapi; 18 kapir. (d) 19 kakéer; 28–29 kakara. (e) 21 othərrək; 22 tharəkən. (f) 24–25 kica. (g) 26–27 kintaan. UR: 4 ipiw; 11 nhandh; 12 athac; 13 olwit; 15 kongəma; 17 ngaykəl; 17' wööthəc; 20 lkiin; 23 waarikan; 30 piithi, taaway.

58. star: (a) 1 unggunggu; 2 nggwulumpangga; 3 nggwupangg. (b) 5 dhwim; 7 ndhwim, (c) 8–10. ongarr. (d) 11, 13 kaktin. (e) 14 thunpa; 15 thönp; 30 thunpi. (f) 17–17' pungər. (g) 23 tawaar; 24–25 tawar. (h) 26–27 kaway. UR: 4 kandkand; 6 ngungkwig; 12 thath; 16 nguca; 18 mer-pork; 19 pathaali; 20 rampirr; 21 oroongətong; 22 arrngəɥlə; 28 kayirra; 29 yirrkincara.

59. wind: (a) 1 alba; 2 aba; 12 alpa; 16 theba. (b) 5–7 yenj; 8 uyanj. (c) 9–10 mburmbwinh. (d) 14 thuun; 15 thöön. (e) 24 muray; 25 muyar. (f) 17–17' muyk. (g) 28 kimpin; 29 kimpirr. UR: 3 aya'; 4 awu; 11 mol; 13 twalt; 18 pun (H and O); 19 makéerr; 20 wiciric; 21 ondhongondh; 22 adhiwngə; 23 kuluwurr; 26 kuyurru; 27 yiway; 30 wunta.

60. water: (a) 1–3 ipi; 5 pi; 30 pi'i. (b) 4, 13 kok. (c) 6–7 pwa'. (d) 8–10, 12 ngog; 11 ngok; 21 oongə; 22 nguw. (e) 14–15, 17–17' ngak; 16 ngaka; 18 ngok. (f) 24–28 pana. UR: 12 awi; 19 yingkáay; 20 waal; 23 puuray; 24 wata (<Eng); 29 kamu.

61. creek: (a) 2 irranhu; 3–4, 8–13 irranh; 5–7 ryanh. (b) 14, 17' punth; 30 puntha. (c) 16 wa'awa; 26 warapa. (d) 28–29 karakal. UR: 1 yati; 4 othakañ (tributary); 15 wo'; 17 ngamp; 16 wa'ap (cog. 16?); 19 manngélp; 20 mantharr; 21 opriganh; 22 ndyə; 23 pirri; 24 patapata; 25 wawupaca; 26 canku; 27 ngancarr.

62. fire: (a) 1 uma; 5–8 mwa; 9–10 mæ; 11 mya; 14, 17–17' thum; 16 thuma; 21 iiMə; 22 mwə; 30 yuma. (b) 2 wukanhu; 3–4, 13 wukanh. (c) 19 peer; 20 wiir; 26 piri; 27 puri. (d) 12 kwu; 23, 29 yuku. UR: 15 wekəñ; 18 paat; 24 wuncu; 24–25 paya (<Eng.); 28 puni.

63. smoke: (a) 1 ucuw; 2 nculu. (b) 3–4 ama. (c) 5–7 bör; 8 ibor; 9 ibör; 10 ibor. (d) 11, 13 wel. (e) 14–15 thok; 16 thoko. (f) 19 peer-kathərr; 20 thirrg. (g) 24–25 kupu. UR: 12 mwunh; 17 kiikəl (?); 17' thiikəl; 18 tomp (C); 21 errkonh; 22 arrju; 23 puluur; 26 cukay; 27 wuncu; 28 karran; 29 punu; 30 nguka.

64. ashes: (a) 2 imp(g)i; 5–7 bi; 8–10, 12 ibi. (b) 15 wekəñ-kayyalp; 17 kayalp. (c) 26–27 kapu. UR: 1 anju; 3 irrinj; 4 ipuun; 11 amamay; 13 ngambay; 14 thum-kurrk; 16 puca; 13 paat-runc (C); 17' thaa'əl; 19 peer-kangkár; 20 riic; 21 onthoogər; 22 ərryəbər; 23 tuuliyar; 24 punci; 25 nulu; 28 cilin; 29 pumpa; 30 purrka.

65. to be burning: (a) 1 wandhyaw (PRES) ~ wandhi-; 2 njinjina (PRES); 3 cici-; 5–7 adhaynd (PRES) ~ adhay-; 8 adhi-; 9 adhayndhi-; 10 nji-; 11 ndhayndh (PRES); 13 njiri-; 14–15 penc-; 16 panci-; 17 pinth-; 17' pec- (TR); 19 pincé-; 20 nca-; 21 ndhi-; 22 ndhiindhənə (PRES). (b) 23 yaaci-; 30 aaci-. (c) 24–25 wacuci-. (d) 26, 28–29 kanta-. UR: 4 iricay (PRES); 12 yicing (PRES); 18 tintarr (C); 27 kupa-; 30 wunta-.

66. meat animal, game: (a) 1, 16 minha; 2 inha; 3 nha; 4, 9–10, 12 ña; 5–7 nhya; 8 ñæ; 14–15, 17–17', 18 minh; 19 miñ; 20 iiñ; 21 inhə; 22 nhyə; 23–27, 30 miña. UR: 11 moth; 13 cipi; 28 calkur; 29 ñalmur.

67. tail: (a) 2 caga; 3, 5–13 cag; 4 thangg. (b) 14–15 mut. (c) 17 thith; 17' thöth. (d) 16 mulu; 18 mul. (e) 28–29 wana. UR: 1 wupu; 11 ulundhak; 19 theen; 20 dhuun; 21 oming; 22 caawnə; 23 yawurriñ; 24 tuki; 25 pici; 26 pulnga, kulal; 27 kampil; 30 pulpan.

68. egg: (a) 2 iwuyu; 3 iwuy. (b) 5–9 paw; 21 apugər. (c) 10–12 ngambay; 13 ngambya. (d) 14 nhepən; 17' nhepən; 18 nhapən. (e) 15 thuk; 16, 30 thuka; 17 thöyk. (f) 24–25 tipurr. (g) 26–27 tingal. (h) 28–29 pampu. UR: 1 unggyini; 4 omarrgandh, mac; 19 miñ-kethém; 20 wuuth; 22 pwəncə; 23 kuntil.

69. dog: (a) 1 utaga; 2 utwa; 3 u'a; 4, 11 twa; 5–7 'wa; 8 0'a; 13 two; 14, 17–17' ku'; 16 ku'a; 18, 23, 28–29 kuta; 19 kutéew; 20 rrwaak; 22 ətwə; 26 kurraa; 27 kutaka; 30 ku'aka. (b) 9 maynd; 10 omindh. (c) 24–23 kaya. UR: 12 atal. 15 ngaakən; 21 iñor.

70. tree: (a) 1 yuku; 2–3 uku; 4 ke; 5–8, 22 ku; 12 kwu; 14–15, 17–17', 18 yuk; 16, 23, 28–30 yuku; 19 yoko; 21 eekə; 24 cuku; 27 cukii. (b) 9–10 kil. (c) 11 cu; 13 cü. (d) 25–26 culpi. UR: 20 lwaanh.

71. leaf: (a) 1 yamba; 11 ambamba. (b) 2 alala; 3–4 alal. (c) 5–7, 9 thundh; 8, 10 thondh. (d) 14 kangk; 30 kangka. (e) 15 thaaləñ; 17 yuk-thaaləñ; 17' thaaləyn. (f) 16 'engk-kona; 18 ringk-kaal, (g) 19 piirr; 23–25 pirra. (h) 27–28 kupu. UR: 12 ithuy; 13 mbiw; 20 lngkurrg; 21 acuc; 22 əriinggəl; 26 pirrk; 29 marra.

72. vegetable food: (a) 1, 16, 24–25, 27, 30 mayi; 2–4, 8–10, 12–13 ayi; 5–7 ay; 11 nji; 14–15, 17–17', 18 may; 19–20 maay; 21 aayə; 22 əyi; 26 maa. UR: 23 kuntil; 28 wucu; 29 mankun.

73. east: (a) 1 awac; 2–3 awæ; 4, 8–10 awar; 5–7 ar; 11 away; 12 awandow; 13 awam; 14–15, 17' kaaw; 16 kawa; 18 irr-kaw; 20 gathing; 30 kaawa. (b) 19 lá-nakay; 21 akan; 22 ka; 23, 27 naka. (c) 28–29 kuliñ. UR: 17 kaampəlk; 26 nuu.

74. west: (a) 1 apuñə ~; 2 puñunu; 3 piñun; 4, 12 ipuñ; 11 poñ. (b) 5–7 nhingthang; 8 inhingthæng; 9 nhinhingthængan. (c) 14–15 kuw; 16, 23–27 kuwa; 18 irr-kuw; 21 uwan; 22 əwwə. (d) 13 icolm; 17–17' iithəl. UR: 10 kar; 19 lá-walpi; 20 lung; 28 kampil; 29 tayu; 30 aacula.

75. north: (a) 1 unggidhu; 2 nggwadhu; 3, 9 nggwadh; 4–7 nggwath; 8 nggath; 10 nggadh; 11 nggwithu; 12 nggwandow; 13 nggwim; 14–15 kungk; 16 kungke; 17–17' kungkiy; 18 irr-ungkarr; 19 lá-kungkurri; 20 nggwarriyang; 21 unggan; 22 nggwərə; 23 kungkaarr; 24–25, 27 kungkarr; 26, 28–29 kungkarri; 30 kungkay. UR: 28 yirrkanci (ALT.).

76. south: (a) 1 ibidhu; 2 ibadhu; 3 3, 9–10 ibadh; 4 ipyath; 5–7 beth; 11 ibithu; 12 ipandow; 13 ipim; 14–15 yiip; 16 yibe; 17–17' thiipiy; 18 irr-iparr; 19 lá-yipərri; 20 piyiying; 21 ipan; 22 pyərə; 23–25 ciparr; 26 ciwarri; 30 yiipay. UR: 27 ngara; 28 kuñil; 29 kuyngkurru.

77. up: (a) 1 ambya; 2 ambi; 3 mbii; 4 mber; 5, 9, 12 mbayr; 6–7 mbayring; 8, 10 mbir; 11 mbay; 13 mbe; 17–17' kempiy. (b) 14 ken; 15 keynəy; 16 kanyi; 18 irr-kan; 19 lá-kani; 30 kani. (c) 20 ngkariy; 23 wangkaangkar; 24–25 wangawangkar; 26 wangkar; 27 wangkii. (d) 28 kiña-taykala; 29 yalu-taykala. UR: 21 awur; 22 əbayrə.

78. down: (a) 2 akæ; 3 kæ; 4–5, 8–10 kar; 6–7 karang; 11 kay; 12 kandow; 13 ka; 14 pek; 15, 17' pak; 16 pake; 17 pak-mancək; 30 pakay. (b) 23 pata; 24–25 patapata. (c) 26–27 cilngku. UR: 1 umənja; 18 irr-kop; 19 lá-yakarri; 20 kulcilang; 21 errmon; 22 ərrwitə; 28 kiña-payici; 29 yalu-kali.

79. tomorrow: (a) 5–9 wangthim; 10 wangdhim; 11 owangap. (b) 17 nguultham; 17' ngooltham; 18 ngul; 19 nguláw; 21 olor; 29 ngulka; 30 ngulkuma. (c) 23 wunkuuñ; 24–25 wunkuñ. UR: 1 rpugunma; 2 nthathim; 3 withim; 4 nggetam; 12 ikum; 13 cinom; 14 ngaathəm əngaa'thəm}; 15 ngutampən; 16 yumu; 20 murrangk; 22 əlpungəw; 26 nguma; 27 ngaca; 28 parrayarran.

80. bye and bye: (a) 1 uta; 9 'wa; (b) 2–4, 12 lwa; 13 lwinj; 14–15, 17–17' ngul; 19 ngeel; 21 olə; 22 lwə; 30 ngula. (c) 5–7 kay. (d) 16 yupa; 18 yuup. (e) 24–25 cuma. (f) 26–27 karru. (g) 28–29 kilu. UR: 8 kithi'; 10 ithig; 11 ica; 20 ñingk; 23 karrku.

81. one: (a) 1 nhipima; 2 ipima; 3, 5–7, 10 pim; 4 mpi; 8–9, 11 piman; 30 ñi'ilama. (b) 14–15 thonəm; 16 thonolu; 17–17' thönönəm; 18 thono; 19 thəningkəl. (c) 23 nupuun; 24–25 ñupun. (d) 28–29 yungkul. UR: 4 iñungg; 12 nogol; 13 niyumam; 20 niib; 21 opol; 22 nhawngkənh; 26 ñiwul; 27 kuman.

82. two: (a) 1 ¬dhyama; 2 udhima; 3 udhim; 4 ociim; 5, 8–9 odhith; 6–7 dhwith; 8–9 odhith; 10 odhithig; 11 ithaym; 13 ocim; 14 kucəm; 15 kööcəm; 16 kucele; 18 kuthirr; 23 kuciirra. (b) 12 lwal; 17 pulnəm; 17' pul(ə)nham; 28–29 pulayi. (c) 21 irrmbə; 22 ərrmyə. (d) 24–25 campul; 27 campuul. UR: 19 kuléntirr; 20 mpaak; 26 mulu; 30 pa'amu.

83. three: (a) 1 wucuma; 2 ucumu; 4 com; 5–11 cum. (b) 14–15 ko'ələm; 16 ko'ele. (c) 3 lwapudhim; 17 pulən-thun; 17' pulənh-thun. (d) 26 tawul; 27 takul. (e) 28–29 karpu. UR: 12 marmam; 13 dom; 18 pinəlam; 19 kənówərr; 20 twaaring; 21 əNjər; 22 ərrawngkə; 23 kuntu; 24 mamarra; 25 kulur; 30 kulntu.

84. many: (a) 1 wucuma; 3 cum. (b) 2 unhirringanhu; 4 onhirringañ. (c) 5 rrwi; 7 rrwi-mcayc; 8–12 orri; 12 orrimcath (ALT.). (d) 14–15, 17' yot; 17 yotəm. (e) 16 uyu; 17' uy. (f) 26–27 ngapi. UR: 6 dhawrind; 13 golt; 18 mong; 19 kaari; 20 kurr; 21 amool; 22 ərrbaanjə; 23 kakuwarr; 24 wuupul; 25 narmpa; 28 yunkarr; 29 mungarrmpara; 30 yali.

85. big: (a) 2 wayiga ~ wayima; 3, 10 wayig; 5–9 weg. (b) 15, 17–17' aw. (c) 24–25 yalpay. UR: 1 amə́nma; 4 ikwali; 11 mway; 12 makwu; 13 ndyak; 14 tha'iy; 16 pi'an; 18 ngamal; 19 thaapəl; 20 ñaamil; 21 awocorr; 22 ku–ngarə; 23 warrkaay; 26 pangkal; 27 ngalal; 28 pulkan; 29 cuki; 30 thu'un.

86. small: (a) 5, 8 pwidh; 6–7 pwidhpwa. (b) 9–10 abog. (c) 17–17' eelən [eedn]; (d) 24 pupay; 25 pupan. UR: 1 acimbətha; 2 abuunggwana; 3 awumbyug; 4 ciw; 11 kic; 12 lög; 13 thith; 14 mañ; 15 pök; 16 mapan; 18 mant; 19 tikipíir; 20 ciikir; 21 ñiñəm; 22 ndəylbaw; 23 pica; 26 pipuy; 27 kitilakay; 28 miti; 29 wurraycakan; 30 cu'ucu'u.

87. far: (a) 1 wanhungu; 12 nhong. (b) 2 unggunu; 4 owol; 5–7 guun; 8, 10 ogon; 9, 13 ogol; 11 onggol; 17–17' uungk. (c) 14 kac; 15 kayc; 16, 27, 30 kaci. (d) 23, 25 kalakalpay; 24 kalalakalpay. UR: 18 raak-thorkorr; 19 kaca-kapée; 20 rwaay; 21 aguwal; 22 ərrcu; 26 kakay; 28 tawulu; 29 wampa.

88. near: (a) 2 ipala; 3 ipay; 4, 11 pyal; 5–7 pe; 8 pe-mam; 9–10 pæy-mam; 12 pal-mam; 13 pæl-mam. (b) 14 thinthinth; 15 thinth; 16 thinthu; 30 yincu. (c) 17–17' piim; (d) 23 yupaayku; 24–25 yupaku. (e) 26 pitir ~ pirri; 27 piti. UR: 1 unggμcma; 18 tongken (H and O); 19 kaca-kéyirr; 20 paarrik; 21 alpə; 22 nəwpə; 28 kiña-taa; 29 puurrin.

89. long: (a) 2 unggumu; 3 ungguum; 4 owom; 5–7 gu'uk; 8 ogo'ok; 8–10, 12–13 ogom; 11 onggom; 14–15, 17' uungk; 16 unggu; 30 uungku. (b) 19 kalkárang; 23 kalpaayku; 24 kalpali; 25 kalkakalpay; 26 kalkalay. UR: 1 rukudhi; 17 engkəc; 18 thorkorr; 20 girrilpinh; 21 ompər; 22 əlbwənə; 27 kurran; 28 calngkay; 29 curina.

90. short: (a) 2 umpama; 4 mpwam. (b) 3 ipuul; 5 mbül; 6–7 mbül-pwa; 8 mböl. (c) 9, 11 pwan; 10 ka-pan (ka extremity); 30 kupan. (d) 16 kocin; 21 ocin.gəg; 23 kucin; 30 kucin (?). (e) 13 ilkom; 24–25, 27 kulka. (f) 17–17' murrkən. UR: 1 mangga; 12 oryal; 14 otəng; 15 kalkanh; 18 kon; 19 teekəpəl; 20 withan; 22 tə¶nə; 26 wanti; 28 kuntun; 29 cutu.

91. hard: (a) 2 pwuthaka; 3–5, 8–13 pwuthak; 7 pwuthuk. (b) 14 yantəmp; 30 yantapa. (c) 15 thayən; 16 thayan; 17–17' tharrən; 18 tharrn. (d) 24–25 tanti. (e) 28–29 kakal. UR: 1 rapan; 6 watrak; 19 kurrcáar; 20 lmbaam; 21 aNhən; 22 ərrciwyə; 23 purrpurr; 26 takil; 27 puyal.

92. this: (a) 5–7 ndrwa'; 8 ndra'. (b) 9 layn; 10 lin. (c) 14–15 in; 16 irr; 18 inh (/i-/ prox, as opposed to /a-/ dist). (d) 17 anth; 17' anh-, nhaanth. (e) 21 unə; 22 nwə. (f) 23–24 yi; 25 yiña; 27 yingu. (g) 28 kiña ~; 29 ngiña ~, UR: 1 urra; 2 tyang; 3 lunh; 4 yin; 11 nggo; 12 iyi, nggit; 13 ana; 19 laa; 20 kul; 26 kulu; 30 ngi'i.

93. what: (a) 1–5, 8–13 ani; 6–7 anay; 14–15, 17–17' ngeen; 16 ngaari; 18 ngaan; 19 ngəntí; 20 ni; 21 anə; 22 nangənə; 23 ngana; 30 ngaani. (b) 24–25 wañu; 26 ñii; 27 wañii; 29 waña. UR: 28 miña.

94. who: (a) 1 arri-dhu (ERG case) ~; 2 arrinha; 3 'inh; 4 ateń; 5–7, 9 'aynh; 8 a'enh; 10 a'inh; 11–12 atinh; 13 ati; 14–15 wee'; 17' wee'iy; 30 waa'i. (b) 16 wayi; 17 weey. (c) 18 waanh; 23 wañu; 24 wancu; 25, 28 waña; 26 cuu; 27 wañaa; 29 wañuna. UR: 19 ngaaniń; 20 nggul; 21 anung ~ okol (ERG); 22 əmawngə.

95. where: (a) 1 andungu; 2 antulu; 3 tyun; 4 andut; 5, 8 ndron; 6–7 ndrong; 9 trongon; 10 tron; 11 tot; 12–13 ndot; 14 want-in; 15 want-inh; 16 wantu; 17 want-iń; 17' want-; 30 wantu. (b) 18 wanthan; 23 wancarra; 24 wancapurr; 25 wancapu; 26 caa; 27 wancaa; 28–29 wuncan. (c) 19 wárrəm; 21 arriin; 22 ərraymbə. UR: 20 thangkal.

96. I: (a) 1 ayʉba; 2 ayunga; 3 ayung; 4 ayong; 5–7 awng; 8–10, 12–13 ayong; 11 njong; 14–15, 17–17', 18 ngay; 16 ngaya; 19 ngántu; 20 ngaay; 21 aayə; 22 yaw; 23–25, 27, 30 ngayu; 26 ngawu; 28 ngaca; 29 ngaca (ERG) ~ ngaypa (NOM).

97. you: (a) 1 andʉba; 2–3 tyu; 4 nti; 5–8 ndru; 9–10 tru; 11 ti; 12 ndyu; 13 ndwin; 14–15 nhint; 16 nhinta; 17–17', 18 nhunt; 19 yeen; 20 aant; 21 eenə; 22 niw; 23, 27 ñuntu; 24–25 yuntu; 26 ñurra; 28 nginta; 29 nginta (ERG) ~ nginpa (NOM); 30 nguna.

98. he: (a) 1 uluba; 2–3, 5–10, 12 lu; 4 lyu; 11, 13 li; 14–15 nhil; 16 nhila; 17-17', 18 nhul; 19 yélu; 20 lab; 21 eelə; 22 liw; 23 ñulu; 24 nulu; 25 yulu; 30 ngula. (b) 28 payi ~; 29 paympayi ~. UR: 26 kuci; 27 ngungu.

99. we dual inclusive: (a) 1 aliba; 2 lingg; 4 leli; 5–7 layngk; 8 lingk; 9 layng; 10 linggay; 11 layl; 12 lil; 13 lel; 14–15, 17–17', 18 ngal; 16 ngale; 19 ngel; 20 ngaal; 21 ali-; 22 laynə; 23–25, 27, 30 ngali; 28–29 ngalici. UR: 3 kwuy; 26 nganci.

100. you dual: (a) 1 ipula; 2 ipulu; 3 ipuy; 4 mpyul; 5–7 piy; 8, 10 poy; 9 pöy; 11, 13 pyul; 12 pol; 14–15, 18 nhip; 16 nhipa; 17–17' nhupəl; 19 yipéel; 20 wal; 21 ipaal; 22 pilə; 23 yupaal; 24–25 yupal; 28–29 ñupalaci; 30 ngu'ula pa'amu. UR: 26 ñurrampa (partially cognate); 27 ñuntumuku (partially cognate).

Appendix B: Other Lexical Materials

1. Umpila-Ya'u comparisons with other Middle Paman languages

This consists of 67 items of 100-word list extracted from Thompson (1976), O'Grady (1976), and Harris and O'Grady (1976); order of items is alphabetical by gloss; numbers followed by period correspond to numbers in Appendix A.

- 85. big mukana; 44. bite patha- 14, 15, 16, 17, 17', 18, 30; 31. black thungku 30; 65. burn 'unta-, aaci- (tr) 30; 38. climb piingka- 30; 61. creek 'atapa 16, 26 ((?));

- 47. cry 'ungka-; 45. cut muunga- 30; 28. die maka- 30; 53. dig wa'i- 14, 16, 30; 69. dog ku'aaka 14, 16, 17, 17', 18, 30; 78. down pakaya 14, 15, 16, 17', 30; 27. eat yangku- 30; 68. egg thun.ka, wuympa 15, 16, 17, 30 ((?)); 4. eye ku'un 30; 37. fall pungka-; 22. fat ku'i 30; 62. fire yuma 14, 16, 17, 17', 30; 42. give ngangka- 30;

- 35. go waatha- 30; 49. good miintha 14, 15, 16, 17, 17', 18 ((?)); 16. hand ma'a 14, 15, 16, 17, 17' 30; 98. he ngulu 14, 15, 16, 17, 17', 18, 30; 1. head pa'an;

- 30. hear ngami- 30; 43. hit tha'i-; 26. hungry 'uuli 30; 96. I ngayu 14, 15, 16, 17, 17', 18,30; 18. knee pungku 14, 15, 16, 17, 17', 18, 30; 48. laugh ngaaci- 30; 71. leaf kangka 14, 30; 40. leave wana- 14,

15, 16, 17, 17' 18, 30; 89. long 'uungku 14, 15, 16, 17', 30; 84. many kulima, yuthu, mukamukan; 66. meat miña 14, 15, 16, 17, 17', 18, 30; 7. mouth kaama; 88. near (y)iñcu, kaayina 14, 15, 16, 30; 5. nose nhiyi 30; 75. northeast kungkay 14, 15, 16, 17, 17', 18, 30; 81. one ñi'i- 30; 51. person pama 14, 15, 16, 17, 17', 18, 30; 36. run pintipinti(i)-; 29. see kiiki-, kuuca-; 34. sit nhiina- 14, 15, 17, 17', 18; 24. skin kulkul; 86. small cu'uci 30; 76. south yiipalu 17, 17', 30; 73. southeast kaaway 14, 15, 16, 17', 18, 30; 32. speak kuupatha-; 46. spear wuthaa-, yina- (*thatha*) 30; 33. stand paa'i-; 13. stomach thul'i 14, 15, 17, 17', 30;

- 54. stone kul'a 30; 67. tail pulpan 30; 39. take ala-; 92. his ngi'i 30; 83. three kukuthi; 41. throw waayi-; 70. tree yuku 14, 15, 16, 17, 17', 18, 30;
- 82. two pa'aamu 30; 77. up kani 14, 15, 16, 18, 30; 72. vegetable food mayi 14, 15, 16, 17, 17', 18, 30; 99. we (incl) ngampula [*ngali* not found]; 93. what ngaani 14, 15, 16, 17, 17', 18, 30; 95. where wantuna 14, 15, 16, 17, 17', 30; 52. woman wayimu;
- 97. you ngunu 14, 15, 16, 17, 17', 18, 30.

2. Cognation judgements

The number in parenthesis represents the language; numbers following that correspond to the Umpila-Ya'u items assumed to be cognate with the corresponding item in the language indicated; shared percentages are indicated in square brackets:

- (14): 44, 53, 69, 78, 62, 49, 16, 98, 96, 18, 71, 40, 89, 66, 88, 75, 51, 34, 73, 13, 70, 77, 72, 93, 95, 97. [26=.388]
- (15): 44, 78, 68, 49, 16, 98, 96, 18, 40, 89, 66, 88, 75, 51, 34, 73, 13, 70, 77, 72, 93, 95, 97. [23=.343]
- (16): 44, 61, 53, 69, 78, 68, 62, 49, 16, 98, 96, 18, 40, 89, 66, 88, 75, 51, 73, 70, 77, 72, 93, 95, 97. [25=.373]
- (17): 44, 69, 68, 62, 49, 16, 98, 96, 18, 40, 66, 75, 51, 34, 76, 13, 70, 72, 93, 95, 97. [21=.313]
- (17'): 44, 69, 78, 62, 49, 16, 98, 96, 18, 40, 89, 66, 75, 51, 34, 76, 73, 13, 70, 72, 93, 95, 97. [23=.343]
- (18): 44. 69, 49, 98, 96, 18, 40, 66, 75, 51, 34, 73, 70, 77, 72, 93, 97. [17=.254]

6. WIK SUBGROUP LEXICAL HISTORY

- (30): 44, 31, 65, 38, 45, 28, 53, 69, 78, 27, 68, 4, 22, 62, 42, 35, 16, 98, 30, 26, 96, 18, 48, 71, 40, 89, 66, 88, 5, 75, 81, 51, 86, 76, 73, 46, 13, 54, 67, 92, 70, 82, 77, 72, 93, 95, 97. [47=.701]

3. Pakanh vocabulary (L14') (from Hamilton and Yam 1994)

- 14. arm puntha; 11. armpit maapu; 64. ashes thuma-nhuuta; 50. bad waya;
- 85. big paapa; 44. bite athang; 31. black nhowantha; 21. blood cookarra; 23. bone yempe; 65. burn ana-pancan; 80. bye and bye ngula; 38. climb kani mathana;
- 61. creek piku; 47. cry paayin, payinga; 45. cut yeka; 28. die uthama;
- 53. dig wa'en; 69. dog ku'a; 6. ear thatu; 73. east kaawo; 27. eat ngolkana;
- 68. egg nhapi; 15. elbow yungka; 4. eye mee'a; 37. fall ancinga; 87. far ana-kaci;
- 22. fat yi'i; 62. fire thuma; 20. foot tha'u; 42. give mamanga; 35. go iyanga;
- 49. good mini; 55. ground aaku; 16. hand polama, ma'a-; 1. head weli; 30. hear ngayanga; 43. hit ingáypikung; 26. hungry maaci; 96. I ngaya; 18. knee pungku;
- 48. laugh thangkina; 71. leaf kangka; 40. leave be wumpa; 12. liver waana;
- 89. long oongko; 84. many yoto; 66. meat minha; 57. moon kapi; 7. mouth thaa;
- 3. nape muci; 88. near pala (hither?) [subtract]; 75. north kungke; 5. nose kaa-kuthu; 81. one thonam; 51. person pama; 29. see thathunga; 34. sit nhiinanga;
- 24. skin aku; 19. shin thuumpa, thumpa-yen.kan; 10. shoulder ingka;
- 86. small maña; 63. smoke thuma-nguka/thoko; 76. south (y)iipe; 32. speak waathinga; 33. stand thangana; 58. star kapi, othorro, thudnpi; 13. stomach ngangka, nhaapaci, thipa (guts); 54. stone muka; 56. sun kinca, punga;
- 67. tail mu(u)yu; 39. take kaalanga; 17. thigh pilu; 92. this ma'a (questionable) [subtract]; 83. three ko'alm; 41. throw thaa'inga; 79. tomorrow manga-nhaathama; 9. tongue thaa-ngantha, thaapa; 8. tooth kanca, kwaanga(?);

- 70. tree yuku; 82. two kucham; 77. up kani; 72. vegetable food mayi;
- 60. water wece; 74. west ku(u)wa, yongko; 93. what nganhi; 95. where wantu;
- 94. who inhu-waa'e; 59. wind wunta; 52. woman wancu.
- [Total viable comparisons: 87]

4. Pakanh comparisons with other Middle Paman

- (14–14'): 14, 50, 44(?), 65, 80, 38, 47, 28, 53, 69, 73, 68, 15, 4, 87, 62, 20, 35, 49, 55, 16, 30, 43, 26, 96, 18, 48, 71, 89, 84, 66, 57, 7, 75, 5, 81, 51, 29, 34, 19, 86, 63, 76, 33, 58, 13, 54, 56, 83, 41, 9, 70, 82, 77, 72, 74, 93, 95, 94, 52. [60=.689]
- (15–14'): 14, 50, 44(?), 65, 80, 47, 73, 4, 37, 87, 20, 49, 55, 16, 30, 43, 26, 96, 18, 48, 89, 84, 66, 7, 75, 5, 81, 51, 29, 34, 19, 10, 63, 76, 33, 58, 13, 56, 83, 41, 9, 70, 82, 77, 72, 74, 93, 95, 94. [49=.563]
- (16–14'): 14, 50, 44(?), 65, 38, 28, 53, 69, 73, 37, 87, 22, 62, 20, 49, 55, 16, 30, 43, 26(?), 96, 18, 48, 12, 89, 66, 57, 7, 3, 75, 5, 81, 51, 34, 24, 19, 10, 63, 76, 33, 56, 83, 41, 9, 70, 82, 77, 72, 74, 93, 95. [51=.586]
- (17–14'): 14, 50, 44(?), 65, 80, 69, 62, 20, 49, 16, 30, 26, 96, 18, 84, 66, 7, 75, 5, 81, 51, 34, 19, 76, 33, 13, 56, 39, 41, 9, 70, 72, 93, 95, 94. [35=.402]
- (17'–14'): 14, 50, 44(?), 65(?), 80, 69, 73, 68, 62, 20, 49, 16, 30, 26, 96, 18, 89, 84, 66, 7, 75, 5, 81, 51, 34, 76, 33, 13, 56, 39, 41, 9, 70, 72, 93, 95, 94. [37=.425]
- (18–14'): 14, 50, 44(?), 47, 45, 69, 73, 68, 4, 49, 55, 16, 30, 96, 18, 48, 66, 57, 75, 5, 81, 51, 34, 19, 76, 33, 56, 39, 9, 70, 82, 77, 72, 74, 93. [35=.402]
- (30–14'): 14, 11, 44(?), 80, 53, 69, 73, 15, 87, 62, 20, 49, 16, 30, 96, 18, 71, 89, 66, 7, 75, 5, 51, 29, 34, 19, 10, 63, 76, 58, 13, 9, 8, 70, 77, 72, 93, 95, 94, 59. [40=.459]

5. Nganhcara (Uwanh patrilect) vocabulary (L16') (from Ian Smith, pers. comm., 1985/1995)

- 2. forehead ngulu ngangka; 3. nape muci thaa; 4. eye thanta; 5. nose kaa kuthu;
- 6. ear kono; 7. mouth thaa; 8. tooth kanu; 9. tongue thaa ngantha;

6. WIK SUBGROUP LEXICAL HISTORY

- 10. shoulder ingki; 11. armpit yiwan; 12. liver kogom; 13. stomach ngangka, thupi; 14. arm puntha; 15. elbow punti; 16. hand ma'a; 17. thigh kuman;
- 18. knee pungku; 20. foot tha'u; 21. blood kamu; 22. fat yi'i, yoko; 24. skin aku;
- 25. headhair yengan; 26. hungry madhji; 27. eat mungga; 28. die uthuma;
- 29. see uwi; 30. hear ngii; 31. black ngunhca; 32. speak thawa; 33. stand thana;
- 34. sit nhiina/e; 35. go uwa; 36. run nunpa, mudba; 37. fall anhci; 38. climb mata; 39. take maa, mama, kalu; 40. leave wanta; 41. throw thii; 42. give waa, adha;
- 43. hit pigu; 44. bite patha; 45. cut umpi; 46. spear yenta; 47. cry paabi;
- 48. laugh thangkangki; 49. good mini; 50. bad waya; 51. person pama;
- 52. woman kuyu; 53. dig wa'i; 54. stone muka; 56. sun punga; 57. moon kapi;
- 59. wind theba; 60. water ngaka; 61. creek wa'awa; 62. fire thuma;
- 63. smoke thoko; 64. ashes puthca; 65. burn panci; 66. meat animal minha;
- 68. egg minha thuka; 69. dog ku'a; 70. tree yuku; 71. leaf enga; 72. veg food mayi;
- 73. east kawa; 74. west kuwa; 75. north kungke; 76. south yibe; 77. up kanhnyi;
- 78. down pake; 79. tomorrow puga; 81. one thono; 82. two kuce; 84. many uyu;
- 85. big yoko; 86. small mepen; 87. far kaci; 88. near thinthu; 89. long unggu;
- 90. short kaarin; 91. hard thayan; 92. this iiru; 93. what waari; 94. who wayi;
- 95. where wantu; 96. I ngaya; 97. you nhinta; 98. he nhila; 99. we du incl ngale; 100. you du nhipa. [92]

6. Uwanh comparisons with other Middle Paman

- (16'–14): 2, 5, 6, 7, 9, 11, 13, 14, 16, 17, 18, 20, 25, 26, 27, 28, 30, 32, 33, 34, 38, 39, 40, 41, 43, 44, 45, 48, 49, 50, 51, 53, 54, 56, 57, 60, 62, 63, 65, 66, 69, 70, 72, 73, 74, 75, 76, 77, 78, 81, 82, 87, 88, 89, 92, 93, 95, 96, 97, 98, 99, 100. [62=.673]
- (16'–15): 2, 5, 6, 7, 10, 11, 13, 14, 16, 17, 18, 20, 26, 27, 30, 32, 33, 34, 37, 39, 40, 41, 43, 44, 45, 48, 49, 50, 51, 56, 60, 63, 65, 66, 68, 70, 72, 73, 74, 75, 76, 77, 78, 81, 82, 87, 88, 89, 91, 92, 93, 95, 96, 97, 98, 99, 100. [57=.619]
- (16'–16): 2, 3, 4, 5, 6, 7, 8, 9, 10, 11, 14, 15, 16, 17, 18, 20, 21, 22, 24, 25, 26, 27, 28, 30, 31, 32, 33, 34, 36, 37, 38, 39, 40, 41, 42, 43, 44, 45, 46, 47, 48, 49, 50, 51, 52(?), 53, 56, 57, 59, 60, 61, 62, 63, 64, 65, 66, 68, 69, 70, 71(?), 72, 73, 74, 75, 76, 77, 78, 81, 82, 84, 86, 87, 88, 89, 91, 92, 93, 94, 95, 96, 97, 98, 99, 100. [82=.89]
- (16'–17): 4, 5, 7, 13, 14, 16, 18, 20, 26, 30, 33, 34, 40, 41, 44, 45, 49, 50, 51, 56, 60, 62, 65, 66, 68, 69, 70, 72, 75, 76, 78, 81, 91, 93, 94, 95, 96, 97, 98, 99, 100. [41=.446]
- (16'–17'): 4, 5, 7, 12, 13, 14, 16, 18, 20, 26, 30, 33, 34, 40, 41, 44, 45, 49, 50, 51, 56, 60, 62, 66, 69, 70, 72, 73, 75, 76, 78, 81, 84, 91, 93, 95, 96, 97, 98, 99, 100. [41=.446]
- (16'–18): 14, 15, 17, 18, 21, 25, 27, 30, 33, 34, 40, 44, 48, 49, 50, 51, 56, 57, 60, 66, 69, 70, 71(?), 72, 73, 74, 75, 76, 77, 81, 82, 91, 92, 93, 96, 97, 98, 99, 100. [38=.413]
- (16'–30): 7, 10, 13, 14, 16, 17, 18, 20, 21, 25, 34, 40, 44, 49, 51, 53, 62, 66, 68, 69, 70, 72, 73, 75, 76, 30, 78, 87, 88, 89, 93, 95, 96, 97, 98, 99, 100. [37=.402]

Uwanh/Wik Averages: (i) Wik minus Muminh: .548; (ii) Mn and Me: .646.

7

Wik Subgroup grammatical history

Ken Hale[1]

In this chapter, linguistic evidence drawn from a particular area of Wik and Middle Paman grammar (specifically, the systems of dependent pronominals) is used to support the following assertions in regard to Wik tenure in the area now associated with the peoples that speak Wik languages:

i. The modern Wik grammatical systems have evolved over a period of time well in excess of that which separates 1788 from the present.

ii. Diversity within the Wik language family requires recognition of at least three subgroups, and simplicity considerations argue in favour of the idea that the observed linguistic diversity must have developed in situ, in the region now occupied by Wik-speaking peoples.

iii. It follows that the Wik-speaking peoples have resided in their present location for a period that certainly exceeds the recent centuries at issue in this case; their residence in the region most probably extends to millennia.

---

1   This was written in 1997.

Introduction

Following approximately the same procedure as in Chapter 6, additional linguistic evidence will be presented here in support of the proposition that the Wik-speaking peoples of Cape York Peninsula have resided in their present location for an unknown period of time beginning long before the landing of the First Fleet in 1788.[2] Here, the evidence will be drawn from the domain of grammar, specifically from the morphology and syntax of pronominal elements. I will take the Wik Subgroup to consist of the clans and communities so identified in Sutton (1978) and in references cited there. For the purposes of the present discussion, I will make use of linguistic material from a representative sample of the Wik languages, including the following:

Mn: Wik-Mungkan(h)
Me: Wik Me'nh, Wik Ep
KN: Kugu Nganhcarra
Nr: Wik Ngatharr, Wik A(a)lkan(h)
Nn: Wik Ngathan(h)

The abbreviations given here follow the usage of Sutton (1978). As the list indicates, members of the Wik group, properly conceived, differ in their use of the Paman terms for language, and accordingly in the name given to the speech-form with which they are associated—some use the term derived from *wika*, others use that derived from *kuuku*.[3] Both are legitimate forms descending from a Paman ancestor language and, as such, are genuine elements of the Cape York Peninsula linguistic heritage. For the sake of simplicity, we will refer to the groups that are of interest here as Wik, following established tradition in the anthropological and linguistic literature.

The five speech-forms listed above have been chosen because they represent reasonably well the extent of linguistic diversity within the Wik group as a whole; and, to some extent, they represent as well the linguistic characteristics of three discernible Wik subgroups, to wit, (i) Mn–Me, (ii) Nr–Nn, and (iii) the Kugu Nganhcarra subgroup (Smith and Johnson

---

2   Hale here uses 'location' broadly. A number of Wik languages have localised but discontinuous associations with particular places. For the details of this partly mosaic pattern, compare Table 5.10 and Maps A2.1–A2.13, this volume: PS.
3   Asterisks denote reconstructed proto-forms in an ancestral stage of the language: PS.

1985, 1986; Smith 1986), abbreviated KN and represented here by Mm (Kugu Muminh, referred to as Wik Muminh in Hale's 1960 notes) and by Kugu Uwanh (Smith and Johnson 1985). In addition to linguistic materials from these Wik groups, we will make reference to materials from other members of the Middle Paman branch of the Paman (or Pama-Maric) language family, and to materials from Paman languages outside the Middle Paman branch. All of this is relevant to the question of the long-term residence of the Wik peoples in Western Cape York Peninsula.

The Wik languages belong to the Middle Paman branch of Paman (cf. Hale 1976c). Other Middle Paman languages include Kuuk Thaayorre (Ta) to the south and the Kaanju-Ya'u-Umpila (Ka, Ya) language to the east. Material from these languages will be involved in our discussions, to some extent. Linguistic data from Middle Paman languages are taken from sources indicated below:

Wik

Mn: Hale notes (1960); Kilham et al. (1986)
Me: Hale notes (1960)
KN: Hale notes (1960); Johnson (English–Nganhcara glossary, 1989, received 1995); Smith and Johnson (1985, 1986); Smith (1986)
Nr: Hale notes (1960)
Nn: Sutton (1995a)

Non-Wik (South)

Ta: Hale notes (1960); Hall (1976a, 1976b)

Non-Wik (East)

Ka: Hale notes (1960)
Ya: Harris and O'Grady (1976); Thompson (1976)

The topic of this discussion is a particular aspect of the grammar of the Wik languages and their Paman relatives of Cape York Peninsula. Specifically, we will be concerned with the grammar of pronouns in the languages, and we will present data that reveal the degree of diversity that exists in the Middle Paman family. As in the first part, we will argue that the diversity observed within the family is relevant to the question of long-term residence of the Middle Paman peoples and, therefore, of the Wik-speaking peoples themselves, in the region they currently occupy. The argument is based on the following premises:

i. linguistic diversity takes time to develop
ii. the Middle Paman diversity at issue here developed in situ
iii. the time required for such diversity to develop is equal to or greater than some number of years.

It will be argued that the diversity found in the Middle Paman and Wik pronominal systems could not have developed in a shorter time than that which separates the year 1788 from the present. The evidence in support of the temporal dimension of this account will be obtained by comparing the Middle Paman situation with comparable situations in other languages for which there are historical records chronicling earlier stages and, therefore, telling us approximately how long it has taken for a given language or language family to progress from one stage to another in the evolution of a particular grammatical system.

Wik and Middle Paman pronominal systems

In addition to a standard Paman system of independent pronouns, the Wik languages, and their Middle Paman relatives to the east (i.e. Kaanju, Kuuku-Ya'u and Umpila), possess systems of dependent pronouns ranging in character from the type commonly termed *clitic pronouns* to the type properly termed pronominal *suffixes* functioning in a system of person *agreement*.

It is the properties and behaviour of the dependent pronouns that will be of primary interest here, since this is an aspect of Middle Paman grammar in which diversity is amply represented. Kuuk Thaayorre (Ta) does not have dependent pronouns,[4] and assuming it to be a true member of Middle Paman, its lack of these elements is relevant to the question of time and the progress of linguistic change in the grammar of pronouns. This issue will be taken up at a later time. The relevant facts of Middle Paman pronominal systems will be presented in four subsections below—three

---

4   A manuscript reader points out that it appears that Thaayorre does have dependent pronouns. See Gaby (2017): PS.

corresponding to languages of the Wik Subgroup (including those using the language classifier Kugu in place of Wik), and another corresponding to the eastern Middle Paman neighbours of the Wik. We begin with Wik-Me'nh and Wik-Mungkan.

Wik-Me'nh (Me) and Wik-Mungkan (Mn) pronominals

These two languages are closely similar in their pronominal systems. The two make use of both *independent* and *dependent* pronouns, also sometimes referred to as free and bound. The former, like full noun phrases, carry stress or accent, and they can be uttered in isolation or in any 'argument position' (e.g. subject, object, indirect object), like any full noun phrase. The latter, however, are unstressed (atonic) and phonologically dependent—they must, so to speak, 'lean' on some other word. Typically, in the Middle Paman languages, and in Cape York generally, dependent pronominals must have a 'host' on their left. That is to say, they are enclitics or suffixes. The properties of Wik-Me'nh and Wik-Mungkan set them slightly apart from their other Middle Paman cousins. They will be treated in two subsections below.

Before actually presenting Wik forms, it is appropriate to make a brief remark about the spelling system used in examples here. Some of the Wik languages, including Wik-Me'nh, Wik-Mungkan, Wik-Ngathan, and Wik-Ngatharr, have undergone an important sound change that has resulted in the reduction of unstressed post-consonantal vowels—i.e. unstressed vowels in the V-position of CV syllables. In the modern spoken languages, these reduced vowels can be realised in three ways: (i) as zero, i.e. deleted altogether, (ii) as a brief central vowel of the type commonly called 'schwa', or (iii) as a full low, or low front, *a*-like vowel. The third of these realisations is found most often word-finally, before a pause, when the utterance terminates in a two-syllable dipping-then-rising intonation characteristic of a common mode of delivery. The other two realisations are typical of non-final positions and of utterance-final position with falling and fading intonation. What is relevant here is that these reduced vowels are omitted in the orthography used in citing examples in this essay. This orthography differs, therefore, from that used in recent standard works on Wik-Mungkan, in which the reduced vowels are represented with the vowel *a* (e.g. in Kilham et al. 1986). The usage adopted here is merely an orthographic convention, and the omission of reduced vowels should not be taken to imply that those segments are entirely absent phonologically—rather, each corresponds to a position (or 'slot') in the syllabic structure, which can be realised as a vocalic nucleus under appropriate prosodic conditions. There is a minor irritation that results from this convention: true consonant clusters must occasionally be distinguished from 'false' clusters resulting from orthographic omission of vowels, the latter being written with an intervening dot where necessary (i.e. 'false' clusters are represented C.C, while true clusters are represented CC, but the distinction is made only where absolutely necessary).[5]

Wik-Me'nh

The following sentences exemplify certain essential features of free and dependent pronominals in Wik-Me'nh:

(1) Wik-Me'nh:
 (a) Ngay   enc-ng-ak.
     1.NOM   fall-1S-FUT
     'I will fall.'
 (b) Nhip   aak   ngeen   thath-nh-ip.
     22.NOM time   what   see-PST-22S
     'When did you two see him.'
 (c) Pathpath-nh-ny   ngaakn-ng.
     bite-PST-1O   dog-ERG
     'The dog bit me.'
 (d) Ngany   pam-ng   peeyk-nh-ny.
     1.ACC   man-ERG   hit-PST-1O
     'The man hit me.'
 (e) Ngany   peeyk-nh-pul(-ny).
     1.ACC   hit-PST-33s(-1O)
     'They (two) hit me.'

---

5   Note that in my chapters I use the Kilham et al. (1986) orthography for Wik-Mungkan, but for Wik-Ngathan and Wik-Ngatharr I use the following system. Schwa is represented by /e/. But there is also a phoneme /e/ that occurs in the first syllable of a word. That is the vowel with primary word stress. It may also appear in the first syllable of the second part of a compound. In that case, I place a hyphen just before the second part of the compound. Hence in my script *kampel* 'quickly' is pronounced [kampəl], *kethen* 'yamstick' is pronounced [kɛthən], and *key-elp* 'unclear water' is pronounced [kɛjɛlp]: PS.

(f) Ngal   wonk   in   wak-l-ak.
    12.NOM   bank   this   follow-12S-FUT
    'We (you and I) will follow this river bank.'

The free pronouns will be considered first. With just the sample of pronouns appearing in (1a–f), it can be seen that pronouns express three grammatical categories: *person*, *number* and *case*. Thus, for example, the pronominal form *ngay* embodies the following categories:

(2) Grammatical categories expressed in the Wik-Me'nh first person singular pronoun *ngay*:

   (a) first person (glossed 1);

   (b) singular number (glossed with single digit, 1, in contrast to dual number, glossed with double digit, 11, and plural, glossed with triple digit, 111); and

   (c) nominative case (glossed NOM, as opposed to accusative case, glossed ACC, e.g. *ngany* in [1d–e]).

Wik-Me'nh, like all Wik languages, has the case system that has come to be called 'split ergative'. It is referred to in this way because nouns and pronouns exhibit different patterns of case inflection—nouns show an ergative pattern, while pronouns use the nominative-accusative system. According to the ergative system employed by nouns the subject of a transitive clause is in the ergative case (ERG), while the subject of an intransitive and the object of a transitive are in the unmarked case, which we call the nominative (NOM) here, though it is also called the 'absolutive' in much linguistic literature. The ergative pattern of case marking is exemplified in the following sentences:

(3) Wik-Me'nh:

   (a) Pam   wu'-nh.
       man   whistle-PST
       'The/a man whistled.'

   (b) Ngaakn   enc-ny.
       dog   fall-PST
       'The/a dog fell.'

(c) Pam-ng   ngaakn   thath-nh.
    man-ERG   dog   see-PST
    'The man saw the/a dog.'

(d) Ngaakn-ng   pam   thath-nh.
    dog-ERG   man   see-PST
    'The dog saw the/a man.'

In (3a–b) the nouns *pam* 'person, man' and *ngaakn* 'dog' appear without an overt case ending, as required where a noun functions as the subject of an intransitive clause. The same nouns appear as object in the transitive sentences (3c–d), and here as well they are uninflected for case, as required. In both cases, we say that these nouns are in the *nominative* case. But when a noun appears as the subject of a transitive clause, as in (3c–d), it is overtly marked for case, by means of the *ergative* case ending *-ng*, hence *pam-ng* 'man-ERG', *ngaakn-ng* 'dog-ERG':

(4) The case of Wik-Me'nh nouns (N) in subject and object function.

Ergative:	*Nominative*:
N-ng	N-Ø
pam-ng	pam-Ø
ngaakn-ng	ngaakn-Ø
(subject of transitive)	(subject of intransitive, object of transitive)

By contrast with the situation just described, pronouns conform to the nominative-accusative pattern exemplified by the first person singular pronoun in the following sentences:

(5) Wik-Me'nh:

(a) Ngay   enc-ng-ak.
    1.NOM   fall-1S-FUT
    'I will fall.'

(b) Ngay   ngaakn   thath-nh-iy.
    1.NOM   dog   see-PST-1S
    'I saw the/a dog.'

(c) Ngany   pam-ng   peeyk-nh-ny.
    1.ACC   man-ERG   hit-PST-1O
    'The man hit me.'

Here, the pronominal subject is invariably *ngay*, taking the form traditionally called nominative whether the clause is transitive or intransitive. The pronominal object in (5c) is specially marked, however, appearing in the accusative case, *ngany*. This is the general pattern for Wik-Me'nh pronouns, as set out in (6):

(6) Wik-Me'nh subject and object pronouns:

	Subject (Nominative)	*Object* (Accusative)
1	ngay	ngany
2	nhint	nhin
3	nhil	nhin
12	ngal	ngal-n
22	nhip	nhip-n
33	pul	pul-n
11(1)	ngan	ngan-n
122	ngamp	ngamp-n
222	nhiy	nhiy-n
333	than	than-n

As mentioned earlier, a single-digit gloss is for singular number, a two-digit gloss is for dual number, and a three-digit gloss is for plural. First, second and third persons are represented by 1, 2 and 3 respectively; 11(1), abbreviating 11 and 111, is for first person exclusive (i.e. a group including speaker but excluding the addressee), while 12 and 122 are for first inclusive (i.e. a group including both the speaker and the addressee).

The non-singular pronouns in (6) show clearly that it is the accusative that is overtly marked for case, being extended by the accusative suffix *-n*. The nominative, by comparison, is relatively unmarked. In addition to the forms tabulated here, Wik-Me'nh also possesses oblique pronominal forms, e.g. the dative (DAT): 1 *ngath*, 2 *nhungk*, 3 *nhung*; 12 *ngal-nt*; 22 *nhip-ng*; 33 *pul-nt*; 11(1) *ngan-nt*; 122 *ngamp-r*; 222 *nhiy-nt*; 333 *than-nt*. Here again, it is clear that the non-singular forms are overtly marked by means of perspicuous suffixes attached to the pronominal base identical to the unmarked form used in the nominative.

Our primary interest, of course, is in the *dependent* pronominal elements of Wik-Me'nh. The sentences of (1) illustrate the basic pattern, according to which dependent pronominals are suffixed to the verb. In (7), pronominal suffixes corresponding to the subject and the object are presented. They conform to the nominative-accusative pattern, as indicated—accordingly, the suffixes in the left-hand column are construed with the subject, whether the clause is transitive or intransitive, while those in the right-hand column are construed the object of a transitive clause (as in the case of the free pronominals, dependent non-singular accusative pronominals bear an overt case ending):

(7) Wik-Me'nh subject and object dependent (suffixed and enclitic) pronominals:

	Subject (Nominative)	*Object* (Accusative)
1	-ng [~ -(i/a)y, -l-]	-ny
2	-(i)nt [~ -ngkan-]	-((nh)i)n
3	-Ø	-Ø
12	-((ng)a)l	-(ng)al-n
22	-(nh)ip	-(nh)ip-n
33	-pul	-pul-n
11(1)	-n	-ngan-n
122	-((ng)a)mp	-(ng)amp-n
222	-(nh)iy	-(nh)iy-n
333	-n [~ -than-, -ngan-]	-than-n

Although the fundamental paradigm here is straightforward, being identical to that of the free pronouns in relation to the grammatical categories represented (person, number, and case), there is a certain amount of extra complexity in the dependent pronominals—they exhibit a considerable amount of morphophonological alternation; that is to say, they are not consistently of the same shape in all environments. To be sure, some of the suffixes are stable, showing no alternation (i.e. 1O(bject) -*ny*, 3S(ubject)/o(bject) -*Ø*, 33S -*pul*, 33O -*pul-n*, 11(1)S -*n*, 11(1)O -ngan-n, 333O -*than-n*). But apart from these 'regular' forms, it is generally the case that Wik-Me'nh dependent pronominals exhibit a certain amount of contextually determined alternation. The first person singular nominative suffixes (glossed 1S), for example, has three alternants, as exemplified in (8):

(8) Wik-Me'nh:
   (a) Ngay   nhiy-n   ngul   thath-ng-ak.
        1.NOM   222-ACC   anon   see-1S-FUT
        'I will see you (plural) anon (bye-and-bye).'
   (b) Ngay   ngul   thath-l-iy-n.
        1.NOM   anon   see-1S-222-ACC
        'I will see you (plural) anon.' (an alternative to (a))
   (c) Ngay   minh   yint-nh-iy.
        1.NOM   fish   spear-PST-1S
        'I speared the fish (animal).'
   (d) Ngay   thath-nhan-ng,   ngay   peeyk-nhan-ng.
        1.NOM   see-IRR-1S,   1.NOM   hit-IRR-1S
        'If I could see it I could hit it.'

The alternant *-ng* appears before the future tense suffix (*-ak* FUT, as in (8a)) and following the irrealis suffix (*-ngan* IRR, used in conditionals, as in (8d)); the alternant *-l-* appears before a second person object suffix, as in (8b), and the alternant *-iy* appears following the past tense ending (*-nh* PST, as in (8c)).

The foregoing is intended merely as an example of the contextual conditioning of Wik-Me'nh dependent pronominals. We will not be concerned to any great degree with the full details of the alternations observed in these elements, but there is one further observation that should be made in this regard, as it will be relevant at a later point. In general, it is possible to relate Wik-Me'nh dependent pronominals to their free pronominal counterparts. In some cases, the segmental phonology of the suffix is identical to that of the free pronoun, e.g.:

(9) Wik-Me'nh unreduced dependent pronominals:

	Free Pronoun	*Dependent Pronominal*
33s	pul	-pul
33o	pul-n	-pul-n
11(1)o	ngan-n	-ngan-n
33o	than-n	-than-n

In the majority of the remaining cases, the dependent pronominal is a reduced form of the free pronoun, lacking the initial consonant, and in some cases, the entire first syllable of the latter, as in the following:

(10) Wik-Me'nh dependent pronominal alternants with initial reduction:

	Free Pronoun	Dependent Pronominal
1o	ngany	-ny
12s	ngal	-(a)l
12o	ngal-n	-al-n
22s	nhip	-ip
22o	nhip-n	-ip-n
11(1)s	ngan	-n
122s	ngamp	-(a)mp
122o	ngamp-n	-(a)mp-n
222s	nhiy	-iy
222o	nhiy-n	-iy-n

There is one important exception to the generalisation that phonological reduction in the evolution of Wik-Me'nh dependent pronominals is from left to right. The first singular nominative (glossed 1s) has a highly prominent alternant in which the initial consonant is retained, the remainder being lost:

(11) Wik-Me'nh dependent pronominal with final reduction:

	Free Pronoun	Dependent Pronominal
1s	ngay	-ng

This may seem to be a minor detail of little or no interest, but there is some evidence that this exceptional alternant represents a retention from an archaic stage in the history of Middle Paman and, if so, it is of great interest to the matter at issue here—i.e. the question of the time-depth implied by the linguistic diversity within Middle Paman. Another aspect of the Wik-Me'nh system that is interesting is the relationship between tense and the suffixed pronominals. As the examples show, pronominal suffixes may precede the future ending (-*ak* FUT), and they generally follow the past tense ending (-*nh* PST). In the present tense, the relation between the tense morphology and the pronominal suffixes is slightly more complex, and in two instances quite irregular. The present appears to be built upon the suffix -*nh* (but with an alternant -*n* sometimes heard), probably a general non-future, from which the past tense also arises. In conjunction with the dependent pronominals, the resulting combination is not always straightforward—the first singular, second singular, and third plural show unexpected alternants (-*ay*, -*ngkan*, and -*ngan*, respectively).

(12) Wik-Me'nh nominative pronominal suffixes in the present tense

1	-nh-ay
2	(-n)-ngkan
3	-Ø
12	-n-ngal
22	-nh-nhip
33	-n-pul
11(1)	-nh-n
122	-nh-ngamp
222	-nh-nhiy
333	(-n-)ngan

This is of interest to us in relation to the question of time-depth, because irregularities often signify relative antiquity in the evolution of grammatical systems, by comparison with highly regular systems that are often recent in origin. Thus, for example, the relatively regular initial reduction in Wik-Me'nh pronominal suffixes could be quite recent, but the irregular second person singular form in (12) is almost certainly an archaic residue from an early period in Middle Paman history.

In the preceding paragraphs, we have given the basic inventories of the dependent subject and object pronominals of Wik-Me'nh and, to some extent, we have documented the phonological alternations they exhibit. We turn now to morphological and syntactic properties of the system. The following points will be relevant in later sections in which comparative observations are made:

(13) The grammar of Wik-Me'nh dependent pronominals:
   (a) The use of subject dependent pronominals is obligatory—i.e. for any person and number category associated with the subject, the corresponding dependent pronominal must appear in the position designated for such elements (see (c) below), as exemplified in (1a), where the pronominal suffix *-ng* is construed with the first person singular subject *ngay*. This principle holds 'visibly' for all person-number combinations except third person singular, where it is assumed to hold abstractly, since that person is non-overt (Ø) in Wik-Me'nh (as it is in most Australian languages).
   (b) The use of object dependent pronominals is optional, as exemplified in (1e), where the first person object dependent pronominal *-ny* (construed with the first person object *ngany*) may appear, or not appear, a circumstance represented notationally by the use of parentheses.
   (c) Both subject- and object-dependent pronominals are suffixed to the verb, as can be seen in all examples so far cited. And the subject suffix precedes the object suffix.
   (d) Both subject and object suffixes may co-occur with overt free nominals (pronouns or noun phrases) in the corresponding argument function—e.g. *-ng* co-occurs with its corresponding subject argument *ngay* in (1a) and *-ny* co-occurs with its corresponding object argument *ngany* in (1d). In the case of objects, however, there is a slight preference for the free and dependent pronominals to occur in complementary distribution—in particular, if the free pronominal occurs, the corresponding suffix is preferably (but not necessarily) omitted. And, in general, Wik-Me'nh is a so-called pro-drop language, permitting free omission of the independent argument, as in (1e), where the subject is omitted, being represented only by pronominal suffix.
   (e) Wik-Me'nh subject dependent pronominals represent a fully standard *agreement* system. That is to say, a particular category in the sentence—to wit, the inflected verb—*agrees* with its subject.

(f) Object-dependent pronominals represent a system of pronominal enclitics. This is virtually an object agreement system, differing from a true agreement system in that the use of the enclitics is optional. The closest parallel is the phenomenon known as 'clitic doubling' in the study of Romance languages, and it will be referred to by this name (Jaeggli 1982).

Wik-Mungkan

Wik-Mungkan nominative and accusative free pronouns are tabulated in (14). They are, clearly, very similar to their Wik-Me'nh cognates. As in that language, so also in Wik-Mungkan, the formation of accusative non-singulars is completely regular. The accusative case ending *-ng* differs slightly from its Wik-Me'nh counterpart, but it is added directly to the unmarked (nominative) form without modification of either element. In the singular accusative, Wik-Mungkan differs from Wik-Me'nh in extending this regular inflection to the second person.

(14) Wik-Mungkan subject and object free pronouns:

	Subject (Nominative)	*Object* (Accusative)
1	ngay	ngany
2	nhint	nhint-ng
3	nhil	nhunh
12	ngal	ngal-ng
22	nhip	nhip-ng
33	pul	pul-ng
11(1)	ngan	ngan-ng
122	ngamp	ngamp-ng
222	nhiy	nhiy-ng
333	than	than-ng

The distribution of Wik-Mungkan accusative and nominative pronominals follows the same pattern as in Wik-Me'nh, as illustrated in the following sentences:

(15) Wik-Mungkan:
   (a) Ngay   punth-ak   iy-a-ng.
       1.NOM   creek-ALL go-FUT-1s
      'I will go to the creek.'

(b) Ngay   kemp   mungk-a-ng.
   1.NOM   meat   eat-FUT-1s
   'I will eat the meat.'

(c) Ku'-ng   ngany   ngul   path.
   dog-ERG   1.ACC   anon   bite
   'The dog will bite me presently.'

(d) Ku'-ng   path-ny.
   dog-ERG   bite-1o
   'The dog bit me.'

(e) Ku'   kan   uthm.
   dog   already   die
   'The dog has died.'

Pronouns follow the nominative-accusative pattern, according to which the subject (whether of an intransitive or of a transitive) is in the nominative (cf. (15a–b)), while the object is in the accusative (cf. (15c)). Nouns represent the ergative system of case inflection, with the ergative appearing on the transitive subject (cf. (15c–d)) and the unmarked (i.e. nominative) case on the intransitive subject (cf. (15e)) and on the object (cf. (15b)).

As seen in (15a–b, d), Wik-Mungkan has dependent subject and object pronominals, which, as in Wik-Me'nh, are suffixed to the verb. Subject suffixes appear obligatorily, construed with their corresponding full pronominal or nominal subject arguments; these latter may, of course, be omitted optionally. Object clitics are not obligatory, occurring preferably in complementary distribution with overt syntactic arguments (i.e. full pronominals or nominals in the object function; cf. the pair (15c–d), showing complementarity of full pronominal *ngany* and clitic *-ny*). Wik-Mungkan suffixed pronominals are somewhat more regular than the corresponding elements in Wik-Me'nh. They consistently follow tense and mode suffixes, and the present-tense paradigm is regular, with minor exceptions.

(16) Wik-Mungkan subject- and object-dependent (suffixed and enclitic) pronominals:

	Subject	Subject (with present)	Object
1	-ng	-ng	-ny
2	-n	-n-n	-(nh)int-ng
3	-Ø	-n	-Ø
12	-l	-n-l	-(ng)al-ng
22	-w	-n-ip	-(nh)ip-ng
33	-pul	-n-pul	-pul-ng
11(1)	-n	-n-n	-ngan-ng
122	-mp	-n-mp	-ngamp-ng
222	-nh	-n-iy	-(nh)iy-ng
333	-yn	-n-tn	-than-ng

In the second person singular, the portmanteau *-ngn* (phonetic [-ˀn]) typically appeared in place of regularised *-n-n* in material collected in 1960. This is reminiscent of the Wik-Me'nh second singular present tense form *-(n)ngkan* in (12). The third plural also has a slight irregularity: the lamino-dental initial assimilates to the *-n-* of the present, giving the combination *-ntn* (phonetic [-nd\n]). Finally, the first person singular subject suffix *-ng* shows a minor irregularity that it shares with the second person singular *-ngn*. Both of these suffixes appear without the preceding present tense marker *-n-*.

The grammatical properties of Wik-Mungkan dependent pronominals are essentially identical to those listed in (13) for their Wik-Me'nh counterparts. They are given in abbreviated form in (17):

(17) The grammar of Wik-Mungkan dependent pronominals:
  (a) The use of subject dependent pronominals is obligatory.
  (b) The use of object dependent pronominals is optional.
  (c) Both subject and object dependent pronominals are suffixed to the verb.
  (d) Both subject and object suffixes may co-occur with overt free nominals (pronouns or noun phrases). For objects, free and dependent pronominals tend to be complementary.

(e) Wik-Me'nh subject dependent pronominals represent a fully standard *agreement* system.

(f) Object-dependent pronominals represent a system of pronominal enclitics.

Wik-Ngathan (Nn) and Wik-Ngatharr (Nr)

These Wik entities are closely similar, and can be treated as dialects of a single language. Like the languages discussed in the previous subsection, and like Wik languages generally, Wik-Ngathan (from Sutton 1978) and Wik-Ngatharr (from Hale 1960 notes) have both free and dependent pronominals. Subject and Object free pronouns are tabulated in (18)—forms which are specific to Wik-Ngatharr are in curly braces {}):

(18) Wik-Ngathan and Wik-Ngatharr subject and object free pronouns:

	Subject (Nominative)		*Object* (Accusative)	
1	ngay		nganh	{ngany}
2	nhunt		nhin	{nhunh}
3	nhul		nhin	
11	ngan		ngan-nh	
12	ngal		ngal-nh	
22	nhupl		nhup-ny	
33	pul		pul-nh	
111	nganthn	{nganthᶦmp}	nganth-ny	
122	ngampl		ngamp-ny	
222	nhiy		nhiy-nh	
333	than		than-nh	

Again, the formation of the accusative is quite regular and transparent in the non-singular. The inventory of free pronouns departs little from the general Wik pattern seen in Wik-Mungkan and Wik-Me'nh, with the slight difference that in Wik-Ngathan/Ngathharra dual and plural numbers are distinguished in the first person exclusive (thus, Nn 11 *ngan*, 111 *nganthn*), these categories being merged (as *ngan*) in Mn/Me.

The grammatical distribution of these free pronominal forms conforms, as expected, to the nominative-accusative pattern (i.e. nominative for all subjects, accusative for objects of transitive verbs, as in (19a–b) and (19c)). Accordingly, they contrast with the ergative-nominative pattern found with noun-based arguments (i.e. with ergative case on transitive subjects, as in (19c), and nominative on intransitive subjects and transitive objects, as in (19f–g)). Example sentences follow:

(19) Wik-Ngathan and Wik-Ngatharr:

   (a) Ngay   pak=k-ang   pönyc-k.   (Nn)
         1.NOM   down=PURP-1S   descend-FUT
        'I will (want to) go down.'

   (b) Ngay   ngul=ng   (p)alk(-k).   (Nr)
         1.NOM   anon=1S   hit(-FUT)
        'I will hit someone'

   (c) Ngany   pam-nth=ny   (pa)lk-nh.   (Nr)
         1.ACC   man-ERG=1O hit-NF
        'A man hit me.'

   (d) Palk-nh=ny.   (Nr)
         hit-PST=1O
        'He hit me.'

   (e) Nhin=ng   (p)alk(-k).   (Nr)
         3.ACC=1S hit-(-FUT)
        'I will hit him.'

   (f) Ngay   yuunh=k-ang eep-eep-k.   (Nn)
         1.NOM   bag=PURP-1S weave-RDP-FUT
        'I will (want to) weave a bag.'

   (g) Ku'   anth   way.ngk(n)-nh. (Nr)
         dog   this   die-NF
        'The dog died.'

   (h) Ma'ak(-k)=nt-nh.   (Nn)
         help-FUT=2S-1O
        'Help me.'

The inventory of recorded dependent subject and object pronominals is given in (20). Parenthetic a-vowels in subject pronominals represent the full vowels recorded by Sutton (1978) for Wik-Ngathan; these are generally reduced in Wik-Ngatharr, and accordingly not written in that dialect:[6]

(20) Wik-Ngathan and Wik-Ngatharr subject and object dependent (enclitic) pronominals:

	Subject	Object	
1	-(a)ng	-nh	{-ny}
2	-nt	-nhin	
3	-Ø	—	
12	-(a)l	-l-nh	
11	-ngan	—	
22	—	—	
33	-pul	—	
122	-mp	—	
111	-(a)nthn	—	
222	-nh	—	
333	-(a)n	-n-nh	

A special, and highly relevant, feature of Wik-Ngathan and Wik-Ngatharr is the placement of these elements. Their preferred position is *enclitic to an immediately preverbal constituent*. This constituent may be: (i) a spatial or temporal/aspectual adverb, as in examples (19a–b); (ii) the subject, as in (19c); (iii) a pronominal or nominal object, as in (19e–f); in general, any preverbal constituent may host a pronominal enclitic (or subject-object enclitic sequence, as in (19f)). Enclitic pronominals may also be hosted by the verb, and they must be if the verb is initial in the clause, as in (19d), where the verb is the sole non-clitic constituent. As in Wik-Mungkan and Wik-Me'nh, so also here, dependent pronominals may be construed with an overt nominal or pronominal argument, as in (19a–c).

There is an additional feature of Wik-Ngathan and Wik-Ngatharr dependent pronominals that distinguishes them from those of Wik-Mungkan and Wik-Me'nh. While all of these languages share the property

---

6   The difference is actually only orthographic. Both dialects have the same reduced vowels. Since 1978 I have used /e/ instead of /a/ for these reduced vowels: PS.

that object enclitics are optional, available data on Wik-Ngathan and Wik-Ngatharr indicates that optionality is not limited to object enclitics there; *subject enclitics are also optional*. The following Wik-Ngatharr sentences differ in this respect: the second singular subject enclitic *-nt* is construed with the subject argument *nhunt* 'you' in (21a), but in (21b), the free pronoun stands alone in representing the grammatical subject.

(21) Wik-Ngatharr:

   (a) Nhunt   kan=nt   mooenc-ny-ey.
         2.NOM   PERF-2S   swim-NF-Q
         'Did you have a swim?'

   (b) Nhunt   ngeen   kan   ngayc-ny.
         2.NOM   what   PERF   see-NF
         'What are you looking at?'

Similarly, in the Wik-Ngathan sentence (22a), from Sutton (1978:306), the first person subject enclitic *-ang* is construed with the corresponding free pronoun *ngay* 'I', while in (22b), from Sutton (1978:277), the subject enclitic is absent:

(22) Wik-Ngathan:

   (a) Ngay   ke'-m=ang   ngayc-ny.
         1.NOM   NEG-ABL=1S   see-NF
         'I didn't see it/them.'

   (b) Ngay   ke'-m   ngayc-ny.
         1.NOM   NEG-ABL   see-NF
         'I didn't see it/them.'

A remarkable Wik-Ngatharr concomitant of the preverbal positioning of pronominal enclitics is the optional *phonological 'fusion' of the enclitic and its host with the verb itself*, with attendant reduction of the initial syllable of the latter (indicated informally by means of parentheses in (19b–c,e)). Thus, for example, the following alternation has been observed:

(23) Wik-Ngatharr:

   (a) Ngay   ngul=ng   palk(-k).
         1.NOM   anon=1s   hit(-FUT)
         'I will hit him.'

(b) Ngay   ngul=nga·lk(-k).
1.NOM   anon=1s+hit(-FUT)
'I will hit him.'

In the second alternant here, the initial consonant of the verb is deleted and the remainder of the verb's initial syllable is merged with the underlying vowel of the first person enclitic, giving a lengthened a-vowel, represented [a·]. The underlying vowel of the enclitic is probably dominant here, as suggested by the following pair, where it is clear (from (24b)) that the vowel of the verb loses its quality in favour of that of the enclitic (evidently /a/ underlyingly, as expected on the basis of its Proto-Middle Paman ancestor *-*nga*):

(24) Wik-Ngatharr:

(a) Ngay   ngul=ng   wump-k.
1.NOM   anon=1S   climb-FUT
'I will climb up.'

(b) Ngay   ngul=nga·mp-k.
1.NOM   anon=1S+climb-FUT
'I will climb up.'

A preceding enclitic-cum-host is not the only conditioning factor in this optional reduction of the initial syllables of verbs. There is an additional class of elements that can trigger this effect, including, among others, the negative *ke'* and a content question word, as shown in (25):

(25) Wik-Ngatharr:

(a) Ngay   ka'+a·yc-ny.
1.NOM   NEG+see-NF
'I can't (don't) see him.'
(< ke' ngayc-ny (NEG see-NF))[7]

(b) Kalk   ngath   weey-ngk+a·r-n.
spear   1.GEN   who-ERG+take-NF
'Who took my spear?'
(< kaar-n (take-NF))

---

[7]   In this variety's sister dialect Wik-Ngathan I have recorded both *ka'* and *ke'* for the negative particle, see Sutton (1995a:23): PS.

The grammar of Wik-Ngathan and Wik-Ngatharr dependent pronominals differs in interesting ways from that observed in the previous subsection for Wik-Mungkan and Wik-Me'nh.

(26) The grammar of Wik-Ngathan and Wik-Ngatharr dependent pronominals:

  (a) The use of subject-dependent pronominals is optional.

  (b) The use of object-dependent pronominals is optional.

  (c) Subject- and object-dependent pronominals are preferably enclitic to the constituent immediately preceding the verb. They may alternatively (though much less commonly) attach to the verb, and must do so if the verb is initial.

  (d) Both subject- and object-dependent pronominals may co-occur with overt arguments (free pronouns or noun phrases).

  (e) Wik-Ngathan and Wik-Ngatharr subject- and object-dependent pronominals are clitics (specifically, enclitics); neither represents an agreement system, properly speaking.

  (f) In Wik-Ngatharr, certain preverbal elements, including host elements with an enclitic, may 'fuse' with the verb, causing phonological reduction of the initial syllable of the latter.

Kugu Nganhcara (KN)

Kugu Nganhcara shares grammatical properties with the languages discussed in the previous two subsections. In relation to its dependent pronominals, it represents a partial blending of the grammars of Wik-Mungkan/Me'nh, on the one hand, and Wik-Ngathan/Ngatharra on the other. The subject and object free pronominals of Kugu Nganhcara are set out in (27):

(27) Kugu Nganhcara subject and object free pronouns:

	Subject (Nominative)	*Object* (Accusative)
1	ngaya	nganyi
2	nhinta	nhina
3	nhila	nhunha
11	ngana	ngana-na
12	ngale	ngale-na

22	nhipa	nhipa-na
33	pula	pula-na
111	nganhca	nganhca-rra
122	ngampa	ngampa-rra
222	nhiya	nhiya-rra
333	thana	thana-na

As before, these conform to the nominative-accusative pattern, unlike noun-based arguments, which conform to the ergative pattern. The following sentences exemplify, in part, these principles of case marking together with other aspects of Kugu Nganhcara grammar of relevance to the issue of diversity within the family as a whole—examples are from Smith and Johnson (1985), except for those identified as specifically Kugu Muminh (Mu), taken from Hale (1960 notes).

(28) Kugu Nganhcara:

   (a) Nhila   pama-ng   nga'a=la   yenta.
       3.NOM   person-ERG fish=3S   spear
       'The man speared the fish.'

   (b) Nhila   nganyi   yupa=nyi   yenta.
       3.NOM   1.ACC   FUT=1O   spear
       'He will spear me.'

   (c) Nhagu-wu=nhca   wico.
       there-DAT=111S   travel
       'We (exclusive plural) travelled to that place.'

   (d) Nhinta   puyu=li=nta   uwa-n.
       2.NOM   away=then=2S   go-2S
       'Did you go away then?'

   (e) Poje-dha-nga=nha=la.
       dry-INCH-CAUS=3O=33S
       'They (two) dry him.'

   (f) Ngaya   nhina   piigu-nga.   (Mu)
       1.NOM   2.ACC   hit-1S
       'I will hit you.'

(g) Nhint   ngaarri-m=nh   piigu-ngan?   (Mu)
    2.NOM   what-ABL=3O   hit-PRES.2S
    'Why are you hitting him?'

(h) Ngaya   ka'i=nh   nhaawa-ng.   (Mu)
    1.NOM   NEG=3O   see-1S
    'I didn't see him.'

(i) Thana   munji-yin.   (Mu)
    333.NOM   swim-PRES.333S
    'They are swimming.'

(j) Thana   kana   munje-dhan.   (Mu)
    333.NOM   PERF   swim-333S
    'They swam.'

Two sets of dependent pronominal elements must be recognised in Wik-Nganhcara (cf. Smith and Johnson 1985:fn.3). In addition to those elements identified as *enclitics* (by means of the = sign in the example sentences of (28)), there is a residue of historically prior *subject agreement suffixes* (identified notationally by means of a hyphen in the example sentences). The two sets of dependent pronominals are tabulated in (29). The subject agreement suffixes are set off in square brackets (and where there is a second alternant, it is a portmanteau embodying the categories of person and present tense). Subject agreement is represented overtly only in the first and second persons singular and in the third person plural. The second person singular subject is represented both by an enclitic (*-nta*) and by agreement (*-n ~ -ngan*). First singular and third plural are represented only by agreement (*-ng(a)* and *-dhan ~ -yin*, respectively)—the overlap between the agreement and enclitic systems is therefore rather slim, being in the second person singular only (cf. (28d), where agreement and enclitic co-occur).

(29) Kugu Nganhcara subject and object dependent pronominals:

	Subject	Object
1	[-ng(a)]-nyi	
2	-nta [-n ~ -ngan]	-na
3	-la-nha	-li-n
12	-le	

11	-na	-na-n
22	-pa	-pa-n
33	-la	-la-n
122	-mpa-mpa-rra	
111	-nhca	-nhca-rra
222	-ya	-ya-rra
333	[-dhan ~ -yin] -rra-n	

Available evidence indicates that agreement is preferred, if not obligatory, in Kugu Nganhcara—that is to say, for any subject whose category matches that of one of the agreement suffixes enclosed in square brackets in (29), overt agreement is expected. In this respect, Kugu Nganhcara conforms to the pattern seen in Wik-Mungkan and Wik-Me'nh. By contrast, enclitic pronominals are optional, and in this Kugu Nganhcara is like Wik-Ngathan and Wik-Ngatharr. Subject agreement morphology is suffixed to the verb, while subject and object enclitic pronominals alternate, as in Wik-Ngathan/Ngatharra, between attachment to an immediately preverbal host and attachment to the verb itself, the first being more usual than the second. If the verb is initial or the unique non-clitic constituent in the clause, as in (28e), attachment to the verb is required. The subject enclitic follows the non-subject in the example just cited, though the order is in fact free (cf. Smith and Johnson 1985:107). In this respect, Kugu Nganhcara differs from Wik-Ngathan and Wik-Ngatharr.

(30) The grammar of Kugu Nganhcara dependent pronominals:

   (a) Subject agreement is preferred, possibly obligatory.

   (b) Subject and object enclitics are optional.

   (c) Subject and object enclitics are preferably attached to the constituent immediately preceding the verb. They may alternatively attach to the verb, and must do so if the verb is initial or alone in the clause.

   (d) Both subject agreement and enclitic pronominals may co-occur with overt arguments (free pronouns or noun phrases).

   (e) The relative order of subject and object enclitics is free.

Other Middle Paman

The eastern Middle Paman languages, Kaanju, Kuuku-Ya'u, and Umpila, like the Wik languages themselves, have both free and dependent pronominals. However, Kuuk Thaayorre, a putative Middle Paman language to the south, does not have a developed system of dependent pronominals.

Kaanju, Kuuku-Ya'u and Umpila

A partial inventory of dependent pronominals is found in Umpila field notes supplied by O'Grady (1959–60) and in brief Kaanju notes of Hale (1960):

(31) Umpila and Kaanju dependent pronominals:

1	-nga	-nyi
2	-ntu ~ -n -ni	-Ø
3	-Ø	
12	-li	—
11(1)	-na	—
22(2)	-nhu	—
122	-mpu	—
33(3)	-'a	-la-n

Example sentences are given in (32), with Kaanju (Ka) from Hale (1960 notes), and Umpila (Um) from Harris and O'Grady (1976):

(32) Kaanju and Umpila:
- (a) Nguna=ni   ku'aka-lu   patha-n?   (Ka)
      2=2S   dog-ERG   bite-PST
      'Did the dog bite you?'
- (b) Nganyi   ku'aka-lu   patha-n.   (Ka)
      1.ACC   dog-ERG   bite-PST
      'The dog bit me.'
- (c) Ku'aka-lu   patha-na=nyi. (Ka)
      dog-ERG   bite-PST=1O
      'The dog bit me.'
- (d) Nguna   kuna   alngki-ka=n. (Ka)

	2.NOM	FUT	fall-FUT=2S

'You are going to fall.'

(e) Ngaya (*sic:* ngayu)   kuna=nga   ngaaci-ku   yuta-ka. (Ka)
    1.NOM   FUT=1S   place-DAT   go-FUT

'I am going to (my) place.'

(f) Ngaani-ku=nhu'u   wuntuu-nu-ngka?   (Um)
    what-DAT=22(2)S   see-PROG-PRES

'What are you (plural) looking for?'

The dependent pronominals here evidently fall into the category of enclitics, and their use is not obligatory. Their placement is much less constrained than in the Wik languages. When they are not attached to the verb, they appear on some pre-verbal constituent, not necessarily that which is in immediate pre-verbal position.

2.4.2. Kuuk Thaayorre

Data available for this language (Hale 1960 notes; Hall 1976a, 1976b) give no evidence of any evolved system of dependent pronouns. However, like other languages to the south, Kuuk Thaayorre does have atonic pronouns which, like enclitics, depend phonologically upon a preceding host:

(33) Kuuk Thaayorre:

(a) … waat   ke'e-rr   (n)unh   (ng)ay.   (Hall)
     … wrong   spear-PST   3.ACC   1.NOM

'… I speared him in error.'

(b) Ngay   ngat   ke'e-rr.   (Hale)
     1.NOM   fish   spear-PST

'I speared a fish.'

(c) Ngay   thiik-arr   (ng)ay.   (Hall)
     1.NOM   break-PST   1.NOM

'I broke it, I did.'

(d) Kuuk   (nh)unt   ngeene   yiik?   (Hale)
     language   2.NOM   what   speak

'What language do you speak?'

Atonic pronouns show their relative reduced character not only by their accentual weakening and their dependence on a preceding host but also, optionally, by loss of their initial consonants (indicated in example (33) by the use of parentheses). In terms of position within the clause, they may be final (following the verb) or in some pre-verbal position, e.g. following the first constituent. An atonic subject pronoun can and typically will appear finally, as in (33a), while a fully accented subject pronoun will appear in the characteristic subject position, i.e. initially, as in (33b). Non-subject pronouns in Kuuk Thaayorre are often final in either case, with atonic pronouns being distinguished accentually and by initial consonant deletion. Interestingly, atonic pronouns may co-occur with corresponding full pronouns, as in (33c). This is a common feature of languages in the region south of the Wik area, as we shall see.

Other Paman languages of Cape York Peninsula

The Wik languages (including as usual, the Nganhcara cluster), are arguably unique in relation to the systems of dependent pronominals that have developed there. No other languages of Cape York Peninsula duplicate precisely the Wik situation as a whole or the principal subtypes pertaining to it.

Northern Paman languages generally lack dependent pronouns, the only exception coming to mind being the single atonic form found in Linngithigh:

(34) Linngithigh:

  (a) Nggoy=ang   nji-n.
       wallaby=1S   spear-PST
      'I speared the/a wallaby.'

  (b) Ayong   nggoy   nji-n.
       1.NOM   wallaby   spear-PST
      'I speared the/a wallaby.'

The enclitic first singular subject pronoun in (34a) is the atonic counterpart of the full pronoun *ayong* 'I' in (34b). Other Linngithigh pronouns lack enclitic forms of this type.

South of the Wik language region, as we have seen, atonic pronouns are found in Kuuk Thaayorre. But this is not the extent of their distribution. They are found as well in Kunjen (Ku; Sommer 1972), Aghu Tharrnggala (AT; Jolly 1989), and Rimanggudinhma (Ri; Godman 1993). These are all southern 'initial dropping languages', and their atonic pronouns closely resemble full pronouns. Examples follow (atonic forms are identified by means of the grave accent):

(35) Upper South CYP Paman:

(a) Uy urb idu-r ày. (Ku)
fish barramundi spear-PST 1.NOM
'I speared a barramundi.'

(b) Abm ày eray ija-r. (Ku)
person 1.NOM some eat-PST
'I ate some.'

(c) Ud-al inh-pigipigi adhen atha-r il ingùn.
dog-ERG meat-pig 1.GEN bite-PST 3.NOM 3.ACC
'The dog bit my pig.' (Ku)

(d) Mawng-əl twə-n lì=nəng. 3.NOM=2.ACC (AT)
who-ERG hit-NF
'Who hit you?'

(e) Nay nhï-l twə-n lì này. (AT)
1.ACC that-ERG hit-PST 3.NOM 1.ACC
'That one hit me.'

(f) Yaw ninh twə-gə. (AT)
1.NOM 2.ACC hit-FUT
'I will hit you.'

(g) Lpung ə w ta-nhəgə yàw nành. (AT)
tomorrow see-PURP 1.NOM 2.ACC
'I will see you tomorrow.'

(h) Ba aðerr pa-n dyù. (Ri)
person two see-PST 1.NOM
'I saw two men.'

(i) Ba:dhi-l   ndo-n   nì   là?   (Ri)
    who-ERG   hit-PST   1.ACC   3.NOM
    'Who hit me?'

(j) Alka   tha-l   ndò   ngàn.   (Ri)
    spear   tie-IMP   2.NOM   3.ACC
    'Tie the spear up!'

(k) Ndo   thùm   ina-l.   (Ri)
    2.NOM   1.DAT   sit-IMP
    'Wait for me!'

(l) Dyu   ngòn   ari   ndo-n.   (Ri)
    1.NOM   3.ACC   NEG   hit-PST
    'I didn't hit/hit him.'

A shared feature of these languages is the essential identity (except for accent) of full and atonic pronouns—atonic pronouns are not reduced or eroded in any noticeable way, a minor exception being the vocalically modified alternative second and third singular accusative forms in Aghu Tharrnggala, in which schwa replaces the original vowel. Another common feature is the relative prevalence of atonic over fully accented pronouns—in Kunjen, this is taken to something of an extreme, in that while pronouns can appear in accented positions (e.g. initial), they are often provided instead with a lexical host and left in atonic form (e.g. *abm ày* (person 1.NOM) 'I'). In distribution, atonic pronouns favour post-verbal position, though they may appear on a pre-verbal host as well; a full pronoun will often attract an atonic one, as in examples (35 l–m).

In these languages, atonic pronouns can, and often do, co-occur with the corresponding argument (pronoun or noun phrase) in pre-verbal position. This resembles the relation that holds in agreement, of course. However, this is not true agreement of the obligatory type seen in Wik-Mungkan and Wik-Me'nh subjects. This southern co-occurrence pattern is not obligatory. It is therefore more akin to the relation that holds between object enclitics and corresponding arguments in the Wik languages just mentioned, or the relation between enclitics and arguments generally in Wik-Ngathan and Wik-Ngatharr: co-occurrence is possible, but optional. We can say, then, that an argument can be 'doubled' by an enclitic, but need not be.

There are at least two other languages that must be mentioned in this connection. They are Yir-Yoront (YY; Alpher 1991) and the Flinders Island Language (FI; Sutton 1980). These differ from the foregoing in that they possess two sets of reduced pronominals. One of these (not necessarily atonic) shows the simple modification of initial consonant loss (e.g. YY *nholo ~ ngolo, olo* '3.NOM'), the other shows a much more substantial reduction to an item properly termed enclitic (e.g. YY *-'l* '3.NOM'):[8]

(36) Yir-Yoront and the Flinders Island Language:

   (a) Waqa-nn   kirr='y=ungnh. (YY)
       go-PRT   see:P=1.NOM=3.ACC
       'I saw him going along.'

   (b) Ngoyo   minha   wa-l.   (YY)
       1.NOM   meat.DAT   go-NPST
       'I am going for meat.'

   (c) Makur   ncilabi-ya   atha=yu. (FI)
       oyster   MoMo-ABL   eat.NPST=1.NOM
       'I am eating my grandmother's oysters.'

   (d) Ngayu=dun   aathi-n   uka-niya. (FI)
       1.NOM=2.ACC see-PST   go-SUBORD
       'I saw you going.'

These sentences exemplify the first person singular subject enclitics (YY *-'y*, FI *-yu*) and their full pronoun counterparts (YY *ngoyo*, FI *ngayu*). As the examples show, the use of enclitics is not obligatory—hence, this is not an agreement system, strictly speaking. In general, enclitics appear (most frequently) on the verb, but also on the first constituent of the clause.

What is important for present purposes is the fact that these southern dependent pronominal systems are historically independent from those of the Wik languages to the north. That is to say, while the morphemes involved are, for the most part, cognate, the dependent enclitic forms developed locally through processes of reduction characteristic of the southern languages. Thus, for example, the reduction of the first person singular from *ngayu* to *-yu* in the Flinders Island language, and the parallel

---

8   'l is [əl], 'y is [əy] [etc.]: PS.

reduction from *ngoyo* to *-'y* in Yir-Yoront, cannot be related directly to the historical derivation of generalised Wik and Middle Paman *-nga*, presumably related to the Proto-Paman reconstruction **ngayu*. Thus, while this reconstructed form is no doubt valid for the Paman family as a whole, the reduced forms must be understood as local developments, peculiar to the individual sub-families. A similar conclusion must be drawn in relation to the initial dropping languages, Kunjen, Aghu Tharrnggala, and Rimanggudinhma. Their atonic pronominals developed in a time period quite separate from that of the remote Paman ancestor they share with Wik and Middle Paman. They can only have developed at a time subsequent to the process of initial dropping so characteristic of these languages; only in this way can the near perfect identity of full and atonic pronominals be understood.

While there are clear similarities between Middle Paman and these more southerly Paman languages in relation to the grammar of dependent pronominals, these similarities are to be attributed not to common ancestry but rather to universal principles of pronominal reduction and clisis that have been observed and studied in languages of the world generally (cf. the ample 'clitic literature' of recent decades, including Borer 1986; Everett 1996; Halpern 1992; Halpern and Zwicky 1996; Klavans 1995; Zwicky 1977; Zwicky and Pullum 1983). The special features of Wik and Middle Paman dependent pronominals, though constrained by universal principles, are, in their details, specific to that subfamily. In the next section, we will describe the most probable historical processes involved in their development and we will attempt to assess the associated temporal dimension.

The grammar and evolution of Wik dependent pronominals

The opinions that have appeared in the linguistic literature, including the references cited above, are many and varied concerning the proper conception of the grammar and historical development of pronominal clitic and agreement systems. There is a picture that emerges, however, in relation to the evolutionary processes involved. A fully established true agreement system appears to represent the advanced stage in an evolution beginning with the prosodic weakening of pronominal elements, proceeding through clisis and clitic doubling, and culminating in agreement. In relation to the Wik languages and their Middle and general Paman relatives, the following evolutionary schema is indicated, based on the evidence available:

(37) Stages in the evolution of Wik and Middle Paman dependent pronominal systems:

Stage 0: Free pronouns only.

Stage I: Atonic (weak) pronouns in complementary distribution with free pronouns.

Stage II: Clitic (enclitic) pronominals with a S(entence)-position host, with optional clitic doubling.

Stage III: Clitic (enclitic) pronominals with a C(lause)-position host, with optional clitic doubling.

Stage IV: Agreement morphology.

No Wik or Middle Paman language represents Stage 0, but this stage is nonetheless relevant, since it is without doubt represented by the more remote Paman and Pama-Nyungan ancestors of Wik. Many Paman languages represent Stage 0—most Northern Paman languages do, and many southern Paman languages belong to this stage (e.g. Guugu Yimidhirr, Yidiny, Dyirbal); even some dialects of Kunjen appear to belong here (e.g. Ogondyan, as found in Hale 1960 notes).[9] In any event, the Wik and Middle Paman languages are past this stage.

The processes of interest in the present context are those that can be detected when there is 'movement', so to speak, in the development of a grammatical system, i.e. when there is some change, such as the prosodic weakening of pronouns, forcing their displacement to an appropriate host, as in Stage I. A pure representative of this stage is the Linngithigh example cited in (34). The pronominals of Kunjen, Aghu Tharrnggala, and Rimanggudinhma have been termed atonic pronouns in the preceding discussion primarily because they differ from full pronouns in accent only (with the minor exceptions noted). However, the grammatical systems of these languages are probably more advanced in historical development, i.e. they are probably beyond Stage I and into Stage II, since doubling is

---

9   Publisher's reader commented: '"Kunjen" is not a phylogenetic group of languages, and the nearest linguistic relatives of Uw-Oykangand (illustrated above) and those of Ogondyan are in separate subfamilies': PS.

possible (e.g. (33c)). The same is true of Yir-Yoront and Flinders Island, where the dependent pronominals are, in addition, phonologically more reduced.

The stages that characterise Middle Paman languages are II–IV. The evidence available for Kaanju-Umpila-Ya'u and for Kuuk Thaayorre suggests that they are representative of Stage II, with enclitic pronouns attached to an S-position host, a feature these Middle Paman languages share with Yir-Yoront. An S-position is a location identified in relation to the sentence as a whole. The most renowned S-position is so-called 'Second Position' or 'Wackernagel's Position' (cf. Halpern and Zwicky 1996, and references cited therein). This is normally defined as 'after the first constituent' of the clause—it is not defined in terms of a particular category (e.g. noun phrase (NP, DP), verb phrase (VP), inflectional projection (IP)), but rather in terms of a *position* within the clause. Another popular position is 'at the end of the sentence', common in verb-final languages, like most of the Paman languages of Cape York Peninsula. In both cases, there the dependent pronoun is an enclitic, it attaches to the constituent immediately to its left—(i) to the verb, when the enclitic appears in S-final position; or (ii) to some S-initial phrase or lexical item, when the enclitic occupies second position within S. The latter position is generally abbreviated P2 (i.e. 'position two') in the literature on clitics. These patterns (P2 and S-final) are amply exemplified in sentences cited in section 2.4.

The stage just described differs from the next in respect to the exact definition of the 'landing site' of dependent, or clitic, pronominals. In Stage III, clitic pronominals are positioned in relation to a category (e.g. noun (N), verb (V), Inflection (Infl), or a projection of these, NP, VP, IP). The enclitic object pronouns of Wik-Mungkan and Wik-Me'nh exemplify this—they are regularly attached to the inflected verb.

A rare but well-documented C-position pattern is that according to which enclitics are positioned in relation to the verb, but allowed to appear either *before* or *after* that category. When a clitic follows the verb, it is hosted phonologically by the verb. When it precedes the verb, it is dependent *syntactically* on the verb but it is hosted *phonologically* by the constituent immediately to its left. Observationally, at least, this is the situation represented by both subject and object enclitics in Wik-Ngathan, Wik-Ngatharr, and Kugu Nganhcara.

While it is relatively certain that these languages represent Stage III, it must be said that there is some ambiguity inherent in the surface forms at Stages II and III. Setting aside the case of post-verbal enclitic attachment, both of these intermediate stages are characterised by a surface form in which an enclitic appears immediately before the verb. And often, as it turns out in actual textual usage, this preverbal position is also *second* position in the clause, since more often than not just one non-clitic constituent precedes the verb. And, of course, if the verb is initial, then the two stages are observationally identical, since enclitics will necessarily coincide as P2. The distinguishing factor, of course, is the notion 'second position':

(38) Second Position (P2):
    (a)   XP=Cl … V.   (Stage II, P2 enclitic)
    (b)   … XP=Cl V.   (Stage III, V-dependent enclitic)

Where the ellipsis (…) is empty, the linear arrangements at these stages coincide entirely. Where overt material appears in the position of the ellipsis, the linear arrangements are, of course, distinct. Therefore, the matter is easy to decide, in principle—if a language proffers examples of, say, YP^XP=Cl^V, then, presumably, it represents Stage III. But the matter is not trivial, in fact, because in some examples of the type just cited, YP could in fact be a fronted element, not relevant to the positioning of the enclitic (Cl). However, on the basis of the careful work of Smith and Johnson (1986) and Sutton (1978), we feel confident in assuming that the Wik-Ngathan, Wik-Ngatharr, and Kugu Nganhcara enclitic pronouns belong to Stage III, rather than Stage II.

An important feature of dependent pronominals at stages II and III is the phenomenon known as 'Clitic Doubling' (see Everett 1996, for much discussion). Clitic doubling represents a certain degree of separation of a dependent pronominal from its syntactic 'argument position' (A-position)—that is to say, the clitic is no longer simply the reduced and phonologically dependent realisation of the argument itself. Instead, in clitic doubling, the clitic appears in its designated clitic (Cl) position, and the corresponding argument position is itself filled by an overt full and unreduced argument expression construed with the clitic. This situation, amply exemplified in the 'Other Middle Paman' section above, is similar in nature to agreement, in which an argument is obligatorily construed with person and number morphology in the verb, or other relevant head. A difference is that clitic doubling, particularly as it is represented in the languages at issue here, is optional—an overt argument need not be 'doubled' by an enclitic. Clitic doubling evolves from Stage I through a number of means, a familiar one being the reanalysis of structures resulting from a fronting process of the type called 'clitic left dislocation', according to which a fronted (dislocated) argument is 'resumed' by a (weak) pronoun.

Before discussing the final stage, we locate the Wik and related grammatical systems within the evolutionary scheme suggested above:

(39) Stages in the evolution of Wik and Middle Paman dependent pronominal systems:

Stage 0: Northern Paman, many Southern Paman.

Stage I: Linngithigh *-ang* '1.NOM'.

Stage II: Yir-Yoront, Kunjen, Aghu Tharrnggala, Rimanggudinhma.

Stage III: Wik-Mungkan/Me'nh object enclitics; Wik-Ngathan/Ngatharra and Kugu Nganhcara subject and object enclitics.

Stage IV: Wik-Mungkan/Me'nh subject agreement; Kugu Nganhcara residual subject agreement.

This sequence represents an evolution toward maximal synthesis in the grammatical expression of the relationship between a verb and its direct arguments (subject and object). It arrives at an end-point, in an important sense, as subsequent developments from a system of true agreement often involve the loss of inflections and movement toward a more analytic morphosyntactic system (cf. Hodge 1970). The relevant high point of synthesis is reached in the form of subject agreement, according to which erstwhile pronominal enclitics have evolved into verbal morphology expressing a true agreement relation between the verb and its subject. Everett (1996:46) attempts to distinguish agreement from the looser clitic doubling relation in the following terms:

(40) Agreement:

> The co-occurrence of a tautaphrasal, coreferent NP-AGR° pair, which refers to a single theta-role and where AGR is included within its host, i.e. [is] m-subcategorised by it.

What this means, in effect, is that agreement is the joint realisation of a single argument (e.g. the subject) by a pair of elements, one of which is a nominal argument (NP), occupying an argument position in syntax (e.g.

the position of the subject) and the other of which is dependent morphology (symbolised AGR°, a suffix, prefix, or infix, depending on the language) expressing person and number (and possibly gender) features integrated into the word-morphology of its host (e.g. the verb, in the cases of interest here. Since the two pieces jointly realise an argument, the relation is one that we have characterised as 'obligatory'. The m-subcategorisation clause of (40) refers to the notion that agreement morphology is 'integrated' into the morphology of the host. The host 'selects' (or 'subcategorises') the agreement morphology, in the sense that the host word is incomplete without it.

It is relatively clear that Wik-Mungkan/Me'nh and Kugu Nganhcara have arrived at this maximal degree of synthesis in relation to subject agreement. Subject agreement is fully functional in Wik-Mungkan and Wik-Me'nh, and it is inextricably integrated into the morphology of the inflected verb in those languages. There are, evidently, two layers of subject agreement morphology, historically speaking—an early layer involving some synchronically opaque morphology of the type seen in the Wik-Me'nh present tense forms in (12), and an evidently more recent layer involving suffixes that are transparently related to the corresponding free pronouns. This historical layering is strikingly evident in Kugu Nganhcara, since the elements involved are different syntactically and morphologically. The old layer of subject agreement is suffixed to the verb and enters into the verbal morphology in a manner that is clearly cognate to the subject agreement system of Wik-Mungkan/Me'nh. It is greatly eroded and gives evidence of being on its way to extinction, in keeping with the popular tendency of inflectional systems to evolve away from synthesis and to move in the direction of analysis. At the same time, a system of subject-oriented dependent pronominals has arisen to replenish Kugu Nganhcara grammar with a new set of enclitics transparently derived from their free pronoun counterparts.

To summarise, the Wik languages represent an evolution toward the maximal degree of synthesis, with prior stages also represented. The maximal stage is reached in subject agreement in Wik-Mungkan and Wik-Me'nh. And an important prior stage is reached in the form of C-positioned clitic doubling—by subject and object enclitics in Wik-Ngathan, Wik-Ngatharr, and Kugu Nganhcara, and by object enclitics in Wik-Mungkan and Wik-Me'nh. Kugu Nganhcara may have progressed beyond the maximal stage of synthesis in its subject agreement morphology, which is reduced and appears to have undergone loss of original forms.

The time-depth of Wik dependent pronominal grammars

Having presented some picture of the diversity that exists within the Wik dependent pronominal systems, we turn now to a consideration of the temporal dimension. We ask now how long it takes for grammatical systems of this sort to evolve. Years of work in historical linguistics, and in the study of clitic and agreement systems specifically, lead us to assume that a language that evolves to Stage IV must have passed through earlier stages. This follows from the fact that Stage IV is an advanced point in an evolution toward synthesis. On the basis of historiographic records and historical reconstruction, we know that the evolution of an agreement system of the type found in the Wik family involves a progression through the stages of (37), allowing of course for differences in approach among comparative and theoretical linguists. Our question, therefore, is this: How long does it take to progress through these stages?

There are two problems with this question. First, we know from the most superficial observation that rates of change vary enormously. Thus, our answer cannot be absolute. We should rather put our question this way: How *fast* can a language or language family progress through these stages? What is the shortest interval in which the relevant changes can be completed? This sets the limits in a more realistic way—while there is in theory no *longest* period within which this evolution can be achieved, there is surely a *shortest* period, given the obvious fact that linguistic change takes time. Our eventual goal here is to argue that the time-depth within the Wik family is substantially greater than two centuries, i.e. that the evolution of the Wik systems of dependent pronominals has taken more than that period of time.

The second problem with our question, of course, is that we have no direct evidence concerning the temporal dimension. Wik-family linguistic records do not predate the first decades of the twentieth century, and, moreover, the records that exist from earlier periods do not include the grammatical information that is crucial here. We have no historiographic evidence, in short. We must make use of indirect evidence.

We have two things working in our favour. First, general principles of grammar and linguistic change lead us to believe that the progression set out in (37) is real, and the study of a large number of languages substantiates this belief. Details vary, of course, but in broad outline, this picture appears to be essentially correct. Second, we possess relevant historical records for a number of languages, and we can determine by examination of documented cases how much time a particular evolution has actually taken. We propose to look at some relevant documented cases here, in order to gain some appreciation of the time-depth implied by the evolution embodied in (39). This will give us a comparative perspective from which to assess the time factor in the Wik and Middle Paman cases.

Greek (Rivero, pers. comm.)

Homeric Greek (sixth century BCE) had clitic pronouns appearing in second position within the clause, i.e. P2 or Wackernagel's position. Two hundred years later (fourth century BCE), in the language of Aristotle and the major tragedies, clitic pronouns are moving away from strict P2 and show variable positioning, sometimes immediately preverbal, sometimes P2—a mixed situation. In the Middle Ages (twelfth to fifteenth century CE), clitic pronouns are V-positioned—V+Cl when the verb is clause initial, and Cl+V following material that has been moved forward to a position on the left of the verb.

What is described here is an evolution from Stage II to Stage III. The process began in the years preceding the Christian Era and it was completed some time in the Middle Ages, a period of well over a millennium. The process culminates in a Greek grammar, which is essentially that represented by the enclitic pronouns of Wik-Ngathan, Wik-Ngatharr, and Kugu Nganhcara.

Spanish (Rivero 1983, pers. comm.; Otero 1976; Nishida 1996)

In Old Spanish (twelfth century CE to 1450), clitic pronouns show variable positioning, P2 or adjacent to the verb. During the three centuries following, and in the language of Miguel de Cervantes' *Don Quijote* (1605), clitic pronouns are V-based, before or after the verb, as in mediaeval Greek. After 1750, the current Spanish system developed— clitics are still V-based, but the relative position of the clitic is determined by verbal inflection (finite, infinitive, or imperative). Dependent pronominals become proclitic to the finite verb and are, therefore, no longer constrained by the so-called 'Tobler-Mussafia Law', which blocked clitics in clause initial position prior to the modern Spanish period.

Again, the evolution that is of interest to us is from Stage II to Stage III. In the history of Spanish, this process may have been completed with greater speed than in the Greek case, but we cannot tell exactly, given that written records in Spanish do not predate the twelfth century, by which time the changes were well under way. In any event, the documented Stage II period for Spanish lasted approximately three centuries, though its inception was surely earlier, as it was firmly established in the twelfth century.

Bulgarian (Izvorski 1995)

In Bulgarian of the ninth century CE, clitic pronouns appear in P2. The use of P2 continued to the seventeenth century when it began to decline in favour of pre-verbal clitics, whose use developed and grew through the following centuries resulting in the fully evolved pre-verbal clitic pattern found in nineteenth-century Bulgarian. The system is virtually identical to that of Wik-Ngathan, Wik-Ngatharr, and Kugu Nganhcara. As pointed out by Klavans (1995), the situation represented jointly by these languages is interestingly uncommon, since the dependency is to the left, while syntactic dependency is to the right (except where the verb is clause-initial).

The Bulgarian evolution also represents the passage from Stage II to Stage III. Because of the careful work of Izvorski (1995), it is possible to identify the temporal junctures rather clearly—she shows, among other things, that the use of P2 clitics arose in Bulgarian as a result of an independent change in syntactic structure and that it increased in the period from the ninth to the thirteenth century. Thus, the linguistic record extends from the beginning of Stage II to the full achievement of Stage III, a period of approximately a millennium.

Egyptian (Loprieno 1995)

Earlier Egyptian (3000 to 1300 BCE) possessed a set of clitic pronouns, enclitics occupying P2. In Later Egyptian, from 1300 BCE to the Middle Ages (1300 CE), enclitic pronouns become restricted and gradually disappear, and new object pronouns develop with orientation to the verb, rather than to second position.

The evolution evidently proceeds from Stage II to Stage III, or possibly Stage IV. But the evolution of P2 clitics is not continuous, unlike that of the corresponding elements in the Wik languages. In Later Egyptian, the development of new V-oriented object pronouns involves a source other than the earlier enclitics.

The temporal scope in Egyptian is rather impressive, involving several millennia.

Northern Italian dialects (Rizzi 1986; Brandi and Cordin 1988)

In their evolution from their Early Romance ancestors, some Italian languages, or 'dialects', including Trentino and Fiorentino, have developed an apparent system of subject agreement, attached to the inflected auxiliary, and involving morphological material that originated as clitic pronouns. These Northern Italian elements are 'subject' clitics, evidently, and they are considered to be agreement by the authors cited, understandably, since they enter into the relation depicted in (40). If so, this case may represent an evolution to Stage IV within a family that elsewhere generally shows evolution of dependent pronominals just to Stage III—with an additional evolutionary development of proclisis in some languages, to be sure. The Northern Italian evolution would presumably proceed through all four stages, with a time-depth equivalent to that of the Romance languages which reach Stage III. The Northern Italian situation is reminiscent of Kugu Nganhcara, in which new subject enclitics coexist with older subject agreement suffixal morphology. The recently evolved Northern Italian subject clitics, coexist, of course, with subject agreement derived from Latin and Indo-European.

Summary and conclusion: Time, space, and Wik grammatical diversity

Our handle on the time dimension derives from comparative examples of the type represented in the section above. These examples all involve the evolution of dependent pronominals to Stage III, the stage that predominates in the Wik family. The shortest documented evolution is some three centuries—but this is artificially short, because of the historical accident that Spanish written records begin in the twelfth century. In the other cases, the evolution is longer, up to a millennium. If the Wik evolution is comparable, then it has taken three centuries at least, using the shortest of the historiographically dated comparison cases. Though the temporal scope is surely greater than this, we will assume it as a minimum.

We can be relatively certain that this evolution took place in situ in an area of Cape York Peninsula encompassing the region now occupied by the Wik-speaking peoples.

First, the Wik developments in relation to dependent pronominals are entirely local and cannot be traced to any other area in Cape York Peninsula or any other part of Australia occupied by Pama-Nyungan languages.

Second, the Wik languages represent an internal diversity that requires recognition of three subgroups. In relation to the evolution of dependent pronominal systems these are the following:

i. Wik-Mungkan and Wik-Me'nh: Dependent pronominals are exclusively verb-based and either suffixed or enclitic, never preverbal. Subject-dependent pronominals constitute an agreement system. Object- (and oblique-) dependent pronominals are enclitics showing optional clitic doubling. Dependent pronominals appear in the sequence subject–object.

ii. Wik-Ngathan and Wik-Ngatharr: Dependent subject and object (and oblique) pronominals are verb-based enclitics, showing optional clitic doubling. They are preferably preverbal (attached to a preverbal host), but they may also attach to the verb. Enclitics appear in the sequence subject–object.

iii. Kugu Nganhcara: There is a residual and reduced agreement system involving suffixes to the verb. In addition, a newer verb-based enclitic system is fully established involving optional clitic doubling. Enclitics are preferably attached to a preverbal host, though they may also attach to the verb. Ordering of enclitics is variable.

This is just one aspect of Wik diversity; the languages also show important differences in phonology (e.g. vowel reduction and umlaut), in morphology (e.g. the modern reflexes of the case endings, and other morphological inventories), and in the lexicon (as observed extensively earlier in this essay). A simplicity argument persuades us that this diversity developed in the present Wik area. To assume otherwise would require a complex system of migrations into the present area on the part of linguistic communities already distinct—i.e. essentially separate in-migrations. The simpler theory is that the observed diversity developed locally over a period of time that, taking all factors into consideration, greatly exceeds the time which separates 1788 from the present.

8

Conclusion

Peter Sutton

It has become a truism that classical Australian societies employed among the simplest ranges of material technology found among the world's peoples, yet they also developed perhaps the most complex systems of kinship relations ever recorded.

In the present study, we have added to the evidence of high sociocultural elaboration first established by kinship studies of Aboriginal Australia. Linguistic organisation is a comparable classical field of rich elaboration. We have complemented the few descriptions of comparable sociolinguistic complexity from other regions, especially that of north-east Arnhem Land (e.g. Schebeck 2001). These studies have been carried out in regions less heavily impacted by colonisation than others, and they suggest the likelihood that comparably complex orderings of Aboriginal linguistic geopolitics and their interweaving with traditional religion and cosmology were once found in all parts of Australia.

Ethnographic mapping of the kind we have employed here largely begins with the specific site, and works upward from there to where collectivities of those sites constitute larger entities, including the clan estate. The clan estate in the Wik Region is in classical terms the elementary linguistic country unit, and the linguistic identities of people are conferred by birth into a clan whose estate holds that language from its creation. Only by mapping a significant number of specific sites in an estate can one be precise about where that estate begins and ends. Only by having specific data on where estates of a common language begin and end can one be precise about where a broad language country or 'tribal territory', in the sense of Tindale (1974), might extend to. It also reveals cases where there is no single continuous country associated with a particular language or dialect. Environmentally based shared geopolitical identities also can only be precisely described on the basis of detailed mapping of estates onto ecological zones and watercourse systems.

In this way, we have in effect proceeded in reverse to the kind of ethnography that begins with the broad language country or 'tribal territory' and looks for language boundaries and then personal membership of the language group. This makes a point that can often be generalised in the Aboriginal case: that complicated nested sociocultural structures are better analysed not as macro-groups with subdivisions, but as micro-entities that are collocated in increasing scales to constitute broader social and cultural identities.

Rather than merely present generalisations, with perhaps cherry-picked examples as supporting evidence, we have chosen here both to describe the salient aspects of the classical linguistic anthropology of the Wik Region and also to present much of the ethnographic detail that underpins that description. For the descendants of the Old People whose cultures are glimpsed here, the factual details will outlive academic analyses by a very long time, and be far more important from the beginning. Offering factual details here will also allow future scholars to revisit the data and come to their own, hopefully more advanced, conclusions.

This study rests critically on the articulation of intensive and geographically extensive ethnographic field mapping by anthropologists with comparative and historical studies of the Wik Region's languages by linguists. Just as critically it rests on the dedication of Wik people to the task of mentoring the anthropologists and linguists. Much of that mentoring took place under remote and physically arduous conditions, as the Wik land tenure system and its interlocking with linguistic geography could only be studied in detail by relying on a rich basis of ethnographic mapping carried out on the ground, travelling by four-wheel drive, by dinghy, on foot, by plane, by helicopter, and on horseback.

8. CONCLUSION

It would be difficult to exaggerate the extent to which classical Cape York Peninsula peoples were obsessed with language. Whether it was in the domains of geopolitics, local organisation, landscape mythology, speech etiquette, singing, place-names, naming of people and their dogs, narrative traditions, joking, or verbal combat, they were unsurpassed among First Australians in the elaboration of everything to do with language. The loss of so much of this baroque heritage as daily practice is only weakly compensated for by the richness of the record.

Appendix 1: Wik clans

Peter Sutton, David Martin, John von Sturmer, Ursula McConnel, John Taylor, Athol Chase, Roger Cribb

Compiled by Peter Sutton

Sources

This appendix rests on field data recorded primarily by myself, David Martin and John von Sturmer, but also by John Taylor and Athol Chase, in the period 1969–97. Some older data are also included from mission records, and from the inter-War work of Donald Thomson and especially Ursula McConnel, and these cases are specifically acknowledged.

The clan entries in *Aak* (Sutton et al. 1990:51–99) have been much revised and augmented here. Von Sturmer's data in this document are largely those drawn from his PhD thesis (1978) by Roger and Alice Cribb for the *Aak* project, although his field work relating to entries here spans the period 1969–97. Most of the remaining information comes from raw field data or mapping reports prepared by David Martin or Peter Sutton in the period 1976–97.

The entries here are only those for clans whose primary estate affiliations lie either within or up to about 10 kilometres from the boundaries of the Wik native title claim.

Conventions

Clan number

Each clan has been assigned a number. This is sometimes the same as an estate number, sometimes not. It is therefore not possible to know the corresponding estate number simply by knowing the clan number. A clan/estate numbering cross-reference list is provided at the end of the document but similar cross-references are also embedded in each clan record.

Surnames

In most cases, a patrilineal clan is associated with one or several surnames that have come into use in the last century and that may often be used as a shorthand means of referring to the clan. The reader is reminded that this does **NOT** mean that any Wik person who carries a particular surname is necessarily a member of the clan concerned. This obviously includes the many women who have acquired surnames from husbands, but may also include, for example, some children who belong to the clan of their father but retain the surname of their mother. In a number of cases of extinct clans, no surname became established. Accordingly, in the cross-reference lists, we cite a first name (such as Cockatoo, Clan 1) or a name based on a principal totem such as Kugu Wayn-gan ('Curlew Language').[1]

There are a number of cases where people of different clans have the same surname. In some cases it is because they have common male totemic names on which the mission surnames became based—for example, the Woollas of Oony-aw (northern Woollas) and the Woollas of Kendall River (southern Woollas), who share Blowfly totem (*Wul*). In other cases, people may have the same non-Aboriginal surname such as Kepple, but again this does not mean they have the same clan or estate—there are four different Kepple families in the Wik Region, each with distinct estates.

---

1   Technically speaking, this type of nomenclature is a reference to a 'patrilect', i.e. a patrilineally transmitted linguistic identity at the clan or sub-clan level, in contrast with a 'communalect' or set of dialects known by a single name such as Wik-Mungkan, Kugu Muminh, and so on.

Descendants

Here we first deal with whether the clan has descendants of any kind, and second with whether or not the clan also has patrilineal descendants and is thus still viable as a clan. In the event that the relevant patrilines have become extinct, it is common for non-patrilineal descendants to assert particularly close rights and interests in the country of the clan.

Core estate interests

This is not the place to attempt to list all countries in which all members of any single clan might have rights and interests. Clan members have a range of different mothers, and fathers' mothers, and mothers' mothers, for example, in whose various countries those members always have some kind of interest, even a profound one. But the scope here is deliberately kept narrowed down just to the core estate (sometimes two estates) corporately associated with the clan under consideration. Maps A2.1–A2.13 in this volume are of core estates.

Ceremony

This refers just to the regional cult-ceremony with which the clan and its estate is most closely associated; the many other ceremonial affiliations of groups are here omitted. As explained elsewhere, this form of categorisation works most neatly for clans with estates between the Embley and Holroyd rivers, where the ceremonial groups, running from north to south, are Shivirri (Saarra, Chivirri), Winchanam, Apelech, Puch and Wanam (Map A1.1).[2]

---

2   There are sub-categorisations for some such affiliations, such as 'Three Stripe' Winchanam and Thu'-Apelech (aka Apelech-Thu').

LINGUISTIC ORGANISATION AND NATIVE TITLE

Map A1.1: WCYP ceremonial groupings

APPENDIX 1

Clan totems

The rather artificial nature of the present exercise is most apparent here. Clan members may have many totems, as these lists attest. Different members of the same clan may lay emphasis on some totems more than others, genealogically distinct clan segments (or sub-clans) may have slightly different sets of totems, and on occasion there is incomplete agreement on the question of whether a clan has a certain totem or not. These factors, combined with the limitations of memory, mean that lists of totems offered by a clan's members tend to vary about a common core, and the lists may come in different orders. Variation in the ordering of the first few totems is often significant. For the most part, we do not attempt to reproduce that degree of complexity here. These lists for the most part merely contain those totems that have been recorded as belonging to the clan concerned. They are often, not always, in some kind of order of importance. One principal or main totem is often used as the basis of naming the clan or clan segment as the bearer of a distinct dialect (totemic patrilect).

Wherever possible we provide the list of clan totems in the language of the clan concerned, together with an English translation. If exceptions to this occur, the name of the language is noted.

Totemic names

These are names of people or names of dogs. They are references, usually oblique, to totems of the clan. The human names are distinguished as to whether they are designated in local languages to be 'Big Names' or 'Small Names'. Records of such names, including this distinction between big and small, go back to the late 1920s in the numerous personal data cards kept by missionaries at Aurukun. Some are quite distinctive of a particular clan and thus connote a particular estate. Many are shared by members of more than one clan, but these name-sharing clans tend to have estates that are linked, or contiguous, or at least within the same wider sub-region, and the names may thus also have connotations with a specific sub-region rather than a single estate.

Where a name has been translated then the translation is provided in inverted commas—for example, '[Whale] threw spume'. Where the name itself occurs in mission or other early records this spelling is distinguished by also being placed between inverted commas. If the early spelling relates to a name for which we have modern records in a more accurate orthography, it is placed in square brackets after the modern spelling—for example, Wike-thaken ['Wikatukkan'].

Dog names are distinguished as to whether their bearer is male or female. In most cases the dog name is an oblique and poetic reference to a patrilineal clan totem of the dog's owner. In a few cases a dog name is the same as the name of a clan totem of its owner, such as Thunggan ('Flying Fish', Clan 63). Dogs are kin in Wik tradition, and their names reflect their membership in patrilineal totemic descent groups. They are typically the daughters and sons of their owners.

Language(s)

Most clans have a single linguistic affiliation, but some have two or three. The languages listed here are only those of affiliation, not those actually spoken by clan members, which may run to half a dozen or more. A language normally has several different names depending on the various languages in which it is named, but here, in general, the name of the language is given only in a single form, its own. Where the name is being superseded, as in the case of Andjingith becoming generally known as Wik-Ayengench (see Clan 1), we provide both names.

Focal sites

Here we often provide the name of one or two main places in the estate of a clan, partly as a means of distinguishing it. At different eras, the 'main place' in a clan's estate may shift from one site to another, possibly due to the influence of different individuals, but in general the focal role of certain sites in each estate tends to be stable. This can be deduced from the number of important places listed on old Aurukun Mission personal data cards (usually only one placename per person), which have retained their salience into the present.

Nickname(s)

Here we give, where known, the 'nickname' of the clan's members. As explained in greater detail in Chapter 3, these names usually refer to distinctive environmental features of one or several estates, or to a major placename in or close to certain estates.

APPENDIX 1

McConnel

Wherever possible, we have reproduced here the typewritten data of Ursula McConnel relating to what she called 'local groups of the Wik-Munkan tribe' (1930b), managing in most cases to identify her 'local groups' or 'totemic groups' with one of the clans of our own records. Her list of 25 'local groups', consisting of 38 'totemic groups' altogether, was later published but in a much abbreviated form (McConnel 1930a:204–5), so here we rely on the fuller typescript. We retain her spellings but have rearranged her material so as to make it more readable. As discussed in Chapter 5, a number of the clans McConnel referred to as being of the 'Wik-Munkan tribe' actually belonged to other varieties such as Wik-Iiyanh.

McConnel assigned each local group a Roman numeral. Where McConnel was unsure whether two groups were distinct, she placed them under a single Roman numeral and called them (a), (b), (c), etc. She believed that all Wik estates were, or had been until recently, distinguished by a handful of 'totem centres' for phenomena that were also the major totems of the local group owning the estate. This is the inland pattern, but does not obtain on the coast.

Here McConnel gives the names of the totem centres, followed by the totem for each site, followed by the clan names that are based on the same totem. Male names are marked (m), female names (f). These all appear to be human names only. Her translations of the names—mostly provided by her informants, some apparently containing her own guesswork—are next to them. Finally, under each clan heading we reproduce her estimates of how many members of the group survived in 1929.

Clan list

CLAN 1

Surnames: (Old Murray, Cockatoo)

Descendants: descendants include Clan 58 q.v.; Clan 1 patriline extinct

Core estate interests: Estate 1 (Thoekel)

Ceremony: Apelech

Clan totems:	**Translation:**
Thum	Fire
Minh War	Mangrove Oyster
Yaatemay	Carpet Snake
Thinelpal	Dugong
Maantalent	Sea Turtle
Walemoericheyn	Whale
Piipep(-piip)	Pied Oystercatcher
Minh Walepayn (Piich)	Big Scale Mullet
Thoeche Ngempiy	Happy Family Bird

Totemic names:

Ku'-thiikel-ee'enh '[Whale] threw spume'	Male	Human
Wuypeng-ee'enh '[Whale] threw [bones] on bank'	Male	Human
Thiinethe-ngaycheyn 'Saw a Coconut' ['Teentanycha', 'Teentingeitchina']	Male	Human
Kaalep ['Carlippe']	Female	Human
Thaankup ['Thancoupie']	Female	Human

Language(s):
Andjingith (Wik-Ayengench)
Wik-Ngatharr
Wik-Paach

Focal sites:
239 Thoekel

Nickname(s):
Thoekelem ('From Thoekel')

CLAN 2

Surnames: Peinkinna

Descendants: yes; patriline extant; see also closely linked Clan 29 (Taismans)

APPENDIX 1

Core estate interests: Estate 2 (Top Love River)

Ceremony: Apelech

Clan totems:	**Translation:**
Nhomp	Wedgetailed Eagle
Theelinh	Two Young Women

Totemic names:

Peynken, rarely Pengkyen ['Peinkinna']	Male	Human
Piimongk [ref. Carpet Snake]	Female	Human
War-maken 'Squeezing Oysters'	Male	Dog
Oonem-thee'enh 'Squirting' [ref. Oysters?]	Female	Dog

Language(s):
Wik-Ayengench
Wik-Mungkan
Wik-Paach

Nickname(s):
Pil-Man-ik-en (obscure; reference to mangroves?)

McConnel
Local group XI (b)

Totem-centre(s):
Tokali trees with snakes' holes etc.
Totems oingorpan carpet snake

Names:

Kukantin (m)	snake has its hole in a tree, comes out when poked
Painkan (m)	snake's skin
Tutthawitua (m)	meat from snake's back
Pamuka (f)	pam – man, uka – go down, snake goes down a hole when man approaches
Pamietjan (f)	pam – man, ietjan – vomits
Pamiwanta (f)	pam – man, wanta – leaves, snake leaves a hole when disturbed

Names:

<u>Akatonamamata</u> (f)   <u>aka</u> – towards, <u>tonama</u> – another, <u>mata</u> – moves, snake moves to another hole when disturbed

<u>Wiwa</u>   little bird frightened by snake

1929 pop. [12–15] (in combination with Clan 29)

CLAN 3

Surnames: (Coconut)

Descendants: yes; patriline extinct

Core estate interests: Estate 3 (Small Lake, Uthuk Eelen) (cf. Clan 59)

Ceremony: Apelech

Clan totems:	Translation:
Minh Nguyempang	Magpie Goose

Totemic names:

| Wike-thakenh ['Wikatukkan'] | Female | Human | Big |
| Chaalemnganh | Female | Human | Small |

Language(s):
Wik-Ayengench
Wik-Ngatharr

Focal sites:
35 Munpunng (Kempiy)

Nickname(s):
Uthuk-Eelenem, Weenem-Eelenem ('From Small Lake')

CLAN 4

Surnames: Ampeybegan, (Bowenda)

Descendants: yes; patriline extant

Core estate interests: Estate 4 (Big Lake, Uthuk Aweyn), also Estate 3 (Uthuk Eelen)

Ceremony: Apelech

APPENDIX 1

Clan totems: **Translation:**
Eleyepeyn   Fresh Water Shark
Minh Kalpay   Magpie Goose
Minh Poowkenh   Pelican
Minh Aarrench   Black Duck
Minh Kechech   Water Snake Species
Puunchelken   Death Adder
Minh Ngum   Black Cormorant
May Mathenngay   Fruit Tree Species
May Ka'err   Hairy Yam Species
May Wooerngk   Arrowroot
Minh Thikiy   Water Hen
Nhathe Pachenyak   Dawn

Totemic names:

Ampe-peeypengan ['Ampeybegan']	Male	Human	Big
Pungk Kalpay 'Goose Knees'	Male	Human	Small
Thiineth-ngaycheyn 'Saw a Coconut' ['Teentingetcha']	Male	Human	Small
Keewethen ['Keevatan']	Female	Human	
Nyal'aath ['Nyarlot', sometimes Naalet]	Female	Human	
Mampen-ow 'Isn't it Rich!' [Ref. pulverised yams][3] ['Mumpowan']	Female	Human	

Language(s):
Wik-Ayengench (long ago)
Wik-Ngatharr (now)

Focal sites:
8 Uthuk Aweyn

Nickname(s):
Uthuk-Awenyem, Weenem-Awenyem ('From Big Lake')

---

3   In this clan's language *mamp* = 'mash, ooze' (nouns), hence *kun-mamp* 'diarrhoea'.

CLAN 5

Surnames: Wikmunea (possibly Nobbelin also)

Descendants: yes; patriline extant

Core estate interests: Estate 5 (Kencherrang)

Ceremony: Apelech, Thu'-Apelech

Clan totems:	Translation:
May Ka'err (BL) May Nham (SL)	Hairy Yam Species
Thiiweth	White Cockatoo
Minh Thechel	Sand Goanna
Uk	Brown Snake
Thuuk Pool	Carpet Snake sp.
Minh Kalpay	Magpie Goose
May Wooerngk	Skin of Arrowroot,
Minh Kechech	Water Snake Species
Minh Aarrench	Black Duck
May Mathenngay	Fruit Species
Minh Thi'er	Bony Fish Species
Minh Mithen (?Moenthen)	?
Ele-yepeyn	Fresh Water Shark
Kuyen	Wild Honey
Thiweth	Owl Species [cf. Nn thiiw 'owl sp', thiiweth 'white cockatoo']

Totemic names:

Wik-man-ey (now often Wikmunya) – ['Wikmunea'] [from White Cockatoo totem – 'It Cried Out']	Male	Human	
Mamp-wa'en 'Leaching Half Salty Yams'	Male	Human	Big
Ampe-peeypengan ['Ampeybegan']	Male	Human	Small

'Wolmby' [Ref. Shark because of site interests at Koe']

APPENDIX 1

Totemic names:

Thum-munhtheng 'In the Ashes'	Male	Human	
Pam-nhumey-echeyn ['Pamnamietna'] [from White Cockatoo totem]	Female	Human	Big
Pam-poonchel-pathenh [from White Cockatoo totem]	Female	Human	Small
Mampen-ow 'Isn't it Rich!' [Ref. pulverised yams] ['Mumpowan']	Female	Human	
Iing ['Eeng', 'Inga']	Female	Human	
Mangke-puunch ['Munkapornch'] 'Long Grass Stems'	Female	Human	
Wooerngke-thupen 'Arrowroot Flower'	Male	Dog	
With-yeeypenh [Ref. Hairy Yam]	Female	Dog	

Language(s):

Wik-Alken (also known as Wik-Ngatharr)

Focal sites:

333 Woowkeng Nr (Kencherreng)

Nickname(s):

Information from Archiewald Otomorathin: 1. Pethem ('From the Saltplains'), 2. Thook[em?] (obscure; said to be from thok 'bushfire' but cf. thook 'long, tall' (Mn)). Information from Eva Pootchemunka and Edna Pootchemunka: Kuth-kempem ('Topside People').

CLAN 6

Surnames: Wolmby, Peemuggina A*

Descendants: yes; patriline extant

Core estate interests: Estate 6 (Aayk); parts of Estate 11 (Kaapathenh)

Ceremony: Thu'-Apelech

Clan totems:[4]	**Translation:**
Eleyepeyn, Kuunger, Theelecheyn	Estuarine Sharks
Minh Chiiynchiiyn	Rat Species of Grass Plains
Thupenaw	Silver Salmon
May Maach	Red Wallaby Fruit, *Eugenia carissoides*
Minh Thiiw	Owl Species
Minh Nguk	Owl Species
May Murrken	Fruit Species, *Canthium sp.*
Aak-ngut	Small Snake Species
Minh Meerp	Hawk Species
Minh Kalpay	Magpie Goose
May Kookenpay	Fruit Species, *Mallotus polyadenus*
Kuump	Blackfruit
Kalk Thu'	Single-barb Hardwood Spear
Thaaleny-engkech	Tree sp. (name given for both *Litsea glutinosa* and *Ixora klanderana*)

---

4   Details recorded for the senior segment, that of descendants of Wikmunea Wolmby:

Surnames: Wolmby

Descendants: yes; patriline extant

Core estate interests: Estate 6; strong custodial interests in Estate 24 (Chaaperreng)

Ceremony: Apelech, Thu'

Clan totems:	**Translation:**
Minh Piith	Grassbird
Ngo'ench	Bushfire
Karrekurr	Rat Species
Minh Thantekuch	Bony Bream
Pawkiy	Shark Species
Keech (Mn)	White Crane
May Kuump	Blackfruit
May Iith	Red Wallaby Fruit

Totemic names: Ku'-Thiikarem   Male   Human   Big

Language(s): Wik-Ngathan

APPENDIX 1

Totemic names:

Waalempay ['Wolmby'] [Ref. Shark Fin Ripples]	Male	Human	Big
Ku'-thiikarem [Ref. Bushrat]	Male	Human	Big
Piim-akenh* [Peemuggina] 'Swore up Close'?	Male	Human	
Wik-maney ['Wikmunea']	Male	Human	Small
Thiineth-ngaycheyn 'Saw a Coconut' ['Teentingeitchina']	Male	Human	
Uthikeng ['Big-headed Catfish'] ['Ootekna']	Female	Human	Big
Yuuymuk ['Yewimuk']	Female	Human	Big
Nguteng-wiiykenh 'Spoke in the Night'	Female	Human	
Aanchemalkenh ['Anjimullken', 'Anchamalkn']	Female	Human	Small
Aakpeyn ['Arkpenya']*	Female	Human	Small
Wituk	Female	Human	Small
Yemp-unchelkenh '[Rat] Heaps up Grass'	Male	Dog	
Kaangk-wuu'enh '[Rat] Likes to Clean Out [Nest]'	Male	Dog	
Kuump-paathe'rr 'Blackfruit Flower'	Male	Dog	
May-thupenh 'Flower: Red Wallaby Fruit'	Female	Dog	
Ngak-kuy-ee'anh '[Shark] Makes Ripples'	Female	Dog	
Thiikarpenh	Female	Dog	

Language(s):
Wik-Ngathan

Focal sites:
85 Aayk

Nickname(s):
Kuuchenm ('From the Lancewood [Ridges]')

[*Inclusion of Peemuggina branch widely but not universally accepted.]

LINGUISTIC ORGANISATION AND NATIVE TITLE

CLAN 7

Surnames: Toikalkin (former generations)

Descendants: yes; patriline extant but see Clan 32

Core estate interests: Estate 7 (Iincheng) but see Clan 32 (core interests now Estate 5, Kencherrang)

Ceremony: Apelech

Clan totems:	Translation:
May Ka'err	Hairy Yam
Mow, Chaanchaan	White Cockatoo
Thiweth	Owl Species
Minh Thechel	Sand Goanna

Totemic names:

Pam-poonchel-pathenh   Female Human

Language(s):
Wik-Ngatharr

Focal sites:
88 Iincheng

Nickname(s):
Kuuchenm ('From the Lancewood [Ridges]')

CLAN 8

Surnames: Namponan, Karntin, Walmbeng (latter in former generations only)

Descendants: yes for all; Namponan patriline extant; Karntin patriline extant; Walmbeng patriline extant but core estate interest now Estate 1 (see Clan 58)

Core estate interests: Estate 8 (Warpang)

Ceremony: Thu'-Apelech

APPENDIX 1

Clan totems:	Translation:
Minh Thiiynchiiyn	Bush Rat
Eleyepeyn	Freshwater Shark
Kalk	Spear
Peel	Small Carpet Snake
Kurraw	Salmon
Pungk	Knee
Kalk Thu'	Single-barb Hardwood Spear
Maach?	Red Wallaby Fruit?

Totemic names:

Kanhtheyn ['Karntin']	Male	Human	Big
Waalmpay ['Walmbeng']	Male	Human	Big
?Nhampuninh ['Namponan']	Male	Human	
Piim-akenh ['Peemuggina']	Male	Human	
Themperring	Male	Human	
May-ngoonch-keempenh	Female	Human	Big
Maach-thupenh 'Flower of Red Wallaby Fruit'	Female	Dog	

Language(s):
Wik-Elken
Wik-Ngatharr

Focal sites:
114 Warpang

Nickname(s):
Kuuchenm ('From the Lancewood [Ridges]')

CLAN 9

Surnames: Comprabar, Pootchemunka B.

Descendants: yes; patriline extant

Core estate interests: Estate 9 (Eer-en)

Ceremony: Apelech

Clan totems:	**Translation:**
Minh Taltal	Plover
Minh Thinthaw	Water Python
May Kuthel (Thoeng)	'Pandja', Boolgooroo
Minh Imp	Freshwater Fish Species
Minh Pelkem	Small Lagoon Jewfish
Minh Intiyn	Jewfish Species
Minh Oolp	Jewfish Species
May Athun	Leichhardt Tree
Yuk Akwel	Tree sp.

Totemic names:

Puche-mangk ['Pootchemunka']	Male	Human	Big
Ngak-yangk-wok ['Ngakyunkwokka']	Male	Human	Small
Math-athenh ['Martuttna']	Female	Human	

Language(s):
Wik-Elken/Wik-Ngatharr

Nickname(s):
Thiik-Winchenm ('From the Sweetgrass Ridges')

CLAN 10

Surnames: Koonutta B

Descendants: yes; patriline extinct

Core estate interests: Estate 10 (Waayeng)

Ceremony: Apelech, Thu'-Apelech

Clan totems:	**Translation:**
Minh Thawel	Wallaby
Minh Warrk	Short-necked Tortoise
Kuchicheyn	Lizard Species

APPENDIX 1

Clan totems: | **Translation:**
May Errk | Lily Species
May Keenchok | Unidentified Plant
May Ka'err Ngunhthem | Half Salty Hairy Yam
Upel | Jabiru
Kuur | Poison Tree
Ngalpe-ngalpen | Emu Hunter Hero

Totemic names:
Minh-yangkeng-unhthenh — Male Human
Pam-theepkanh — Female Human
Tha'-piik — Female Human

Language(s):
Wik-Ep, also known as Wik-Iit

Focal sites: 204 Waayeng

Nickname(s):
Waayengem ('From Waayeng [Lagoon]')

CLAN 11

Surnames: (One man remembered as Wik Piith—i.e. 'the Grassbird Man')[5]

Descendants: yes; patriline extinct

Core estate interests: Estate 11 (Kaapathenh)

Ceremony: Apelech

Clan totems: | **Translation:**
Piith (main totem) | Grass Bird
Yuul' | Bailer Shell
Keren | Conch Shell

---

[5] He may have been Henry, father of Laura, who was mother of Rhoda Pootchemunka.

Clan totems:	**Translation:**
Minh Chirrn	Kite Hawk
May Kuth	Long Yam Species
Minh Ngaypathenh	White Tern?
Yuul' Thoengoen	Baler Shell Species
Puun Paal'	Fish Species
Minh Puuch (= Theepenh)	Edible Seashell Species

Totemic names:

Nyoopelen	Male	Human
Errkema-mamenh 'Quickly Grabbed'	Male	Human
Thiinethe-ngaycheyn 'Saw a Coconut' ('Teetaneetcha')	Male	Human
Wik-thaken ['Wikatukkin']	Female	Human
Mithamngan [cf. 'Mitanguttin']	Female	Human
Chaalemenh (?Chaalemnganh)	Female	Human

Language(s):
Wik-Ngatharr

Focal sites:
676 Yu'engk

Nickname(s):
Ngamp-Thew-enem ('From the Mouth of Kirke River')

CLAN 12

Surnames: Yunkaporta (A) (northern Yunkaportas)

Descendants: yes; patriline extant

Core estate interests: Estate 12 (Um-thunth, Moving Stone)

Ceremony: Apelech

APPENDIX 1

Clan totems:	Translation:
Minh Korr'	Brolga
May Umpey	Lily Species
Minh Marrp	Sleepy Fish
Yuk Marrp	Acacia Species
May Kooth	Lily Species, including Stock, Stalk, Flower
Yangk	Lower Leg, including Foot of any Species
Chaaperr	Blood
Ochengan	Mudshell
[not recorded]	Young Black Duck

Totemic names:

Yangke-poot ['Yunkaporta'] '[Brolga] Lower Leg Tendon'	Male	Human	Big
Kaa'-wop '[Brolga's] Beak Whistle'	Male	Human	Small
Ngangke-chaaperr 'Heart's Blood'	Male	Human	Small
May-wurrpem-mungk '[Brolga] Eating Food From Nest'	Female	Human	Big
May-komp ['Mikompa', 'M.K.']	Female	Human	Small

Language(s):
Wik-Mungkan

Focal sites:
169 Um-thunhth
881 Moving Stone

Nickname(s):
Thomp-Ompemem ('From the Beach in Between [Two Rivers]')

CLAN 13

Surnames: Marbendinar

Descendants: yes; patriline extant (see also linked Clan 16)

Core estate interests: Estate 13 (Thinthaw-aw)

Ceremony: Apelech

Clan totems:	**Translation:**
Minh wooep	Swamp Snake
Ma'	Hand
Upen	Milky Mangrove
Yangk	Lower Leg
Thuut	Breast
Yuk Ngucheman	Turpentine Tree
Thuuk Thinhthaw	Water Python
Thuuk Thayen	Black Snake Species
Minh Wath	White-tailed Water Rat
May Ma'-put [= Ma'-pinch, Mn]	Arrowroot
Thuuk Wunt	Whip Snake
Yuk Thiimpin	Hibiscus Species
Minh Paap	Cheeky Hawk (Kite)
Kakelang	Hawk Species
Minh Pik-Kuchiy	Jewfish
[not recorded]	People Performing Malp Ceremony
Minh Kekuyeng	Echidna
Nyeeyn	Fly

Totemic names:

Ma'-pentenh ['Marbendinar'; 'Hand Come Out']	Male	Human	
Minh-yankeng-unhthenh	Male	Human	Big
Ku'-nhat ['Koonutta']	Male	Human	Big
Ku'-wuy-thee'en [Ref. Water Rat]	Male	Human	Big
Wany-matan ['Wynmuttin'; High-climber]	Male	Human	
Thip-kakalang 'Greedy Hawk'	Female	Human	Big
Yuk-wayenh-thee'enh ['Yukwainten'] [Ref. Echidna Quills]	Female	Human	Small
Upen-peeth 'Flower of Milky Mangrove'	Female	Dog	

APPENDIX 1

Totemic names:

| Upen 'Milky Mangrove' | Male | Dog |
| Maaken 'Greedy Hawk Pouncing' | Male | Dog |

Language(s):
Wik-Ep
Wik-Me'enh

Focal sites:
567 Thinhthaw-aw

Nickname(s):
Pin-Poeykelem ('From Waterlily Leaf [Country]')

CLAN 14

Surnames: Pootchemunka (A)

Descendants: yes; patriline extant

Core estate interests: Estate 14 (Wanke-nhiyeng), Estate 32 (Yongk-uyengam), combined as one; see also Clans 35 (Ngakyunkwokka, Kawangka, Bell) and 37 (Koo'oila).

Ceremony: Winchenem

Clan totems:	**Translation:**
Minh Oolp	Freshwater Jewfish
Yuk Yongk	Ironwood
Yuk Put	Bloodwood
Yuk Puch	Swamp Mahogany
Minh Akul	Freshwater Jewfish
Minh Kaa'-kucheng	Mature Minh Akul
Minh Ponchath	Frill-necked Lizard
Minh Ngaamp	Black Water Snake
Taltál	Plover
May Kuthel	Boolgooroo (vegetable)
Thinthaw	Water Python
Kelmpang	Galah

Totemic names:

Puche-mangk ['Pootchemunka'] 'Swamp Mahogany-Base'	Male	Human	Big
Ku'-kathempang	Male	Human	Small
Mathepuuk ['Marthapook']	Female	Human	Big

Puukiy ('Porky' in mission records) also a Female Human Big Name, but may be familiar form of Mathepuuk

Puukew ['Red Berry, *Abrus precatorius*']	Female	Human	Big
Nhuken-pech [Ref. Grass Tree]	Male	Dog	
Waathiy-kathenh [Ref. Cocky Apple String?]	Male	Dog	
Akul-pech 'Hole of Tree Sp.'	Male	Dog	
Put-pech 'Hole of Bloodwood Tree'	Female	Dog	
Peel'-pech 'Hole of *Leptospermum*'	Female	Dog	

Language(s):

Wik-Mungkan

Focal sites:

120 Wanke-nhiyeng
746 Yongk-uyengam

Nickname(s):

May-Mangkem ('From Abundant Vegetable Food [Country]')

CLAN 15

Surnames: Landis, Gothachalkenin, Eundatumweakin

Descendants: yes; patriline extant

Core estate interests: Estate 15 (Thaangkunh-nhiin)

Ceremony: Apelech

Clan totems:	Translation:
Ngamel	Mature Flat-tailed Stringray
Yuumel	Immature Flat-tailed Stringray
Kalk	Spear

APPENDIX 1

Clan totems: **Translation:**
Wul Blowfly
Thaach Breakers
Puthen Beach
Thap-kulath Hammerhead Shark
Wuuleth Catfish Species
Apelech Clear Water
Yuk Wenthen Lancewood
Yuk Oelaan *Hibiscus tiliaceus*

Totemic names:

(Ku'-)Thaach-elkenh ['Gothachalkenin'] '[Dog +] Breakers Rising'	Male	Human	Big
Ku'-pel-empenh 'Dog + Spearshaft Lumps'	Male	Human	Small
Ooentetham-iincheyn '[Ray] Goes on Belly'; [cf. Mission surname 'Eundatumweakin' clearly from Ooentetham-weykenh: '[Ray] Travels on Belly'	Male	Human	Small
Wul 'Blowfly'	Male	Human	Small
Thoelp-won ['Telpoanna']	Female	Human	
'Kornamnayuh' ('K.O.')	Female	Human	
?Thak-nhooyngk	Female	Human	
?Iimpen-pon ['Eembinpawn']	Female	Human	
Yuumel-pu' 'Flat-tailed Ray Vagina'	Female	Dog	
Kaay-tha'eyn 'Removing Stringray Barb'	?	Dog	
Makenh 'Squeezing [Ray Flesh]'	?	Dog	

Language(s):
Wik-Ngathan (for a time 'Wik-Iincheyn')

Focal sites:
130 Thaangkunh-nhiin

Nickname(s):
Puthen Nhikenem ('From the Beach in Between [Two Rivers]')

CLAN 16

Surnames: Marpoondin

Descendants: yes; patriline extant (see also linked Clan 13)

Core estate interests: Estate 16 (Am, Bullyard)

Ceremony: Mixed Apelech

Clan totems:	Translation:
Ngaaken Mut	Dog Tail
Upen (?)	Poison tree
Minh Thiiw	Owl Species
Kekuyeng	Echidna
Tawetaw	Nightjar ('Carpenter Bird')
Miintin	Sea Turtle
Kuyeng	Leaden flycatcher

Totemic names:

Ma'e-pantiyn	Male	Human
['Marpoondin', 'Marpoondinyar'] '[Echidna] Making a Fist'		
'Korwuthaen/Korweartin'	Male	Human
Yuk-wayenh-thee'enh ['Yukwainten']	Female	Human
(cf. May Yukway 'Blackfruit'		
Minh Yukway 'Mudfish')	?	Human
Thoeyp-keykel 'Black Greedy-Hawk'	Female	Human
Wonhth-athenh ['Wontatin']	Female	Human
Mak-waa'en	Male	Human

Language(s):
Wik-Me'enh

Focal sites:
124 Am

Nickname(s):
Pin-Poeykelem ('From Waterlily Leaf [Country]')

APPENDIX 1

CLAN 17

Surnames: Pamtoonda

Descendants: yes; patriline extant

Core estate interests: Estate 17 (Wal-ngal)

Ceremony: Winchenem

Clan totems:	Translation:
Minh Aarrench	Black Duck
Minh Keemp	Flying Fox
Thaypen	Taipan
May Po'el	Nonda Fruit
Yuk Thanchel	Milky Pine
Ngangk-wik-thawen	Heartbeat
Minh Wooep	'Stormbird'
Pam	Man
Yuk Kom	File Leaf Tree, *Ficus opposita*
Punhth	Creek/Arm
Ngaay	Lightning
Ngooy	Rainbow (= Taipan)
Mee'	Eyes
Minh Pe'	Australasian Grebe
Minh Woy	Whistler Duck
Minh Puypenhthang	White-eyed Duck
Minh Miwen	Green Pygmy Goose
Yuk Upen	Milky Mangrove (Poisonous)
Minh Waliy	Swamp Fish Species
Minh Wooech	Freshwater Crayfish
Minh Kompel	Swamp Fish Species (?Rainbow Fish)

Totemic names:

Pam-t(h)uunt ['Pamtoonda'] [Ref. Man + Arm/Creek]	Male	Human	Big
Pam-alken ['Pamulken'] ?'Man Being Struck'	Male	Human	Big
Thaypen-kump ['Tybingoompa'] 'Taipan's Urine [=Rain]'	Male	Human	Big
Thante-kul 'Angry Eyes'	Male	Human	Big
Ku'-wooepeth ['Koowearpta'] [Ref. Dog + Stormbird]	Male	Human	Small
Punhthe-nhethenh 'Arm/Creek-?'	Male	Human	
May-nhuuth ['Minoota'] 'Smelling Fruit' [Ref. Flying Foxes Scent Food]	Female	Human	Big
Maame-ngooy ['Marmoya'] [Ref. Rainbow]	Female	Human	Small
Thum-pe' ['Fire' + 'Aust.Grebe']	Female	Human	Small
Wump-Piiken ['Hitting Flying Foxes']	Male	Dog	
Mem-maaken [Ref. Crushing Flying Fox]	?	Dog	

Language(s):
Wik-Mungkan

Focal sites:
2101 Wal-ngal

Nickname(s):
Kon-Koothem ('From Waterlily Leaf [Country]')

CLAN 18

Surnames: Koomeeta, Pamulkan, Tybingoompa

Descendants: yes; patrilines extant

Core estate interests: Estate 18

APPENDIX 1

Ceremony: Apelech

Clan totems:	**Translation:**
Ngooy	Rainbow
Thaypen	Taipan
Ngaay	Lightning/Thunder
Thulepath	Jabiru
Minh Wuungkem (= Wuchen-thak)	Barramundi
Minh Wel	Blue-tongue Lizard

Totemic names:

Thaypen-kump ['Tybingoompa'] 'Taipan's Urine [=Rain]'	Male	Human	Big
Ku'-miith ['Koomeeta'] 'Dog + Juvenile Taipan'	Male	Human	Small
Pam-alken ['Pamulkan'] Male 'Man Struck [by Lightning]'		Human	Small
May-thip-kompen	Male	Human	

('Uki' a common male name this clan - Yukay? Totemic?)

'Nunkatiapin' possibly belongs here (Ngangka-thaypen?) probably name of deceased husband of Gladys Nunkatiapin (Gilbert 1977:292), usually known as Gladys Tybingoompa (Thaypen-kump, see above); her husband Timothy was of this clan.

Kum-yelem-wucheyn ['Koomeyalmootina'] ('File Fig Crawling')	Human Female	Big	
Piinmer-athenh ['Peemerratan'] 'Taipan Bitten/Coiling'	Female	Human	Small
Nhath-thi'eng-ooethenh 'Thunder Calling Out West'	Female	Human	Big
?Yooerentanen	Female	Dog	

Language(s):
Wik-Elken
Wik-Ngatharr

Focal sites:
127 Oonem-ee'enh

Nickname(s):
Eere-mangkem ('from the mouth of Knox River')

CLAN 19

Surnames: Peemuggina B (e.g. Arkapenya deceased)

Descendants: patriline extinct (but see Clan 6 disputed inclusion of segment C, Peemugginas)

Core estate interests: Estate 19

Ceremony: Apelech, Thu'

Clan totems:	Translation:
Minh Kurraw	Salmon
May Kuump	Blackfruit
May Iith (May Maach, Nn)	Red Wallaby Fruit
Minh Thaw (= Minh Wath)	Water Rat
Nyiingk-kuchen	Shark species

Totemic names:

Piim-akenh ['Peemuggina'] '?Swearing Close'	Male	Human
Uthikeng ['Oothekna']	Female	Human
[Ref. 'Curry' of Salmon; however uthik(eng) also means big-headed catfish]		
Yuuymuk ['Yewimuk']	Female	Human
Aanchemalkenh ['Anjimullken']	Female	Human
Nguteng-wiiykenh	Female	Human
Aak-peyn ['Arkpenya']	Female	Human

Language(s):
Wik-Ngathan

APPENDIX 1

Focal sites:
2006 Ngak-pungericheng

Nickname(s):
Eere-mangkem ('from the mouth of Knox River')

CLAN 20

Surnames: Yunkaporta B. (southern Yunkaportas)

Descendants: yes; patriline extant

Core estate interests: Estate 20

Ceremony: Apelech

Clan totems:	Translation:
Korr'	Brolga
Ku'	Dog
May Umpey	Lily Root, *Nymphaea lotus*
May Wum	Lily Seeds ('Rice'), *Nymphaea lotus*
May Kooth	Water Lily, *Nymphaea lotus*
Yaalecheyn	Mudshell
Wopenh	Bamboo Species
Keelp	Leichhardt Tree, *Nauclea orientalis*
Marrp	Acacia Species, *Thryptomene oligandra*
Minh Mee'	Ectoparasite Found on Brolgas
Chaaperr, Wewem	Blood
Woopen	Flesh of Mudshell
Minh Yuumpach	? [?Snake, Yuumech?, cf. yuum 'Black-headed Python']

Totemic names:

Kaa'-wop '[Brolga's] Beak Whistle'	Male	Human	Big
Minha Ngangke-chaaperr 'Animal's Heart's Blood'	Male	Human	Big
Yangke-poot ['Yunkaporta']	Male	Human	Small

Totemic names:

'Brolga Lower Leg Tendon'			
Ku'-nhiich 'Dog-Curry Tree'	Male	Human	Big
Pam-kooch ['Pamcotch']	Female	Human	Big
May-wurrpem-mungk	Female	Human	Big
'[Brolga] Eating Food From Nest'			
May-komp ['Mikompa']	Female	Human	Small
'Brolga Glad Plenty Tucker' (?)			
Tha'-ichman ['Taisman']	Male	Human	Big
'Foot [Toe?] of [Brolga]'			
Piiwiyn [Ref. Brolga Whistle]	Male	Human	
Aak-thoneng-uk	Female	Human	
Empeey	Female	Human	
'Marmoya'	Female	Human	

Language(s):
Wik-Mungkan

Focal sites:
222 Piithel
226 Ku'-mut
226 Mangke-puypeng
692 Ngak-yoompenh

Nickname(s):
Eeye-mangkem ('from the mouth of Knox River')

CLAN 21 (see also 101)

Surnames: Korkaktain

Descendants: yes; patriline extant

Core estate interests: Estate 21 (= 101)

Ceremony: Key-elp (Puch)

APPENDIX 1

Clan totems: | **Translation:**
Minh Mookethaw | Salmon
Ngo'ench | Bushfire
Thante-kuch | Bony Bream
Yoomen | Women's Fighting Stick
Waangk [Doubtful] | Woven Bag

Totemic names:

Yaal-muk-mamen(h)	Male	Human	
Ku'-keeketheyn ('Korkaktain')	Male	Human	Big
Yaal-mukiy	Male	Human	Small
Wik-nguth	Female	Human	Big
Wathengow ['Watingowa']	Female	Human	Small
[Ref. White-tailed Rat Minh Wath]			
Keeketheyn	Female	Dog	
Kech-yuungk	Male	Dog	

Language(s):
Wik-Elken
Wik-Ngathan

Focal sites:
2019 Kuchenteypenh

Nickname(s):
Kunchenm ('From Scrub Country [at Lower Kendall River]')

CLAN 22 (*see also* 103)

Surnames: Woolla (B)

Descendants: yes; patriline extant

Core estate interests: Estate 22 (= 103)

Ceremony: Key-elp (Puch)

Clan totems: | **Translation:**
Minh Aarrench | Black Duck

Totemic names:

Wul 'Blowfly' ('Woolla')	Male	Human
Ku'-pel-empenh ('Ku'a pel-umpin')	Male	Human
Ku'thaach-elkenh ('Gothakchalkenin')	Male	Human

Focal sites:
964 Thaa'-puuntiy

Nickname(s):
Punyelem (meaning not recorded)

CLAN 23 (see also 104)

Surnames: (None recorded—people referred to as Wik Waangk (Woven Bag Language))

Descendants: Unclear; may have been clan of mother of Old Diamond Koowearpta.[6]

Core estate interests: Estate 23 (= 104)

Ceremony: ?

Clan totems:	**Translation:**
Waangk	Woven Bag

Totemic names:

Yuk-wayenh-thee'enh ['Yukwainten']	Female	Human

Language(s):
Wik-Me'enh

Focal sites:
180 Dish Yard
180 Weten

---

6   The mother of Mulloch Wolmby and of James Kalkeeyorta were two sisters, Ma'-muy and Ma'-kenen, totemic dialect Wik Waangk, and from west of Dish Yard (i.e. west of Weten, Estate 23). Silas Wolmby to David Martin, thence Martin to Sutton, 2 May 1997. But see also Clan 38.

CLAN 24 *see* 107

CLAN 25 *see* 110

CLAN 26 (*see also* 102)

Surnames: Ornyengaia, Bandacootcha

Descendants: yes; patriline extant

Core estate interests: Estate 102

Ceremony: Apelech, Puch

Clan totems:	Translation:
Minh Theelecheyn	Freshwater Shark
Minh Thap-Kulath	Hammerhead Shark
Minh Yuumel	Flat-tailed Ray
Wooeper	Jellyfish
Minh Monk	Bandicoot
Minh Pinyel-pinyel	Sea Bird Species ('Canary')
Kaa'-ngengych	Westerly Wind
Ngaypathenh	Tern Species
Minh Moenchen	Barramundi
Minh Wuchengolpeng	River Mullet
Minh Ichen	Jewfish?
Uncheyn	Tree Used for Spear Handles, *Hibiscus tiliaceus*
Ngoepenh	Edible Sedge from Saltpans
Pul Ochengan tharrn	Two Initiates

Totemic names:

Paantekuch ['Bandacootcha']	Male	Human	Big
Yiim	Male	Human	Big
Unyengay ['Ornyengaia']	Male	Human	Small
Ookemaakanh	Female	Human	Big
Palpakempath ['Palpak']	Female	Human	Small

Totemic names:

Weecheyn	Male	Dog
Pu'alanh	Male	Dog
Thapekul	Male	Dog
Ngoepenh Paatherr	Female	Dog
Uncheyn Paatherr 'Hibiscus Flower'	Female	Dog

Language(s):
Wik-Keyenganh

Focal sites:
637 Wiykath-ooemoeth
[5/5/95] Thuuyenh

Nickname(s):
Kunchenm ('From Scrub Country [at Lower Kendall River]')

CLAN 27 see 109

CLAN 28

Surnames: Yantumba A, Holroyd A

Descendants: yes; patriline extinct?

Core estate interests: 1970s/early 1980s: pursued tenure of Estate 23, but original estate said to be (SIL genealogies) 'timber place' north of Holroyd River and vicinity of Thuuk River; cf. clans and estates 112, 141

Ceremony: Wanam

Clan totems:	Translation:
Minh Achemp	Emu
Waayngkan	'Night Bird' (Curlew)

Totemic names:

Yantemp ['Yantumba']	Male	Human
?Wakanji	Male	Human

Language(s):
Wik-Iiyanh
Pakanha

Focal sites:
177 Thanmel
180 Weten

Nickname(s):
1. Pimp-thuurrpenham ('From Reed-grass and Melaleuca [Country]');
2. Pachem ~ Pechem ('From Open [Country]'; Mackenzie spelling: Patchim)

McConnel

possibly: Curlew (map); and see Clan 112 for clan data

CLAN 29

Surnames: Taisman

Descendants: yes; patriline extant

Core estate interests: Estate 2 (see also Clan 2)

Ceremony: Apelech

Clan totems:	Translation:
Thuulk	Brolga

Totemic names:

Tha'-ichman ['Taisman'] [ref. foot/talons of Brolga?]	Male	Human
Piimongk [ref. Carpet Snake]	Female	Human
War-maken 'Squeezing Oysters'	Male	Dog
Oonem-thee'enh 'Squirting' [ref. Oysters?]	Female	Dog

Language(s):
Wik-Mungkan
Wik-Ayengench [Andjingith] (formerly)

Focal sites:
551 Tha'-achemp; Waakem

Nickname: Waakemem; also Pil-man-iken?

McConnel
Local group   XI(a)
Totem-centre(s): 1. <u>Kokam</u> (swamp)
Totems: <u>min</u> <u>kora</u> native companion

Names:

<u>Taitjaman</u> (m)	<u>ta</u> foot
<u>Kuwampa</u> (m)	<u>wampa</u> – wing
<u>Kokokala</u> (m)	<u>kokala</u> – sinew in leg [cf. poot?]
<u>Miname'a</u> (m)	<u>Me'a</u> – eye, <u>mina</u> – meat, seeks about for food
<u>Wikyulnegan</u> (m)	<u>wik</u> – voice, call
<u>Wikyuanbajan</u> (m)	
<u>Wikyungana</u> (m)	
<u>Kawoppa</u> (m)	[Kaa'-wop]

<u>Minwonkatjabara</u> (m) [?Minh ngangke-chaaperr]

<u>Pamkotjinbatta</u> (f) pam – man, batta – bites, feeds, katja – far off, sees a man far off when feeding

<u>Akatonamabentan</u> (f) <u>Aka</u> – ground, <u>tonama</u> – by itself, <u>bentan</u> – comes out, one native companion comes out by itself into the open

<u>Manangauja</u> (f)	puts its beak into mud to pick up panja
<u>Manbentan</u> (f)	<u>man</u> – neck, neck comes out
<u>Iinga</u> (f)	[cf. mission spelling 'Eeng' (Clan 20)]
<u>Maiwutmanka</u> (f)	
<u>Maikompan</u> (f)	
<u>Pamkotja</u> (f).	

Totem-centre(s): 2. <u>Yukbekan</u> (trees)

Totems: <u>mai</u> <u>po'alam</u>   yellow fruit

APPENDIX 1

Names:
Koaligan (m)
Noinyamanka (f)
1929 pop. [?]

CLAN 30 – deleted

CLAN 31

Surnames: Woolla (A), Kongotema

Descendants: yes; patriline extant [Clan 30 in *Aak* is actually just a branch of 31]

Core estate interests: Estate 28 (Oony-aw)

Ceremony: Winchenem (Three Stripes)

Clan totems:	Translation:
Ooyn	Ghost
Wooynpey	Lovers
[not recorded]	'Sparrow'
Wak Poonch	Grass Species
May Kuyen	Sweet Sugarbag (wild honey sp.)
May Thiw	Wild Honey Species
Minh Panhth	Goanna Species
Yuunch Thinkem	Red Gum
Thul	Woomera
Think	Lower Back
Minh Ichen	Spangled Perch
Wol	Blowfly Species – has Yellow Eyes

Totemic names:

Wol ['Woolla'] [Wul?] 'Blowfly'	Male	Human	Big
Ku'-pel-empenh	Male	Human	Big
'Dog + Tree Lumps [Ghost]'			
Kumen-umpenh 'Cut the Thigh'	Male	Human	Big

Totemic names:

Ko'engothem ['Kongotema'] [Ref. 'Sparrow' Bird Species]	Male	Human	Small
Mangk-poonch ['Munkapornch'] 'Grass (*Perotis rara*) Stems'	Female	Human	Big
Panyaaw ['Panyawa'] 'Greedy Ghosts Racing'; [Lou Yunkaporta defined Panyaaw as Female Human Big Name]	Female	Human	Small
Pam-kooep	Female	Human	Big
Mee'-yimen	Female	Human	Small
Ngeke-thee'enh 'Lovers' Trysting Signal'	Male	Dog	
Tha'-ukathenh '[Ghost] Lowering Feet'	Male	Dog	
Nhenchenhan 'Having Intercourse'	Female	Dog	

Language(s):

Wik-Mungkan

Focal sites:

469 Oony-aw

McConnel

Local group   X

Totem-centre(s):   1. <u>Ornyanuwa</u>

Totems: <u>ornya</u> male ghosts

Names:

<u>Koowana</u> (m)	<u>ko</u> – prefix, <u>owan</u> – meet, ghosts meet together between the two lagoons
<u>Panyauwa</u> (f)	<u>pantia</u> – sweethearts

1929 pop. [10–20]

CLAN 32

Surnames: Toikalkin (Current—see also Clan 7 for previous generations)

Descendants: yes; patriline extant

APPENDIX 1

Core estate interests: Estate 5

Ceremony: Apelech

Clan totems:	Translation:
May Ka'err	Yam Species
Chaanchaan, Mow	White Cockatoo
Yuk Punpel	Tree Species
Wooerngk-kalk	Shoot of Arrowroot
Pi'	Antbed
Yaal	Fresh Floodwater
Yuk Punpel	Tea Tree Species
Thechel	Sand Goanna
Keenthinh	Corn (on Foot)
Thiweth	Owl Species

Totemic names:

Thuykalkenh [Ref. Sand Goanna]	Male	Human	Big
Ku'-keenhthin 'Dog + Corns on Feet'	Male	Human	Big
Uuk-wun-mamenh 'Front-Lay-Grabbed' [Ref. Crest of White Cockatoo]	Male	Human	Small
Pam-nhumey-ethenh ['Pamnamutna'] [Ref. Armpit powder used to disguise odour when fishing]	Female	Human	
Yuuymuk ['Yewimuk']	Female	Human	
Pam-poonchel-pathenh	Female	Human	
Aak-pop	Female	Human	Small
Punpel-thupen 'Tea Tree Species Flower'	Male	Dog	
Um-micheyn [Ref. Antbed]	Male	Dog	
Yaal-moerang [Ref. Fresh Floodwater]	Male	Dog	
Man-than 'Neck Standing' [Ref. Goanna]	Male	Dog	
Muwem-penh [Ref. White Cockatoo]	Female	Dog	

Language(s):

Wik-Elken/ Wik-Ngatharr

Focal sites:

333 Woowkeng (Nr) (= Kayncherrang = Kencherrang)

CLAN 33

Surnames: Pambegan

Descendants: yes; patriline extant

Core estate interests: Estate 31 (Mukiy)

Ceremony: Winchenem

Clan totems:	**Translation:**
Walkaln	Bonefish
Chicherrak	Willy Wagtail
Tiin-tiin	Peewee
That	Green Frog
Mal	Bat
Yuum	Black-headed Snake
N(y)eeyn	Fly
May Kurrp	Grey Mangrove (*Avicennia marina*)
May Yuunch	Black Mangrove (*Bruguiera gymnorhiza*)
[from McConnel:	
Muuy	Bullroarer
Wanch-komen	Unmarried Girl at Puberty

Totemic names:

Pam-piiken 'Man Being Struck'	Male	Human	Big
Pam-kuchethen (cf. 'Pamkochitta')	Female	Human	Big
Thum-pipem	Male	Human	
From Thomson:			
'Yänk omp'n'	Male	Human	
(Yangk-umpen, 'cuts leg', ref. bonefish)			
'Kangkutjatta' (genealogies)	Male	Human	Small
Thip-ngut (genealogies)	Female	Human	Small
Thip-unt [ref. belly of bonefish]	Female	Human	Small
Pämkottjätta [ref. peewit Thomson 1946:161–3]	Female	Human	Big
('Pamkochitta')			

APPENDIX 1

Totemic names:

'Yatut' [ref. bonefish bones Thomson 1946:162]   Dog

Language(s):

Wik-Mungkan (however, place-names indicate that their estate was formerly associated with a Northern Paman language)

[language of Billy Mammus known to JS Karntin as Ya'ali, PS Book 37:39, probably a voice-quality term like Chiliko; note this dialect as recorded by McConnel in 1928 had stem-final vowels, unlike the present variety]

Focal sites:

2031 Mukiy

McConnel

Local group II

Totem-centre(s): 1. Potjamamana (amongst mangrove trees)

Totems: mai korpi black mangrove

Names:

Kontutthan (m) konta – head, tutthan – sticks into, i.e. 'in the head the spear sticks'… The stalk of the mangrove beam sticks into the red sepals which resemble hair' (McConnel 1935:75–76; 1957:40)

Totem-centre(s): 2. Adeda (small creek running into lower Archer)

Totems: min wolkollan bone-fish

Names:

Bambegan (m)	pam – man, began – beats, heart of bone-fish beats at approach of man
Yangkambin (m)	yanka – tail, ampan – cuts, the tail is cut off first
Tipiwunta (f)	tipi – guts, wunta – leaves, guts of bone-fish are left aside, not eaten [cf. Thip-unt above]

Totem-centre(s): 3. Nernpanyinna

Totems: neanya fly

Totem-centre(s): 4. Tatfigunan

Totems: <u>min tatta</u> frog

Totem-centre(s): 5. <u>Kulepan</u>

Totems: <u>moiya</u> bullroarer

1929 pop. [8]

CLAN 34

Surnames: Koondumbin

Descendants: yes; patriline extinct

Core estate interests: Estate 42

Ceremony: Winchenem

Clan totems:	Translation:
Kang-káng	White-breasted Sea Eagle
Minh Themp	Black Duck
Minh Koon	Burdekin Duck
Waangk	Woven Bag

Totemic names:
Ku'-theempen ['Koondumbin']   Human   Male
'Munukka'   Human   Male
[cf. 'Monako' below, and 1891 Aurukun birth record, father 'Manako']
'Anjumbin' [Andyimban, Anch-umpan]   Human   Female

Language(s):
Wik-Mungkan

McConnel

Local group III
Totem-centre(s): 1. <u>Merokman</u> (nests in trees)

Totems:
<u>kong kong</u> white fish-hawk,
<u>nun parkanjan</u> small hawk

APPENDIX 1

Names:

<u>Monako</u> (m)	carries meat to nest in tree
<u>Omikam</u> (m)	outstretched wings in flying
<u>Wutthayepinnna</u> (f)	sinew of hawke's [sic] leg
<u>Wikatauwa</u> (f)	<u>wika</u> – voice <u>tauwa</u> – talks, calls out

Totem-centre(s): 2. <u>Wikatama</u> (lower reaches of Archer River)

Totems:
<u>min</u> <u>tempi</u> swamp duck,
<u>min</u> <u>mantaba</u> plains turkey

Names:

<u>Nakwantana</u> (m)	<u>nak</u> – water, <u>wantan</u> – leaves behind, duck leaves tracks behind in water as it swims
Kuandambin (m)	
<u>Tatempanmeya</u> (f)	<u>ta</u> – foot, <u>meya</u> – lifts, duck lifts its foot to paddle itself along

Totem-centre(s): 3. <u>Amboinam</u>

Totems: <u>min</u> <u>wunkam</u> rock cod

Totem-centre(s): 4. <u>Eida</u>

Totems: <u>min</u> <u>tut</u> <u>tha</u> parrot

Totem-centre(s): 5. <u>Taimanir</u> [Cf. 'Timinie Creek']

Totems: <u>maiariki</u> swamp water lily -(1)

Totem-centre(s): 6. <u>Waiyuya</u> (anthills),

Totems:
<u>wanka</u> string dilly-bag
<u>puntamen</u> fishing-net

Names:

<u>Mewutthanbunkan</u> (f)	<u>me</u> – eye or hole, <u>bungan</u> make, refers to pattern of bag

1929 pop. [5]

CLAN 35

Surnames: Ngakyunkwokka, Kawangka, Bell

Descendants: yes; patrilines extant

Core estate interests: Estate 27 (Yongk-uyengam), Estate 14 (Wanke-nhiyeng), combined as one (see also linked Clans 14, 35)

Ceremony: Winchenem

Clan totems:	Translation:
Minh Oolp	Freshwater Jewfish
Yuk Yongk	Ironwood
Yuk Put	Bloodwood
Minh Akul	Freshwater Jewfish
Minh Kaa'-kucheng	Mature Minh Akul
Minh Ponchath	Frill-necked Lizard
Minh Ngaamp	Black Water Snake
Taltál	Plover
May Kuthel	Boolgooroo (vegetable)
Thinthaw	Water Python
Kelmpang	Galah
Oy' [respect form]	Water

Totemic names:

Ngak-yangk-wok ['Ngakyunkwokka'] Male Human Big
[said to mean 'Tail Cuts Water', 'Walking in the Water'; Water ref. here is to totem]
Kushan[7] ['Koorchine'] Male Human Big
Mathe-Puuk ['Marthapook'] Female Human Big
Kel-weencheyn [Ref. Kelmpang – Galah] Female Human Big

Language(s):
Wik-Mungkan
Formerly (a long time ago) Wik-Ep

---

7 Possibly in error for Kuchan, given there are no sibilants in the relevant language.

APPENDIX 1

Focal sites:
120 Wankeniyeng
746 Yongk-uyengam

CLAN 36

Surnames: Koo'ekka

Descendants: yes; patriline extinct

Core estate interests: Estate 29 (Watson River)

Ceremony: Iinch, Malp?

Clan totems:	Translation:
Pikuw	Saltwater Crocodile
Minh Punchiy	Long-Necked Swamp Turtle
Parrp	Hawk Species
Kekuyeng	Echidna

Totemic names:

Ku'-kunentangen [Ref. Crocodile]	Male	Human	Big
Keke-thee'enh 'Spears Thrown [At Echidna]'	Male	Human	Big
Ku'-ek 'Dog + [Swamp Turtle] Shell' ['Koo'ekka']	Male	Human	Small
Thipiy-mat '[Crocodile] Going Up On Belly'	Female	Human	Big
Yuk-wayenh-thee'enh 'Spears Thrown At [Echidna]'	Female	Human	Big
Eke-than '[Swamp Turtle] Shell Stands'	Female	Human	Small
Koom [Ref. Small Eagle Species]		Dog	
Ku'-ek 'Dog+[Swamp Turtle] Shell'		Dog	
Ngek-wunpen '[Crocodile] Puts Jaw [On Log]'		Dog	
Keke-tha'en 'Removing Spears [Quills]'		Dog	

Language(s):
Wik-Mungkan
(formerly 'Wik-Ompom', i.e. Mbiywom)

McConnel

Local group I

Totem-centre(s): 1. Konga (a swamp) [= *Aak* site 2321/3829 Korng(a)]

Totems: pikua salt water crocodile

Totem-centre(s): 2. Nakapanpang (on the river) [= *Aak* site 2362 Ngake-pampeng]

Totems: minwunkam 'night-fish'

Names: Tipimuta(f) tipi – guts, muta – tail

Totem-centre(s): 3. Ankainanwa

Totems: mai anka white fruit

Names: Koanka (m)

1929 pop. [2]

CLAN 37

Surnames: Koo'oila

Descendants: yes; patriline extant; incorporated into Ti Tree group through adoption of late Eric Koo'oila; original estate ?37?; but totems very close to those of clans 14 and 35.

Core estate interests: Estates 27, 14

Clan totems:	Translation:
Note: Eric Koo'oila to J von Sturmer 1969:	
Taltál	Plover
Ponchath	Frill-necked Lizard
Minh Oolp	Freshwater Dewfish
Kaykachi	Big Freshwater Dewfish
Yongk	Ironwood
Yuk(ew) Pach	Gumplant (? Tree parasite) [may be Ngukew, see Dog names]
Minh Okol	Spotted Freshwater Dewfish

APPENDIX 1

Clan totems:	Translation:
Thinthew	Freshwater Snake
Thaypen	Taipan
Uk	Brown Snake
Thuuk Ngamp	Small Black Water Snake
Thinkam	Tree Gum
Puunch	Xanthorrea Gum
Mulayng	Brown Freshwater Snake [?File Snake]
Implied by dog names:	
Yuk Okol	Swamp-growing Tree sp.
Yuk Put	Bloodwood

Totemic names:

Ku'-koyl 'Koo'oila'	Male	Human
Okol Pach ('Okol Flower')		Dog
Ngukuw Pach ('Ngukuw Flower')		Dog
Wukulpun [Ref. Taipan]		Dog
Kothomangk [Big Name Ref. Plover]		Dog
Yongk Pach ('Ironwood Flower')		Dog
Put Pach ('Bloodwood Flower')		Dog

Ceremony: Winchenem

Language(s):
Wik-Mungkan

CLAN 38

Surnames: Marbthowan, Marbdaw

Descendants: yes; patriline extant

Core estate interests: Vicinity of Dish Yard and Ti Tree, possibly estate 37 Kuympay-aw, but Mission cards give 'Tanmilla' (Thanmel) and 'Peemungkum' (Pi'emangkem) and 'Ngoia' (?) as well as Ti Tree, thus giving the emphasis to the wider area about Dish Yard (Estate 23). Possibly same clan as 41 as Mission cards give 'Kowerrpita' as a Small Name for

Billy Marbdaw. Joyce and Evelyn and Akay née Marbthowan were the children of two brothers whose country was 'from Pi'emangkem down to the Knox', which places them very close to, or even overlapping with, the Dish Yard estate (23).

Clan totems: **Translation:**
As for Clan 17 (Pamtoondas) (Flying Fox, Taipan, Heartbeat, etc.)

Totemic names:

'Marbdaw', 'Marbthowan', also 'Marbdowan'	Human	Male	Big/Small
'Pamtoonda'	Human	Male	Big
'Kowerrpita'	Human	Male	Small
'Ngorngimullina'	Human	Female	

Ceremony: Winchanam (?)

Language(s):
Wik-Mungkan

CLAN 39

Surnames: Koowarta, Pahimbung

Descendants: yes; patriline extant

Core estate interests: Estate 49 (Ku'-aw)

Ceremony: Winchanam

Language(s): Wik-Mungkan

Clan totems:	Translation:
May Mach	Wild Ginger
Yakalpa	Red Kangaroo
Ngaankam-mut	Kangaroo Tail
Kuyngkiy	Livistona Palm
Ularrk	Leech
Ku'-ngekanam	Dingo, Wild Dog

APPENDIX 1

Totemic names:

Ku'-waat ['Koowarta']	Human	Male	Big
['Dog-larrikin', ref. to Leech][8]			
Pa'ampang ['Pahimbung']	Human	Male	Small
[ref. Livistona Palm (kuyngkiy)]			
Ngak-mangk-?weeka	Human	Female	
[see McConnel's Nakmankwerka; SIL Mn 'swim' is wookaman]			

Focal sites:

Ku'-aw	(Dingo Story Place)
Ngaankam mut	(Kangaroo Tail)
Ularrk-aw	(Leech Story Place)
Kuyngkiy-aw	(Livistona Palm Story Place)

McConnel

Local group IX (a)

Totem-centre(s): 1. <u>Tean</u>

Totems:

<u>olavika</u> male leech [typo for 'olarika', i.e. *Ularrk*, PS]
<u>uwa</u> female leech

Names:

<u>Kuwatean</u> (m)	<u>ku</u> – prefix, <u>uwa</u> – leech, <u>tean</u> – take off
<u>Omanya</u> (m)	<u>uwa</u> – leech, <u>manya</u> – small
<u>Kuwota</u> (m)	
<u>Nakmankwerka</u> (f)	<u>naka</u> – water, <u>mank</u> – back, <u>werka</u> – swims, leech swims behind a person and gets on her back

Totem-centre(s): 2. <u>Kuauwa</u>

Totems: <u>Ku'a</u> – dingo

---

8   The Leech is a larrikin (promiscuous one) because it becomes distended like an erection and may get inside the vaginas of women foraging in swamps, against which they used to wear a bark 'utility pad' (term from McConnel; the one she collected is in the SA Museum).

Names:

<u>Mintaangala</u> (m)   <u>min</u> – meat, <u>ta</u> – paw, <u>angala</u> – gnaws, dingo gnaws meat held by its paw

<u>Alputa</u> (m)   <u>puta</u> – hollow log, dingo finds animal in hollow log

<u>Punkameya</u> (m)   <u>punka</u> – <u>meya</u> – lifts

Totem: <u>mai</u> <u>koinkan</u> edible palm stem

Names:

<u>Waakatan</u> (m) <u>katan</u> – cuts, soft part of stem is out out and eaten

Totem: <u>mai</u> <u>epanna</u> small root

Name:

<u>Yankatipan</u> (f) <u>yanka</u> – stem, <u>tipan</u> – dries up, stem dries up then root is ready for eating).

Local group: IX(b)

Totem-centre(s): 3. <u>Kuimpiauwa</u> (swamp near melon-hole country),

Totems: <u>min</u> <u>kuimpi</u> kangaroo

Names:

<u>Taambeya</u> (m)   <u>ta</u> – foot, <u>beya</u> – hops

<u>Unkapipa</u> (f)   <u>unka</u> – breast bone, <u>pipa</u> – broken, kangaroo sits up, looks as if breast-bone were broken

<u>Pampointjalama</u> (f)   <u>pam</u> man, <u>pointjalama</u> – sniffs, kangaroo sniffs the air when a man is near

1929 pop. IX(a): [8–10]; IX(b): [1 woman]

CLAN 40 *see* 113

CLAN 41

Surnames: Kowearpta

Descendants: yes; patriline extant

Core estate interests: Estate 23? Nearby?

Ceremony: Winchanam (?)

Language(s): Wik-Mungkan

Clan totems:	Translation:
Minh Wuk	Flying Fox
Minh Mont	Jabiru
Yuk Thuumpiy	Paperbark
Yuk Wuuy	Guttapercha
Minh Themp	Black Duck
Minh Woy	White Duck
Minh Thaypen	Taipan

Totemic names:
possibly *Ku'-weepatha   Male   Human [see mission spelling Kowearpta]

CLAN 42: number not in use

CLAN 43

Surnames: Mapissa (first name, female)

Descendants: yes; patriline extinct

Core estate interests: Estate 24

Ceremony: Puch?

CLAN 44

Surnames: Chii'iiy (Samuel)

Descendants: none recorded

Core estate interests: Estate 44

Ceremony: Apelech?

CLAN 45 – deleted

CLAN 46

Surnames: Fruit (also just first names: Dan and Hope)

Descendants: yes; see Clan 65, probably same clan

Core estate interests: Estate 30 (probably same as Estate 75)

Ceremony:

Clan totems:	**Translation:**
Minh Kolet	Peaceful Dove

Language(s):
Wik-Mungkan

Focal sites:
2338 Kolet-aw

Aurukun Mission card for Hope gives her country area as 'Ortwalle, Emmy Landing'—i.e. site 2341 Otwale-nyin?; one for a Dan gives his as Cheyyim (cf. Cheyam); one for Polly Fruit gives Panun, lower than Pooeya [Puuy], Archer River.

CLAN 47

Surnames: Charcoal

Descendants: none recorded

Core estate interests: Estate 32?

Language(s):
If this is the Charcoal who was the late Roy George's mother's cousin-brother, he was Mbiywom according to Annie George.

CLAN 48

Surnames: George, Parker, Day

Descendants: yes; patrilines extant

Core estate interests: Estate 33 (Oyónton)

APPENDIX 1

Ceremony:

Clan totems:	Translation:
Tungtung 1 (Ilkutj)	Soft-backed Long Necked Turtle
Tungtung 2 (Ilkutj)	Hard-backed Long Necked Turtle
Korrop	Black-nosed Wallaby
Took	Snail (lives in hollow ironwoods)
Utjányang	(All) Flowers (mainly messmate)
[not recorded]	Echidna
Andjal	Goanna sp.
Mepen	Red-legged Bushman (Sorcerer) known as Torritha in Ngkoth, and as Laek(ay) in Anathangayth.

Totemic names:

Trakawa (F of Robert Day)　　Male　　Human

Language(s):

Mbaywum (= Mbiywum, Mbiywom, Wik-Ompom, Wik-Ompam)

Alice Mark calls their language Trotj; Annie George confirms more widely grounded view that Mbaywum, Trrotj [/rr/ – cf. AM's /r/], and Ngkoth are neighbouring and similar but distinct languages/dialects.

CLAN 49

Surnames: Old Luke

Descendants: none recorded

Core estate interests: Estate 30? Note: Mission cards have 'Hey River'

Focal sites:
2345 Kuympay-Awenyin

CLAN 50

Surnames: Motton

Descendants: yes; patriline extant

Core estate interests: Estate 51

Ceremony:

Clan totems:	Translation:
Achemp [in Mn]	Emu
Theynwaw [in Ngkoth]	Eagle sp. (red, white neck)

[see also Arthur Pambegan Jr bio for Pizzi Gallery Wik War i.e. Oyster Lg]

Names (said to be afterbirth names in this case, not clan totemic, but still primary names):

Twitharran	Male	Human
Mathawan	Male	Human
Nggolpenden [cf. 'Golpendun']	Female	Human
Aachwal	Female	Human

Language(s):
Ngkoth, Chaa-Ngkoth ('Ngkoth Language')

CLAN 51

Surnames: Mark, Kangaroo

Descendants: yes; patriline extant

Core estate interests: Estate 52 (Onhánggun)

Ceremony:

Clan totems:	Translation:
Indjwon [Burringan in Anathangayth]	Red Kangaroo
Korrop [Kwatjan in Anathangayth]	Grey Kangaroo
Ku [Ngoomp in Anathangayth]	Firestick
Iway	Owl sp.
Wungwung	Ibis sp. (like a jabiru, only eats dewfish from creeks)
[wife of Wungwung]	Black Ibis
[wife of Wungwung]	White Ibis

APPENDIX 1

Names (possibly afterbirth names rather than clan totemic):

Atjótin [Andrew Mark]	Male	Human
Wongay [Andrew Mark]	Male	Human
Narredjan [MM of Joyce Hall]	Female	Human

Language(s):

Arraythinngith (= Arrithinngithigh, Arreythinwum depending on language used)

CLAN 52

Surnames: Doughboy, Blowhard

Descendants: yes; Blowhard patriline extant.

Note: Main country interests are those of the late Noel Blowhard's patriline, and descendants of Ida (née Doughboy) Paul (in particular, Joyce Hall and Thancoupie). Blowhards also have country interests in the Pepen (Peppan) area (not assigned an estate number or entry in this system, as too far north), but they are recognised as having interests in the area south of Embley River on the basis of an ancestral connection to the Hey River area, probably a patrilineal one as Billy Blowhard's Aurukun Mission card gives his country area as 'Weipa mouth', and also possibly one traced via the late Noel Blowhard's mother Polly (long deceased), whose country is listed on Aurukun Mission cards as 'Ngolga, near Weipa mouth'. Wik native title applicant Polly Ann Blowhard identified (in 1995) as part of the 'Wik-Way' grouping.

This estate may extend to Moyngom (Hey Point), a matter of some controversy. The Aurukun Mission card for Saul, brother of Doughboy, gives his country area as 'Myngump'.

Core estate interests: Estate 53 (West Side Middle Hey River)

Ceremony: Chivirri

Clan totems:	Translation:
Achemp (Mn)	Emu
Twal	White-breasted Sea Eagle

Names (possibly afterbirth names here):
Adhheylpan, Adhheylpin   Female   Human
['Atholpan', 'Ethelpen']

Language(s):
Latumngith (older records)
also given as Liningith (i.e. Linngithigh?—possibly in an extended sense as dialectal typifier) (PS Field Book 84:23)

CLAN 53 see 51

CLAN 54

Surnames: none recorded

Descendants: none recorded

Core estate interests: Estate 55

CLAN 55

Surnames: none recorded

Descendants: none recorded

Core estate interests: Estate 59 (Thaa'-pulnh); Clan 113 (Peinyekka/Jingle) are now main custodians.

Language(s):
Wik-Iiyanh?

CLAN 56

Surnames: none recorded

Descendants: none recorded

Core estate interests: Estate 56 (Yagalmungkenh), part of Wik-Way area

APPENDIX 1

CLAN 57

Surnames: none recorded

Descendants: none recorded

Core estate interests: Estate 57 (Ikeleth, Waterfall), part of Wik-Way area

Focal sites:
Ikeleth
Waterfall
Alichin

CLAN 58

Surnames: Walmbeng

Descendants: yes; patriline extant

Core estate interests: Estate 1

Ceremony: Apelech

Language(s): Wik-Elkenh

Clan totems:	Translation:

[Note: These are totems of Rex and Cecil Walmbeng's patriline. Rex also asserted an identification with his mother's totems (see Clan 1), principal ones of which include Thinhelpal (Dugong), Maantalnt (Sea Turtle), Walemoericheyn (Whale), and Yaate-mey (= Kaa'-nguunthaw 'Snorer', = Woekelaw 'Big Neck', i.e. mythic Carpet Snake Oyengorrpen, all terms in Wik-Elkenh/Wik-Ngathan]:

Theelicheyn	Juvenile Freshwater Sharks
Chiiynchiiyn [Karrkurra]	Bush Rats
Ele-yepeyn	Mother Shark
Kuunger	Adult Sharks (both sexes)
May Murrken	Blackfruit (*Canthium odoratum*?)
May Kuump	Blackfruit (*Mallotus polyadenus*)
May Mathenngay	Blackfruit (similar to *M. polyadenus*)
May Maach	Red Wallaby Fruit (*Eugenia carissoides*)

Clan totems: **Translation:**
Minh Paak — King Parrot (red wings)
Minh Muukethaw — Whiskered Salmon

Totemic names:

'Walmbeng'	Male	Human	
Wikman(iya)	Male	Human	Small
Thiineth-ngaycheyn ['Saw a Coconut'] 'Teentanytcha'	Male	Human	
May Yuunch Keempenh	Female	Human	Small
Mangk Nhayenh	Female	Human	Big
Yuuymuk	Female	Human	Big
Uthikeng	Female	Human	Big

CLAN 59

Surnames: Bowenda

Descendants: yes; patriline extant

Core estate interests: Estate 3, Estate 4 (originally incorporated into Clan 4)

Ceremony: Apelech

Clan totems: Translation:
[see Clan 4]

Totemic names:
[see Clan 4]

Language(s):
Wik-Ngathan

Focal sites:
Wath-nhiin, Uthuk Aweyn

CLAN 60

Surnames: Owokran (A)

Descendants: yes; patriline extant

Core estate interests: Estate 34 (Lower Ward River)

Note: Country interests of descendants span several of the old estates in the Wik-Way area. Estate 34 is the patri-estate of Cyril Owokran, Alma Moon's mother, and Alison Woolla's mother's mother. The same people have particular succession interests in estates 56 (Yagalmungkenh), 35 (Ubun), 57 (Ikeleth), an interest in 36 (Wuthan), and in Alison Woolla's (and siblings') case a preeminent interest in Estate 43 (Yaaneng/Wallaby Island), the estate of their mother's father. As part of a general Wik-Way alliance—even though Alison Woolla, for example, did not identify herself and family as such—they also share interests in coastal estates to the north, but leave the talking for e.g. Mbang to others.

Ceremony: Chivirri

Clan totems:	Translation:
Keerrk (Mn)	Black Cockatoo
Korr' (Mn)	Brolga

Totemic names:

Wewamang (Mn)	Male	Human
[Ref. Brolga, wewam = 'blood']		
'Owokran' [Ref. Black Cockatoo]	Male	Human

Language(s):
Andjingith (Wik-Ayengench)

CLAN 61

Surnames: none recorded

Descendants: none recorded; custodial interests mainly now collectively those of primary holders of estates 34, 57, 36, 43.

Core estate interests: Estate 35 (Uwbun), part of Wik-Way area

Focal sites:
2399 Uwbun

CLAN 62

Surnames: (last woman Mookerr-ethenh)

Descendants: patriline extinct; interests in the estate contested in former times especially between Fred Kerindun and Geraldine Kawangka, now under general custodianship of southern Wik-Way families

Core estate interests: Estate 36 (Wuthan)

Ceremony: Chivirri?

Clan totems:	Translation:
Minh Thaa'-kuuk	Diamond Stingray
May Wu'emp	Arrowroot

Totemic names:
Mookerr-ethenh ('Mokereten')   Female   Human   Big

Language(s):
Andjingith (Wik-Ayengench)

Focal sites:
649 Wuthan

CLAN 63

Surnames: Matthew

Descendants: yes; patriline extant

Core estate interests: Estate 45 (Moyngom)

Ceremony: Chivirri

Clan totems:	Translation:
Thunggan	Flying Fish

Totemic names:

Thunggan ['Flying Fish']   Dog

Language(s):
Linngithigh

CLAN 64

Surnames: Go'olfree (Norman)

Descendants: none recorded

Core estate interests: Estate 38 (Amban)

Language(s):
Ndra'ngith

CLAN 65

Surnames: Chevathen (Albert)

Descendants: yes; patriline extant.

Note: The Chevathen family has multiple ancestral connections to old clan estates within the area between the Embley and Archer rivers. The birthplace of Andrew Chevathen at Malnyinyu (at Pera Head, Estate 66), where the afterbirth was buried next to a particular tree (see photo facing p104 in Sutton et al. 1990), is widely known and this form of association is one regarded as bringing special responsibilities (even though Pera Head is in an adjoining estate to that of his Aboriginal father, 41 Thud Point). (His natural father was European.) His birth association with Pera Head passes down to his own immediate descendants.

Core estate interests: Estate 41 (Thud Point)

Ceremony: Chivirri

Clan totems:	Translation:
Chiith	Fish Hawk
[not recorded]	Sharks (all)
[not recorded]	Green Sea Turtle

Totemic names:

Nggolpanam	Male	Human

Language(s):
Ndra'ngith

CLAN 66

Surnames: Clark (Jimmy Clark, also Mabel neé Taisman, later Pamulkan)

Descendants: yes; patriline extinct

Core estate interests: Estate 40 (Malnyinyu, Pera Head; Malinu?)

Ceremony: Chivirri

Clan totems:	Translation:
Keech (Mn)	Crane
[not recorded]	Shooting Star

Totemic names:

'Ndorndorin'	Male	Human	Big
'Kowkan'	Male	Human	Small
Animbi	Female	Human	Big
'Awunka'	Female	Human	Big
'Datanjinu'	Female	Human	Small

Language(s):
Adithangath (= Adithinngithigh, latter probably in Linngithigh)

Focal sites:
2452 Pera Head

CLAN 67

Surnames: Chevathun (Joseph), Kelinda

Descendants: yes; patriline extant

APPENDIX 1

Note: The surname Chevathun is said to have been assigned in Aurukun Mission times on the basis of a 'navel-name' relationship. Some Aurukun mission records spell the name 'Chevachun', but 'Chevathun' is now normalised. In terms of common descent and the old clan system these Chevathuns are not of the same group as the Chevathens (see Clan 65, note spelling difference), although on a wider regional basis they both form part of the Wik-Way people with shared interests in land. Chevathuns are primarily based at Aurukun, Chevathens at Napranum. The late Joseph Chevathun's father is said to have been a brother of Dick Kelinda, father of Jean George, and to be of the same estate, totems and language.

There have been suggestions that Kelindas' country is south of Aurukun. Not only the statements of living authorities but all the old records indicate clearly that this is quite incorrect. The Aurukun Mission cards from the 1920s and 1930s indicate the country of Kelindas to be Anyiyam (Roberts Creek), as there are entries for members of the Kelinda Family which contain the entries: 'Anyeeyum', and 'Anyiema, Weipa Mouth' and 'Weipa Mouth'. Donald Thomson's field notes of 1933 (File no. 276) list 'Old Dick [Kelinda]' as being of 'Alingit' language, and the mission cards lists his country area as 'Weipa Mouth, Mission' ('Mission' here most likely refers to the 'Mission River' in the sense common to Aurukun usage, i.e. the Embley).

Core estate interests: Estate 46 (Anyiyam)

Ceremony: Chivirri

Clan totems:	**Translation:**
A'oy	Arrowroot
Paandj	Gecko (large, black striped)
Paandj	Night, Darkness
Kambal	Saltwater Crocodile
Kandhak	Oyster
[not recorded]	Porpoise
Ino, Inong?	Cyclone
Kambin	Silver Mullet
Motmot	Scaly Mullet
Tjakil	Bonefish

Clan totems: **Translation:**
Ndhonogh Frill-necked Lizard
Nggaantj White Cockatoo
Waath Crow
La Wattle Tree sp.
Ambaatjil Small Mullet spp.

Totemic names:

Awun	Male	Human	?Big
'Rossa'	Male	Human	Small
Yepinyi	Male	Human	
Rruchuk	Male	Human	
'Kelinda' [Kel-ndun?]	Male	Human	
Ólandan ['Ollondin'] [Ref. La (Wattle) Story]	Male	Human	
Awompan ['Awumpun', 'Avumpun'] [Ref. Porpoise]	Female	Human	Big
Peendj [Ref. Gecko; Aurukun pron.?]	Female	Human	Small
'Gawanka'	Female	Human	

Language(s):
Alngith (Alengathiy in Wik-Mungkan)

CLAN 68

Surnames: Kerindun

Descendants: yes; patriline extant.

Note: Kerinduns have long been associated with the area south of Embley River and west of Hey and Watson rivers. This is attested to by independent records going back to the early 1930s. They also have some kind of ancestral connection to the Mission River area. Occasionally one hears people from Napranum say that is where their true country lies. The widest consensus, and their own view, is that they belong south of the Embley in the Wik-Way area, and have a classical estate there still fairly well known to a number of people. The senior Kerinduns trace their link to this estate via their father and father's father's father. Their father's mother was a Kelinda (Clan 67), also of this same area, their mother's mother's estate was at Pera Head (Clan 66, Estate 40), and their father's father's father had a wife from Wuthan (mouth of Archer, Clan 62, Estate 36). They are multiply connected to the wider area.

Core estate interests: Estate 47 (Winda Winda Creek, interests in Mbang)

Ceremony: Chivirri

Clan totems:	Translation:
(Sutton 1995 field notes:	
[not recorded]	Crow
[not recorded]	Darkness
[not recorded]	White Cockatoo
[not recorded]	Gecko
[not recorded]	Vagina ('Woman Front')
Yakel (Mn)	Wattle (*Acacia crassicarpa*, a Lancewood)
(cf. Sam Kerindun to John von Sturmer early 1970s:	
Paantj	(Gecko? = Kochen Ngaa' Mn; cf. Paandj below)
Adha	Crow
Lorr	Red Schnapper
Errong	Sunfish
Oyon	Sleeping Fish [Cod?]
Tjarra	Bird (Seagull?), Dance Of Bird,
[not recorded]	Cloud

Totemic names:

Awun	Male	Human
Ma'-duk (Old Anthony)	Male	Human
[*duk* = 'woomera' in Andjingith; totemic or nickname?]		
Kaawnggwingan	Female	Human
Paandj [Ref. Night; cf. Paantj above]	Dog	

Language(s):

Linngithigh (Liinengathiy in Wik-Mungkan)

LINGUISTIC ORGANISATION AND NATIVE TITLE

CLAN 69

Surnames: Warnkoola, Kepple (B)

Descendants: yes; patriline extant

Core estate interests: Estate 48 (Meripah Homestead area)

Ceremony: Winchenem, Nhomp

Clan totems:	Translation:
Minh Panhth-engkepanch	Sand Goanna
Minh Kuypang	Black Bream
Waangk	Dillybag
Akwala	Dewfish

Totemic names:

Waangk-kul 'Dillybag Handle'	Male	Human	Big
Man-pent '[Goanna] Sticks Up Neck'	Male	Human	Small
Eempen [Ref. Goanna Closing Lair]	Female	Human	Big
Mut-tuuth [Thuth?] [Ref. Goanna Tail]	Female	Human	Small
Mut-tuuth [Thuth?] [Ref. Goanna Tail]		Dog	
Panhth-wuut 'Old Man Sand Goanna'		Dog	
Panhth-mayn 'Young Sand Goanna'		Dog	
Panhth-engkepanch 'Inland Goanna Species'		Dog	

Focal sites:
697 Miirrp

Language(s):
Wik-Iyeyn (also Wik-Iiyenh)

CLAN 70

Surnames: Dick, York(?)

Descendants: yes; patriline extant for Dicks; York situation needs checking

Core estate interests: Estate 39 (Mbang)

Ceremony: Not recorded

Clan totems:	Translation:
A'oy	Arrowroot*
Paandj	Gecko (large, black striped)
Paandj	Night, Darkness
Kambal	Saltwater Crocodile
Kandhak	Oyster
[not recorded]	Porpoise
Ino	Cyclone
Tjakil	Bonefish
Ndhonogh	Frill-necked Lizard
Nggaantj	White Cockatoo
Waath	Crow
La	Wattle Tree sp.
Ambaatjil	Small Mullet spp.

*Note: First totem supplied by Esther (née Dick) Coconut; the same one plus rest of list supplied by Jean George.

Language(s):

Mamangathi (also known as Mamangayth, Mamngayth depending on language) (multiple records over some decades)

Note: See also Clan 84 (descendants of Charlie Committy, same totems and area but different language).

CLAN 71

Surnames: none recorded (Old Bamboo People)

Descendants: none recorded

Core estate interests: Estate 44 (Minh-wuthel; Big Bamboo)

Clan totems:	Translation:
Ngak	Water

Totemic names:

Mipanganh [cf. Mn *thaa'(ang) mipangan* 'to test or try']

Language(s):

Wik-Paach (= Wik-Ngaangungker in Wik-Ngathan)

Focal sites:

414 Minh-wuthel

CLAN 72

Surnames: Otomorathin

Descendants: patriline extinct

Core estate interests: Estate ? [Jean George says: from Paydan; Silas Wolmby says he was from the inland highland country of upper Hey River, not from the coast (SW to PS83:59); Uki Otomorathin's totems on the whole certainly imply the inland]

Ceremony: Chivirri

Clan totems:	Translation:
Thaypen [Mn, Nn]	Taipan
Aghórringan [in Alngith, = Kuyen, Mn]	Long-mouth Sugarbag (*Trigona* sp.)
May Polp	Small Sugarbag (*Trigona* sp.)
Achemp (Mn)	Emu

Totemic names:

Themoyerredhayn ['Otomorathin']   Male   Human

Language(s): [a Wik-Way variety]

CLAN 73

[Seems to be same as Clan 93 Ngakapoorgum]

Surnames: Koo'agga (Neeyum Yunkaporta)

Descendants: [see Ngakapoorgum; Neeyum Yunkaporta has descendants]

APPENDIX 1

Core estate interests: [information not available]

Ceremony: Wanam

Clan totems:	Translation:
Thoyo	Hammerhead Shark

Totemic names:
Nhii'em ['Neeyum']   Female   Human

CLAN 74

Surnames: Nancy Of Ward R.

Descendants: none recorded

Core estate interests: not precisely recorded

Ceremony: not recorded

Clan totems:	Translation:
Oyengorrpen	Carpet Snake
Piipep	Bird Species (?Oystercatcher)
Thadiy	Sea Turtle
[not recorded]	Flesh of Sea Turtle

CLAN 75

Surnames: Kepple (A), Brodie

Descendants: yes; patriline extant

Note: Connie Clark and Polly Perkin were sisters, whose country was on the upper Archer River and is understood to be the same country as that of old Charlie Kepple and Alfred Brodie (Clan 75, Estate 65). Connie Clark's daughter Bessie Savo is particularly associated with her mother's Top Archer country. Connie's sister Polly was married to Charlie Fruit of Watson River, whose descendants (e.g. Lawrence Fruit) thus have associations with both Top Archer and Watson River, but particularly the latter.

Core estate interests: Estate 65 (Top Archer); see also Estate 30.

Ceremony: Not recorded

Clan totems [puul-ay]:   **Translation:**
Minh Ka'enth Thinth   Large Freshwater Catfish sp.
Minh Ko'en   Magpie Goose
Minh Achemp   Emu
Kangkang   White Breasted Sea Eagle

Language(s):
Mbiywom (Wik-Ompom [wik-ompəm] in Wik-Mungkan)

CLAN 76

Surnames: Lawrence

Descendants: yes; patriline extant

Core estate interests: Estate 66 (Puuy, Mid Archer River (north))

Ceremony: Winchanam (possibly Carpet Snake)

Clan totems: **Translation:**
Ooyngorrpen   Mangrove Carpet Python
Kanpuk   White Swamp Lily, *Nelumbo nucifera*

Totemic names:
Tha'ichman	Male	Human	
Peynken ['Bankana']	Male	Human	
'Koopolla'	Male	Human	
Mee'-wachenh-thathen ['Eye-distant-seeing']	Female	Human	Big
'Pampornch'	Female	Human	
'Pamient'	Female	Human	

Language(s):
Wik-Mungkan
formerly Mbiywom?

APPENDIX 1

McConnel

Local group: VI

Totem-centre(s): 1. Potjauwa (lagoon)

Totems: mai kan puka   water-lily (white)

Names:
Kopala (m) pala – white ko – prefix
Filiteni (f)
Papauwa (f)
Apinkina (f)

1929 pop. [3]

McConnel

cf. the following [may be another clan with company interests in Puuy]. This was the clan of Johnny Pic Pic and his son James.

Local group: VII Poiya

Totem-centre(s): 1. Kanmulaua (circle of ant beds)

Totem-centre(s): 2. Pokauwanauwa (tree with lump like cuscus going up tree)

Totems:
1. minkanmula – male cuscus,
2. min pokauwan – female cuscus

Names:

Wikwota (m)	wik – voice, wata – green ant, ant bites cuscus and makes it cry out
Natonka (m)	nata – back bone onka – long
Pipaninna (f)	pipa – breaks, bends, ninna – sits, cuscus sits as if its back were broken with weight of young in pouch
Pukapapa (f)	puka – baby, papa – teat, baby cuscus sucks its mother's teat for milk
Koimamama (f)	koi – string, vine, mamama – holds on by hands to vine to pull it up tree

1929 pop. [5]

CLAN 77

Surnames: Old Sullivan ('Chaleben'), Old Kooman [cf. Kumama below]

Descendants: patriline extinct

Core estate interests: Estate 58

McConnel
[see her map location for Bushnut and Night Fish]
Local group V

Totem-centre(s): 1. Panam (holes in rocks in creek)

Totems: mai maitji – 'bush-nut' or swamp root

Names:

Kumama (m)	ku – prefix, mama – pick up
Kuwipa (m)	wipa – washed up, roots are washed up against trees in flood time
Tipnguta (f)	tip – root, refers to mashing of roots for food

Totem-centre(s): 2. Tatjapián

Totems:

min jintan	night-fish
min ekka	fresh-water mussel
mainyeana	black fruit
mai neitja	red and white fruit

Names:
Tipdutan (m) tipi – guts
Koekka (m) ko – prefix, ekka – fresh-water mussel

1929 pop. [2]

CLAN 78

Surnames: Ahlers (e.g Douglas)

Descendants: yes; patriline extant

Core estate interests: Estate 64 (Thornbury Creek)

Ceremony: [information not available]

Clan totems:	Translation:
Keerrke	Sparrowhawk
Thithilang	Peewee
Nguyimpa	Magpie Goose
Poyenang	[? Translation]
Ma'-unthu	Jewfish
Nga' Engka	Jardine (fish)

Language(s):
Information apparently differs: Mungkanhu, also identified as Ayapathu ('Mungkanhu', however, may be a term that includes the variety Ayapathu from an upper Kendall perspective).

CLAN 79

Surnames: (Blind Cockatoo, Topsy Wolmby nee Koo'ekka)

Descendants: patriline extant

Core estate interests: Estate 67

Clan totems:	Translation
Minh Wel, Minha Waliy	Blue-tongue Lizard

Language(s):
Wik-Iyanyi (Wik-Iyeyn)

CLAN 80

Surnames: John, Brown*

Descendants: yes; patriline extant

Core estate interests: Estate 146 (western Weipa Peninsula)

Ceremony: [information not available]

Clan totems: **Translation:**

[Language terms here are in Anathangayth, supplied by Alice Mark, not in the clan's own language Laynngith ~ Alngith]

[not recorded]	Cyclone
Nwidham	'Swordfish' 'Black-finned Shark'
Tja'angk	Long-tailed Stingray
[not recorded]	Crab
Ka'andhak	Rock Oyster
[not recorded]	Mangrove Oyster

Totemic names:

Rruchuk

Language(s):

Alngith, Layngith, Laynngith (alternate names)

Focal sites:

Napranum, Nggonban (Evans Point), Oningan,

Note: * In terms of the old clan system, Dick Brown's patriline seems to have been a branch of the same clan as that of Ronnie John's father and father's father, as they have the same language and totems, and are associated focally with the same core land at western Weipa Peninsula. Some of Dick Brown's descendants may express an interest in a wider definition of country, Susie Madua extending her claims as far north as Duifken Point and Pine River, north-east to Luwaeng and Andoom, east to the old mission site at Twenty Mile, south-east to Watson River, and south to Pera Head. While the outliers of this set of claims would be disputed by many, her family's core association with the Weipa area is not seriously disputed.

CLAN 81

Surnames: Mitherropsen ('Mister Robinson')

Descendants: none recorded (Mitherropsen died 1953)

Core estate interests: Estate 60 but see also Clan 144?

APPENDIX 1

Clan totems: **Translation:**
Achemp Emu
Keemp Flying Fox

Totemic names:
Ngak-weentathenh   Male   Human

Language(s):
Wik-Iiyanh

Focal sites:
285 Achemp-aw

CLAN 82

Surnames: Owokran B (Old Stephen)

Descendants: none recorded

Core estate interests: Estate 43 (Yaaneng)

Clan totems: **Translation:**
Thinelpal Dugong

Totemic names:
'Theetaneecha'   Male   Human
[probably 'Saw a Coconut']

Language(s):
Andjingith (= Wik-Ayengench)
Wik-Paach

Focal sites:
662 Yaaneng

CLAN 83

Surnames: Coconut

Descendants: yes; patriline extant

Core estate interests: Estate 68 (Wathayn)

Ceremony: [information not available]

Clan totems:	Translation:
Ndraengwud	Long-nosed Sugarbag (*Trigona* sp.)
[not recorded]	Blind Shark
[not recorded]	File Stingray

Totemic names:
Awungka

Language(s):
Ndrrangith

Focal sites:
Wathayn

CLAN 84

Surnames: Committy

Descendants: yes; patriline extant. The late Charlie Committy was from 'Mbang side', his totems included Gecko and Crow, and his language was Linngithigh. On all three factors he looks most likely to have been from a branch of the same clan as Kerinduns. His descendants include Sylvia Charger, who is his daughter, and her descendants.

Core estate interests: Estate 149 (possibly same sites as Estate 39)

Ceremony: [information not available]

Clan totems:	Translation:
According to Jean George:	
A'oy	Arrowroot

Clan totems:	Translation:
Paandj	Gecko (large, black striped)
Paandj	Night, Darkness
Kambal	Saltwater Crocodile
Kandhak	Oyster
[not recorded]	Porpoise
Ino	Cyclone
Tjakil	Bonefish
Ndhonogh	Frill-necked Lizard
Nggaantj	White Cockatoo
Waath	Crow
La	Wattle Tree sp.
Ambaatjil	Small Mullet spp.

According to Roy Jingle and Alice Mark:

Waath	Crow
Paandj	Gecko (large, black striped)

Language(s):

Linngithigh (from two independent senior sources)

One view, not widely held, is that their language was Nda'ngith, called by some others Ndrra'ngith

Language seems to be the main or even only difference between this lineage and those of Clan 70 (Dick, York), and there is no detail suggesting their country was either separate from or the same as that of Clan 70.

CLAN 85

Surnames: English (descendants of Okolkon)

Descendants: yes; patriline extant

Core estate interests: Estate 69 (Myall Creek)

Ceremony: Not recorded

Clan totems: **Translation:**
Nguul — Stork
Mbaekay — Saltwater Crocodile
Ivivri — Echidna
Mangki — Cuscus

Totemic names:
Okolkon	Male	Human
Amomanka	Male	Human
Twitarran	Male	Human
Kwintji	Female	Human

Language(s):
Anathangayth

Focal sites:
Meyka (Twenty-Mile)

CLANS 86–89: Numbers not in use

CLAN 90 see also 105

Surnames: Koonutta A

Descendants: yes; patriline extant

Core estate interests: Estate 105

Ceremony: Key-elp (Puch)

Clan totems: **Translation:**
Upen — Milky Mangrove
Nyeeyn — Fly

Totemic names:
Ku'-nhat ['Koonutta']	Male	Human

Language(s):
Wik-Ngathan

CLAN 91 *see* 134

CLAN 92 *see* 124

CLAN 93 (*see also* 127)

[data recorded in Wik-Ngathan by PS, see 127 for Kugu Muminh version recorded by John von Sturmer]

Surnames: Ngakapoorgum

Descendants: yes; patriline extant

Core estate interests: Estate 127 (Thampench)

Ceremony: Wanam

Clan totems:	Translation:
Minh Yuumel	Flat-Tailed Stingray
Thape-kulath	Hammerhead Shark
Kaa'-Ngench	Westerly Wind
Uncheyn	Hibiscus (Spear Handles)
Ngak Milp	Saltwater
Wol	Blowfly
Yuk Wenthen	Lancewood

Totemic names:

Ngake-buugem ['Ngakapoorgum']	Male	Human	
Thip-Yuumel 'Belly of Flat-tailed Ray'	Female	Human	Big
Wanggamagan	Female	Human	
Nhii'em ['Neeyum']	Female	Human	

Language(s):
Wik-Muminh

CLAN 95 see 119

CLAN 96 (see also 118)

Surnames: Tarpencha (= Aurukun-based branch of 118)

Descendants: yes

Core estate interests: Origins Estate 118; interests in succession Estate 23 (Dish Yard)

Ceremony: Wanam

Clan totems:	Translation:
Kenha	Freshwater Crocodile
Nhomp	Wedgetailed Eagle

Totemic names:

Thaha-panchi ['Tarpencha'] 'Whiskers'	Male	Human	Big
Aak-mangdhan	Male	Human	Small
Wanggo	Female	Human	Small

Language(s):
Pakanha
Wik-Iiyenh

CLAN 97 (= 123, q.v.)

Surnames: Ngallametta, Wunchum

Descendants: yes; patriline extant

Core estate interests: Estate 123 (Thugu, Pu'an)

Ceremony: Wanam

Clan totems:	Translation:
Pama Uthu	Dead Body
Konkon, Chinpu (Clan = 123)	Jackass
Nga'a Umbi	Jewfish

APPENDIX 1

Clan totems:	Translation:
Minh Thukan	Scrub Turkey
Minh Monte	Jabiru
Kek-wayeng [in variety of Mn]	Echidna

Totemic names:

Wancham ['Wunchum']	Male	Human	Big
Kaha-nguka	Male	Human	Big
Ngalamata ['Ngallametta']	Male	Human	Small
Omborromb	Female	Human	Big
Munyim	Female	Human	Small
Yipa ['Yippah']	Female	Human	Small

Language(s):
Kugu Uwanh

CLAN 98 see 130

CLAN 101 (= 21, q.v.)

Surnames: Korkaktain

JvS name: Kendall R. Nth.1

Descendants: yes; patriline extant

Core estate interests: Estate 21 (= 101) (Kuchent-eypenh)

Ceremony: Puch

Principal totem: Kugu Kala, Kugu Chiichi

Clan totems:	Translation:
Kugu Kalu	Rat
Minha Thukan	Cape York Scrub Fowl
Minha Kuuku	Cape York Brush Turkey
Madhe-awu	Australian Pelican

Language(s):
Wik-Ngathan

Focal sites:
Nguyunga
Kuchund-eypanh
Kumbanhin
Aambeng

CLAN 102 (= 26, q.v.)

Surnames: Ornyengaia, Bandacootcha

JvS name: Kendall R. Nth.2

Descendants: yes; patriline extant

Core estate interests: Estate 102 (Thuuyenh)

Ceremony: Puch [*and* Apelech?]

Principal totem: Kugu Keka, Spearhandle

Clan totems:	Translation:
Kugu Keka	Spearhandle
–	Spear
–	Fresh Water Sharkfish

Language(s):
Wik-Keyenganh

CLAN 103 (= 22, q.v.)

Surnames: Woolla B

JvS name: Kendall R. Nth. 3

Descendants: yes; patriline extant; (early origins lost, but some ultimate connection with Clan 15)

Core estate interests: Estate 103 (= 22)

APPENDIX 1

Ceremony: Not recorded

Principal totem:

Clan totems:	Translation:
Wiikath-Aw	Fairy Story
Yuumel	Flat-tailed Stingray
Thap-kulath	Cross-chark
Nhiiy'	White-chested Brown Eagle
Thaamel	Spear Handle

Totemic names:

Wul 'Blowfly'	Male	Human
Ku'-pel-empenh 'Dog + Spearshaft Lumps'	Male	Human
Nhi'iyam	Female	Human
Pal-pek-pathenh (ref. Freshwater Shark, Kuunger)	Female	Human
Ku'-nham-ney ['Kornamnayuh']	Female	Human

Language(s):
Wik-Ngathan

Focal sites:
Punyelang
Thuyunh
Thaa'-pundi
Pu'andha

CLAN 104

JvS name: Kendall R. Nth. 4

Descendants: patriline extinct; succession interests by members of Clan 96

Core estate interests: Estate 23/104 (Weten, Dish Yard)

Principal totem: Kugu Wangga, Dillybag

Clan totems:	Translation:
Wangga	Dilly Bag
Katanyak (Nn), Pintili (Uw, Mum)	Bonefish
Nga'a Pinya (Uw), Minh Pinyi (Mum)	Nailfish
[not recorded]	Jewfish
[not recorded]	File Stingaree
[not recorded]	Spotted Stingaree
[not recorded]	Diamond Stingaree
[not recorded]	Big Silver Mullet

Totemic names:

Mayi Manu   Female   Human

Language(s):
Wik-Iinchenya (JvS)
Wik-Ngathan (JvS)
Wik-Me'enh (PS)

Focal sites:
Ya'ing; Weten (Dish Yard)

CLAN 105 (= 90)

Surnames: Koonutta A

JvS name: Kendall R. Nth.5

Descendants: yes; patriline extant

Core estate interests: Estate 105

Ceremony: Not recorded

Principal totem: Wik-Upun; Kugu Minha

Clan totems:	Translation:
Yuk Upun	Poison Milk-tree
Yuk Nguchaman	Turpentine
Minha Koona	Mangrove Duck, Burdekin Duck

APPENDIX 1

Clan totems:	Translation:
Minh Ko'ina	Magpie Goose
Minh Arinja	Iron Duck, Black Duck
Minh Mayanh	Diver Duck
Minh Warrka	Smelly Swamp Turtle
Ingk Pikiya /Kek Uyak	Porcupine
Minha Panhthiyan (Uw)	Diver Duck
Waka Winchin (Uw)	Sugarcane Grass (associated with Geese)
Kunche-mut-ongk	Yellow Storm Bird, Yellow Oriole

Totemic names:

Ku'a Nhat ('Koonutta')	Male	Human	
Thanhthidha	Male	Human	Big
Minh Manu	Female	Human	Big
Wunt (K)Enhthanh (cf. 'Wontuttin')	Female	Human	Small

Language(s):
Wik-Me'enh (JvS)
Wik-Ngathan (from M in the case of Jack Koonutta) (PS)

CLAN 106

Surnames: Not recorded

JvS name: Kendall R. Sth.1

Descendants: patriline extinct

Core estate interests: Estate 106 (Kuli-anychan?)

Ceremony: Not recorded

Principal totem: Kugu Pangku, Wallaby

Clan totems:	Translation:
Minha Pangku	Agile Wallaby
Minha Yangki	Amethyst Python
Minha Wudhu/Pupan	Possibly *Protemnodon bicolor*

Clan totems:
Yuku Thokele
Minha Madhe

Translation:
Unidentified Swamp Plant, Red Flower
Australian Pelican

Totemic names:

Ku'a Thokele	Dog
Ku'a Wudhu	Dog

Language(s):
Kugu Ugbanh

Focal sites:
Puntum
Ngaka Kaychim
Mukum-awu
Itha Thaha Ngululu
Kuli-anchan
Yomen-awu

CLAN 107 (= 24, q.v.)

Surnames: Poonkamelya

JvS name: Kendall R. Sth.2

Descendants: yes; patriline extant

Core estate interests: Estate 107

Ceremony: Not recorded; probably Puch

Principal totem: Kugu Ngutu, Bushfire

Clan totems:
Minha Thupan/Ancha (Thu)pan
Pungku
Ngo'onji, (Mu) Ngutu
Minha Chiichi, Minha Kopatha
Waka Kek Yuta

Translation:
Salmon
Knee-Cap
Grass Fire
Bush Rat
Grass

Clan totems:	Translation:
Mayi Ku'uwa	Red Fruit in Scrub
Mayi Kumba	Black Fruit (*Ficus* sp.)
Minha Pawe	Catfish, Short and Fat, Divided Tail
Minha Yiwa	White Owl, Probably Barn and/or Grass Owl
Kempepan	Black Water Snake, Yellow Belly
Wubandu	Small Carpet Snake, White and Black Spotted
Yuku Mali	Bats, Live in Hollow Logs
Ngu'unji Waka	Small Hawk (Sparrow)
Minha Ngome	Salt Water Shark; Yellow

Totemic names:

Pungk-melyidha (= Mn. Pungk Melya = 'Knee ?Staggers'[9]) [Ref. Salmon]	Male	Human	Big
Ngutu Waka ['Ngoortokka'] 'Grass Fire'	Male	Human	Big

Language(s):

Kugu Muminh

Focal sites:

Kengge
Ku'a-awu

CLAN 108

Surnames: Not recorded

JvS name: Kendall R. Sth.3

Descendants: yes; patriline extant in 1978

Core estate interests: Estate 108

Ceremony: Not recorded

---

9 cf. *melya* and *mel-mel* 'wobbly' (Wik-Mungkan).

Principal totem: Kugu Atu; Kugu Wun-ga

Clan totems:	**Translation:**
Mayi Atu	Sugarbag
Minha Thuntu	Frill-necked Lizard
Minha Wiingu	Little Bird
Minha Mangan	Little Possum
Minha Waga	Small Possum
Mayi Wun-ga	Sugarbag (Alternative List)
Minha Mangan	Morning Bird (Honey Eater)
Minha Mangan 2	Squirrel (Sugar Glider)
Minha Thuchi Workom (2)	Blue Crane
Minha / Ku'a Waaga (2)	Possibly Native Cat (*Dasyurus*)
Minha Mulinpu (2)	Torres Strait Pigeon

Totemic names:

Pindha Mun-kayi	Female	Human	Big
Mayi Kugu Ngangka	Female	Human	Small
Mayi Mangka	Female	Human	Big

Language(s):
Kugu Muminh

Focal sites:
Pi'am
Adham
Ponche
Mangka Pomponi
Iiy
Kapi-awu
Kanggani

CLAN 109 (= 27)

Surnames: Kalkeeyorta

JvS name: Kendall R. Sth.4

Descendants: yes; patriline extant

Core estate interests: Estate 109

Ceremony: Puch

Principal totem: Kugu Chiichi, Bushrat

Clan totems:	Translation:
Minha Chiichi/Minha Kupatha	Rat (Mocking Name)
Minh Thupan Pi'an	Salmon; Big Curry Part in Guts
Waka Yutu	Grass, Eaten by Rats
Ngo'onji	Bushfire
Pungk	Knee, Kneecap, 'Bones in Fish'
May Ku'uwa	Red Fruit
May Kumbe	Black Fruit
Thuchi Ngu'unji	Small Bird (Hawk?)
Yiwa	Barn Owl (*Tyto alba*), Grass Owl
Minha Ngome	Saltwater Shark

Totemic names:

Ngutu Waka 'Grassfire'	Male	Human
Kek Yutu ['Kalkeeyorta']	Male	Human
'Grass Spear'		
'Telpoanna'	Female	Human
'Eempinpawn'	Female	Human

Language(s):
Kugu Muminh

Focal sites:
Puntum
Ngaka Kachim

Nickname(s):
In Wik-Ngathan: Kunchenm ('From Scrub Country [at Lower Kendall River]')

CLAN 110 (= 25, q.v.)

Surnames: Karyuka, Marbunt

JvS name: Kendall R. Sth.5

Descendants: yes; patriline extant

Core estate interests: Estate 110

Ceremony: Puch

Principal totem: Kugu Toho-Toh, Barramundi

Clan totems:	Translation:
Nga'a Wunggam/Thaku (1)	Barramundi Big/Small
Nga'a Angk (1)	Rock Cod
Nga'a Pooya (1)	Mud Crab
Manyire (1)	File Stingray
Galah (1)	Galah
Miji (1)	Seagull
Miji (1)	Black Bream
Miy-Miy (1)	Red Schnapper
Minha Pupu (1)	Pheasant Coucal
Nga'a Wunggam (List 2)	Barramundi
Nga'a Angk (2)	Rock Cod
Nga'a Pooy (2)	Mud Crab
Nga'a Miya-Miya (2)	Red Snapper
Nga'a Tha'u-Wunkam (2)	File Stingray
Nga'a Miji (2)	Little Black Bream
Nga'a Molbe (2)	Long Grunter
Mayi Thunhtha (2)	White Fruit (*Eugenia eucalyptoides*)
Yuku Puchim (2)	Mangrove Species (Floating Log)
Nga'a Konalinh (2)	Butterfish

Totemic names:

Kaha-yuga 'Bridge of Barramundi Nose'   Male   Human   Big

APPENDIX 1

Totemic names:

('Karyuka')

Nga'a Kaha-kuli 'Wild Face of Barramundi'	Male	Human	Small
Kaha Peke Thanan	Male	Human	Small
['Barramundi Looking Down']			
Pungk-Miji 'Knee of Black Bream'	Male	Human	Small
Nga'a Punta 'Barramundi Bladder'	Male	Human	
Thaha-Muwa ('Tarmowa')	Female	Human	Big
Nguchuw 'Skinned File Stingray'	Female	Human	Big
Kuw Wankin	Female	Human	
Pudhi	Female	Human	
Mayi Kunga Thuka	Female	Human	
Ngawi Thiin	Male	Dog	
Wakanh	Male	Dog	
Atha Pathanh	Male	Dog	
Patananh	Male	Dog	
Yegananh	Male	Dog	
Yee'-Mipe	Male	Dog	
Tananh	Male	Dog	
Miji Thuka	Male	Dog	
Puchim Bedha	Male	Dog	
Konalinh	Male	Dog	
Pooya Thuka	Female	Dog	
Konhtho Thuka	Female	Dog	
Kalim Thuka	Female	Dog	

Language(s):

Kugu Uwanh

Focal sites:

Agu Thunhtha, Mangaynyi (= Mengeyn, Mn), Milbe, Nga'adha, Pangkam, Thuke, Thunhtha Pangkam, Umam, Wuki-awu, Wuyinh-awu

McConnel: Not listed but see map: Crab and Barramundi.

CLAN 111

Surnames: Not recorded

JvS name: Kendall R. Inland 1

Descendants: patriline extant in 1978

Core estate interests: Estate 111

Ceremony: Not recorded

Principal totem: Not recorded

Clan totems:	Translation:
[not recorded]	Flying-Fox

Language(s):
Wik-Iiyanh

Focal sites:
Region of Koka and at Kuthe and Ngakwi-awu.

CLAN 112

Surnames: Not recorded

JvS name: Kendall R. Inland 2

Descendants: patriline extant in 1978

Core estate interests: Estate 112

Ceremony: Not recorded

Principal totem: Kugu Wayn-gan, Curlew

Clan totems:	Translation:
Minha Wayn-gan	Curlew (Southern Stone Curlew?)
Mayi Payan	Water-Lily

Totemic names:

Yank Thipin [cf. 'Yankabina' below]	Female	Human	Big
Yangk Waninh	Female	Human	Small
Pindha Kulawi	Female	Human	

Language(s):
Wik-Iiyanh

McConnel

Local group XIIIc

Totem-centre(s): Ko'cha, (open country near waterlily lagoons of lower Holroyd River)

Totems: min wainkan curlew

Names:

Minkaboiya	min – meat, ka – not, boiya – meat, curlew, disappears as one tries to spear it
Ngutan Wokanje (m) wokan -	walks about, ngutan – night time
Yantampa (m)	Ian – there goes, tampa – legs, there go his legs!
Minwula (m)	min – meat, wuta – two lie down, two legs of curlew lie together on the ground when it sits on them
Yankabina (f)	yanka – tail, bina – shakes, curlew shakes its tail as it runs
Wapin (f)	
Iipaiyan (f)	

1929 pop. [3]

CLAN 113 (= 40, q.v.)

Surnames: Peinyekka, Jingle

JvS name: Kendall R. Inland 4

Descendants: yes; patriline extant

Core estate interests: Estate 113 (formerly also listed as Estate 50)

Ceremony: Wanam

Principal totem: Kugu Keke, Nankeen Kestrel

Clan totems:	**Translation:**
Minha Keke (Kakelang in Mn)	Sparrow Hawk (? Nankeen Kestrel *Falco cench.*) [Also Kerrkiy in ?Mungkanho]
Minha Engka (Thochen in Mn)	Jardine, Saratoga (*Sclerophages leichhardti leichhardti.*) [Also Thochin in ?Mungkanho]
Kun-tul	Rifle Fish
Minh Paak	King Parrot
Ma'a-wunta	Freshwater Crayfish

Totemic names:

Pany-ek ? ['Peinyekka']	Male	Human
Aak-kup	Male	Human
Ku'a Nhampa Magan	Male	Dog

Language(s):
Wik-Iiyanh

Focal sites:
Agu Tha'u Kakalang = Tha'e-Kakel
Kakalang Ngannga

McConnel

Local group Possibly McConnel's XIII(d); if so, then:

Totem-centre(s): [not stated]

Totems: min kerki chicken-hawk

Names: Nompinam ngana (m)

1929 pop. [not stated]

APPENDIX 1

CLAN 114

Surnames: Not recorded

JvS name: Kendall R. Inland 5

Descendants: patriline extant in 1978

Core estate interests: Estate 114

Ceremony: Not recorded

Principal totem: Bandicoot

Clan totems:	Translation:
Minh Monke	Bandicoot
Pinya Pinya	Little Bird; Yellow Chest
Minha Nhompi	Wedgetailed Eagle

Totemic names:

| Ku'a Yija | Male | Dog |

Language(s):
Wik-Iiyanh

McConnel
Cf. Bandicoot cult centre on map.

CLAN 115

Surnames: Quinkin

JvS name: Kendall R. Inland 6

Descendants: yes; patriline extant

Core estate interests: Estate 115

Ceremony: Winchinam

Principal totem: Kugu Nhompi, Wedgetailed. Eagle

Clan totems: **Translation:**
Minha Nhompi   Wedgetailed Eagle, *Aquila audax*
[Nhompo in ?Mungkanho]
Minha Akul   Jewfish
[Akwela in ?Mungkanho]
Yuk Akwela [in ?Mungkanho]   Tree sp.
Yuk Po'olo   Yellowfruit (*Parinari nonda*)
Yuk Yongka   Cooktown Ironwood
Nyarrka (Mn: Nyerrk)   Small Owl-like sp.
Nguurrku   Big Owl sp.
Chepanang   Quail

Totemic names:
cf. mission card for Louisa:
'Takwybattowan'   Male   Human
'Pambattan'   Female Human
[cf. 'Ta'abatabata' below]

Language(s):
Wik-Iiyanh (formerly?); given to PS by Koppa Eempan Yunkaporta as Wik-Mungkanh in 1990.

Focal sites:
Thaachenyin, Thaa'-ngupa, Paamp Puuti, Chew'eng (all southern end Meripah block).

McConnel
Local group XVI

Totem-centre(s): (Zarven [sic: Barren] country of Upper Kendall River)

Totems: <u>min</u> <u>nompi</u> eagle-hawk

Names:
<u>Kontantja</u> (m)
<u>Ngemin</u> (m)
<u>Mintanganta</u> (m) <u>min</u> – meat, <u>ta</u> – beak
<u>Kopipan</u> (m) <u>pipan</u> – breaks

Ta'abatabata (f) ta'a – claw, bata – bites, eats meat from claw
Ngaientja (f)
Mitjangunta (f)

1929 pop. [1]

CLAN 116

Surnames: Kepple (C)

JvS name: Kendall R. Inland 7

Descendants: yes; patriline extant

Core estate interests: Estate 116

Ceremony: Winchanam

Principal totem: Mumpa (Nhinkalo), Devil

Clan totems:	Translation:
Thaha-panchi	Beard
Mumpa, Nhinkalo	Devil
Chepingka	Quail
Chiiwo'	Bird sp. (like a cockatoo)
Mowa	White Cockatoo
Waath	Crow

Totemic names:

Thaha-panchi	Human	Male	Big
Ku'-iicha [Ref. Emu]	Human	Male	Small
Mithaboy	Human	Male	Small
[e.g. Noble Kepple—probably from 'Mr Boyd']			
Ku'-wonya	Human	Female	Small
A'-itha	Human	Female	
Ngekathayan	Dog		

Language(s):
Wik-Iiyanh

McConnel

Identifies two clans and estates covered by our Clan and Estate 116:

Local group XVII

Totem-centre(s): 1. (Ridgy country where Kendall River rises)

Totems:

mintjipin	quail
patja	shooting-star or meteor

Names:

Akabattan (f) aka – the ground, battan – bits, meteor falls to earth
1929 pop. None

Local group XVIII

Totem-centre(s): 1. (Barren country of Upper Kendall River)

Totems:

min wata	crow
mantianka	praying mantis
min tatji	Iguana (large)

Names:

Tumintjaka (m)
Nointjauwaka (m)

1929 pop. [1]

CLAN 117

Surnames: Kepple (D) (Old Mosey Kepple)

JvS name: Kendall R. Inland 8

Descendants: patriline extant in 1978; extinct now; Quinkins and Warnkoola/Kepples have ancestry from this clan.

Core estate interests: Estate 117

Ceremony: Not recorded

Principal totem: Kugu Yome, Possum

APPENDIX 1

Clan totems:　　　　　　**Translation:**
Minha Kulan (Mn) -Yome (Mu)　　Possum

Totemic names:
Pungk Kulan　　　　Male　　Human　Big
Minha Untu　　　　 Male　　Human　Big
Agu Wuk Rampe　　 Male　　Human　Small

Language(s):
Wik-Iiyanh

McConnel
Local group XIV (a)

Totem-centre(s): Wutji

Totem: minkulan opossum (male)

Names:
Ko'olan (m)
Mawumpan (f) opossum uses its hands
Totem: min wutjiga opossum (female)

Names:
Tananya (m)
Maitjauwa

1929 pop. [2]

CLAN 118 (*see also* 96)

Surnames: Kendall, Edwards, Tarpencha

JvS name: Kendall R. Inland 9

Taylor code: 18

Descendants: yes; patriline extant

Core estate interests: Estate 118

Ceremony: Wanam

Principal totem: Kugu Kanhe, Freshwater Crocodile

Clan totems:	**Translation:**
Minha Kanhe	Freshwater Crocodile, *Croc. johnstonii.*
Yuku Thaynchelu	Milk Tree
Yuk Wontoje	Cottonseed; Yellow Flower
Yuk Odho	Beefwood/Nutwood
Muk	Stone
Minha Thuchi Thayma	Sparrow
Thugu Pool	Similar to Blue-tongue Lizard
Nga'a Mankan	Freshwater Cod

Totemic names:

Kanhe Wudu	Male	Dog	
Thuka Kambanh	Female	Dog	
Ngeke Wunpan	Male	Dog	
Ma'a Wunpan	Female	Dog	
Mutu Ngaka Kumpinh	Male	Dog	
Thayma	Male	Dog	
Muk Kanke	Female	Human	Big
A'etha	Male	Human	Big
Agu Manga Thana	Male	Human	Big
[Dougal Tarpencha's version: Aak-Mangdhan]			
Meelyo	Female	Human	

Language(s):
Wik-Iiyanh (but cf. 96: Pakanh)

CLAN 119

Surnames: Shortjoe, Kemthan

JvS name: Kendall R. Inland 10

Descendants: yes; patriline extant

Core estate interests: Estate 119

Ceremony: Winchinam

Principal totem: Blue-tongue Lizard

Clan totems: **Translation:**
Wali (Awu)   Blue-tongue Lizard Awu
Maanyi (Awu)   Water Lily Awu
Thaanchil/Agu Yuku Tha' (Awu)   Milky Tree (Story)
Wuut   Greybeard
Ku'   Dog

Totemic names:
Manhintha   Male   Human   Big
Kenthen 'Fled' ['Kemthan'][10]   Male   Human

Language(s):
Wik Iyanh

McConnel
Local group XXI

Totem-centre(s): 1. (Curved line of natural stones colour resembling that of native cat and spotted)

Totems: min yungatang native cat

Names:
Panyaka (m)

Totem-centre(s): 2. (Heap of stones)

Totems: min wala Blue-tongue lizard

Names:
Kopotja (m)
Manpunka (m)
Unku (m)

1929 pop. [3]

---

10   Reference to a Totemic Being who fled in the story, name of Being not recorded. Said to have been a name derived from Roddy Shortjoe's 'uncle', hence possibly a *kuuten* (navel string) name rather than a clan name for men of Clan 95.

CLAN 120

Surnames: Not recorded

JvS name: Kendall R. Inland 12

Descendants: patriline extinct

Core estate interests: Estate 120

Ceremony: Not recorded

Principal totem: Kugu Poykol, Freshwater Catfish

Clan totems:	Translation:
Nga'a Poykola	Freshwater Catfish

Language(s):
Ayepath (Ayapathu)

CLAN 121

Surnames: Not recorded

JvS name: Thuuk R. 1

Descendants: patriline extinct

Core estate interests: Estate 121

Ceremony: Not recorded

Principal totem: Kugu Thinhthaw, Snake

Clan totems:	Translation:
Minha Thinhthaw	Freshwater Snake, *Liasis fuscus*
Ngaka Yee	Flowing Water
Mayi Kumba	Black Fruit (*Ficus* sp.)

Language(s):
Kugu Muminh

CLAN 122

Surnames: Possibly Koowootha (e.g. Dennis, sent to Yarrabah ?1940s)

JvS name: Thuuk R. Inland 1

Descendants: patriline extant in 1978

Core estate interests: Estate 122 (east of Ongorom)

Ceremony: Not recorded

Language(s):
Wik-Iiyanh

CLAN 123 (= 97 q.v.; see also linked Clan 130)

Surnames: Ngallametta and Ngallapoorgum (segment A), Wunchum (segment B)

JvS name: Thuuk R. 2

Descendants: yes; patriline extant

Core estate interests: Estate 123; see also linked Estate 130

Ceremony: Wanam

Principal totem: Kugu Uthu [Dead Body], alt. Kugu Muchua

Clan totems:	**Translation:**
Pama Uthu	Dead Body
Kompo	Devil
Minha Manu Wunpan	Scrub Turkey, *Megapodius freycinet*
Minha Thukan	Brown Scrub Turkey, *Alectura*
Wangayj	File Snake, *Acrocordus javan.*
Mayi Munyim	Bush Onion
Waba	Green Frog
Mayi Winggu	Arrowroot, *Tacca pinnatifida*
Mayi Kannga	Wild Grape
Monke	Bandicoot, *Isoodon macrurus*?

Clan totems: **Translation:**
Minha Kimpu   Jackass
Kuunku (2)   Scrub Turkey
Umbe/Waaying (2)   Jewfish
Munyam/Ichare (2)   Onion, *Typhonium brownii*
Kugu Nyincham (2)   Ghost

Totemic names:

Name	Sex	Type	Size
Ngalam-Bugam ('Ngallapoorgum')	Male	Human	Big
Wancham ('Wunchum')	Male	Human	Big
Wobe	Male	Human	
Minha Badha	Male	Human	Small
Keenge	Male	Human	
Ngalameta ('Ngallaametta')	Male	Human	Small
Warpa		Human	
Chuuchi		Human	Small
Thapa(N) Echinam	Female	Human	Big
Omberamp	Female	Human	
Yipa	Female	Human	
Manu Thukan	Female	Human	
Panyimpan	Female	Human	Small
Pama Thupi	Male	Human	Big
Aya Kominan	Female	Human	
Kuya Dhiin	Male	Dog	
Mukpin	Male	Dog	
Thukan Kugu	Male	Dog	
Thumu Thuka	Female	Dog	
Woyjengon	Female	Dog	
Kiiwula		Dog	

Language(s):
Kugu Uwanh

Focal sites:
Pu'an

APPENDIX 1

CLAN 124

Surnames: Mimunyin

JvS name: Holroyd R. 1

Taylor code: 1415

Descendants: yes; patriline extant in 1978

Core estate interests: Estate 124

Ceremony: Wanam

Principal totem: Kugu Nga'a, Stingray

Clan totems:	Translation:
Nga'a Wanggin	Long-tailed Stingray
Mayi Mugam	Long Hairy Yam
Minha Kaha-Yuwa	White Ibis
Wela Niku	Big Baler Shell

Totemic names:

Mayi Manyim	Male	Human	Big
Wumpu	Female	Human	
Yangkam		Human	Small
Mayi Ma'a Pugam		Human	

Language(s):
Kugu Ugbanh

CLAN 125

Surnames: Not recorded

JvS name: Holroyd R. 2

Descendants: patriline extinct 1978

Core estate interests: Estate 125

Ceremony: [Wanam]

Principal totem: Kugu Thu'a

Clan totems:	**Translation:**
Minha Yewo	Whale
Minha Wadha	Crow
Waka Wuthu	Grass Seed
Yongk (Awu)	Ironwood (Woomera Tree)
Wanam (Awa)	Ceremonial Ground

Language(s):
Kugu Ugbanh

Focal sites:
Ku'a Wunen
Thaha-Kungadha 2
Aye

CLAN 126

Surnames: Not recorded

JvS name: Holroyd R. 3

Descendants: patriline extant in 1978

Core estate interests: Estate 126

Ceremony: Not recorded

Principal totem: Kugu Poole, Carpet Snake

Clan totems:	**Translation:**
Minha Poole	Carpet Snake
Minha Kukun-Ngu	Little Bird (Dove)
Yuk Pindi	Small Lizard
Minha Pawra	Fish Species
Minha Kaha-Miji	Sea Turtle
Minha Kuuluwan	Diamond Dove, *Geopelia cuneata*

APPENDIX 1

Totemic names:

Kukun-nga	Male	Human

Language(s):
Kugu Mu'inh

CLAN 127

Surnames: Ngakapoorgum, Ngallapoorgum

JvS name: Holroyd R. 4

Descendants: yes; patriline extant

Core estate interests: Estate 127

Ceremony: Wanam

Principal totem: Kugu Keka, Spearhandle

Clan totems:	Translation:
[not recorded]	Flat-tailed Stingaree
[not recorded]	Spear
[not recorded]	Lancewood
[not recorded]	Saltwater
[not recorded]	Tide
[not recorded]	Whistle Wind
[not recorded]	Jelly Fish

Totemic names:

Thupi Yomel	Female	Human
Ngaka Kumen Mento	Female	Human
Ngaka Puugam ('Ngakapoorgum')	Male	Human
Pelempinh		Dog
Thaha-Apanh		Dog
Yeth-Umpinh		Dog

Language(s):
Kugu Muminh

Focal sites:
Thampench

CLAN 128

Surnames: Not recorded

JvS name: Holroyd R. 6

Descendants: patriline extinct

Core estate interests: Doubt whether distinct from Clan 132 (JvS).

Ceremony: Not recorded

Principal totem: Kugu Minha, Diver

CLAN 129

Surnames: Holroyd C (e.g. Robert Holroyd Snr aka *Benenh Yi'iyam*), Edwards A

JvS name: Holroyd R. 8

Taylor code: 1415

Descendants: patrilines extant

Core estate interests: Estate 129

Ceremony: Not recorded

Principal totem: Kugu Kujin, Freshwater Shark

Clan totems:	Translation:
Minha Kujin	Fresh Water Shark
[not recorded]	Snake
Kampanya	Swordfish (Sawfish)
Minha Thowo	Storm Bird
Minha Ngathalje	Spangled Drongo

APPENDIX 1

Clan totems: | **Translation:**
Minha Kaha-je | Egret, *Egretta* sp.
Minha Engk-l-piya | White-Necked Heron
Minha Kopo | Small Black Crane
[not recorded] | Little Blue Grasshopper

Totemic names:

Name	Sex	Type	Size
Mayi Kempa	Male	Human	Big
Nga'a Murgan	Male	Human	Small
Yi'iyam '[Sea Breakers] go on and on' ['Yeium']	Male	Human	
Benenh ref. 'Little Blue Grasshopper'	Male	Human	
Ngaka-pugam ('Ngakapoorgum')	Male	Human	
Wulu 'Salty Water' ['Woolla']	Male	Human	
Thith-unchan 'Big Breaker Runs all along [Shore, With Crackling Sound]'	Female	Human	
Thupi-yomelo [Ref. Stingray]	Female	Human	
Nhihiyam	Female	Human	
Kaha-Je Kugu [Ref. White Crane]	Male	Do	
Kaha-Je Thaku		Dog	
Thoyowo [Ref. Hammerhead Shark]	Male	Dog	
Pungk-unchan 'Sea Breakers Break Bank'	Male	Dog	
Thayja '[Sea] Froth'	Male	Dog	
Pelempinh 'Lump/Knot [on Spear Handle]'	Male	Dog	
Thaha-apanh	Male	Dog	

Language(s):
Kugu Muminh

CLAN 130

Surnames: Yantumba (B), Minpunja, Toby, Holroyd, Thompson

JvS name: Holroyd R. Inland 1

Taylor: Clan 16

335

Descendants: yes; patriline extant

Core estate interests: Estate 130 (linked to Estate 123, see Clan 123)

Ceremony: Wanam

Principal totem: Kug-Uthu, Dead Body

Clan totems:	**Translation:**
Pama Uthu	Dead Body
Minha Monte	Jabiru
Mimpa	Clothes, Bush Blanket
Minha Konkon	Jackass, Kookaburra
Minh Punba	File Snake
(Minh) Thugu Ngamba	Black, White-bellied, Swamp Snake
Mayi Payan	Mate to Waterlily
Yuku Thata	Frog (Generic Term)
Minh Manu Wunpan	Black Scrub Turkey
Minh Thuchi Yidu	Kingfisher
Minh Thukan	Brown Turkey
Yuku Payan	Tree Species

Totemic names:

Yentamba ('Yantumba')	Male	Human	Big
Mimpa Puugam	Male	Human	Big
Mimpanji	Male	Human	Big
Thali	Female	Human	Small
Iinjin	Female	Human	
Payan Payche	Female	Dog	
Konkon	Male	Dog	
Tukan		Dog	

Language(s):
Wik-Iiyanh

APPENDIX 1

CLAN 131

Surnames: Not recorded

JvS name: Christmas Ck. 1

Descendants: patriline extant in 1978

Core estate interests: Estate 131

Ceremony: Not recorded

Principal totem: Kugu Yome, Possum

Clan totems:	Translation:
Minha Yome	Possum
Minha Pinba	Squeaker
Monto/Kulam	Road, Track, Where Possum Makes Road
Yuku Wongbe	Rhinoceros Beetle
Nga'a Malidha	[type of fish]
Nga'a Kulang	[type of fish]

Totemic names:

Pungkundu	Male	Human	Big
Minha Tha'u Pipi	Male	Human	Small
Komben		Human	
Umu Thupan	Male	Dog	
Waamanh	Female	Dog	

Language(s):
Kugu Mu'inh

CLAN 132

Surnames: Brian

JvS name: Christmas Ck. 2

Taylor code: 12

Descendants: yes; patriline extant

Core estate interests: Estate 132

Ceremony: Not recorded

Principal totem: Kugu Minha, Diver

Clan totems:	**Translation:**
Minha Ko'an/Minha Nguyumba	Geese, Goose Egg (Magpie Goose)
Minha Thampe	Iron Duck
Minha Koonu	Burdekin Duck
Panhthiyan	Diver
Umele	Diver
Nguma	Diver
Ngache Thugu	Red-bellied Black Snake
Kapi/Peengan	Moon
Ngache Thuthuwa	Death Adder
Thumu Pupi	Firestick
Aag Eka	Heaps of Shell on Beach
Ngaka Uthi	Freshwater Mussel
Minha Yapi	Pee Wee, *Grallina cyanoleuca*

Totemic names:

Pungku Ko'an	Male	Human
Minha Yimba	Female	Human
Minha Manu	Female	Human
Manu Katha	Female	Human

Language(s):
Kugu Yi'anh

Focal sites:
Yangku

APPENDIX 1

CLAN 133

Surnames: Not recorded

JvS name: Christmas Ck. 4

Descendants: patriline extant in 1978

Core estate interests: Estate 133

Ceremony: Not recorded

Principal totem: Kugu Yome, Possum

Clan totems:	**Translation:**
Yome (List 1)	Possum, Brown
Pinba (1)	Squeaker
Yuku Ngada (1)	Spider (Generic)
Thochon (also Nga'a Engka) (1)	Jardine
Maykun (1)	Rifle-fish
Poykolo (1)	Catfish, Long Pointy Nose, Freshwater
Wongbo (1)	Beetle (Rhinoceros Beetle)
Yuk Thochon (1)	Tree (used for making coolamon)
Minha Yome (List 2)	'Possum'
Minha Penjon (2)	Probably Brush Cuckoo
Windi (2)	Stingray
Margala (2)	Stingray
Nga'a Kulang (2)	King Fish
Minha Pinba (2)	Squeaker
Minha Thuchi Mayanga (2)	Probably Varied Lorikeet
Minha Thuchi Maychigam (2)	Probably Red-winged Parrot
Nga'a Poykolo (2)	[type of fish]
Nga'a Engka (2)	[type of fish]
Nga'a Lutu (2)	[type of fish]
Yuku Windi (2)	?[type of tree]
Yuk Wongwo (2)	Rhinoceros Beetle

Clan totems: **Translation:**
Yuku Thochon (2)   Unidentified Tree Species
Ngache Upun (2)   Rifle-fish
Untu (2)   Scrotum, Testes
Tha'u (2)   Foot, Paw
Agu (2)   Ground
Nga'a Maykun (2)   Rifle-fish
Yuku Ngada (2)   Spider (Generic)
Yuk Yome (2)   Unidentified Tree Species, in Vine Forest

Totemic names:
Tha'u Nhaanyi	Male	Human	Big
Walule	Male	Human	Big
Ayncha Tha'u Kuuwa	Male	Human	Big
Perret	Male	Human	Small
Tha'u-Majin	Female	Human	
Wucha Kiga	Female	Human	Big
Minha Tha'u	Female	Human	Big
Yuk Upun Waalang	Male	Dog	
Thayje Waalang	Male	Dog	

Language(s):
Kugu Mu'inh

CLAN 134 (= 91)

Surnames: Arkwookerum, Holroyd D, Lowdown, Coleman

JvS name: Christmas Ck. 5

Taylor code: 13

Descendants: yes; patrilines extant

Core estate interests: Estate 134

APPENDIX 1

Ceremony: Wanam

Principal totem: Kugu Yome, -Chaawana

Clan totems:	**Translation:**
Minha Yome	Possum, Brown
Pinba	Squeaker [Rainbow Lorikeet]
Yuku Ngada	Spider (Generic)
Thochon	Jardine
Maykun	Rifle-Fish
Poykolo	Catfish, Long Pointy Nose; Freshwater
Wongbo	Rhinoceros Beetle
Yuk Thochon	Tree (used for making coolamons)
Yuk Yome	Unidentified Tree Species, in Vine Forest

Totemic names:

Minha Untu	Male	Human	Big
Agu Wuk Rampe	Male	Human	Big
Perret	Male	Human	Small
Thaha-Majin	Female	Human	Big
Tha'u-Majin	Female	Human	Big
Wucha Kiga	Female	Human	Big
Minha Tha'u	Female	Human	Big
Thayje Ku'a-l-wunan	Male	Dog	
Nga'awu	Male	Dog	
Wayche Yee	Female	Dog	
Waga Unggu	Male	Dog	

Language(s):
Kugu Mu'inh

Focal sites:
Waalang

CLAN 135

Surnames: Not recorded

JvS name: Christmas Ck. 6

Descendants: patriline extant in 1978

Core estate interests: Estate 135

Ceremony: Not recorded

Principal totem: Kugu Yome, Kugu Chaawana

Clan totems:	Translation:
Minha Yome	'Possum'
Minha Penjon	Probably Brush Cuckoo
Windi	'Stingray'
Margala	'Stingray'
Nga'a Kulang	'King Fish'
Minha Pinba	'Squeaker' [Rainbow Lorikeet]
Minha Thuchi Mayanga	Probably Varied Lorikeet
Minha Thuchi Maychigam	Probably Red-winged Parrot
Nga'a Poykolo	[Catfish]
Nga'a Enka	[type of fish]
Nga'a Lutu	[type of fish]
Yuku Windi	[not recorded]
Yuk Wongwo	Rhinoceros Beetle
Yuku Thochon	Unidentified Tree Species
Ngache Upun	Long-tailed Eel
Untu	Scrotum, Testes
Tha'u	Foot, Paw
Agu	Ground
Nga'a Maykun	'Rifle-Fish'
Yuku Ngada	Spider (Generic)

APPENDIX 1

Totemic names:

Muchuchan	Male	Dog
Kach Uganh	Male	Dog
Muninh	Male	Dog
Thayje Waalang	Male	Dog
Walu Yi'i	Male	Dog
Minha Kiga Puugam	Male	Human Big

Language(s):
Kugu Mu'inh

CLAN 136

Surnames: Not recorded

JvS name: Christmas Ck. 7

Descendants: patriline extinct

Core estate interests: Estate 136

Ceremony: Not recorded

Principal totem: Kugu Thinthaw, -Wube

Clan totems:	**Translation:**
Minha Thinthaw	'Water Snake', *Liasis fuscus*

Totemic names:

Kargo	Female	Human	Big

Language(s):
Kugu Mangk

CLAN 137

Surnames: Not recorded

JvS name: Christmas Ck. 8

Descendants: patriline extinct

Core estate interests: Estate 137

Ceremony: Not recorded

Principal totem: Kugu Kujin, Freshwater Shark

Clan totems:	Translation:
Nga'a Kujin	Freshwater Shark

Language(s):
Kugu Muminh

CLAN 138

Surnames: Not recorded

JvS name: Christmas Ck. Inland 1

Descendants: patriline extant in 1978

Core estate interests: Estate 138

Ceremony: Not recorded

Principal totem: Kugu Atu, Sugar Bag

Clan totems:	Translation:
Atu	'Sugarbag', Native Honey/Bee, *Trigona* sp.

Language(s):
Wik-Iiyanh

CLAN 139

Surnames: Not recorded

JvS name: Breakfast Ck. 1

Descendants: patriline extant in 1978

Core estate interests: Estate 139

Ceremony: Not recorded

Principal totem: Kugu Toho-Toh, Barramundi

Clan totems: **Translation:**
(See Kendall R. Sth 5) Not elicited separately

Totemic names:

Nga'a Margin	Male	Human
Nga'a Elpen	Female	Human
Mangkarana Thanan	Female	Human
Mangk-(Th)Anan	Female	Human
(Nga'a) Nguchu	Female	Human
Pama (P)Indha Unggan	Female	Human

Language(s):
Kugu Mangk

CLAN 140

Surnames: Ned

JvS name: Breakfast Ck. Inland 1

Taylor code: 17

Descendants: yes; patriline extant

Core estate interests: Estate 140

Ceremony: Not recorded

Principal totem: Kugu Monte, Kug-Uthu

Clan totems: **Translation:**
Minha Monte (Mu) 'Policeman Bird', Jabiru
[not recorded] Freshwater Crocodile

Totemic names:
'All in one' with T2, HU1 (see John von Sturmer 1978)

Language(s):
Wik-Iiyanh
Pakanha

McConnel

Local group XXIV

Totem-centre(s): 1. (On upper reaches of Edward River where crocodile is found),

Totems: min kena – fresh-water crocodile

Names:

Akamandana (m)	(aka – ground, mana – neck, tana stands, crocodile puts head up to look about)
Aeta (m)	(ta – foot, crocodile covers eggs in sand with foot to keep them warm and dry),
Kentan (m)	(kena – crocodile, tana – stands, there is a crocodile! or a crocodile stands there),
Tejola	
Taanjaiya (f)	(ta ontia – crocodile moves legs as he goes across sand)
Winkan (f)	
Worbako (f)	
Noitji (f)	
Mainmanka (f)	(mai – food, mankan – eats)

1929 pop. [10–12].

CLAN 141

Surnames: Not recorded

JvS name: Christmas Ck. Inland 2

Descendants: patriline extant in 1978

Core estate interests: Estate 141

Ceremony: Not recorded

Principal totem: Curlew

Clan totems:	Translation:
[not recorded]	?Crow, *Corvus orru salvatorii*
[not recorded]	Probably southern Stone Curlew
[not recorded]	Magpie Lark, *Grallina cyanoleuca*

Language(s):
Pakanha

CLAN 142

Surnames: see 129 – conjoint?

JvS name: Holroyd River 5

Taylor code: 1415

Descendants: yes; patriline extant in 1978

Core estate interests: Estate 142

Ceremony: Not recorded

Principal totem: Kugu Yome

Clan totems:	Translation:
Minha Yome (List 1)	Possum, *Trichosurus vulpecula*
Minha Pinba (1)	Squeaker [Rainbow Lorikeet]
Monto/Kulam (1)	Road, Track, Where Possum Makes Road
Yuku Wongbe (1)	Rhinoceros Beetle
Nga'a Malidha (6)	King Fish (Alligator Gar)
Nga'a Kulang (1)	King Fish (Alligator Gar)
Yome (List 2)	'Possum, Brown'
Pinba (2)	'Squeaker'
Yuku Ngada (2)	Rifle-fish, *Toxotes chatareus*
Thochon (2)	Jardine, *Sclerophages leichhardtii*
Maykun (2)	Rifle-Fish, *Toxotes chatareus*
Poykolo (2)	Catfish, Long Pointy Nose, Freshwater
Wongbo (2)	Rhinoceros Beetle

Clan totems:	**Translation:**
Yuk Thochon (2)	Tree (Used For Making Coolamon)
Yuk Yome (2)	Unidentified Tree Species, In Vine Forest
Minha Yome (List 3)	'Possum'
Minha Penjon (3)	Probably Brush Cuckoo
Windi (3)	Stingray
Margala (3)	Stingray
Nga'a Kulang (3)	'King Fish'
Minha Pinba (3)	'Squeaker'
Minha Thuchi Mayanga (3)	Probably Varied Lorikeet
Minha Thuchi Maychigam (3)	Probably Red-Winged Parrot
Nga'a Poykolo (3)	[Catfish]
Nga'a Engka (3)	[type of fish]
Nga'a Lutu (3)	[type of fish]
Yuku Windi (3)	–
Yuk Wongwo (3)	Rhinoceros Beetle
Yuku Thochon (3)	Unidentified Tree Species
Ngache Upun (3)	Long-tailed Eel
Untu (3)	Scrotum, Testes
Tha'u (3)	Foot, Paw
Agu (3)	Ground
Nga'a Maykun (3)	'Rifle Fish'
Yuku Ngada 3)	Spider (Generic)

Totemic names:

Pungku Pinba   Male   Human

Focal sites:

Pabim

Language(s):

Kugu Mu'inh

CLAN 143

Surnames: Not recorded

JvS name: Christmas Ck. 3

Descendants: patriline extinct

Core estate interests: Estate 143

Ceremony: Not recorded

Principal totem: Kugu Pooli

Clan totems:	Translation:
Minha Pooli	Carpet Snake
Minha Kaha-Miji	Sea Turtle (All Species)

Language(s):
Kugu Mu'inh

Focal sites:
Yangku

CLAN 144

Surnames: Moses, Edward

JvS name: Holroyd River 7

Taylor code: 11

Descendants: patriline extant 1978

Core estate interests: Estate 144

Ceremony: Not recorded

Principal totem: Kugu Toho-Toh (JvS)

Clan totems:	Translation:
Achamp	Emu
[not recorded]	Groper
[not recorded]	Barramundi

Totemic names:

| Ku'a Toom | Male | Dog |
| Ku'a Yija | Male | Dog |

Focal sites:

Thaa'-pulnh, Achemp-aw area (cf. JvS KU3)

Language(s):

Not recorded

McConnel: ?XIIIa

CLAN 145

Surnames: Not recorded

JvS name: Holroyd River 9

Descendants: patriline extant in 1978

CLAN 146: Number not in use

CLAN 147

Surnames: Not recorded

Descendants: Not recorded

Core estate interests: Estate 147 (McConnel's XV)

CLAN 148

Surnames: Not recorded

Descendants: Not recorded

Core estate interests: Estate 148 (Beagle Camp)

APPENDIX 1

Surname/name/clan/estate cross-reference

Table A1.1: Modern surnames and their clan and estate affiliations up to c. 1978

Name	Type	Clan	Estate	Comments
Ahlers	surname	78	64	
Ampeybegan	surname	4	4	
Arkwookerum	surname	91	134	
Arkwookerum	surname	134	134	
Atu 1 (Kugu)	totem ref.	108	108	
Atu 2 (Kugu)	totem ref.	138	138	
Bandacootcha	surname	26	102	
Bandacootcha	surname	102	102	
Bell	surname	35	14	
Bell	surname	35	27	
Blowhard	surname	52	53	
Bowenda (formerly)	surname	4	4	
Bowenda (now)	surname	4	4	
Bowenda (now)	surname	59	3	
Brodie	surname	75	65	
Brown	surname	80	146	
Charcoal	first name	47	32	
Chevathen	surname	65	41	Mainly at Weipa
Chevathun	surname	67	46	Mainly at Aurukun
Chii'iiy	totem ref.?	44	44	
Clark	surname	66	40	
Cockatoo	first name	1	1	
Coconut	first name	3	3	
Coconut	surname	83	68	
Committy	surname	84	149	
Comprabar	surname	9	9	
Day	surname	48	33	
Dick	surname	70	39	
Doughboy	surname	52	53	
Edward A	surname	129	129	

LINGUISTIC ORGANISATION AND NATIVE TITLE

Name	Type	Clan	Estate	Comments
Edward B	surname	144	144	
English	surname	85	69	
Eundatumweakin	surname	15	15	
Fruit	surname	46	30	
George	surname	48	33	
Go'olfree	surname	64	38	
Gothachalkenin	surname	15	15	
Holroyd (A)	surname	28	112?	e.g. Joe
Holroyd (B)	surname			
Holroyd (C)	surname	129	129	e.g. Robert
Holroyd (D)	surname			
Jingle	surname	113	113	
John	surname	80	146	
Kalkeeyorta	surname	27	109	
Kalkeeyorta	surname	109	109	
Kangaroo	surname	51	52	
Karntin	surname	8	8	
Karyuka	surname	25	110	
Karyuka	surname	110	110	
Kawangka (formerly)	surname	35	14	
Kawangka (formerly)	surname	35	27	
Kawangka (now)	surname	35	31	
Kelinda	surname	67	46	
Kemthan	surname	119	119	
Kendall	surname	96	118	
Kendall	surname	118	118	
Kepple (A)	surname	75	65	Top Archer Kepples
Kepple (B)	surname	69	48	Warnkoola Kepples
Kepple (C)	surname	116	116	Mump-awu Kepples
Kepple (D)	surname	117	117	Yome-awu Kepple
Kerindun	surname	68	47	
Kongotema	surname	31	28	
Koo'ekka	surname	36	29	
Koo'oila	surname	37	14	
Koo'oila	surname	37	27	
Koomeeta	surname	18	18	

APPENDIX 1

Name	Type	Clan	Estate	Comments
Koondumbin	surname	34	42	
Koonutta (A)	surname	90	105	Kendall River
Koonutta (A)	surname	105	105	Kendall River
Koonutta (B)	surname	10	10	Waayeng area
Koowarta	surname	39	49	
Koowootha	surname	122?	122?	e.g. Dennis
Korkaktain	surname	21	101	
Korkaktain	surname	101	101	
Kowearpta	surname	41	23?	
Kujin 1 (Kugu)	totem ref.	129	129	
Kujin 2 (Kugu)	totem ref.	137	137	
Landis	surname	15	15	
Lawrence	surname	76	66	
Luke	first name	49	30?	
Mabel	first name	66	40	
Marbendinar	surname	13	13	
Marbthowan	surname	38	23?	see also Estate 37
Marbthowan	surname	38	37?	
Mark	surname	51	52	
Marpoondin	surname	16	16	
Matthew	surname	63	45	
Mimunyin	surname	124	124	
Minha 1 (Kugu)	totem ref.	128	132?	
Minha 1 (Kugu)	totem ref.	132	132	
Minpunja	surname	130	130	
Mitherropsen	first name	81	60	
Monte (Kugu)	totem ref.	140	140	
Mookerrethenh	first name	62	36	
Moses	surname	144	144	
Motton	surname	50	51	
Namponan	surname	8	8	
Nancy	first name	74	?	
Neeyum	first name	73	?	
Ngak (Wik-)	totem ref.	71	44	
Ngakapoorgum	surname	93	127	
Ngakapoorgum	surname	127	127	

LINGUISTIC ORGANISATION AND NATIVE TITLE

Name	Type	Clan	Estate	Comments
Ngakyunkwokka	surname	35	14	
Ngakyunkwokka	surname	35	27	
Ngallametta	surname	97	123	
Ngallametta	surname	123	123	
Ngallapoorgum	surname	97	123	
Ngallapoorgum	surname	123	123	
Not recorded		106	106	
Not recorded		111	111	
Not recorded		114	114	
Not recorded		122	122	
Not recorded		141	141	
Not recorded		145	145	
Ornyengaia	surname	26	102	
Ornyengaia	surname	102	102	
Otomorathin	surname	72	?	
Owokran (A)	surname	60	34	e.g. Cyril
Owokran (B)	surname	82	43	From Yaaneng
Pahimbung	surname	39	49	
Pambegan	surname	33	31	
Pamtoonda	surname	17	17	
Pamulkan	surname	18	18	
Parker	surname	48	33	
Peemuggina (A)	surname	6	6	e.g. Peter
Peemuggina (B)	surname	19	19	e.g. Arkapenya
Peinkinna	surname	2	2	
Peinyekka	surname	113	113	
Piith (Wik-)	totem ref.	11	11	
Poole (Kugu)	totem ref.	126	126	
Pooli (Kugu)	totem ref.	143	143	
Poonkamelya	surname	24	107	
Poonkamelya	surname	107	107	
Pootchemunka (A)	surname	14	14	Ti Tree P's
Pootchemunka (A)	surname	14	32	Ti Tree P's
Pootchemunka (B)	surname	9	9	C Keerweer P's
Poykol (Kugu)	totem ref.	120	120	
Quinkin	surname	115	115	

Name	Type	Clan	Estate	Comments
Shortjoe	surname	119	119	
Sullivan	first name	77	58	
Taisman	surname	29	2	
Tarpencha	surname	96	118	
Tarpencha	surname	118	118	
Thinthaw 1 (Kugu)	totem ref.	121	121	
Thinthaw 2 (Kugu)	totem ref.	121	121	
Thu'a (Kugu)	totem ref.	136	136	
Toho-Toh 1 (Kugu)	totem ref.	139	139	
Toho-Toh 2 (Kugu)	totem ref.	144	144	
Toikalkin (former)	surname	7	7	
Toikalkin (now)	surname	32	5	
Tybingoompa	surname	18	18	
Waangk 1 (Wik-)	totem ref.	23	104	
Waangk 2 (Wik-)	totem ref.	104	104	
Walmbeng	surname	58	1	
Warnkoola	surname	69	48	
Wayn-gan (Kugu)	totem ref.	112	112	
Wikmunea	surname	5	5	
Wildfellow	surname	15	15	
Wolmby	surname	6	6	
Woolla (A)	surname	31	28	Oony-aw Woollas
Woolla (B)	surname	22	103	e.g. Jackson
Woolla (B)	surname	103	103	e.g. Jackson
Wunchum	surname	97	123	
Wunchum	surname	123	123	
Yantumba (A)	surname	28	112?	Aur. Yantumba
Yantumba (B)	surname	130	130	Por. Yantumbas
Yome 1 (Kugu)	totem ref.	131	131	
Yome 2 (Kugu)	totem ref.	133	133	
Yome 3 (Kugu)	totem ref.	135	135	
Yome 4 (Kugu)	totem ref.	142	142	
York	surname	70	39	
Yunkaporta (A)	surname	12	12	Northern Y's
Yunkaporta (B)	surname	20	20	Southern Y's

Clan/estate cross-reference list

Table A1.2: Estates and related surnames as at c. 1978

Clan	Estate	Name	Type	Comments
1	1	Cockatoo	first name	
2	2	Peinkinna	surname	
3	3	Coconut	first name	
4	4	Ampeybegan	surname	
4	4	Bowenda (formerly)	surname	
4	4	Bowenda (now)	surname	
5	5	Wikmunea	surname	
6	6	Peemuggina (A)	surname	e.g. Peter
6	6	Wolmby	surname	
7	7	Toikalkin (former)	surname	
8	8	Karntin	surname	
8	8	Namponan	surname	
9	9	Comprabar	surname	
9	9	Pootchemunka (B)	surname	C Keerweer P's
10	10	Koonutta (B)	surname	Waayeng area
11	11	Piith (Wik-)	totem ref.	
12	12	Yunkaporta (A)	surname	Northern Y's
13	13	Marbendinar	surname	
14	14	Pootchemunka (A)	surname	Ti Tree P's
14	32	Pootchemunka (A)	surname	Ti Tree P's
15	15	Eundatumweakin	surname	
15	15	Gothachalkenin	surname	
15	15	Landis	surname	
15	15	Wildfellow	surname	
16	16	Marpoondin	surname	
17	17	Pamtoonda	surname	
18	18	Koomeeta	surname	
18	18	Pamulkan	surname	
18	18	Tybingoompa	surname	
19	19	Peemuggina (B)	surname	e.g. Arkapenya
20	20	Yunkaporta (B)	surname	Southern Y's
21	101	Korkaktain	surname	

APPENDIX 1

Clan	Estate	Name	Type	Comments
22	103	Woolla (B)	surname	e.g. Jackson
23	104	Waangk 1 (Wik-)	totem ref.	
24	107	Poonkamelya	surname	
25	110	Karyuka	surname	
26	102	Bandacootcha	surname	
26	102	Ornyengaia	surname	
27	109	Kalkeeyorta	surname	
28	112?	Holroyd (A)	surname	e.g. Joe
28	112?	Yantumba (A)	surname	Aur. Yantumba
29	2	Taisman	surname	
31	28	Kongotema	surname	
31	28	Woolla (A)	surname	Oony-aw Woollas
32	5	Toikalkin (now)	surname	
33	31	Pambegan	surname	
34	42	Koondumbin	surname	
35	14	Bell	surname	
35	27	Bell	surname	
35	14	Kawangka (formerly)	surname	
35	27	Kawangka (formerly)	surname	
35	31	Kawangka (now)	surname	
35	14	Ngakyunkwokka	surname	
35	27	Ngakyunkwokka	surname	
36	29	Koo'ekka	surname	
37	14	Koo'oila	surname	
37	27	Koo'oila	surname	
38	23?	Marbthowan	surname	see also Estate 37
38	37?	Marbthowan	surname	
39	49	Koowarta	surname	
39	49	Pahimbung	surname	
41	23?	Kowearpta	surname	
44	44	Chii'iiy	totem ref.?	
46	30	Fruit	surname	
47	32	Charcoal	first name	
48	33	Day	surname	
48	33	George	surname	

Clan	Estate	Name	Type	Comments
48	33	Parker	surname	
49	30?	Luke	first name	
50	51	Motton	surname	
51	52	Kangaroo	surname	
51	52	Mark	surname	
52	53	Blowhard	surname	
52	53	Doughboy	surname	
58	1	Walmbeng	surname	
59	3	Bowenda (now)	surname	
60	34	Owokran (A)	surname	e.g. Cyril
62	36	Mookerrethenh	first name	
63	45	Matthew	surname	
64	38	Go'olfree	surname	
65	41	Chevathen	surname	Mainly at Weipa
66	40	Clark	surname	
66	40	Mabel	first name	
67	46	Chevathun	surname	Mainly at Aurukun
67	46	Kelinda	surname	
68	47	Kerindun	surname	
69	48	Kepple (B)	surname	Warnkoola Kepples
69	48	Warnkoola	surname	
70	39	Dick	surname	
70	39	York	surname	
71	44	Ngak (Wik-)	totem ref.	
72	?	Otomorathin	surname	Uki
73	?	Neeyum	first name	Married Clive Y.
74	?	Nancy	first name	Of Ward River
75	65	Brodie	surname	
75	65	Kepple (A)	surname	Top Archer Kepples
76	66	Lawrence	surname	
77	58	Sullivan	first name	
78	64	Ahlers	surname	
80	146	Brown	surname	
80	146	John	surname	
81	60	Mitherropsen	first name	

APPENDIX 1

Clan	Estate	Name	Type	Comments
82	43	Owokran (B)	surname	From Yaaneng
83	68	Coconut	surname	
84	149	Committy	surname	
85	69	English	surname	
90	105	Koonutta (A)	surname	Kendall River
91	134	Arkwookerum	surname	
93	127	Ngakapoorgum	surname	
96	118	Kendall	surname	
96	118	Tarpencha	surname	
97	123	Ngallametta	surname	
97	123	Ngallapoorgum	surname	
97	123	Wunchum	surname	
101	101	Korkaktain	surname	
102	102	Bandacootcha	surname	
102	102	Ornyengaia	surname	
103	103	Woolla (B)	surname	e.g. Jackson
104	104	Waangk 2 (Wik-)	totem ref.	
105	105	Koonutta (A)	surname	Kendall River
106	106	Not recorded		
107	107	Poonkamelya	surname	
108	108	Atu 1 (Kugu)	totem ref.	
109	109	Kalkeeyorta	surname	
110	110	Karyuka	surname	
111	111	Not recorded		
112	112	Wayn-gan (Kugu)	totem ref.	
113	113	Jingle	surname	
113	113	Peinyekka	surname	
114	114	Not recorded		
115	115	Quinkin	surname	
116	116	Kepple (C)	surname	Mump-awu Kepples
117	117	Kepple (D)	surname	Yome-awu Kepple
118	118	Kendall	surname	
118	118	Tarpencha	surname	
119	119	Kemthan	surname	
119	119	Shortjoe	surname	

Clan	Estate	Name	Type	Comments
120	120	Poykol (Kugu)	totem ref.	
121	121	Thinthaw 1 (Kugu)	totem ref.	
121	121	Thinthaw 2 (Kugu)	totem ref.	
122	122	Not recorded		
123	123	Ngallametta	surname	
123	123	Ngallapoorgum	surname	
123	123	Wunchum	surname	
124	124	Mimunyin	surname	
126	126	Poole (Kugu)	totem ref.	
127	127	Ngakapoorgum	surname	
128	132?	Minha 1 (Kugu)	totem ref.	
129	129	Kujin 1 (Kugu)	totem ref.	
129	129	Edward A	surname	
130	130	Minpunja	surname	
130	130	Yantumba (B)	surname	Pormpuraaw. Yantumbas
131	131	Yome 1 (Kugu)	totem ref.	= Taylor 13?
132	132	Minha 1 (Kugu)	totem ref.	
133	133	Yome 2 (Kugu)	totem ref.	= Taylor 13?
134	134	Arkwookerum	surname	cf. Taylor's 13
135	135	Yome 3 (Kugu)	totem ref.	= Taylor 13?
136	136	Thu'a (Kugu)	totem ref.	
137	137	Kujin 2 (Kugu)	totem ref.	
138	138	Atu 2 (Kugu)	totem ref.	
139	139	Toho-Toh 1 (Kugu)	totem ref.	cf. Taylor 11
140	140	Monte (Kugu)	totem ref.	cf. Taylor 16
141	141	Not recorded		
142	142	Yome 4 (Kugu)	totem ref.	= Taylor 13?
143	143	Pooli (Kugu)	totem ref.	
144	144	Moses	surname	
144	144	Edward B	surname	
145	145	Not recorded		
146				Not in use
147	147	Not recorded		McConnel's XV
148	148	Not recorded		Beagle Camp mob

APPENDIX 1

Figure A1.1: Victor Wolmby, Apelech ceremony leader, 1972
Source: John von Sturmer

Figure A1.2: Estate 40 site: Malnyinyu (Pera Head), Barracuda and Bluefish Story Place, 1988
Source: David Martin

Figure A1.3: Estate 34 site: Yagalmungkan, red ochre source, 1988
Source: David Martin

APPENDIX 1

Figure A1.4: Estate 34 site: aak penchiy (danger place) behind mangroves, Norman River, 1988
Source: David Martin

Figure A1.5: Estate 1 Thikel-aampeyn base camp and rich resource site, 1985
Source: Peter Sutton

Figure A1.6: Estate 1 site: Waathem, with Cecil Walmbeng, 1985
Source: Peter Sutton

APPENDIX 1

Figure A1.7: Estate 3 Isobel Wolmby mapping site Thooerpenith, 1976
Source: Peter Sutton

Figure A1.8: Estate 3 Johnny Ampeybegan mapping base camp site Wachnyathaw, 1976
Source: Peter Sutton

Figure A1.9: Estate 3 mapping party at Wachnyathaw, 1976
Source: Peter Sutton

Figure A1.10: Estate 3 Fred Chaney at Watha-nhiin (Peret) Outstation 1979
Source: Peter Sutton

APPENDIX 1

Figure A1.11: Estate 4 site: Uthuk Aweyn (Big Milky Way, aka 'Big Lake'), 1976
Source: Peter Sutton

Figure A1.12: Estate 4 Johnny Ampeybegan at his birthplace site Yaal, Big Lake, 1976
Source: Peter Sutton

Figure A1.13: Estate 5 Lomai Woolla at Kencherrang, Brown Snake Story Place, 1985
Source: Peter Sutton

Figure A1.14: Estate 5 mapping Kencherrang area, David Martin with Raymond and Lomai Woolla, 1985
Source: Peter Sutton

APPENDIX 1

Figure A1.15: Estate 6 site: Aayk swamp, Estuarine Shark Story Place, 1977
Source: Peter Sutton

Figure A1.16: Estate 6 site: Kuthenhthang cremation mound, 1977
Source: Peter Sutton

Figure A1.17: Estate 6 mapping site: Wiip-aw (across river), shade camp, 1977
Source: Peter Sutton.

Figure A1.18: Estate 6 Noel Peemuggina at Waathanem-ompenh, wet season base camp, 1977
Source: Peter Sutton

Figure A1.19: Estate 6 Silas and Caleb Wolmby digging Aayk well, 1977
Source: Peter Sutton

APPENDIX 1

Figure A1.20: Estate 7 site: Mithenthathenh cremation mound, 1977
Source: Peter Sutton

Figure A1.21: Estate 11 site: Thew-en (Cape Keerweer), Woven Bag Story Place, 1977
Source: Peter Sutton

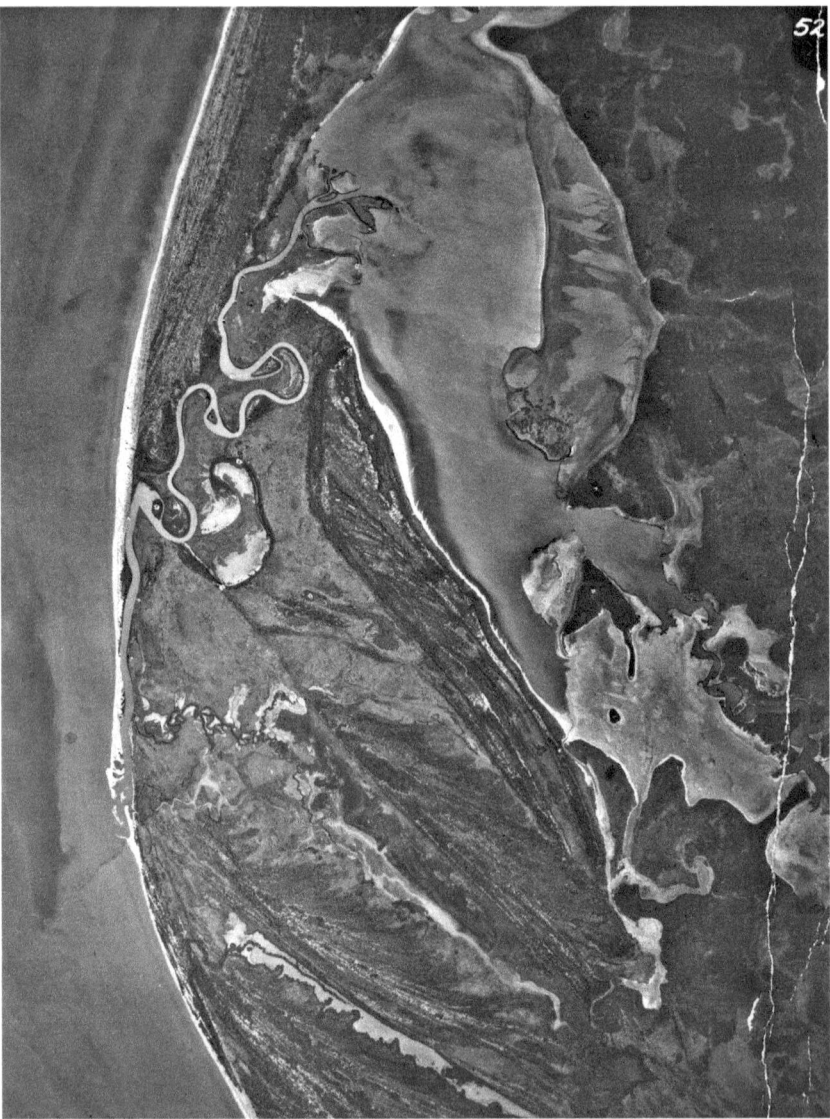

Figure A1.22: Kirke River area aerial photo used in field mapping; pinpricks are site locations

Source: © Commonwealth of Australia (Geoscience Australia) 2021. This product is released under the Creative Commons Attribution 4.0 International Licence

APPENDIX 1

Figure A1.23: Estate 12 site: Um-thunth (Moving Stone, Story Place), 1977
Left to right: Clive Yunkaporta, Peter Sutton, Jack Spear, Roy Yunkaporta
Source: Peter Sutton (photo taken by Francis Yunkaporta)

Figure A1.24: Annie Kalkeeyorta, Estate and Clan 12, Aurukun, 1987
Source: David Potter

APPENDIX 1

Figure A1.25: Mortuary ceremony, Aurukun, 2009
Source: Wendy Cull

Figure A1.26: Estate 14 mapping party, Ti Tree area, 1990
Left to right: Dugal Tarpencha, Jim Pootchemunka, John Kelly Pootchemunka, Billy Panjee Koo'oila, Neville Pootchemunka, Nigel Stuart Pootchemunka, Donald Pootchemunka, Nigel Pootchemunka
Source: John Adams

Figure A1.27: Estate 14 Ti Tree Outstation, 1979
Source: Peter Sutton

Figure A1.28: Estate 14 Francis Yunkaporta observes as Bob Massey introduces Fred Chaney to spirits at Wanke-nhiyeng (Ti Tree Lagoon), Two Girls and Moon Story Place, 1979
Source: Peter Sutton

APPENDIX 1

Figure A1.29: Estate 15 Rupert Gothachalkenin, Thaangkunh-nhiin well, wet season base camp and danger place, 1977
Source: Peter Sutton

Figure A1.30: Estate 15 Thaangkunh-nhiin, inner camp site, 1977
Source: Peter Sutton

Figure A1.31: Estate 20 Mapping Kuu'eneng base camp, Knox River area, 1978
Source: Peter Sutton

APPENDIX 1

Figure A1.32: Estate 20 Mangk-puypeng, Dog Story Place, Knox River, 1977
Source: Peter Sutton

Figure A1.33: Estate 20 Piithel, wet season base camp, with Jack Sleep and others, 1977
Source: Peter Sutton

Figure A1.34: Estate 23 site: Thanmel, all-season base camp with cremation and fighting grounds close by, 1977
Source: Peter Sutton

Figure A1.35: Estate 23 mapping site: Weten (Dish Yard), all-season base camp, 1977
Source: Peter Sutton

APPENDIX 1

Figure A1.36: Ron Yunkaporta, middle Archer River, 1990
Source: Peter Sutton

Figure A1.37: Estate 49 John Koowarta, Clan 39, Archer River, 1990
Source: Peter Sutton

Figure A1.38: Inland forest mapping, Kendall River Holding, 1991
Source: Peter Sutton

APPENDIX 1

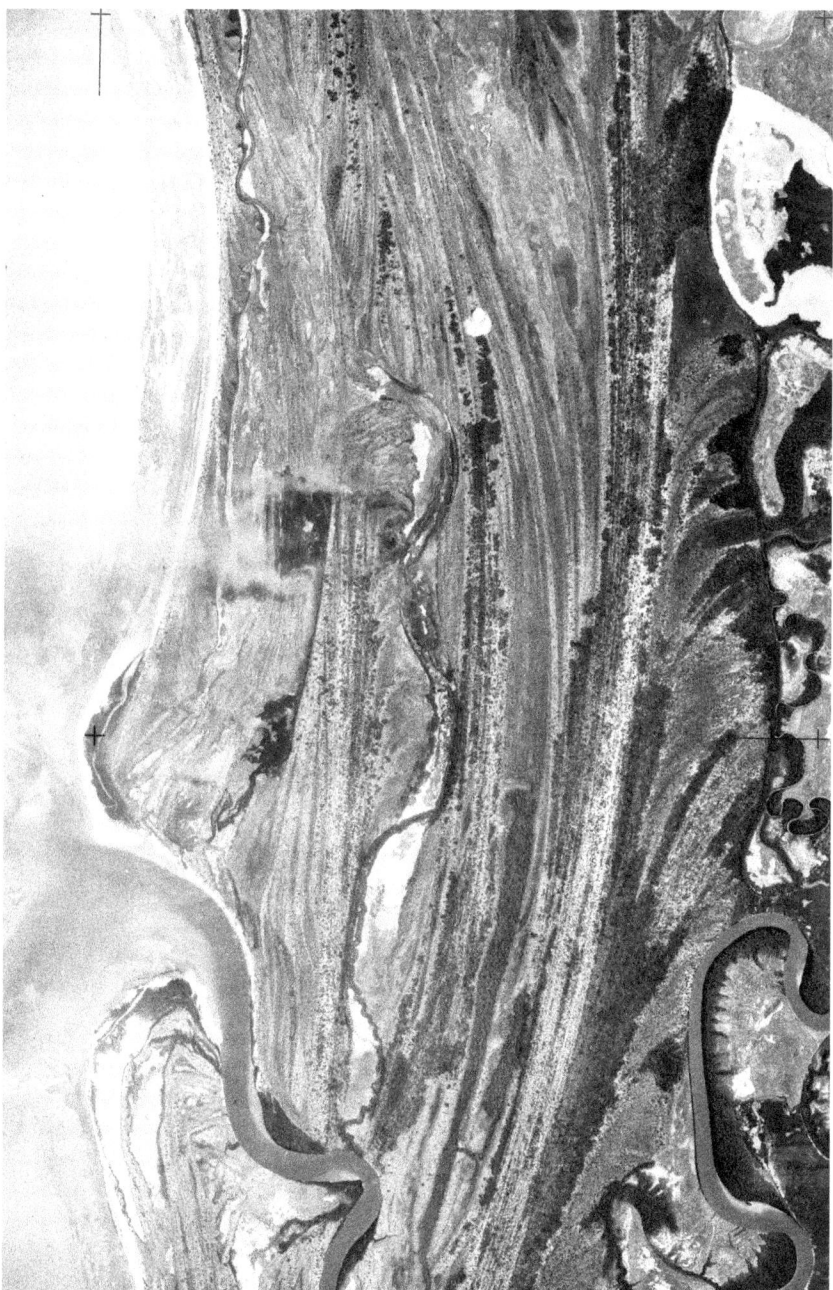

Figure A1.39: Aerial photo of Kendall River mouth with likely hunting fires, 1957

Source: © Commonwealth of Australia (Geoscience Australia) 2021. This product is released under the Creative Commons Attribution 4.0 International Licence

Figure A1.40: Estate 21 Sydney Wolmby and others at Ngaateng swamp, 2007
Source: David Martin

Figure A1.41: Estate 106 Empadha, South Kendall Outstation, 1978
Source: Diane Smith

APPENDIX 1

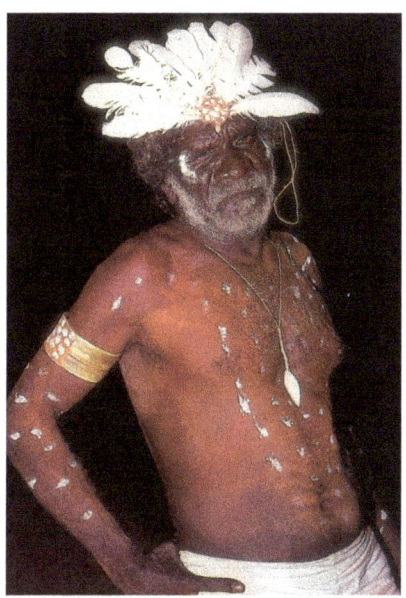

Figure A1.42: James Kalkeeyorta, Clan 109, Aurukun, 1982
Source: Jeanie Adams

Figure A1.43: Estate 123 Pu'an Outstation at Thuuk River, 1978
Source: Diane Smith

Figure A1.44: MacNaught Ngallametta, Clan 97, Aurukun 1987
Source: Dale Chesson

Figure A1.45: Mapping Koepenth swamp, dry season camp site, Estate 3, with Paddy Yantumba, 1977
Source: Peter Sutton

APPENDIX 1

Figure A1.46: Ron Yunkaporta tape recording at the bora tree where he was an initiand in 1970, Aurukun, 2006
Source: Peter Sutton

Figure A1.47: Apelech ritual during mortuary ceremony, Aurukun, 2006
Source: Jane Karyuka

Figure A1.48: Hula dancers, mortuary ceremony, Aurukun, 2009
Source: Jane Karyuka

APPENDIX 1

Figure A1.49: Alan Wolmby (Clan & Estate 6) 'baptising' John von Sturmer near Aayk, 1971
Source: J. von Sturmer (photo by Ken Wunchum)

Appendix 2: Wik estates

Peter Sutton, David Martin, John von Sturmer, Ursula McConnel, Roger Cribb, Athol Chase and John Taylor

Compiled by Peter Sutton

Clan estate maps (Maps A2.1–A2.13) here are based on the Australian 1:100,000 map series, which are arranged thus from north to south and west to east:

	Map A2.1: WEIPA	Map A2.2: YORK DOWNS		
	Map A2.3: AURUKUN		Map A2.4: WENLOCK	
Map A2.5: CAPE KEERWEER	Map A2.6: ARCHER RIVER	Map A2.7: MERAPAH	Map A2.8: ROKEBY	
	Map A2.9: HOLROYD	Map A2.10: KENDALL RIVER	Map A2.11: STRATHBURN	Map A2.12 EBAGOOLA
	Map A2.13: EDWARD RIVER			

On these maps, the estate numbers and dialect abbreviations are placed roughly at the centre of the estate concerned. Estates each contain up to a few score named sites, most but not all of them contiguously distributed, which are not shown here. For example, 87 distinct sites have been identified as belonging to Estate 12, and 148 as belonging to Estate 4. These were among the more intensively mapped estates. For Estate 13, at the other end of the scale, we recorded only 31 sites (Sutton et al. 1990:831–40).

At the head of each estate entry below we give the estate number followed by a map number. The map number refers to the maps within this book.

LINGUISTIC ORGANISATION AND NATIVE TITLE

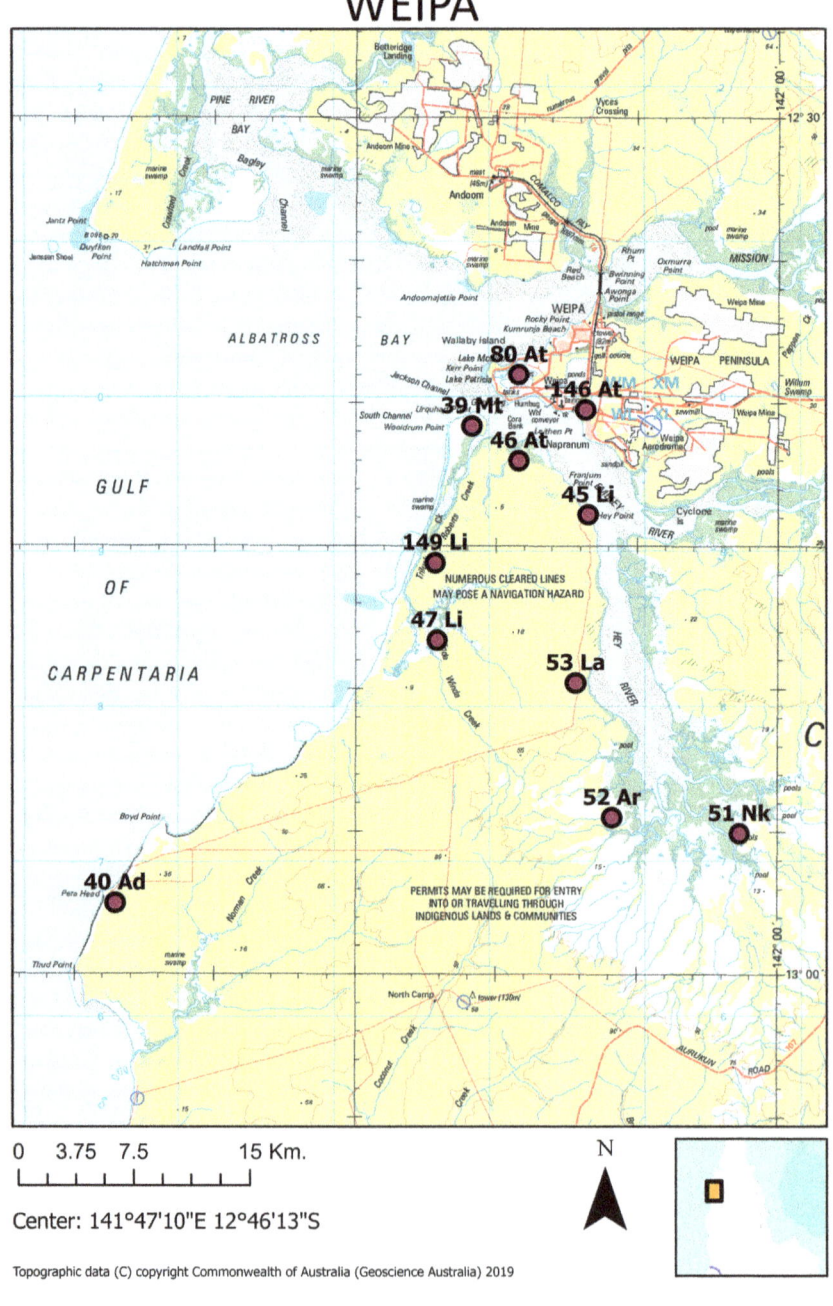

Map A2.1: Clan estates and languages: Weipa sheet
Source: © Commonwealth of Australia (Geoscience Australia) 2019

APPENDIX 2

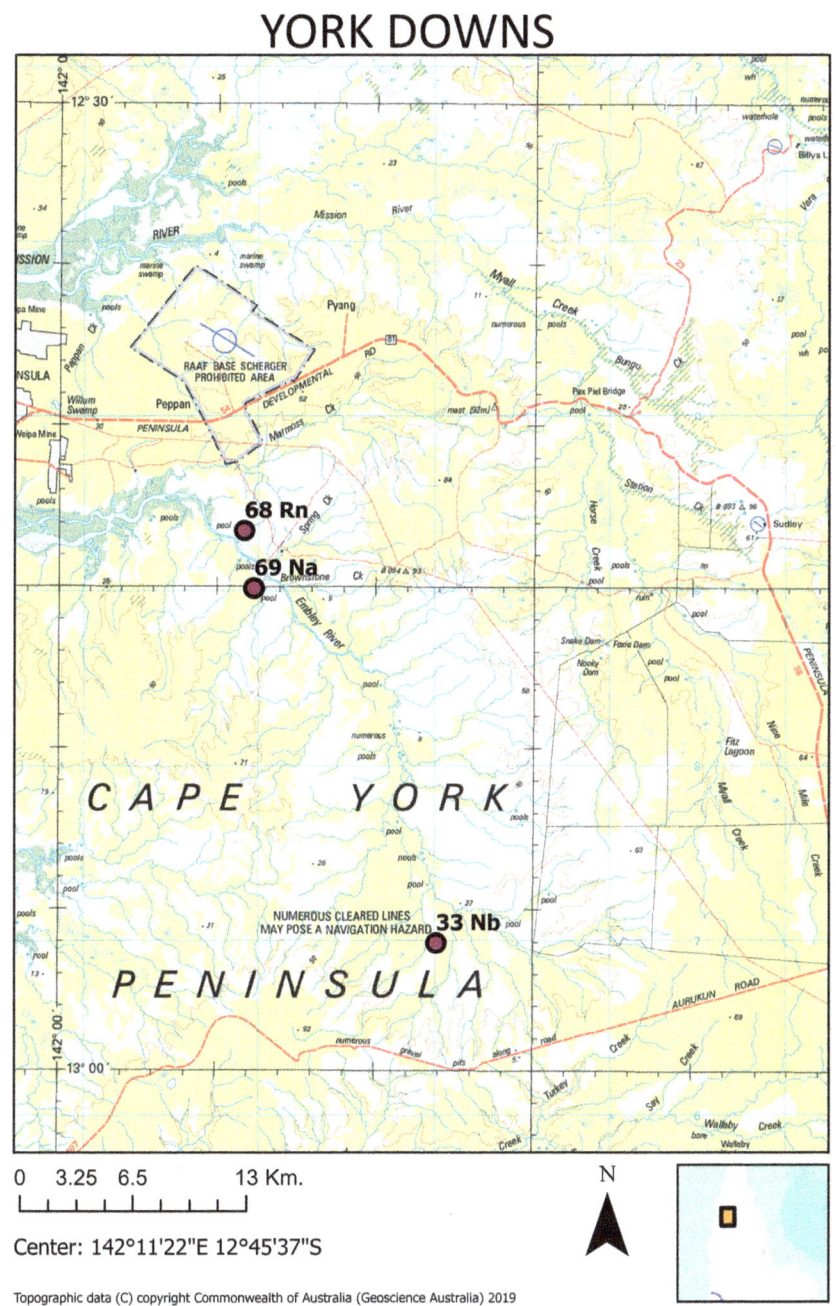

Map A2.2: Clan estates and languages: York Downs sheet
Source: © Commonwealth of Australia (Geoscience Australia) 2019

LINGUISTIC ORGANISATION AND NATIVE TITLE

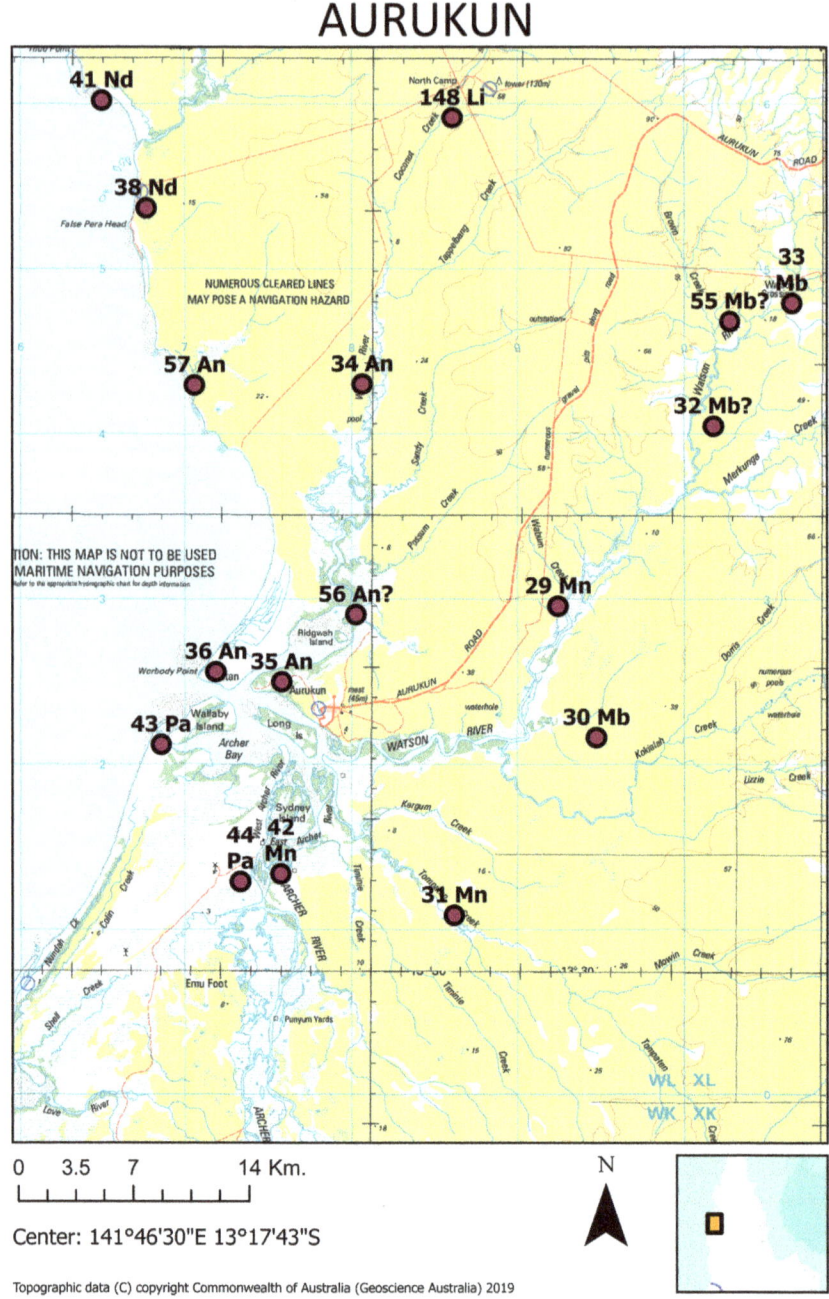

Map A2.3: Clan estates and languages: Aurukun sheet
Source: © Commonwealth of Australia (Geoscience Australia) 2019

APPENDIX 2

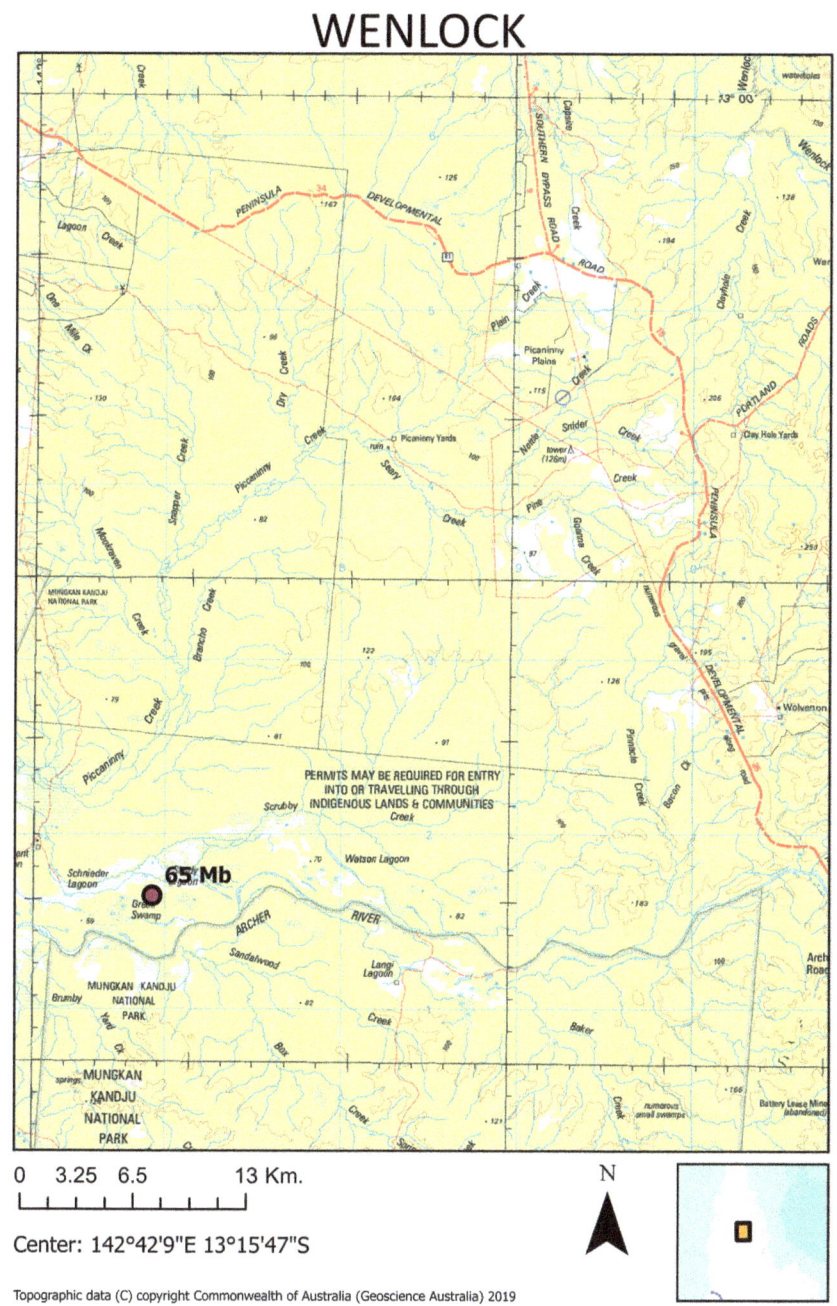

Map A2.4: Clan estates and languages: Wenlock sheet
Source: © Commonwealth of Australia (Geoscience Australia) 2019

LINGUISTIC ORGANISATION AND NATIVE TITLE

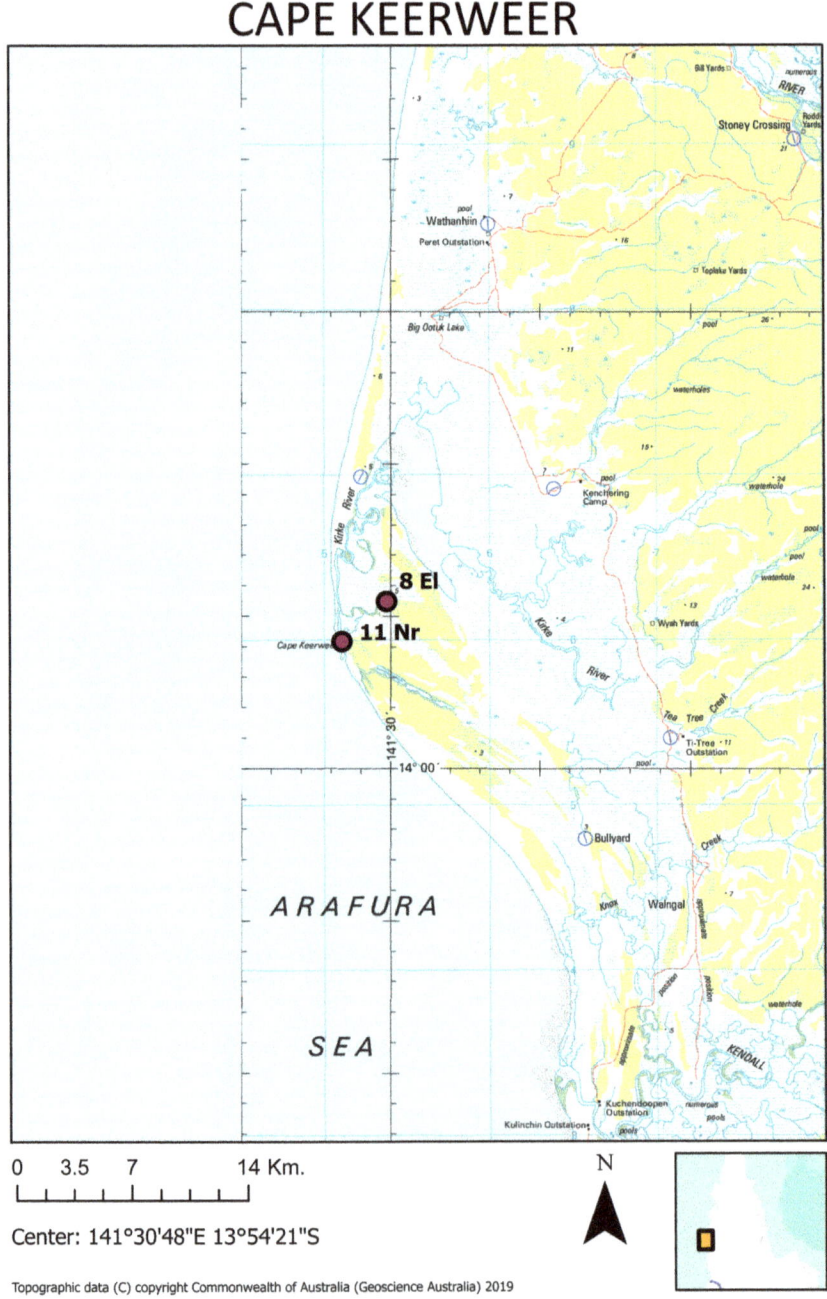

Map A2.5: Clan estates and languages: Cape Keerweer sheet
Source: © Commonwealth of Australia (Geoscience Australia) 2019

APPENDIX 2

ARCHER RIVER

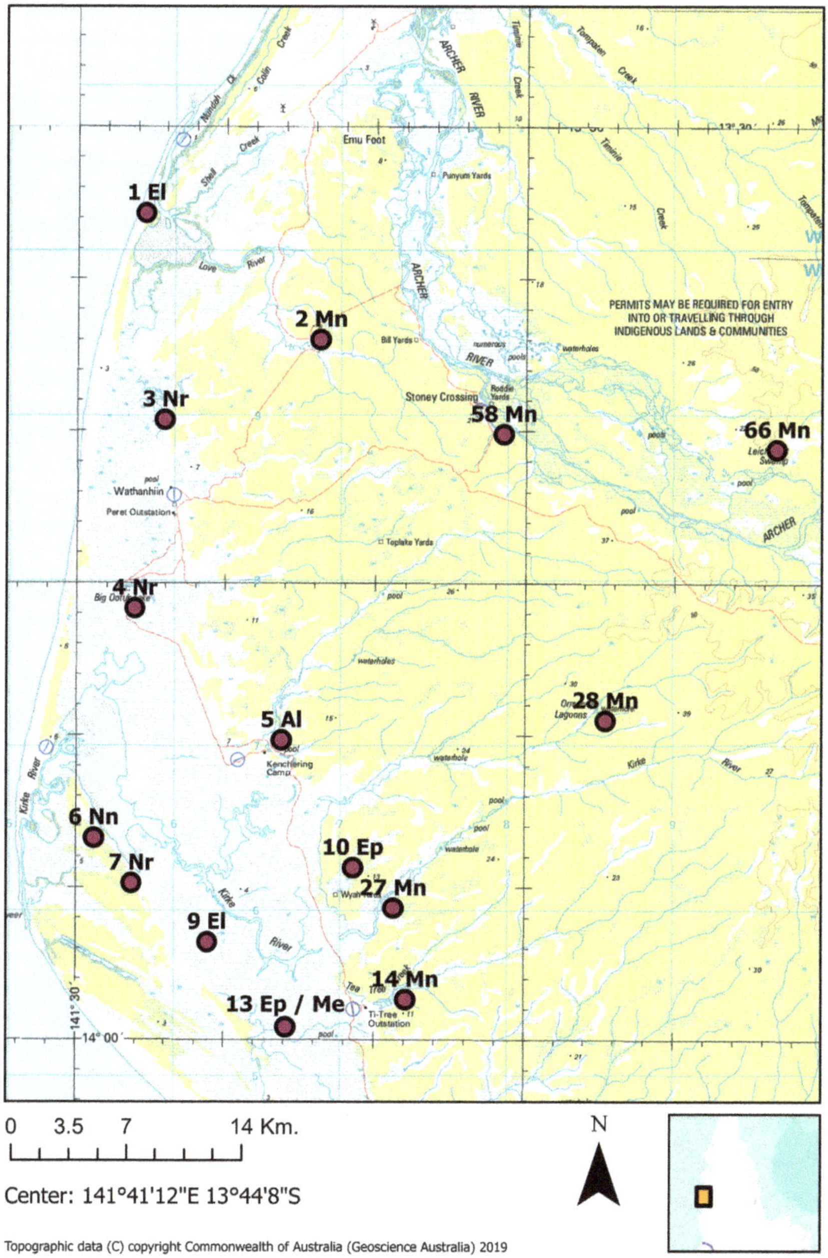

Map A2.6: Clan estates and languages: Archer River sheet
Source: © Commonwealth of Australia (Geoscience Australia) 2019

LINGUISTIC ORGANISATION AND NATIVE TITLE

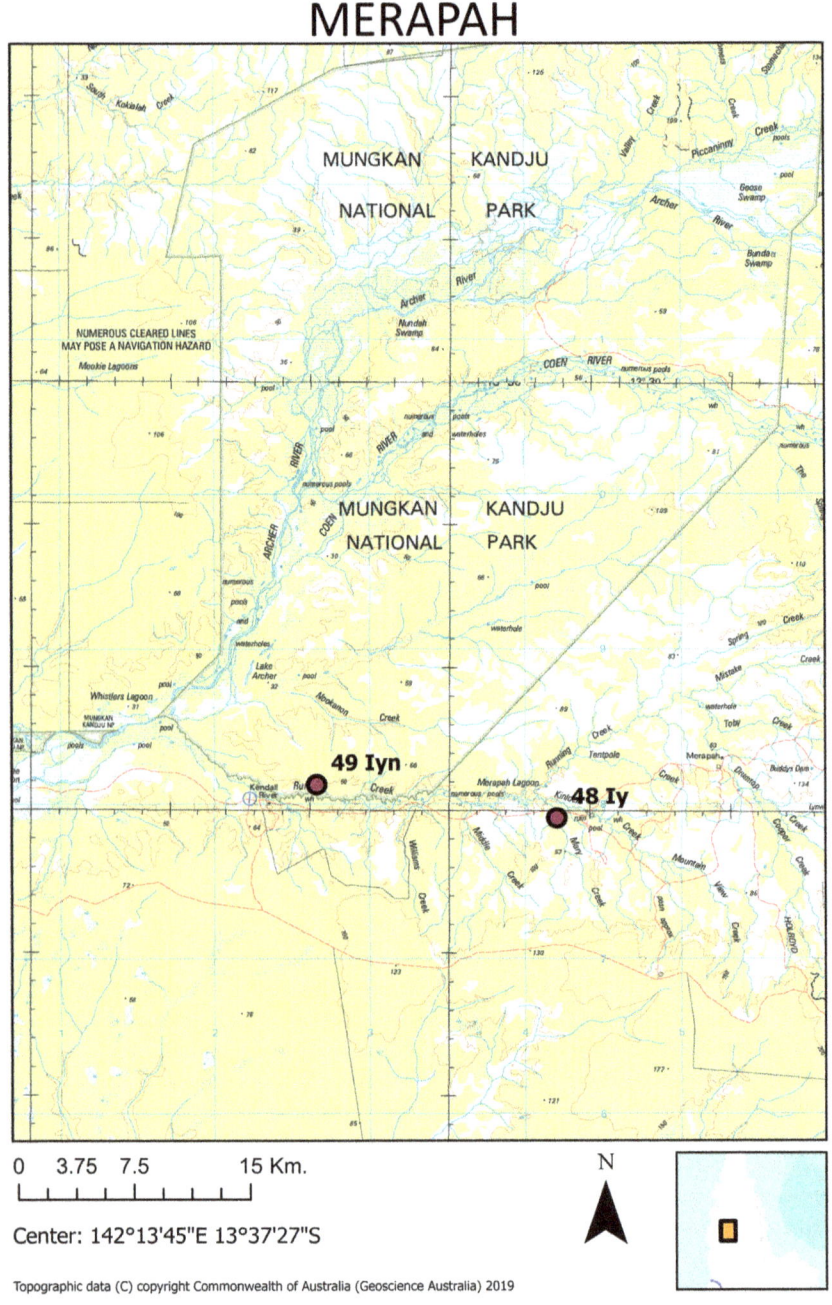

Map A2.7: Clan estates and languages: Merapah sheet
Source: © Commonwealth of Australia (Geoscience Australia) 2019

APPENDIX 2

Map A2.8: Clan estates and languages: Rokeby sheet
Source: © Commonwealth of Australia (Geoscience Australia) 2019

LINGUISTIC ORGANISATION AND NATIVE TITLE

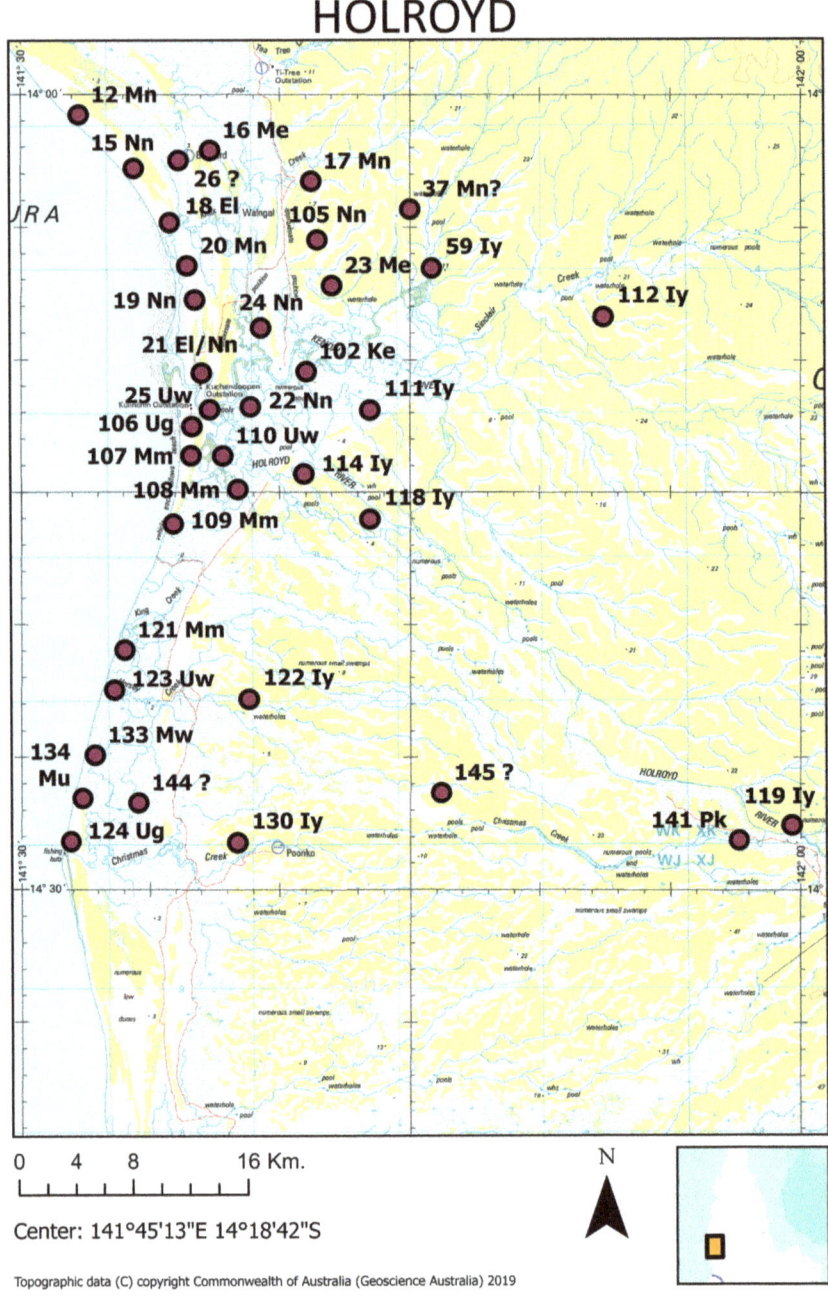

Map A2.9: Clan estates and languages: Holroyd sheet

Source: © Commonwealth of Australia (Geoscience Australia) 2019

APPENDIX 2

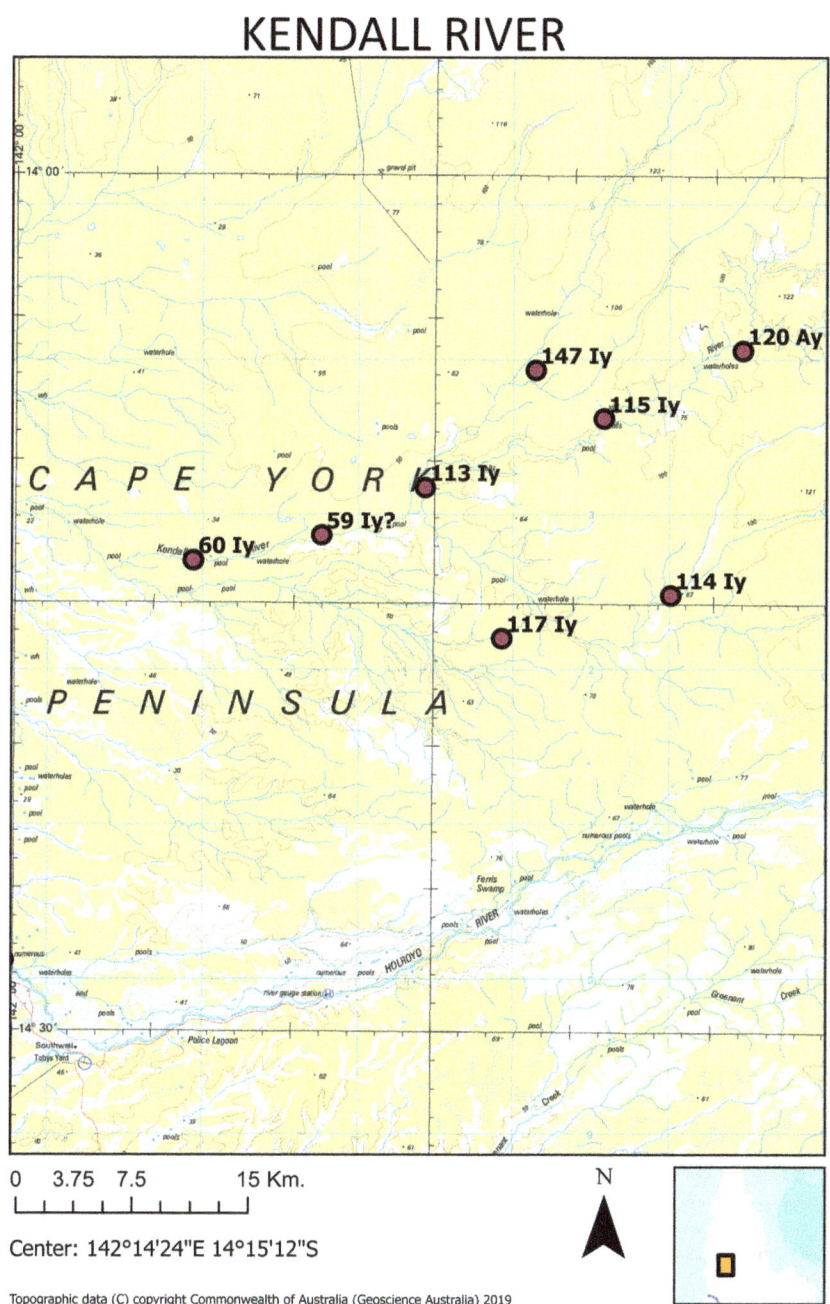

Map A2.10: Clan estates and languages: Kendall River sheet
Source: © Commonwealth of Australia (Geoscience Australia) 2019

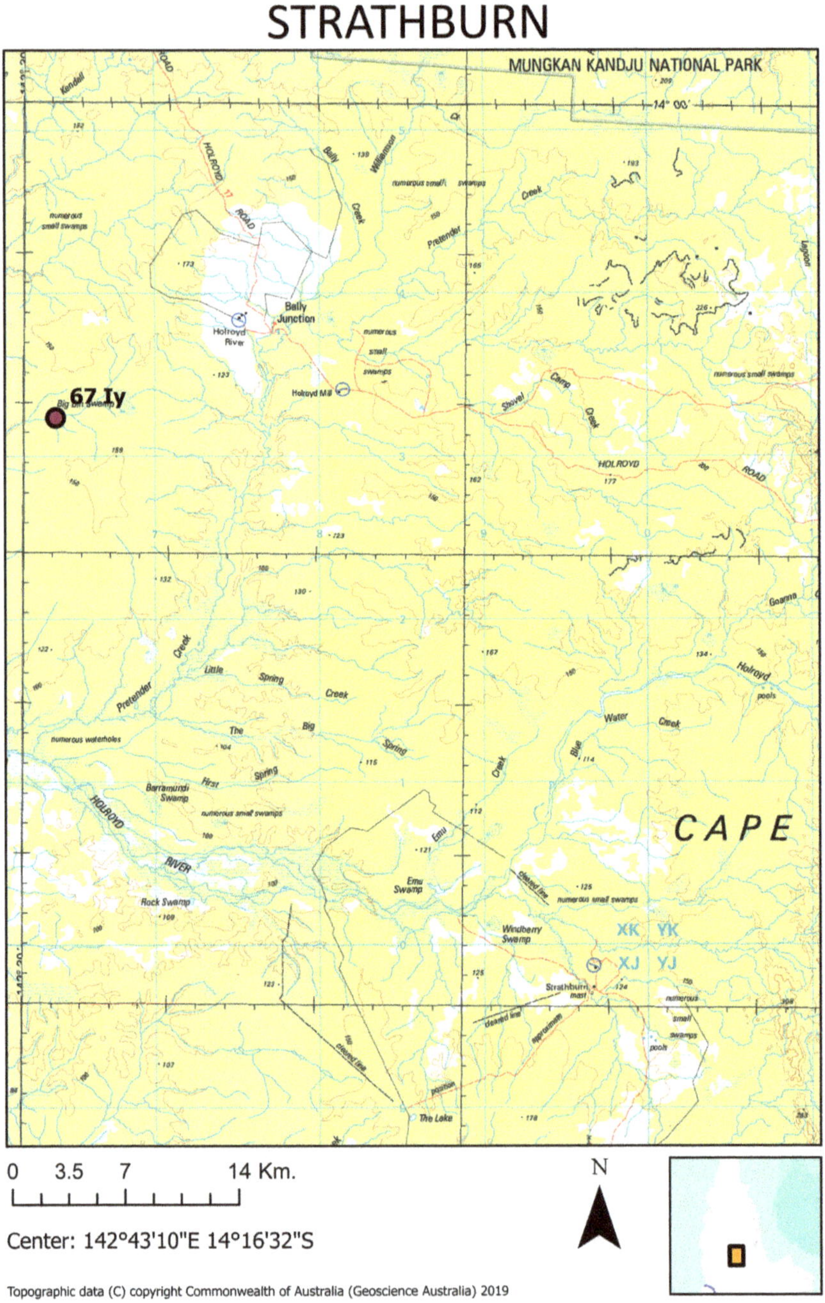

LINGUISTIC ORGANISATION AND NATIVE TITLE

STRATHBURN

Map A2.11: Clan estates and languages: Strathburn sheet

Source: © Commonwealth of Australia (Geoscience Australia) 2019

APPENDIX 2

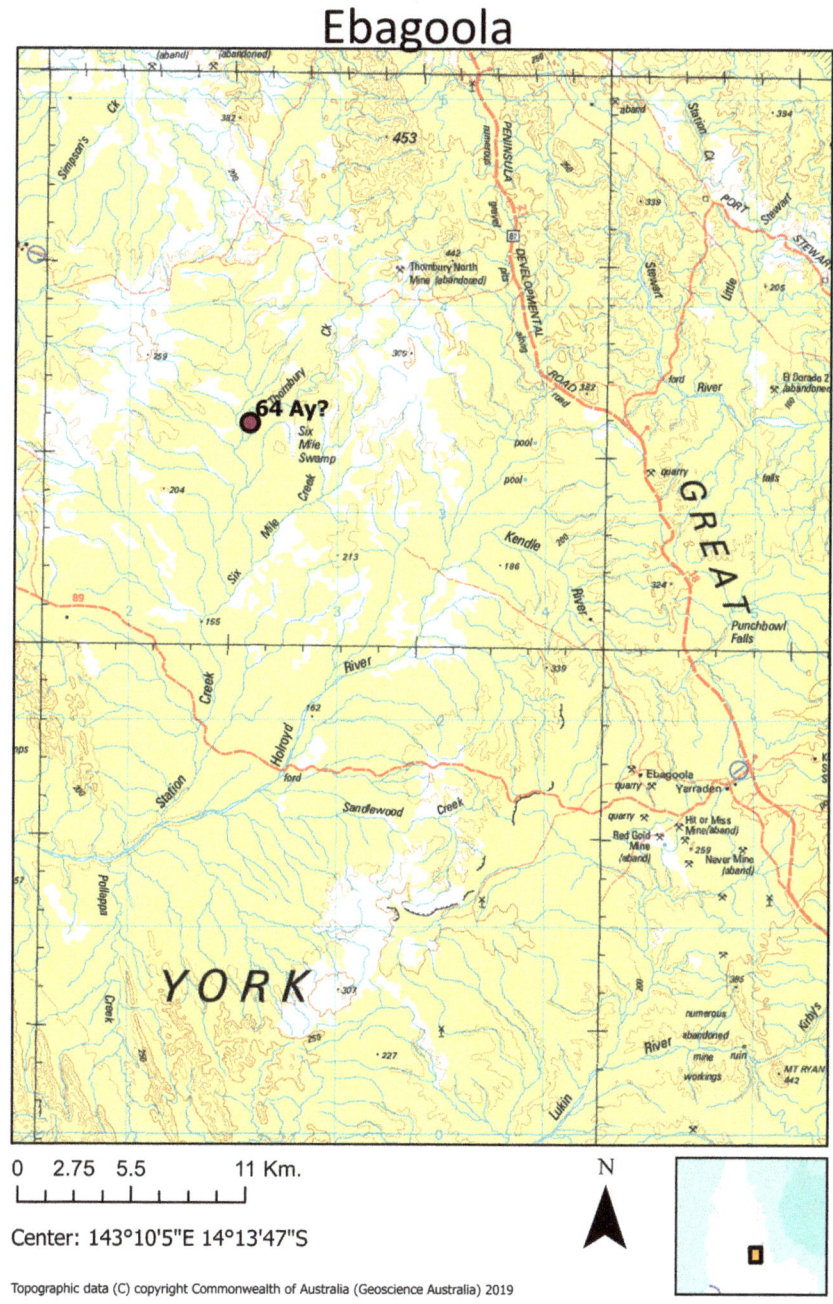

Map A2.12: Clan estates and languages: Ebagoola sheet
Source: © Commonwealth of Australia (Geoscience Australia) 2019

LINGUISTIC ORGANISATION AND NATIVE TITLE

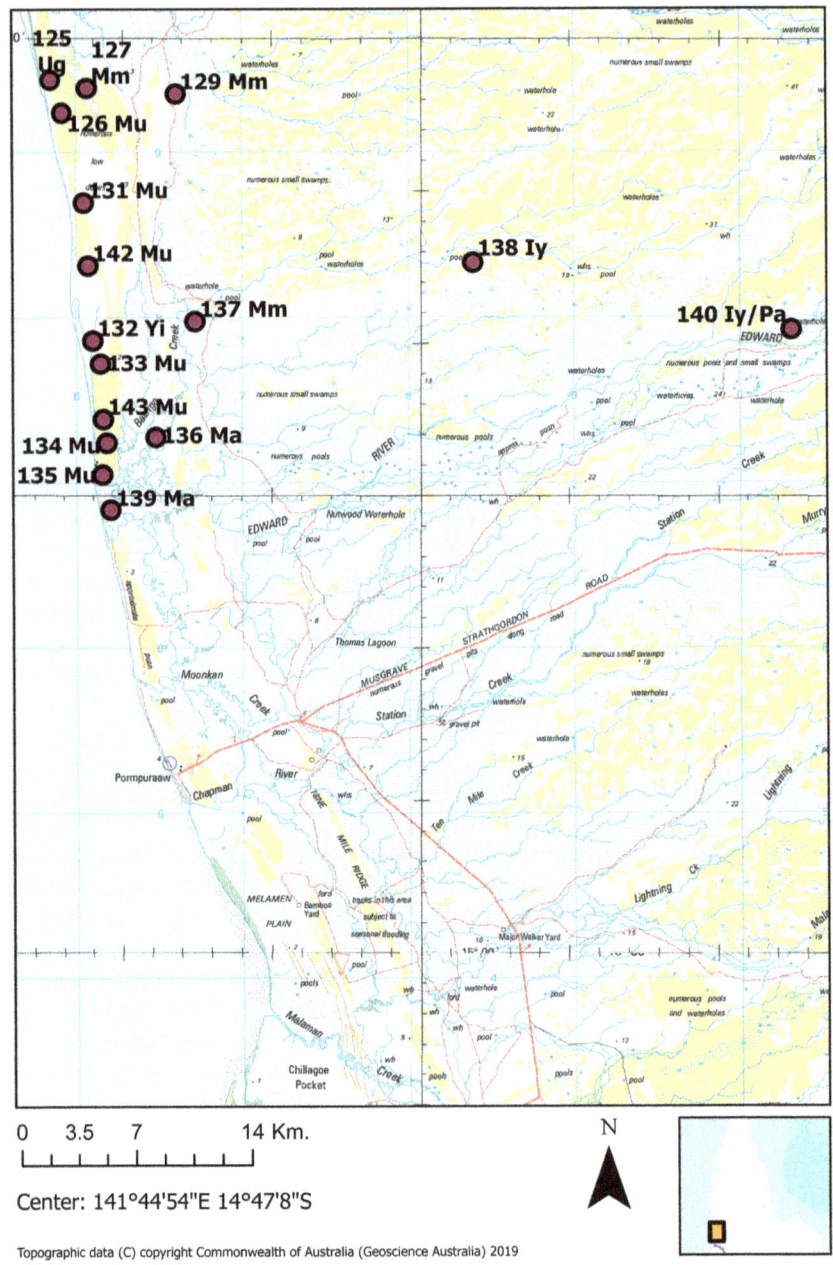

Map A2.13: Clan estates and languages: Edward River sheet
Source: © Commonwealth of Australia (Geoscience Australia) 2019

APPENDIX 2

ESTATE NUMBER 1 (Map A2.6)

Cover terms: Thoekel; Bottom Love River

Locality description: Lower Love River drainage system.

Core tenure interests: Formerly country of Clan 1 (Old Murray, Cockatoo et al.), now extinct. By succession now the country of Clan 58, after some decades of contested succession with members of Clan 2, possibly with the closely linked clans 2 and 29 collectively. (Clan 58 itself was originally a branch of Clan 8 whose country is on the lower Kirke River.) In 1929 McConnel recorded the male clan name 'Painkan' (cf. surname Peinkinna, Clan 2) as being associated with this estate and its Carpet Snake totemic centre (McConnel 1930b), and the male clan name 'Taitjaman' (cf. surname Taisman (*Tha'-ichman*), Clan 29) as being associated with the Kookem (McConnel's 'Kokam') swamp area upstream. Thus, it appears likely that Clan 2 members were making a succession claim to the lower Love River by 1929, while retaining their relative social unity with members of Clan 29 (McConnel listed them joined together as local groups XI(a) and XI(b).) Clans 2 and 29 jointly now claim upper Love River.

A north-eastern portion of old Estate 1, focused on Tha'-achemp (the site of Emu Foot Outstation), has been added to the country of Clan 2/29 (Estate 2) and lost from old Estate 1, by agreement with Clan 58. On the other hand, it appears that southern reaches of the old Yaaneng estate (number 43) have been added to Estate 1 since the demise of its former owners. Thus, in broad terms there has been an extension of Estate 1 northwards along the coast and a contraction of its inland reaches. Such reshaping of estates is not usually documented in this region.

Occupation history: The numerous shell mounds in this estate testify to occupation of some antiquity (Cribb 1986a, 1986b; Cribb et al. 1988; Cribb 1990). Mission cards indicate that 'Tokalie' (= Thoekel, lower Love River) was a common broad designation for the country of origin for a number of people at the time of earliest records (1920s). Site records for this estate indicate high continuity in occupation of the land over recent generations until the present. Its rich hunting and fishing grounds, ideal camping places and plentiful wells, as well as its close proximity to Aurukun, have made it easy for people to maintain contact with it when based at Aurukun. The outstation at Munth on the south bank of the mouth of the Love has been occupied regularly since about 1988.

Language association: Formerly Andjingith and Wik-Paach, possibly also Wik-Ngatharr (see Sutton 1997b). By succession now mainly Wik-Elken (Clan 58's section) and partly Wik-Mungkan (Clan 2/29's section, although their own languages were in the far distant past Andjingith and Wik-Paach).

Area: Love River

Sites: See *Aak* volume: Sites Listed Alphabetically by Estate

McConnel map: Carpet Snake, Oyster

ESTATE NUMBER 2 (Map A2.6)

Cover terms: Top Love River

Locality description: Upper Love River drainage system up to the western side of Archer River.

Core tenure interests: Clan 2/29 (Peinkinna, Taisman).

Occupation history: See site records in *Aak*. Two outstations have been active in this estate: Emu Foot (Tha'-achemp), and Hagen Lagoon (Ochengan-thathenh), both established c. 1990. The former was a former stock camp for the mission cattle operation in the ?1940s–70s, and the latter a sandalwooding camp before World War II.

Language association: Formerly Andjingith and Wik-Paach, now Wik-Mungkan.

Area: Love River

Sites: See *Aak* volume: Sites Listed Alphabetically by Estate

McConnel map: Yellow Fruit, Native Companion

ESTATE NUMBER 3 (Map A2.6)

Cover terms: Munpunng; Wathe-nhiin; Uthuk Eelen ~ Weenem Eelen; Small Lake

Locality description: The Small Lake drainage system which lies between that of Love River and that of Big Lake on the coast. When it overflows in the wet season it empties south into the Big Lake system and thence to the Kirke River, which ends at Cape Keerweer.

Core tenure interests: Formerly Clan 3 (Coconut et al.), on whose demise succession passed to Old Arraman of Estate 4 (Big Lake). By the mid-1970s, succession was again being debated since Arraman's death without surviving offspring, and the main claims being advanced publicly were those of members of the Wolmby family whose father's mother had been a former owner (Clan 3), and those of Callum Woolla (1910–82, Clan 31, from nearby Estate 28, but asserting his own claims independently of the majority of Clan 31, hence he was assigned clan number 55 in Aak; since his death there is probably no need now to identify a distinct Clan 55). By the early 1980s succession had settled in favour of Clan 59 (Bowendas), who had, some decades previously, been incorporated into Clan 4 of the contiguous Big Lake area, the same clan as Old Arraman, after arriving from Doomadgee Mission in north-west Queensland. Clan 59's senior members also maintain an active interest in their ancestral lands in the Nicholson River area of the Northern Territory. By the early 1990s, however, it was clear that Clan 59 (Bowendas) kept a close association with the old Big Lake clan (Ampeybegans) in relation to tenure interests in Small Lake, thus asserting interests over estates 3 and 4 together.

Occupation history: See site records in *Aak*. A cattle outstation called Peret (after the Wik-Mungkan name Piirrith for the site locally named Pooerroeth, after a well at the southern end of the all-season airstrip) was established in this estate in about 1957. It was the centre of cattle operations in the mission lands for some years, until 1975. The following year Peret was occupied mainly by Cape Keerweer people and their spouses and became an outstation. On the death of Peret (i.e. 'parrot') Arkwookerum the outstation was renamed after the well closest to the house and at the northern end of the main airstrip, Watha-nhiin. Details of the populations based here and nearby in the 1970s and 1980s are contained in Sutton (2016b). A number of outstation services, as well as a boys' detention centre, have at times been based at the southern end of the Peret airstrip, probably at Kal-nyin (known in English as Cattle Camp).

Language association: Formerly Andjingith, possibly both Andjingith and Wik-Ngatharr, in the distant past. Wik-Ngatharr by the early twentieth century. Now Wik-Ngathan due to succession by Clan 59, and partly Wik-Ngatharr due to interests of Clan 4.

Area: Cape Keerweer

Sites: See *Aak* volume: Sites Listed Alphabetically by Estate

McConnel map: Goose

ESTATE NUMBER 4 (Map A2.6)

Cover terms: Uthuk (Aweyn); Big Lake

Locality description: The drainage system of Big Lake (Uthuk Aweyn ~ Weenem Aweyn), which collects overflow from the Small Lake system immediately to the north and itself overflows south into the Kirke River.

Core tenure interests: Records indicate a long and stable possessory relationship between this estate and Clan 4 (Ampeybegan, later adding Bowenda). Along the southern edge of the estate there are lands shared with members of Clan 6. In the south-western corner, north of Puunanel to around Kawkey, the northern coastal section of old Estate 11 (patriline extinct) has long been under the custodianship of the owners of Estate 4. Since the 1980s estates 4 and 3 have been closely linked under the effective control of members of Clan 4 (see further Estate 3 and Clan 59).

Occupation history: See site records in *Aak*. The seasonal pattern of use of this estate under pre-settlement conditions is detailed in Sutton (1978). The lake itself lies in a floodplain and was only used, but for months at a stretch, in the dry seasons. During the cattle era the lake was the location for a stock camp and yards. Since the mid-1970s it has been used as a seasonal outstation. Since the 1980s there has been an intermittent outstation at Kawkey, on the south-western edge of the estate.

Language association: Formerly—and a very long time ago—Andjingith (and possibly Wik-Ngatharr as well). For some generations it has been Wik-Ngatharr, but a Wuungk song from Poenp in this estate is still sung in Andjingith.

Area: Cape Keerweer

Sites: See *Aak* volume: Sites Listed Alphabetically by Estate

ESTATE NUMBER 5 (Map A2.6)

Cover terms: Kayncherrang (Kencherang); Woowkeng

Locality description: The drainage system of an unnamed tributary of the Kirke River system that lies east of the Big Lake system and west of the Oony-aw system, downstream until it meets the upper reaches of the permanently filled Kirke estuary.

APPENDIX 2

Core tenure interests: Long recognised as country belonging to members of Clan 5 (Wikmuneas). There has also been a regular presence on this estate by members of Clan 32 (Toikalkins), and at the time it was mapped in 1985 they were also recognised by the mapping informants, including members of Clan 5, as its co-owners. Indeed, senior members of Clan 32 have been the mainstay of this outstation since 1976. Some members of other groups rejected this incorporation and stated that members of Clan 32 should instead simply have maintained their ancestral relationship to Estate 7 (Iincheng).

Occupation history: See site records in *Aak*. There was some kind of intermittent cattle camp here from the ?1940s onwards. There has been an outstation, occupied intermittently, at or near Kayncherrang (Kencherang Outstation), since 1976.

Language association: Wik-Alken. There has been one suggestion from Clifford Toikalkin (Clan 32, 1935 – c. 2012) that the language for this area was formerly Wik-Ep. This would not be surprising, as this was the language of the former owners of adjacent Estate 10 (Waayeng) and was formerly the language of Clan 14 (part-owners of adjacent Estate 14, Ti Tree).

Area: Upper Kirke River

Sites: See *Aak* volume: Sites Listed Alphabetically by Estate

ESTATE NUMBER 6 (Map A2.6)

Cover terms: Aayk

Locality description: The sandridge system on the south-west side of the main Kirke River estuary, and west to the lower Kirke River. On the northeast side of this estuary the estate overlaps with Estate 4 (Big Lake) where a fringing area is held in company with Clan 4. On the coast to the west, from the Kirke mouth north to Puunanel, Estate 6 has assumed custodianship of the northern half of Estate 11 (Kaapathenh) at least *pro tem*.

Core tenure interests: Clan 6 (Wolmby/Peemuggina). Custodianship extends to the northern half of old Estate 11 whose former owners died out some decades ago. The southern part of Estate 11 is held in company with members of Clan 8 and Clan 12. There is the possibility that in time Estate 11 will re-emerge through succession and its present partial incorporation into Estate 6 will then lapse. In the late 1970s the unity of the Wolmby and Peemuggina branches of Clan 6, and their collective tenure of Estate 6, were firm. Some have asserted the Peemugginas 'really' come from Knox River area [possibly Estate 19: PS]. They deny this.

Occupation history: See site records in *Aak*. This estate contains the site of the first outstation development of the then Aurukun Mission, that of Aayk, which was begun with airstrip works under the supervision of the late Victor Wolmby in 1971. It and nearby sites have been occupied under the title of 'Aayk' or 'New Aayk' during most years since then. In the 1990s the outstation on this estate was located close to Mulpa'el-nhiin; another outstation at Wiip-aw on the lower Kirke River has also been occupied. A commercial fisher called Eddie Fisher erected a house and freezing plant at Winchenng in this estate, or in part of old Estate 11 run by the owners of Estate 6, in the early 1980s. He was forced by local government to abandon the site in the mid-1990s but later returned.

Language association: Wik-Ngathan.

Area: Cape Keerweer

Sites: See *Aak* volume: Sites Listed Alphabetically by Estate

ESTATE NUMBER 7 (Map A2.6)

Cover terms: Iincheng

Locality description: The middle Kirke estuary, mainly on the south-western side, south-east of the Aayk area.

Core tenure interests: Clan 7 (Toikalkin [Older]). Younger generations of this clan (referred to here as Clan 32) have shifted their country interests to the adjacent Estate 5, and Kencherang Outstation. See Estate 5 for further details.

Occupation history: See site records in *Aak*.

Language association: Wik-Ngatharr.

Area: Cape Keerweer

Sites: See *Aak* volume: Sites Listed Alphabetically by Estate

APPENDIX 2

ESTATE NUMBER 8 (Map A2.5)

Cover terms: Warpang

Locality description: A small estate, south of the lower Kirke River and west of Estate 6, which lies mainly along the floodplain edge of the sandridge system on the south-western side of the main Kirke River estuary.

Core tenure interests: Clan 8. This formerly consisted of three main branches, known by the mission surnames: Namponans, Karntins, and Walmbengs. Of these, Namponans maintain a key role as custodians. Karntin descendants (e.g. Rebecca Wolmby) do not include any living people of this surname. Walmbengs, while acknowledging their patrilineal origins in the Warpang estate, have succeeded to Estate 1 (q.v.) on the basis of Rex and Cecil Walmbeng's matrifilial connection with that estate and do not actively pursue country interests in Estate 8. Walmbengs are now Clan 58.

Occupation history: Easily and regularly accessed from nearby outstations such as Aayk since the early 1970s.

Language association: Wik-Elken (same dialect form as Wik-Ngatharr).

Area: Cape Keerweer

Sites: See *Aak* volume: Sites Listed Alphabetically by Estate

ESTATE NUMBER 9 (Map A2.6)

Cover terms: Eer-en

Locality description: An area of sandridges and perched swamps with drainage into the lower Kirke River, east of Cape Keerweer and south of the main Kirke River estuary.

Core tenure interests: Clan 9 (Comprabars). Many places in this estate have overlapping interests held by clans with neighbouring estates, particularly 11, 12 and 13.

Occupation history: See site records in *Aak*.

Language association: Wik-Elken (dialect form also known as Wik-Ngatharr).

Area: Cape Keerweer

Sites: See *Aak* volume: Sites Listed Alphabetically by Estate

ESTATE NUMBER 10 (Map A2.6)

Cover terms: Waayeng, Waareng

Locality description: A small drainage system on the middle Kirke River between the Kanycherrang system and the Ti Tree system.

Core tenure interests: Clan 10, patrilineally extinct, but members' interests have been passed down to Ross Douglas Koonutta and Rebecca Karntin.

Occupation history: See site records in *Aak*. This was one of the staging points for cattle when being walked out from Peret and/or Big Lake to the railhead at Mungana hundreds of kilometres to the south-east. There was a yard here during cattle time (roughly 1950s – early 1970s).

Language association: Wik-Ep (also known in this case as Wik-Iit).

Area: Upper Kirke River

Sites: See *Aak* volume: Sites Listed Alphabetically by Estate

ESTATE NUMBER 11 (Map A2.5)

Cover terms: Kaapathenh; Theew-en; (older usage:) Yu'engk (mission spelling 'Yonko'); Cape Keerweer mouth

Locality description: The area both north and south of the mouth of the Kirke River, the central point of which is usually known as Cape Keerweer.

Core tenure interests: Clan 11 became extinct many years ago, and the estate has become divided in its custodianship. To the north custodianship of parts of it have been assumed by owners of Estate 4. Just north of the Kirke mouth parts of it have been under custodianship of owners of Estate 6. South of the mouth areas have been looked after by owners of Estate 12, or in some cases jointly by estates 8 and 12, and east of the mouth some places have been looked after by owners of Estate 6.

APPENDIX 2

Occupation history: See site records in *Aak*, where Wik oral traditions relate events dating back to c. 1885. An outstation was established at Wiip-aw in this estate in the 1980s, and continued to be occupied over several years until the establishment of the nearby outstation at Kawkey.

Language association: Wik-Ngatharr.

Area: Cape Keerweer

Sites: See *Aak* volume: Sites Listed Alphabetically by Estate

ESTATE NUMBER 12 (Map 2.9)

Cover terms: Um-thunth, Moving Stone; sometimes Ngul-mungk.

Locality description: On the coast immediately south of Cape Keerweer and extending inland south-east along parallel ridge systems, including a series of large permanent swamps. The southern reaches of old Estate 11 are looked after by the clan who hold Estate 12, at least for the time being, as Clan 11 is extinct.

Core tenure interests: Clan 12 (northern Yunkaportas).

Occupation history: See site records in *Aak*. An outstation was begun at Kaapathenh in old Estate 11 by members of Clan 12 in early 1976 and the sheets of iron left there for this purpose were still there many years later.

Language association: Wik-Mungkan (coastal variety).

Area: Cape Keerweer

Sites: See *Aak* volume: Sites Listed Alphabetically by Estate

ESTATE NUMBER 13 (Map A2.6)

Cover terms: Thinthaw-aw

Locality description: On the sandridge systems south of the middle Kirke River and creeks that drain north into the middle Kirke. Midway between the coastal estates (mainly 12) and the inland (mainly sclerophyll forest) estate of Ti Tree (14). Closely associated with Estate 14 on its southern side, the waters of which drain south into the Knox River system.

Core tenure interests: Clan 13 (Marbendinars).

Occupation history: See site records in *Aak*.

Language association: Their language is known both as Wik-Ep and Wik-Me'enh.

Area: Knox River

Sites: See *Aak* volume: Sites Listed Alphabetically by Estate

ESTATE NUMBER 14 (*see also* 27) (Map A2.6)

Cover terms: Ti Tree; Wanke-nhiyeng

Locality description: The 'Tea Tree Creek' drainage system (a tributary of the Kirke River), but focused on Ti Tree Lagoon, and extending down to the edge of the saltpans close to the middle Kirke River. In the 1970s the estate was distinguished from Estate 27, which encompassed the next creek system to the north of here, namely the main Kirke channel, with a focus on the large lagoons about Yongk-uyengam. When mapped in 1990, both creek systems were held to be in the same estate.

Core tenure interests: Clans 14, 35, 37—the picture is complicated, however. In the mid-1970s Clan 35 (Ngakyunkwokkas, Kawangkas [originally at least] and Bells) was identified as the main group of owners for Estate 14, and Clan 14 (Ti Tree Pootchemunkas) was identified as the main group for Estate 27 (Yongk-uyengam, the main Kirke channel). When further parts of the area were mapped in 1990, and on subsequent inquiries in 1997, clans 14 and 35 were identified as one group claiming both creek systems together. The *Aak* volume also lists Clan 37 (Koo'oilas) for Ti Tree. This came about through the adoption of Eric Koo'oila.

Occupation history: See site records in *Aak*. There was a cattle camp at Ti Tree for many years from the ?1940s. In 1976 Bob Massey Pootchemunka and others established an outstation there and it has continued to be occupied intermittently since then.

Language association: Wik-Mungkan. (Ngakyunkwokkas are said to have originally been affiliated to Wik-Ep).

Area: Upper Kirke River

Sites: See *Aak* volume: Sites Listed Alphabetically by Estate

APPENDIX 2

ESTATE NUMBER 15 (Map A2.9)

Cover terms: Thaangkunh-nhiin ('Tonkaning')

Locality description: Mainly a series of parallel ridge systems, many containing shellgrit, on the coast between Estate 12 (the southern side of Cape Keerweer) and Estate 18 on the northern side of the mouth of Knox River. Overflow water from Estate 15 flows south into the Knox River system.

Core tenure interests: Clan 15 (Landises, Gothachalkenins, Eundatumweakins)

Occupation history: See site records in *Aak*. An estate with very focused and continuous occupation in the latter years of the life of Clan 15 senior figure Billy Wildfellow, who died nearby and was buried at Thee'engkangk (site 155, *Aak* p. 523) in the late 1940s. He was photographed at Cape Keerweer in 1933 by Donald Thomson (see Sutton 2019:262–63). Thaangkunh-nhiin, the site, appears to have been a major base camp for semi-nomadic Wik people into the 1960s (see Aurukun Mission cards), and an outstation near this site ('Tonkaning') was occupied over a number of years after about 1989. An earlier outstation was set up here and a building erected, at Moomanchem, in 1978, by Billy Landis and others.

Language association: Wik-Ngathan (some senior members of Clan 15 used the alternative name Wik-Iincheyn for some time in the 1970s and 1980s).

Area: Knox River

Sites: See *Aak* volume: Sites Listed Alphabetically by Estate

McConnel map: Spear-handle

ESTATE NUMBER 16 (Map A2.9)

Cover terms: Bullyard; Am; older usage: Nhooyengk

Locality description: A flood plain fringed mainly on the west by parallel sandridges, on the north side of the middle Knox River, into which its waters drain. Midway between the coast and the inland dry sclerophyll country. Closely associated with Estate 13 immediately to its north.

Core tenure interests: Clan 16 (Marpoondins).

Occupation history: See site records in *Aak*. An outstation was established in this estate in c. 1980–81 at Am, a long narrow permanent lagoon. Its original instigators were members of Clan 17, closely related to Clan 16. This outstation is usually known as Bullyard. Its principal occupants for a considerable time were core members of Clan 16 and their families.

Language association: Wik-Me'enh.

Area: Knox River

Sites: See *Aak* volume: Sites Listed Alphabetically by Estate

ESTATE NUMBER 17 (Map A2.9)

Cover terms: Walngal; Top Knox. Older usage: Konkooth, also Komeng

Locality description: The upper Knox River drainage system down as far as the parallel dune system just west of the sclerophyll forest country, at the eastern end of the pericoastal floodplain.

Core tenure interests: 17 (Pamtoondas).

Occupation history: See site records in *Aak*. An outstation was set up here in 1990 and has been intermittently occupied since. Its core occupants were members of Clan 17 and their spouses and other family. A number of this group spent a month here in 1986 during mapping of the estate by David Martin.

Language association: Wik-Mungkan

Area: Upper Knox River

Sites: See *Aak* volume: Sites Listed Alphabetically by Estate

ESTATE NUMBER 18 (Map A2.9)

Cover terms: Eere-mangk ('Errimunka'); Oonem-ee'enh (Wik-Elken), Oonem-thee'enh (Wik-Ngathan, Wik-Mungkan); older usage: Ithenang

Locality description: The coastal ridge systems west of the floodplain, from the north bank of the lower Knox River northwards.

Core tenure interests: 18 (Koomeetas, Pamulkans, Tybingoompas).

Occupation history: See site records in *Aak*. Planning for an outstation in this estate has focused on the site Ooonem-ee'enh (127). Gladys Tybingoompa (Clan 27) was born at Ithenang in this estate in 1946.

Language association: Wik-Elken (Wik-Ngatharr).

Area: Knox River

Sites: See *Aak* volume: Sites Listed Alphabetically by Estate

McConnel map: [Big Tide &] Thunder

ESTATE NUMBER 19 (Map A2.9)

Cover terms: Not recorded

Locality description: A small area about half way between the mouths of the Knox and Kendall rivers on the pericoastal ridge system.

Core tenure interests: Clan 19 (Arkapenya Peemuggina), now extinct. Most of the mapped sites in this estate are looked after by extant clans with neighbouring estates, especially 21 (Korkaktains).

Occupation history: See site records in *Aak*.

Language association: Wik-Ngathan.

Area: Knox River

Sites: See *Aak* volume: Sites Listed Alphabetically by Estate

ESTATE NUMBER 20 (Map A2.9)

Cover terms: Piithel; Eeye-mangk (Wik-Mungkan), Eere-mangk (Wik-Elken)

Locality description: The south side of the lower Knox River, at the mouth, and including ridge systems and creeks draining north into Knox River.

Core tenure interests: Clan 20 (southern Yunkaporta).

Occupation history: See site records in *Aak*.

Language association: Wik-Mungkan (coastal variety).

Area: Knox River

Sites: See *Aak* volume: Sites Listed Alphabetically by Estate

ESTATE NUMBER 21(/101) (Map A2.9)

Cover terms: Kuchent-eypenh

Locality description: The coast and pericoastal sandridge systems on the north side of the mouth of the Kendall River, from which overflow and creeks drain south into the Kendall.

Core tenure interests: Clan 21 (Korkaktains) (= Clan 101).

Occupation history: See site records in *Aak*. Extensive records from 1928 onwards exist for occupation here by traditional owners of countries in the immediate region, many of whom are named in these records. Aurukun Mission maintained an informal mission outstation here in the period between 1928 and c. 1958, run by Archiewald Otomorathin (and her husband Uki until his death in 1948). An outstation was established in this estate at Kuchent-eypenh in 1977. Occupation of this camp was regular until 1985, and has been intermittent subsequently.

Language association: Wik-Elken, Wik-Ngathan.

Area: Lower Kendall River

Sites: See *Aak* volume: Sites Listed Alphabetically by Estate

McConnel map: Pelican

ESTATE NUMBER 22(/103) (Map A2.9)

Cover terms: Not recorded

Locality description: Both sides of the lower middle Kendall River, mainly on the south side in its eastern reaches.

Core tenure interests: Clan 22/103 (Southern Woollas).

Occupation history: See site records in *Aak*.

Language association: Wik-Ngathan.

APPENDIX 2

Area: Middle Kendall River

Sites: See *Aak* volume: Sites Listed Alphabetically by Estate. Von Sturmer 1978: Thuyunh, Pu'anhdha

McConnel map: Baby

ESTATE NUMBER 23 (Map A2.9)

Cover terms: Weten; Dish Yard

Locality description: On the north side of the middle Kendall River from the edge of the floodplain east to near Thaa'pulnh; its creeks and watercourses run south into Kendall River.

Core tenure interests: Formerly Clan 23/104, now extinct. In the mid and late 1970s the estate was subject to a protracted debate over succession. Two senior members of Clan 28 (Yantumba/Holroyd), originally from the upper Christmas Creek area, claimed the estate as that of their father, but more accurately on the basis of intimate knowledge of the area and a long history of use of it. Senior members of Clan 90/105 denied this claim and asserted their own succession through the clan leader, for whom it was mother's country. He also knew the estate intimately. In the late 1970s and early 1980s the two main protagonists died and the issue became quieter. A nephew of the Clan 28 protagonist continued to pursue their claims on his own behalf. Clan 41 (Kowearptas) and Clan 38 (Marbthowans) have customary tenure interests in the area, recorded since the pre-war period, but appear to have refrained from entering discussions over the fate of Estate 23.

Occupation history: See site records in *Aak*. A stock yard and airstrips were constructed here in the 1960s when the Bureau of Mineral Resources had a bulldozer in the area. An outstation was intermittently occupied here from 1978.

Language association: Sutton's informants gave the language of the former owning clan (23/104) as Wik-Me'enh. Von Sturmer's gave it as Wik-Iincheyn (= Wik-Ngathan). Both, however, agreed the totemic name of their dialect was Wik-Waangk ~ Kugu Wangga (Woven Bag Language).

Area: Middle Kendall River

Sites: See *Aak* volume: Sites Listed Alphabetically by Estate. Von Sturmer 1978: Ya'ing

ESTATE NUMBER 24 (Map A2.9)

Cover terms: Chaaperreng

Locality description: Largely on the north side of the lower Kendall River, east of the coastal ridge system, on the pericoastal ridges and east across the floodplain to the first inland ridge system. The water from here flows south into the Kendall. There is an error in the *Aak* volume: Estate 24 is shown on Map 12 south-east of here; this area is that of Estate ?102.

Core tenure interests: Formerly Clan 43. This clan is extinct. The identification of deceased woman Watingowa as a member of this clan in the *Aak* documentation needs correction; she was a member of Clan 21. Certain descendants of members of Clan 6 (branch A, descendants of Mulloch Wolmby), and of Clan 27 (Kalkeeyortas) trace close ancestral connections to the estate's former owners.

Occupation history: See site records in *Aak*.

Language association: Wik-Ngathan.

Area: Lower Kendall River

Sites: See *Aak* volume: Sites Listed Alphabetically by Estate

ESTATE NUMBER 25 (Map A2.9)

Cover terms: Minh-thii'er-pecheng

Locality description: This estate number was used by Peter Sutton and David Martin for land that is also von Sturmer's Estate 110. There are entries in *Aak* under both numbers. See 110 for the major details.

Core tenure interests: Clan 110 (Karyukas). See 110 for details.

Occupation history: See 110.

Language association: See 110.

Area: Lower Kendall River

Sites: See *Aak* volume: Sites Listed Alphabetically by Estate. See 110

ESTATE NUMBER 26 (Map A2.9)

Cover terms: Thum-merriy

Locality description: In the parallel ridge country near the coast between the Kirke and Knox rivers, south-east of Cape Keerweer.

Core tenure interests: Formerly Clan 44 (Samuel Chii'iiy), now extinct. The estate was apparently divided in terms of custodianship between neighbouring estates 15 and 18, in the 1970s.

Occupation history: See site records in *Aak*.

Language association: Not recorded.

Area: Knox River

Sites: See *Aak* volume: Sites Listed Alphabetically by Estate

ESTATE NUMBER 27 (Map A2.6)

Cover terms: Yongk-uyengam

Locality description: The upper middle drainage system of the main Kirke River channel, focused on the large permanent lagoon at Yongk-uyengam and Pe'.

Core tenure interests: Clans 14, 35, 37. See Estate 14 for details. Briefly: at different times this area has been defined as part of the same estate as Estate 14, at other times distinct from it but closely allied to it. When distinct, it was particularly associated with Clan 35. When combined, it is associated with linked clans 14/35 and 37. Current status: combined with 14 under the general title of 'Ti Tree'.

Occupation history: See 14.

Language association: See 14.

Area: Upper Kirke River

Sites: See *Aak* volume: Sites Listed Alphabetically by Estate. 745 Pe', 746 Yongk-uyengam

ESTATE NUMBER 28 (Map A2.6)

Cover terms: Oony-aw ('Ornyawa')

Locality description: The drainage of the creek system that lies just north of the main Kirke channel, focused on the large permanent lagoons at Oony-aw ('Ornyawa Lagoons'), north-west across the upper reaches of several more creek systems to the upper reaches of creeks flowing west into Small Lake and north-west into Love River. It also extends to within a few kilometres of Archer River on the north-east. In that sense it lies between, rather than on, the main defining geographic systems of the region.

Core tenure interests: Clan 31 (northern Woollas). The emergent Clan 55 listed in *Aak* (that of Callum Woolla) can now be re-defined as a branch of Clan 31 since his decease. The Clan 30 (Lou Yunkaporta) of *Aak* seems merely to have been a branch of 31—however, she was laying claim to Oony-aw in 1985 during mapping in the area, but her claims there were not accepted by all. On the other hand, her clan totems match those of 31 and one of them (Ghost) matches the key site in the estate, typical of inland clan/estate relations. Since her passing the issue of whether she was of a separate clan has lapsed.

Occupation history: See site records in *Aak*.

Language association: Wik-Mungkan.

Area: Upper Kirke River

Sites: See *Aak* volume: Sites Listed Alphabetically by Estate

McConnel map: Male Ghosts, Female Ghosts, Baby, Swamp Fish ('*min kiwa* [Silver Jewfish]'), Bird sp. ['min nguttham'])

ESTATE NUMBER 29 (Map A2.3)

Cover terms: Lower Watson

Locality description: The Watson River from about 3 km below the Merkunga Creek junction to the junction of the Watson and the Archer; New Chum Crossing, Police Lagoon, to Oyenten; south-east to Kokialah Creek (at least some interests here, see site 2551 in *Aak*); Aurukun area north to just beyond the airstrips.

APPENDIX 2

Core tenure interests: Clan 36 (Watson River Koo'ekkas), patriline now extinct. Succession principally via offspring of deceased Clan 36 women, hence interests now principally Comprabars, Bandacootchas.

Occupation history: See site records in *Aak*.

Language association: Formerly Wik-Ompom [ie. Mbiywom]. Now Wik-Mungkan.

Area: Watson River

Sites: See *Aak* volume: Sites Listed Alphabetically by Estate

ESTATE NUMBER 30 (Map A2.3)

Cover terms: Kolet-aw (site 2338); Lower Watson east

Locality description: Between the lower Watson River and Kokialah Creek.

Core tenure interests: Clan 46, patriline extinct: Dan and Hope, Connie Clark (mother of Bessie Savo), Polly Fruit (mother of Matthew and Lawrence Fruit). Possibly included Old Luke, listed in *Aak* as Clan 49, focal site 2345 Kuympay-awenyin, listed p. 183 as Estate 30.

Occupation history: See site records in *Aak*.

Language association: Wik-Ompom (Mbiywom). Now Wik-Mungkan?

Area: Watson River

Sites: See *Aak* volume: Sites Listed Alphabetically by Estate. 2338 Kolet-aw (~ Minh-kolet-aw), 2345 Kuympay-awenyin

ESTATE NUMBER 31 (Map A2.3)

Cover terms: Mukiy; Small Archer

Locality description: On the south side of Watson River below the Kokialah Creek junction to where the Watson meets the Archer (Main Archer); up Kokialah Creek at least to its junction with Lizzie Creek; south to include the whole system flowing into the Small Archer (i.e. the lower Tompaten Creek of the official maps), including Kargum, Tompaten and Mowin Creeks. It is possible Kokialah Creek was formerly a distinct estate as it appears in the early literature associated with a language that Clan 33 people do not identify with ('Kokiala—perhaps more accurately Kuuk-Iiyala or similar).

Core tenure interests: Clan 33 (Pambegans). A number of descendants of Geraldine née Pambegan and the late Mittaboy ['Mr Boyd'] Kawangka follow the Pambegan country interest more firmly than the Kawangka one (Clan 35, Ti Tree area).

Occupation history: See site records in *Aak*. An outstation called Mukiy (Mookie) was established on the upper reaches of Kargum Creek in the 1980s, and has been in frequent use since then.

Language association: Wik-Mungkan.

Area: Small Archer

Sites: See *Aak* volume: Sites Listed Alphabetically by Estate. Also: Makarrang (Nundah Yard)

McConnel map: Mangrove, Bonefish, Fly, Frog, Bullroarer

ESTATE NUMBER 32 (Map A2.3)

Cover terms: Upper Watson East

Locality description: [information not available]

Core tenure interests: [information not available]

Occupation history: See site records in *Aak*. See also references to Emmy Landing in Aurukun Mission records.

Language association: [information not available]

Area: [information not available]

Sites: [information not available]

ESTATE NUMBER 33 (Map A2.3)

Cover terms: Watson Crossing

Locality description: Watson Crossing area, Oyónton (also Oyenten ~ Ayónton depending on language; Oyenten is Mn, Oyónton is Mbiywom). *Information from Roy Jingle with Alice Mark*: All of Horse

Creek. (Where Horse Creek meets York Downs Creek, this estate meets that of Alice Mark.) Moonlight Creek, from there up to Leichhardt Yard (lagoon and yard), south to Yokai Yard, south-west along the Merluna boundary fence, hits the head of Twintpen Creek (Aurukun turnoff), hits a rise, straight from there to Oyenten Swamp. Also Alfie Yard, east from Cox Creek Yard. Cox Creek, 4 km north-east of Old York Downs. Kariko [= Keriko]—a lagoon on top from which a creek flows (?Kurracoo Creek), also a Goanna (Andjal) Story Place is nearby at Goanna Lagoon on Goanna Creek. Twintpen (~ Tawínt-pen) is a branch from the same creek. Swamp Turtle (Ilkutj) story is at Oyonton, a swamp on a tableland with no creek, and part of the old mission reserve. Old York Downs (Sudley) is part of this country. Pineapple Lagoon, Pineapple Yard also. From Annie George: Oyonton, Pitj(i) Lagoon ('Pitj' from English 'Fitz', Mbiywom name Uchányang, also = 'Blue Lagoon'), Horse Creek, Moonlight Creek. (Alice Mark also says: at Police Lagoon)

Core tenure interests: Clan 48 (Georges, Parkers and Days).

Occupation history: See site records in *Aak*. On the main road between Aurukun and the outside world including Weipa, hence long frequented, hunted and camped in by custodians and others on a regular basis.

Language association: Mbiywom (= Mbeywom), also known in Wik-Mungkan etc. as Wik-Ompom; also known as Orrkel.

Area: [information not available]

Sites: See above.

ESTATE NUMBER 34 (Map A2.3)

Cover terms: Ward River, Paydan

Locality description: Lower Ward River from about Tappelbang Creek to (below?) the junction of Sandy Creek with the Ward; up the Ward via Paydan to Beagle Camp; includes the farm on Possum Creek. Mapped in some detail, see Aak and 1995 mapping.

Core tenure interests: Clan 60 and descendants (Owokrans), but other interests are acknowledged.

Occupation history: See site records in *Aak*.

Language association: Andjingith (Wik-Ayangench).

Area: Wik-Way

Sites: See *Aak* volume: Sites Listed Alphabetically by Estate. (*Aak* p. 66 has 308 Ikeleth but probably not correct.)

ESTATE NUMBER 35 (Map A2.3)

Cover terms: Uwbun, alt. Ubun

Locality description: The promontory forming the east side of the lower Ward River estuary, and east to near Aurukun.

Core tenure interests: Clan 61, the former owners, are extinct. Custodianship principally by those holding interests in adjacent estates (see Clan 61 for details). Regular use by wider Aurukun population as a kind of commons may be a factor in delaying or preventing full classical type of succession.

Occupation history: See site records in *Aak*. See Roger Cribb's (1986a, 1986b) data on old shell mounds and earth oven remains in the area. In more or less continuous use, at least in dry seasons, since the early days of Aurukun Mission, as it is close to the township.

Language association: Andjingith.

Area: Wik-Way

Sites: See *Aak* volume: Sites Listed Alphabetically by Estate; 2399 Uwbun

ESTATE NUMBER 36 (Map A2.3)

Cover terms: Wuthan

Locality description: From the mouth of Archer River north along the coast and inland to the lower Ward River estuary, north as far as the dunefields and their southward-trending drainage go.

Core tenure interests: Formerly Clan 62 (last member probably the long deceased woman Mookerr-ethenh). In the 1970s the main claimants to succession, long engaged in debate over the question, were the late Fred Kerindun and late Geraldine Kawangka. No longer in serious dispute by 1995, when conjoint interests were asserted by holders of surrounding estates (Owokrans and descendants, e.g. Alison Woolla); regular use by wider Aurukun population as a kind of commons may be a factor in delaying or preventing classical type of succession.

Occupation history: See site records in *Aak*. An army base was operated here at Wuthan during World War II. In the post-War period Aurukun people planted and ran a coconut plantation here. Victor Wolmby, then known as Victor Coconut, was one of the overseers of the plantation work. In regular use most of the year for recreation, fishing etc. by Aurukun residents.

Language association: Andjingith (Wik-Ayangench).

Area: Wik-Way

Sites: See *Aak* volume: Sites Listed Alphabetically by Estate. 649 Wuthan

ESTATE NUMBER 37 (Map A2.9)

Cover terms: Kuympay-aw

Locality description: [information not available]

Core tenure interests: Possibly Clan 38 (Marbthowans—e.g. Akay, Joyce Woolla).

Occupation history: See site records in *Aak*.

Language association: Wik-Mungkan?

Area: Upper Kirke River

Sites: See *Aak* volume: Sites Listed Alphabetically by Estate

ESTATE NUMBER 38 (Map A2.3)

Cover terms: Amban

Locality description: On the coast about Norman Creek and False Pera Head.

Core tenure interests: Formerly Clan 64 (Go'olfree), patriline now extinct. Interests held by Goodman Chevathen, father's father of Andrew Chevathen, but on what basis is not clear (possibly mother's country). Custodial interests include those of Kerinduns (Clan 68), and perhaps others.

Occupation history: See site records in *Aak*. An outstation called Amban (sometimes spelled Umbung) was established here c. 1988.

Language association: Ndra'ngith.

Area: Wik-Way

Sites: See *Aak* volume: Sites Listed Alphabetically by Estate

ESTATE NUMBER 39 (Map A2.1)

Cover terms: Mbang, Urquhart Point

Locality description: On the coast south from the mouth of the Embley River. Urquhart Point (Mbang), to Wulndrrun, Traylak Creek mouth, possibly as far as Thiitj Lagoon and Lwemdjin Lagoon.

Core tenure interests: Clan 70 (descendants of Arthur Dick; also Yorks?)

Occupation history: See site records in *Aak*.

Language association: Mamangathi (Mamngayth).

Area: Wik-Way

Sites: See locality description above.

ESTATE NUMBER 40 (Map A2.1)

Cover terms: Pera Head, Malnyinyu (Mission records: 'Mullino')

Locality description: On the coast at Pera Head and Boyd Point, and towards Winda Winda Creek.

Core tenure interests: Formerly Clan 66, that of Mabel Pamulkan née Taisman, patriline now extinct. Interests held by Mabel's descendants, e.g. through Harold Pamulkan and Mildred Kerindun. Joanne Wolmby's interests came from her mother's mother Maggie, sister of Jimmy Clarke.

Occupation history: See site records in *Aak*.

Language association: Adithinngithigh.

Area: Wik-Way

Sites: See *Aak* volume: Sites Listed Alphabetically by Estate.
2452 Pera Head

ESTATE NUMBER 41 (Map A2.3)

Cover terms: Thud Point, Upu-mren

Locality description: On the coast, focused on Thud Point between Norman River and Pera Head.

Core tenure interests: Clan 65. Also interests now collectively by Wik-Way group.

Occupation history: See site records in *Aak*. Andrew Chevathen and family were visiting from Weipa in the 1990s. He was born at Pera Head, regularly using the surrounding country till age c. 12 (his birthdate: 1938).

Language association: Ndra'ngith.

Area: Wik-Way (Winda-Winda)

Sites: See *Aak* volume: Sites Listed Alphabetically by Estate

McConnel map: [information not available]

ESTATE NUMBER 42 (Map A2.3)

Cover terms: Lower Archer River, Meerokem

Locality description: The estate runs from, and includes, Sidney Island, originally on both sides of the main Archer, up as far as Mach-aw (the northern 'Stoney Crossing'). Mach-aw is held in company with Estate 66. Succession to the area on the western bank of the Archer between Okenychang as far as Kerinth has passed to the Taisman family (see Clan 29), under arrangements made by the late Edward Koondumbin. The Koondumbin estate adjoins that of the Pambegans (Estate 31, see Clan 33) to the east.

Core tenure interests: Clan 34 (Koondumbins).

Occupation history: See site records in *Aak*. Edward Koondumbin vigilantly policed the Archer River. He made complaints about the operations of commercial barramundi fishermen in his waters right up until his death. He directly confronted certain fishermen (e.g. Fred Spore and Fred Zeimer), and told them to get out of his river. Others, he told to move their nets. He would tell them; 'I am boss of this river'. This was as late as Doug Featherstone's time (early 1980s), it is said.

Most of this country, particularly certain important sites along the river, continue to be frequently used. In the mid-1970s, there were large numbers of people camped up the Archer, including at Thudhem. During the mapping trip, there were several camps—on an island opposite Thudhem, and at Achan for instance—as well as at Aegan (Hagan) Lagoon. While the Archer has in some respects become an area where many Wik people go out to camp, all Aurukun people acknowledge that this area belongs to the Koondumbins, and Aurukun people generally ask them permission to come and camp or hunt in this country.

Language association: Wik-Mungkan.

Area: Lower Archer

Sites: See *Aak* volume: Sites Listed Alphabetically by Estate

McConnel map: Fish Hawk, Dilly-bag, Fishing net, Parrot, Rock-cod, Swampduck, Waterlily

ESTATE NUMBER 43 (Map A2.3)

Cover terms: Yaaneng

Locality description: South side of the mouth of Archer River.

Core tenure interests: Formerly Clan 82 (Stephen Owokran). Principal succession at 1994 was to Alison Woolla (her mother's country). Senior members of Clan 58 (Walmbengs) have custodial interests.

Occupation history: See site records in *Aak*. Long in use, in and after mission times, as a base camp area. Formerly site of a major initiation ground. Used regularly by Aurukun residents.

Language association: Formerly Wik-Paach and/or Andjingith.

Area: Lower Archer

Sites: See *Aak* volume: Sites Listed Alphabetically by Estate. 662 Yaaneng

McConnel map: Dugong, also Shark?

ESTATE NUMBER 44 (Map A2.3)

Cover terms: Bamboo, Big Bamboo; formerly Minh-wuthel

Locality description: Area of Bamboo cattle outstation, west wide of lower Archer River.

Core tenure interests: Formerly Clan 71 (Wik Ngak, i.e. Water Totem clan, now extinct).

Occupation history: See site records in *Aak*. Long used in mission times as a cattle yarding, branding, butchering centre, banishment camp from mission etc.

Language association: Former owners Wik-Paach (= Wik-Ngaangungker).

Area: Lower Archer

Sites: Minh-wuthel (Big Bamboo)

ESTATE NUMBER 45 (Map A2.1)

Cover terms: Moyngom (Hey Point)

Locality description: Hey Point area.

Core tenure interests: Clan 63 (Matthews).

Occupation history: See site records in *Aak*.

Language association: Linngithigh.

Area: Wik-Way

Sites: See 1995 mapping data. Moyngom (~ Mayngum, Hey Pt), Praenjim, Tiich

ESTATE NUMBER 46 (Map A2.1)

Cover terms: Anyiyam (Mission cards: 'Anyiema, Weipa mouth')

Locality description: Lower southern side of Embley River.

Core tenure interests: Clan 67 (Chevathun (A), Kelinda).

Occupation history: See site records in *Aak*.

Language association: Alngith.

Area: Wik-Way

Sites: Anyiyam (Roberts Creek), Nggoraynam, Ndrrilkiyach

ESTATE NUMBER 47 (Map A2.1)

Cover terms: [information not available]

Locality description: Mainly inland, between the coast (just south of the lower Embley) and the lower Hey estuary; Winda Winda Creek; interests in Mbang; possibly interests at Hey Point?

Core tenure interests: Clan 68 (Kerinduns).

Occupation history: See site records in *Aak*.

Language association: Linngithigh.

Area: Wik-Way

Sites: [information not available]

ESTATE NUMBER 48 (Map A2.5)

Cover terms: [information not available]

Locality description: Upper drainage system of Running Creek upstream of the junction of Middle Creek and Running Creek, including the Meripah homestead area and south of it.

Core tenure interests: Clan 69 (Warnkoolas/Kepples (B)).

Occupation history: See site records in *Aak*.

Language association: Wik-Iy-eyn (also given as Wik-Iiyenh).

Area: Upper Archer

Sites: Minchakngaateng, Thampoon, Ngooni. Paamp Impen-eng, Thamerr-eng

APPENDIX 2

ESTATE NUMBER 49 (Map A2.5)

Cover terms: Ku'-aw

Locality description: Lower Running Creek downstream from its junction with Middle Creek to its junction with Archer River, and along Archer River, focused particularly on its anabranch lake Ku'-aw ('Tea Tree Lagoon') and the hinterland lagoons to the south that overflow into it. At the homestead area of Kendall River Holding. North to Nhapi (Lake Archer), and possibly on the north side of the Archer below Ku'-aw. South-west to the region of Po'on and towards (but not including) Thaa'-pulnh on a tributary of the middle Kendall.

In 1929 McConnel recorded two linked estates (IX(a) and (b)) for here (see details under Clan 39). At that time the more southerly of the two had only one female survivor while the more northerly one, associated with the Koowarta/Pahimbung patriline, had 8–10 people. It seems most likely that the estate of old IX(b) has been absorbed into that of IX(a) on the extinction of the patriline associated with the former.

Core tenure interests: Clan 39 (Koowartas, Pahimbungs).

Occupation history: See site records in *Aak*, where there is an emphasis on early associations with sandalwooders in this area. In the 1980s/90s there was use of the estate from Meripah, later from Aurukun.

Language association: Wik-Iyenya.

Area: Upper Archer

Sites: See *Aak* volume: Sutton 1990; Sutton, Langton, von Sturmer 1991

McConnel map: Palm, Dingo, Leech; Kangaroo; probably White Water Snake (i.e. File Snake, see Mulayng-aw)

ESTATE NUMBER 50 (= 113, latter is primary number for estate map) (Map A2.10)

Cover terms: Kakelang-aw (also Tha'e-kakel)

Locality description: Upper Kendall River, from the westernmost of two waterfalls downstream for 20 or 30 km, together with swamps and associated local drainage. The focal site in the estate is Agu Tha'u Kakalang

(Sparrowhawk Talons) or Kakalang-ngannga, known in Wik-Mungkan as Tha'e-kakel or Kakelang-aw. Von Sturmer 1978: Head of Kendall, right on top, on south arm; up from Achamb-awu.

Core tenure interests: Clan 40/113 (Peinyekkas/Jingles).

Occupation history: See site records in *Aak*. Roddy Kemthan and Rosie Ahlers had been there while working for Rokeby.

Language association: Wik-Iiyanh.

Area: Upper Kendall

Sites: See *Aak* volume: Sites Listed Alphabetically by Estate

McConnel map: Chicken-hawk

ESTATE NUMBER 51 (Map A2.1)

Cover terms: Chaa'-ngkoth; Upper Hey River

Locality description: The upper drainage system of the Hey River, the south-eastern half, roughly.

Core tenure interests: Clan 50 (Motton).

Occupation history: See site records in *Aak*.

Language association: Ngkoth.

Area: Wik-Way

ESTATE NUMBER 52 (Map A2.1)

Cover terms: Onhánggun

Locality description: The south-western creeks and associated drainage area of the upper Hey River system.

Core tenure interests: Clan 51 (Mark, Kangaroo, Daisy Brodie)).

Occupation history: See site records in *Aak*.

Language association: Arraythinngith (= Arrithinngithigh, Arreythinwum depending on language used).

Area: Wik-Way

Sites: Onhánggun (also Anánggun), Idhholdja, Ndholndjin, Okaw (also Ikaw), Takun, Tjilwin, Moonlight Lagoon

Note: Estate 54 formerly assigned separately, now deleted as this is same estate.

ESTATE NUMBER 53 (Map A2.1)

Cover terms: [information not available]

Locality description: West side of the middle Hey River.

Core tenure interests: Clan 52 (Blowhards; Ida Paul, mother of Joyce Hall and Thancoupie (Gloria Fletcher))

Occupation history: See site records in *Aak*.

Language association: Latumngith.

Area: Inclusion of this land in the Wik-Way area by others was not accepted by Joyce Hall—or was it that she rejected the appellation 'Wik-Way' on the basis that, while a custodian of this estate, she herself was not Wik-Way because her primary identification was with her father's area further to the north?

Sites: Joyce Hall and Thancoupie include Moyngom, disputed.

ESTATE NUMBER 54 *see* 52

ESTATE NUMBER 55 (Map A2.3)

Cover terms: [information not available]

Locality description: South-west of Watson Crossing.

Core tenure interests: Clan 54 (patriline extinct). Custodial interests held by ?

Occupation history: See site records in *Aak*.

Language association: Possibly Mbiywom.

Area: Wik-Way

Sites: [information not available]

Note: This number was originally assigned (in *Aak*) to the Kunche-ku' area north-east of Peret Outstation, which was particularly associated with Callum Woolla. He was, however, a member of Clan 31, owners of the Oony-aw estate (28). Since his death we have not been aware of a distinction being made between Oony-aw and Kunche-ku' areas that resembles an assertion of two estates.

ESTATE NUMBER 56 (Map A2.3)

Cover terms: Yagalmungkan(h) area

Locality description: Lower Ward River from about Cowplace Creek downstream but not as far as Uwbun.

Core tenure interests: Clan 56 (patriline extinct). Succession is subject to ongoing negotiations.

Occupation history: See site records in *Aak*.

Language association: Andjingith?

Area: Wik-Way

Sites: See *Aak* volume: Sites Listed Alphabetically by Estate. Yagalmungkanh

ESTATE NUMBER 57 (Map A2.3)

Cover terms: Ikeleth; Waterfall

Locality description: On the coast north of Archer River from about Ikeleth to Waterfall, Ina Creek and Alichin Point.

Core tenure interests: Clan 57, patriline extinct. Long claimed by Cyril Owokran by succession, in addition to his patrilineal estate on the lower Ward River (Estate 34). Joint interests by southern Wik-Way people, and, some would say, all Wik-Way people. Rexie Wolmby asserted an interest in the Ikeleth area on the basis of his late father's (Alan Wolmby's) birthplace (1930) and afterbirth tree there. Although this assertion had limited support, at Alan Wolmby's house-opening ceremony in c. 1991 the house was unlocked by Andrew Chevathen (Clan 65, Estate 41, Thud Point, Wik-Way).

Occupation history: See site record in *Aak*. In regular use, except when closed for mourning purposes, by residents of Aurukun, especially those from a Wik-Way family.

Language association: Andjingith?

Area: Wik-Way

Sites: See *Aak* volume: Sites Listed Alphabetically by Estate

ESTATE NUMBER 58 (Map A2.6)

Cover terms: Mid Archer River (south)

Locality description: Along the Archer River between Stony Crossing and Ku'-aw. South of the main Archer River; adjoins the Koowarta estate to the east. The large 'island' running from near Stoney Crossing, where the Archer forms two major branches, is held in company with those from north of the Archer (Estate 66, Clan 76).

Core tenure interests: The former owners appear to be extinct in a direct patrilineal sense. Koowartas have expressed custodial interest, possibly Taismans, and more recently Oonyaw Woollas. Extinct clan numbered 77, probably Bushnut and Nailfish (see McConnel below); evidence about them may be in Thomson's 1933 genealogies.

Occupation history: See site records in *Aak*.

Language association: Wik-Mungkan; also ?Chiluk (Noel Peemuggina to PS).

Area: Middle Archer

Sites: See *Aak* volume: Sites Listed Alphabetically by Estate. Includes the helicopter crash site, a well-known landmark. Punth-eempening (Roddie Yard)

McConnel map: Probably: Bushnut, Nailfish (*'min jintan'* [minh chintan])

ESTATE NUMBER 59 (Map A2.10)

Cover terms: Thaa'-pulnh

Locality description:

Core tenure interests: Former owners unidentified. Succession has passed at least to the custodianship of Clan 40/113 (Peinyekkas/Jingles) whose focal estate is immediately upstream at Estate 50 (113).

Occupation history: See site records in *Aak*.

Language association: Wik-Iiyanh?

Area: Middle Kendall

Sites: See *Aak* volume: Sites Listed Alphabetically by Estate Thaa'-pulnh

ESTATE NUMBER 60 (Map A2.10)

Cover terms: Achemp-aw (Achamp-awu?)

Locality description:

Core tenure interests: Formerly Mitherropsen ('Mr Robinson') (Clan 81)? Succession has at least passed to the custodianship of Clan 40/113 (Peinyekkas/Jingles) whose focal estate (50) is upstream of here. Von Sturmer 1978 lists an upper Kendall River clan (KU3) for the Thaa'-pulnh (Estate 59) and Achemp-aw (60) area, which may be Mitherropsen's clan.

Occupation history: See site records in *Aak*.

Language association: Wik-Iiyanh?

Area: Middle Kendall

Sites: See *Aak* volume: Sites Listed Alphabetically by Estate. 285 Achemp-aw

McConnel map: Emu

ESTATE NUMBER 61 *see* 115

ESTATE NUMBER 62 (= 117) (Map A2.10)

Cover terms: Kulan-awu?

Locality description: South and south-east of the two waterfalls on the upper Kendall, adjacent to Estate 50 (Kakelang-aw).

Core tenure interests: Formerly Old Mosey Kepple (Clan 117), a clan listed as extant by von Sturmer 1978 in *Aak* p75.

Occupation history: See site records in *Aak*.

Language association: Wik-Iiyanh

Area: Upper Kendall

Sites: See *Aak* volume: Sites Listed Alphabetically by Estate. [Probably a Possum totemic centre, i.e. Kulan-awu?]

McConnel map: Opossum

ESTATE NUMBER 63(/118) (118: Map A2.9)

Cover terms: [information not available]

Locality description: On the South Kendall River (the 'Holroyd' of the official maps) between the main Kendall and main Holroyd rivers, 'inside' (east?) from Um-po'am.

Core tenure interests: Clan 96/118 (Kendalls/Edwards/Tarpenchas).

Occupation history: See site records in *Aak*.

Language association: Wik-Iiyanh.

Area: Upper Kendall [?]

Sites: See *Aak* volume: Sites Listed Alphabetically by Estate. [Freshwater Crocodile totemic centre?]; probably: 1305 Milinyin (vicinity of 1304 Miindji)

ESTATE NUMBER 64 (Map A2.12)

Cover terms: Thornbury Creek

Locality description: Thornbury Creek area, on the upper Holroyd River system; company connections to Estate 119 to the west.

Core tenure interests: Clan 78 (Douglas Ahlers, Stanley Ahlers).

Occupation history: See site records in *Aak*.

Language association: Ayapathu?; also given as Mungkanhu.

Area: Upper Holroyd

Sites: [information not available]

ESTATE NUMBER 65 (Map A2.4)

Cover terms: Green Swamp

Locality description: Upper Archer River and its drainage from its junction with Piccaninny Creek to near Langi Lagoon, ?mainly on the south side.

Core tenure interests: Clan 75 (Charlie Kepple).

Occupation history: See site records in *Aak*.

Language association: Mbiywom (Wik-Ompom).

Area: Upper Archer

Sites: Green Swamp (Goose Story), Iwiya (Catfish Story Place at Piccaninny Junction; called Eyvya in Alice Mark's language), Thench, Pindling, Bunda Yards, Sandy Lagoon, Shady Lagoon; also: (?) Kontathan, Yuukingka (between Partridge Yard and Iwiya), Layngay

ESTATE NUMBER 66 (Map A2.6)

Cover terms: Mid Archer (north), Puuy

Locality description: This estate runs from Mach-aw (held in company with Clan 34 Koondumbins) up past Puuy ('Leichardt Swamp' on 1:100,000 map). It may extend almost as far as Archer Bend. The large 'island' running from near Stoney Crossing, where the Archer forms two major branches, is held in company with those from south of the Archer (Estate 58, Clan 77).

Core tenure interests: Clan 76, *inter alia* George Rokeby, the descendants of Jimmy Lawrence, Rebecca, Roberta; Goanka; Margaret (mother of the late Charles Taisman), Polly Fruit and Connie Clark.

Occupation history: See site records in *Aak*.

Language association: Wik-Mungkan.

Area: Middle Archer River

Sites: [information not available]

ESTATE NUMBER 67 (Map A2.11)

Cover terms: [information not available]

Locality description: Upper Kendall River system, probably in the area west of Coleman Creek.

Core tenure interests: Clan 79 (Topsy Wolmby).

Occupation history: See site records in *Aak*.

Language association: Wik-Iyanyi.

Area: Top Kendall

Sites: Puchenganpeng, Pukulpanth

ESTATE NUMBER 68 (Map A2.2)

Cover terms: Wathayn

Locality description: North side of Lower Embley River, on lower Mamoose Creek, at Spring Creek, Ndhinggwulung (Spring Creek outstation), west side of old Weipa Mission, Big Wathayn to the Oil Rig, Bellview Creek, Cockatoo Island (probably the 'Cyclone Island' of the official maps), right to Beening Creek.

Core tenure interests: Clan 83 (Coconut).

Occupation history: See site records in *Aak*. Immediate accessibility by a short journey from both old Weipa Mission and from Napranum probably means contact between clan members and their estate has not been too seriously curtailed.

Language association: Ndrrangith.

Area: [information not available]

Sites: See locality description above.

ESTATE NUMBER 69 (Map A2.2)

Cover terms: Mayul (Myall Creek), Twenty Mile (Old Weipa Mission, Meyka)

Locality description: [information not available]

Core tenure interests: Clan 85 (English).

Occupation history: See site records in *Aak*.

Language association: Anathangayth.

Area: Myall Creek

Sites: Core sites: Meyka (Twenty-Mile, Old Weipa Mission; cf. 'Myka Creek'); places listed also by Alice Mark (of Clan 85) but perhaps associated with linked estates upstream: Mayul (Myall Creek), Katjali, Oyónton, Pitji ('Fitz', local name Uchányan), Keriko (cf. 'Kurracoo Creek'), Locky Yard, Shotover Creek, One Mile Creek, Wenlock Creek, Billy Lagoon, Clarinet Yard.

ESTATE NUMBER 70–100 NOT IN USE

ESTATE NUMBER 101 *see* 21

ESTATE NUMBER 102 *see* 26

ESTATE NUMBER 103 *see* 22

ESTATE NUMBER 104 *see* 23

ESTATE NUMBER 105 (Map A2.9)

Cover terms: [information not available]

Locality description: In lower Kendall River area but exact location uncertain. Described as 'round Dish Yard [Weten]; Knock [Knox] River top side' (von Sturmer 1978:597).

Core tenure interests: Clan 105 (= 90) Koonuttas.

Occupation history: See site records in *Aak*.

Language association: Von Sturmer 1978: Wik-Me'enh; PS: Jack Koonutta (Clan 105) took Wik-Ngathan from his mother and this has become the clan's language of affiliation.

Area: Lower Kendall

Sites: [information not available]

ESTATE NUMBER 106 (Map A2.9)

Cover terms: Kuli-aynchan ?

Locality description: On the south side of Kendall River mouth.

Core tenure interests: Von Sturmer 1978 has former owners as Clan 106 (extinct).

Occupation history: See site records in *Aak*. Regular use until about 1957. Outstation (at Empadha) established here in 1977 (see von Sturmer 1980 for photographs of buildings and occupation in 1978).

Language association: Formerly Kugu Ugbanh (Clan 106).

Area: Lower Kendall

Sites: See *Aak* volume: Sites Listed Alphabetically by Estate. Von Sturmer 1978: Puntum, Ngaka Kaychim, Mukum-awu, Itha Thaha Ngululu, Kuli-anchan [see also 3018 Kuli-Aynychan and official map's 'Kulinchin'], Yomen-awu.

ESTATE NUMBER 107 (Map A2.9)

Cover terms: [information not available]

Locality description: On the coast between Kendall River and King [Thuuk] River.

Core tenure interests: Clan 24 (Poonkamelyas, = Clan 107).

Occupation history: See site records in *Aak*.

Language association: Kugu Muminh.

Area: Lower Kendall

Sites: See *Aak* volume: Sites Listed Alphabetically by Estate. Von Sturmer 1978: Kengge, Ku'a-awu

ESTATE NUMBER 108 (Map A2.9)

Cover terms: [information not available]

Locality description: On the coast south of mouth of Kendall River.

Core tenure interests: Clan 108. Von Sturmer 1978 listed patriline as extant.

Occupation history: See site records in *Aak*.

Language association: Kugu Muminh.

Area: Lower Kendall

Sites: See *Aak* volume: Sites Listed Alphabetically by Estate. Von Sturmer 1978: Kanggani, Mangka Pomponi.

ESTATE NUMBER 109 (Map A2.9)

Cover terms: [information not available]

Locality description: On coast south of Kendall River mouth.

Core tenure interests: Clan 109 (= Clan 27, q.v., Kalkeeyortas).

Occupation history: See site records in *Aak*.

APPENDIX 2

Language association: Kugu Muminh.

Area: Lower Kendall

Sites: See *Aak* volume: Sites Listed Alphabetically by Estate. Von Sturmer 1978: Puntum, Ngaka Kachim. Attribution of site 399 Mengeyn to this estate (see *Aak*, p. 61) is probably incorrect; should be in Estate 110.

ESTATE NUMBER 110 (Map A2.9)

Cover terms: Mangaynyi (Mengeyn)

Locality description: On coast south of Kendall River.

Core tenure interests: Clan 110 (= 25, q.v. Karyukas).

Occupation history: See site records in *Aak*.

Language association: Kugu Uwanh.

Area: Thuuk River ?

Sites: See *Aak* volume: Sites Listed Alphabetically by Estate. Von Sturmer 1978: Umam, Agu Thuntha, Thuntha Pangkam, Pangkam, Wuyinh-awu, Wuki-awu.

McConnel map: Crab, Barramundi

ESTATE NUMBER 111 (Map A2.9)

Cover terms: Kok

Locality description: On the middle Kendall River about the major lagoon. Called Kok.

Core tenure interests: Clan 111 (typifying surname? – von Sturmer 1978 listed patriline as extant).

Occupation history: See site records in *Aak*.

Language association: Wik-Iiyanh (Clan 111).

Area: Middle Kendall

Sites: See *Aak* volume: Sites Listed Alphabetically by Estate. Von Sturmer 1978: Kuthe, Ngakwi-awu

ESTATE NUMBER 112 (Map A2.9)

Cover terms: [information not available]

Locality description: North side of middle Kendall River, inland from Thanmul (= site 117 Thanmel)

Core tenure interests: Clan 112 (typifying surname? Von Sturmer 1978 listed patriline as extant)

Occupation history: See site records in *Aak*.

Language association: Wik-Iiyanh.

Area: Middle Kendall

Sites: [information not available]

McConnel map: Curlew

ESTATE NUMBER 113 (= 50) (Map A2.10)

Cover terms: Tha'-kakel

Locality description: Part of upper Kendall River system containing the waterfall Tha'-kakel (Kakelang-aw), upstream from Achemp-aw.

Core tenure interests: Focal estate of Clan 40 (Peinyekkas, Jingles).

Occupation history: See site records in *Aak*. Roddy Kemthan (Shortjoe) and Rosie Ahlers had both been there before its focal point was mapped in 1991.

Language association: Wik-Iiyanh.

Area: Upper Kendall

Sites: Von Sturmer 1978: Agu Tha'u Kakalang (= Kakalang Ngan-nga). RA to DFM: Ungkanang. See PS report list

McConnel map: Chicken-hawk

APPENDIX 2

ESTATE NUMBER 114 (Map A2.10)

Cover terms: [information not available]

Locality description: Between the upper Kendall and upper Holroyd rivers.

Core tenure interests: Clan 114 (von Sturmer 1978 listed patriline as extant).

Occupation history: See site records in *Aak*.

Language association: Wik-Iiyanh.

Area: Upper Kendall

Sites: See *Aak* volume: Sites Listed Alphabetically by Estate

ESTATE NUMBER 115 (Map A2.10)

Cover terms: Nhomp-aw (~Nhompo-awu)

Locality description: On the upper Kendall River focused on the easterly of two waterfalls, at Nhomp-aw; near Kulan-awu; in the southern extent of Meripah pastoral lease.

Core tenure interests: Clan 115 (Quinkins).

Occupation history: See site records in *Aak*.

Language association: Wik-Mungkanh (Mungkanho?) von Sturmer 1978 listed patriline as extant, and has Wik-Iiyanh

Area: Upper Kendall

Sites: Nhomp-aw (von Sturmer 1978: Nhompo-awu near Kulan-awu), Thaachenyin, Thaa'ngupa, Paamp Puuti, Chew'eng, Mee'-Kalwanh

McConnel map: Eagle-hawk [Wedgetailed Eagle]

447

ESTATE NUMBER 116 (Map A2.8)

Cover terms: Mumpa-awu

Locality description: Upper Kendall River, northern branch, near Meripah Station.

Core tenure interests: Clan 116 (Kepples).

Occupation history: See site records in *Aak*.

Language association: Wik-Iiyanh (von Sturmer 1978), Wik-Iiyenya, Wik-Nhinkalo (totemic reference to devil).

Area: Upper Kendall

Sites: Von Sturmer 1978: Mumpa-awu, Wadha-awu.

McConnel map: Shooting Star, Quail, Praying Mantis [= Mumpa, von Sturmer 1978:612], Crow

ESTATE NUMBER 117 (= 62) (Map A2.10)

Cover terms: Kulan-awu?

Locality description: Upper Kendall River, near Kugu Keke (von Sturmer 1978).

Core tenure interests: Clan 117 (Old Mosey Kepple) (listed by von Sturmer 1978 as extant).

Occupation history: See site records in *Aak*.

Language association: Wik-Iiyanh.

Area: Upper Kendall

Sites: Kulan-awu?

McConnel map: Opossum

ESTATE NUMBER 118 (Map A2.9)

Cover terms: [information not available]

Locality description: Middle part of South Kendall River, inside from Um-po'am.

Core tenure interests: Clan 118 (Kendalls, Tarpenchas).

Occupation history: See site record in *Aak*.

Language association: Wik-Iiyanh.

Area: Upper Kendall

Sites: Probably: 1305 Milinyin (vicinity of 1304 Miindji, 1306 Munthaneng)

ESTATE NUMBER 119 (Map A2.9)

Cover terms: [information not available]

Locality description: On upper South Kendall and Holroyd rivers.

Core tenure interests: Clan 119 (Shortjoes, Kemthans).

Occupation history: See site records in *Aak*.

Language association: Wik-Iiyanh.

Area: Upper Kendall

Sites: Von Sturmer 1978: Kuujuru, Yongka Thulum, Agu Koothiya, Thaanychil-awu.

McConnel map: Waterlily, Blue-tongue Lizard

ESTATE NUMBER 120 (Map A2.10)

Cover terms: Agu Poykol-awu ('Catfish Story Place')

Locality description: On main river, upper Kendall River.

Core tenure interests: Formerly Clan 120 (von Sturmer 1978 lists patriline as extinct).

Occupation history: See site records in *Aak*.

Language association: Clan 120 was Ayapathu (von Sturmer 1978).

Area: Upper Kendall

Sites: Von Sturmer 1978: Agu Poykol-awu

McConnel map: Catfish

ESTATE NUMBER 121 (Map A2.9)

Cover terms: [information not available]

Locality description: On the coast north of Thuuk River.

Core tenure interests: Formerly Clan 121, patriline listed by von Sturmer 1978 as extinct.

Occupation history: See site records in *Aak*.

Language association: Clan 121 was Kugu Muminh.

Area: Thuuk River

Sites: See *Aak* volume: Sites Listed Alphabetically by Estate

ESTATE NUMBER 122 (Map A2.9)

Cover terms: [information not available]

Locality description: Upper Thuuk River, east of Ongorom.

Core tenure interests: Clan 122, patriline listed by von Sturmer 1978 as extant.

Occupation history: See site records in *Aak*.

Language association: Wik-Iiyanh.

Area: Thuuk River

Sites: See *Aak* volume: Sites Listed Alphabetically by Estate

ESTATE NUMBER 123 (Map A2.9)

Cover terms: Thugu, Pu'an

Locality description: Lower Thuuk River.

Core tenure interests: Clan 123 (= 97, q.v., Ngallamettas, Wunchums).

Occupation history: See site records in *Aak*. Regular occupation until about 1957. Outstation established at Pu'an 1978 (for photographs see von Sturmer 1980:159, 163).

Language association: Kugu Uwanh.

Area: Thuuk River

Sites: See *Aak* volume: Sites Listed Alphabetically by Estate. Von Sturmer 1978: Anbada, Pidhala, Mongkom-awu, Yenge (~Yengye), Thokey, Matpi-awu, Maka(a)nban, Pathe

McConnel map: Yam

ESTATE NUMBER 124 (Map A2.9)

Cover terms: [information not available]

Locality description: On the coast on the north side of Holroyd River mouth.

Core tenure interests: Clan 124 (= 92, q.v., Mimunyins).

Occupation history: See site records in *Aak*.

Language association: Kugu Ugbanh.

Area: Lower Holroyd

Sites: See *Aak* volume: Sites Listed Alphabetically by Estate. Von Sturmer 1978: Kuutuman, Kuladha, Ku'a-wunen, Wela Niku

ESTATE NUMBER 125 (Map A2.13)

Cover terms: Thaha-kungadha?

Locality description: Lower Holroyd River, south bank.

Core tenure interests: Formerly Clan 125 (patriline listed by von Sturmer 1978 as extinct).

Occupation history: See site records in *Aak*.

Language association: Kugu Ugbanh.

Area: Lower Holroyd

Sites: See *Aak* volume: Sites Listed Alphabetically by Estate. Von Sturmer 1978: Agu Aye, Wanam-awu

ESTATE NUMBER 126 (Map A2.13)

Cover terms: [information not available]

Locality description: On the coast just south of the mouth of Holroyd River.

Core tenure interests: Clan 126 (patriline listed by von Sturmer 1978 as extant).

Occupation history: See site records in *Aak*.

Language association: Kugu Mu'inh.

Area: Lower Holroyd

Sites: See *Aak* volume: Sites Listed Alphabetically by Estate

ESTATE NUMBER 127 (Map A2.13)

Cover terms: Thampench

Locality description: On the coast just south of Holroyd River mouth.

Core tenure interests: Clan 127 (= Clan 93, q.v., Ngakapoorgums).

Occupation history: See site records in *Aak*.

Language association: Kugu Muminh.

Area: Lower Holroyd

Sites: See *Aak* volume: Sites Listed Alphabetically by Estate. Von Sturmer 1978: Kiban, Ka'adha, Yekong, Pukam, Impa

ESTATE NUMBER 128

Cover terms: [information not available]

Locality description: [information not available]

Core tenure interests: Von Sturmer 1978 lists clan as extinct, also commenting that he was doubtful whether this was a separate group from Clan 132.

Occupation history: See site records in *Aak*.

Language association: [information not available]

Area: Holroyd River (?Lower)

Sites: [information not available]

ESTATE NUMBER 129 (Map A2.13)

Cover terms: [information not available]

Locality description: South of Holroyd River, intermediate between the coast and inland environments.

Core tenure interests: Clan 129 (listed by von Sturmer 1978 as extant).

Occupation history: See site records in *Aak*.

Language association: Kugu Muminh.

Area: Middle Holroyd

Sites: See *Aak* volume: Sites Listed Alphabetically by Estate

ESTATE NUMBER 130 (Map A2.9)

Cover terms: Thupi-ijiy ?

Locality description: On the north bank of Holroyd River upstream from Thupi-ijiy.

Core tenure interests: Clan 130 (= 98, q.v., Yantumbas, Minpunjas).

Occupation history: See site records in *Aak*.

Language association: Wik-Iiyanh.

Area: Upper Holroyd

Sites: See *Aak* volume: Sites Listed Alphabetically by Estate. Von Sturmer 1978: Thumba-awu, Ulman, Kuna(nga)-waya, Oygo, Thopenenh, Migu-Awung, Punba-awu, Thugu Ngamba-awu, Payan-awu

ESTATE NUMBER 131 (Map A2.13)

Cover terms: [information not available]

Locality description: North side of Christmas Creek.

Core tenure interests: Clan 131 (patriline listed by von Sturmer 1978 as extant).

Occupation history: See site records in *Aak*.

Language association: Kugu Mu'inh.

Area: Lower Christmas Creek

Sites: See *Aak* volume: Sites Listed Alphabetically by Estate. Von Sturmer 1978: Piching, Mutha-awula, Thugu, Kaha-ngungku-awu

ESTATE NUMBER 132 (Map A2.13)

Cover terms: Yangku

Locality description: On the coast north of Christmas Creek.

Core tenure interests: Formerly Clan 132, listed by von Sturmer 1978 as extinct.

Occupation history: See site records in *Aak*.

Language association: Kugu Yi'anh.

Area: Lower Christmas Creek

Sites: See *Aak* volume: Sites Listed Alphabetically by Estate. Von Sturmer 1978: Ngamba, Kurka Pelen, Piching, Pilu

ESTATE NUMBER 133 (Map A2.12)

Cover terms: Memola ?

Locality description: North of Christmas Creek, along the coast north from Waalang.

Core tenure interests: Clan 133 (patriline von Sturmer 1978 listed as extant).

Occupation history: See site records in *Aak*.

Language association: Kugu Mu'inh.

Area: Lower Christmas Creek

Sites: See *Aak* volume: Sites Listed Alphabetically by Estate

ESTATE NUMBER 134 (Map A2.12)

Cover terms: Waalang

Locality description: Christmas Creek, north of the mouth.

Core tenure interests: Clan 134 (Arkwookerums).

Occupation history: See site records in *Aak*.

Language association: Kugu Mu'inh.

Area: Lower Christmas Creek

Sites: See *Aak* volume: Sites Listed Alphabetically by Estate. Von Sturmer 1978: Kupu, Windidha, Impa, Kunamnga, Wunhthoj, Empa, Ngaka Pukam (= Pinta?), Puuny, Agu Panych, Puunyu [cf. *Aak* site 3512 Poonyowa], Kuja Tha'u, Thacha Poye(ngo), Pempela, Inyenge, Thitha Punhtha, Mayin-ngu, Thanhthula, Ngaka Wi'i'am, Nga'a-awu-ngu

ESTATE NUMBER 135 (Map A2.12)

Cover terms: Waalang south side?

Locality description: At the mouth of Christmas Creek, on the south bank.

Core tenure interests: Clan 135 (von Sturmer 1978 listed patriline as extant).

Occupation history: See site records in *Aak*.

Language association: Kugu Mu'inh.

Area: Lower Christmas Creek

Sites: See *Aak* volume: Sites Listed Alphabetically by Estate. Von Sturmer 1978: Thangkadha, Poompo, Waying, Pipi Mini, Wenka Winggu, Wudu, Kek Thu'ula

ESTATE NUMBER 136 (Map A2.12)

Cover terms: [information not available]

Locality description: On middle part of Christmas Creek.

Core tenure interests: Formerly Clan 136 (patriline listed by von Sturmer 1978 as extinct).

Occupation history: See site records in *Aak*.

Language association: Kugu Mangk.

Area: Middle Christmas Creek

Sites: See *Aak* volume: Sites Listed Alphabetically by Estate. Von Sturmer 1978: Kunalu, Thochon, Pambe, Wu'udha, Thanychun, Thankanyjin, Empay Wakanh, Pempela

ESTATE NUMBER 137 (Map A2.12)

Cover terms: [information not available]

Locality description: On Christmas Creek [probably middle or upper].

Core tenure interests: Formerly Clan 137 (patriline listed by von Sturmer 1978 as extinct).

Occupation history: See site records in *Aak*.

Language association: Kugu Muminh.

Area: Middle[?] Christmas Creek

Sites: Von Sturmer 1978: Pinhdha Mechom, Wuyinh, Inyenge

ESTATE NUMBER 138 (Map A2.12)

Cover terms: [information not available]

Locality description: Large territory on middle section of Christmas Creek, upstream from Pepen.

Core tenure interests: Clan 138 (patriline listed by von Sturmer 1978 as extant).

Occupation history: See site records in *Aak*.

Language association: Wik-Iiyanh.

Area: Middle Christmas Creek

Sites: Von Sturmer 1978: Thacha Poye(ngo), Michere, Koon Inychane

ESTATE NUMBER 139 (Map A2.12)

Cover terms: [information not available]

Locality description: Lower Breakfast Creek.

Core tenure interests: Clan 139 (von Sturmer 1978 listed patriline as extant).

Occupation history: See site records in *Aak*.

Language association: Kugu Mangk.

Area: Breakfast Creek

Sites: Von Sturmer 1978: Pangkadha, Thatanga, Pimpadha, Ku'a Punhthungu, Tha'u Ngukara, Yan-nga, Maalun

ESTATE NUMBER 140 (Map A2.12)

Cover terms: [information not available]

Locality description: Large territory from Strathgordon down the north side of Edward River.

Core tenure interests: Clan 140 (von Sturmer 1978 listed patriline as extant).

Occupation history: See site records in *Aak*.

Language association: Wik-Iiyanh, Pakanha.

Area: Breakfast Creek

Sites: Von Sturmer 1978: Nhandu-ijiy Mimponyje [all one name]

McConnel map: Fresh Water Harmless Crocodile

ESTATE NUMBER 141 (Map A2.9)

Cover terms: [information not available]

Locality description: On upper Christmas Creek, below its junction with the South Kendall.

Core tenure interests: Clan 141 (von Sturmer 1978 listed patriline as extant).

Occupation history: See site records in *Aak*.

Language association: Pakanha (von Sturmer 1978) (= Bakanhu, Ayabakanh, Wik-Pak, etc.).

Area: Upper Christmas Creek

Sites: Von Sturmer 1978: Agu Wayn-gan (Ngan-nga), Yapi-awu

ESTATE NUMBER 142 (Map A2.13)

Cover terms: Pabim ?

Locality description: On the coast south of Holroyd River.

Core tenure interests: Clan 142 (patriline listed as extant by von Sturmer 1978).

Occupation history: See site records in *Aak*.

Language association: Kugu Mu'inh.

Area: Lower Holroyd

Sites: Von Sturmer 1978: Pabim

ESTATE NUMBER 143 (Map A2.13)

Coverterms: Yangku?

Locality description: North of Christmas Creek on or near the coast.

Core tenure interests: Formerly Clan 143 (listed by von Sturmer 1978 as extinct).

Occupation history: See site records in *Aak*.

Language association: Kugu Mu'inh.

Area: Lower Christmas Creek

Sites: 3501 Yangku

ESTATE NUMBER 144 (Map A2.9)

Cover terms: [information not available]

Locality description: On the flood plain area north of the lower Holroyd River.

Core tenure interests: Clan 144 (patriline listed by von Sturmer 1978 as extant).

Occupation history: See site records in *Aak*.

Language association: ?

Area: Lower Holroyd River

Sites: See *Aak* volume: Sites Listed Alphabetically by Estate. Von Sturmer 1978: Thaha-pul-n, Achamp-awu, ?Mamen

McConnel map: Emu

ESTATE NUMBER 145 (Map A2.9)

Cover terms: [information not available]

Locality description: On the north side of the middle Holroyd River.

Core tenure interests: Clan 145 (patriline listed by von Sturmer 1978 as extant).

Occupation history: See site records in *Aak*.

Language association: ?

Area: Middle Holroyd River

Sites: See *Aak* volume: Sites Listed Alphabetically by Estate

ESTATE NUMBER 146 (Map A2.1)

Cover terms: Western Weipa Peninsula

Locality description: From the Oil Rig (Oil Camp) near Beening Creek in the south-east of the Peninsula, north-west via Napranum and Nggonban (Evans Point) to the western end of Weipa Peninsula, north-east via Weipa township and Albatross Hotel to Oningan (see Uningan Reserve); Trunding Creek. Inland extent described by Ronnie John (PS Field Book 83:132) as west of some kind of line going straight across from Oningan to the Oil Rig. Company interests with Estate 45 at Praenjim (Franjum Point) on southern bank of Embley River.

Core tenure interests: Clan 80.

Occupation history: See site records in Sutton et al. 1997.

Language association: Alngith, Layngith, Laynngith (alternate names).

Area: Wik-Way

Sites: Napranum, Mundhing, Nggonban ~ Nggonbayn (Evans Point), Naenam, Trandhing, Mbining (Beening), Oil Rig/Camp, Oningan, Dhenthikaram, first bridge (not second), Barkly Yard, Wallaby Island, Kamrindja, Owang, Ruwrimin

ESTATE NUMBER 147 (Map A2.10)

Cover terms: [information not available]

Locality description: On upper Kendall River.

Core tenure interests: McConnel's local group XV.

Occupation history: See site records in Sutton et al. 1997.

Language association: Wik-Iiyanh.

Area: Upper Kendall

Sites: [information not available]

APPENDIX 2

McConnel map: Messmate and Bloodwood Flowers

ESTATE NUMBER 148 (Map A2.3)

Cover terms: Beagle Camp?

Locality description: The upper Coconut Creek drainage system.

Core tenure interests: Interests attributed to Clan 63 (Matthews) but this is not their focal estate (see Estate 45). General succession by Wik-Way people.

Occupation history: See site records in Sutton et al. (1997). Beagle Camp was established here in the 1960s and some Wik-Way people worked there in that decade. Readily visited by road from Aurukun.

Language association: Linngithigh.

Area: Wik-Way

Sites: See Sutton et al. 1997

ESTATE NUMBER 149 (Map A2.1)

Cover terms: Part of Mbang area

Locality description: In area of Urquhart Point, south side of lower Embley River.

Core tenure interests: Clan 84 (Committy).

Occupation history: See site records in Sutton et al. 1997.

Language association: Linngithigh (but see Clan 84 entry).

Area: [information not available]

Sites: Mbang, Kokanin, Wulndrrun, Traylak [same as Estate 39?]

References

Aboriginal Land Commissioner 1982. *Daly River (Malak Malak) Land Claim*. Canberra: Australian Government Publishing Service.

Aboriginal Land Commissioner 1984. *Nicholson River (Waanyi/Garawa) Land Claim*. Canberra: Australian Government Publishing Service.

Alpher, Barry 1972. On the genetic subgrouping of the languages of southwestern Cape York Peninsula, Australia. *Oceanic Linguistics* 11:67–87. doi.org/10.2307/3622803

Alpher, Barry 1991. *Yir-Yoront Lexicon: Sketch and Dictionary of an Australian Language*. Berlin/New York: Mouton de Gruyter. doi.org/10.1515/9783110872651

Alpher, Barry, and David Nash 1999. Lexical replacement and cognate equilibrium in Australia. *Australian Journal of Linguistics* 19:5–56. doi.org/10.1080/07268609908599573

Ashmore, Louise 2017. Wik-Ngathan and Wik-Alken demonstratives. PhD thesis, School of Oriental and African Studies, University of London.

Bergsland, Knut, and Hans Vogt 1962. On the validity of glottochronology, *Current Anthropology* 3:115–153. doi.org/10.1086/200264

Berndt, Ronald M. and Catherine H. Berndt 1988. *The World of the First Australians. Traditional Aboriginal Life: Past and Present*. Canberra: Aboriginal Studies Press.

Birdsell, Joseph B. 1953. Some environmental and cultural factors influencing the structure of Australian Aboriginal populations. *American Naturalist* 87(834):171–207. doi.org/10.1086/281776

Birdsell, Joseph B. 1957. Some population problems involving Pleistocene man. *Cold Springs Harbor Symposia on Quantitative Biology* 22:47–69. doi.org/10.1101/sqb.1957.022.01.008

Birdsell, Joseph B. 1958. On population structure in generalized hunting and collecting populations. *Evolution* 12:189–205. doi.org/10.1111/j.1558-5646.1958.tb02945.x

Birdsell, Joseph B. 1968. Some predictions for the Pleistocene based on equilibrium systems among recent hunter-gatherers. In R.B. Lee and I. DeVore (eds) *Man the Hunter* (pp. 229–40, 246). Chicago: Aldine Publishing Company.

Birdsell, Joseph B. 1973. A basic demographic unit. *Current Anthropology* 14:337–56.

Birdsell, Joseph B. 1979. Ecological influences on Australian Aboriginal social organization. In I.S. Bernstein and E.O. Smith (eds), *Primate Ecology and Human Origins: Ecological Influences on Social Organization* (pp. 117–151). New York: Garland STPM Press.

Birdsell, Joseph B. 1987. Some reflections on fifty years in biological anthropology. *Annual Review of Anthropology* 16:1–12. doi.org/10.1146/annurev.an.16.100187.000245

Birdsell, Joseph B. 1993. *Microevolutionary Patterns in Aboriginal Australia: A Gradient Analysis of Clines*. New York: Oxford University Press.

Borer, Hagit (ed.) 1986. *The Syntax of Pronominal Clitics*. Syntax and Semantics 19. New York: Academic Press.

Bos, Robert 1973–74. MS. Unpublished Field Notes, Weipa. Canberra: Australian Institute of Aboriginal and Torres Strait Islander Studies Library.

Brandi, Luciana, and Patrizia Cordin 1988. Two Italian dialects and the null subject parameter. In O. Jaeggli and K. Safir (eds), *The Null Subject Parameter* (pp. 111–42). Dordrecht: Kluwer. doi.org/10.1007/978-94-009-2540-3_4

Capell, Arthur 1955. MS. Unpublished field notes, Cape York Peninsula. Canberra: Australian Institute of Aboriginal and Torres Strait Islander Studies.

Capell, Arthur 1963. *Linguistic Survey of Australia*. Canberra: Australian Institute of Aboriginal Studies.

Carnie, Andrew, Eloise Jelinek, and Mary Ann Willie (eds) 2000. *Papers in Honor of Ken Hale*. Cambridge, Massachusetts: MIT Working Papers in Linguistics.

Cervantes Saavedra, Miguel de 1605. *El ingenioso hidalgo Don Quixote de la Mancha*. Madrid: Francisco de Robles.

Chase, Athol, Bruce Rigsby, David Martin, Benjamin Smith and Peter Blackwood 1998. Mungkan, Ayapathu and Kaanju Peoples' Land Claims to Mungkan Kaanju National Park and Lochinvar Mining Field. Claim Book. Aboriginal Land Act 1991 claims AB94–003, AB96–007 and AB96–008. Unpublished report for Cape York Land Council.

Chase, Athol and Peter Sutton 1981. Hunter-gatherers in a rich environment: Aboriginal coastal exploitation in Cape York Peninsula. In A. Keast (ed.), *Ecological Biogeography of Australia* (pp. 1817–52). The Hague: W. Junk.

Chaseling, Wilbur S. 1957. *Yulengor: Nomads of Arnhem Land*. London: The Epworth Press.

Co-ordata Research 1994. Report on Anthropological and Linguistic Research at Weipa 1993–94 for the Napranum Aboriginal Corporation and Quintigan Land Management Aboriginal Corporation. Thuringowa. Unpublished report.

Cribb, R. 1986a. A preliminary report on archaeological findings in Aurukun Shire, western Cape York. *Queensland Archaeological Research* 3:133–58. doi.org/10.25120/qar.3.1986.185

Cribb, R. 1986b. A graphics system for site based anthropological data. *Australian Aboriginal Studies* 1986(2):24–30.

Cribb, R. 1990. The archaeological record. In P. Sutton, D. Martin, J. von Sturmer, R. Cribb and A. Chase (eds), *Aak: Aboriginal Estates and Clans between the Embley and Edward Rivers, Cape York Peninsula*, (pp. 33–7). Unpublished report. Adelaide: South Australian Museum.

Cribb, R., R. Walmbeng, R. Wolmby and C. Taisman 1988. Landscape as cultural artefact: shell mounds and plants in Aurukun, Cape York Peninsula. *Australian Aboriginal Studies* 1988(2):60–73.

Crowley, Terry 1981. The Mpakwithi dialect of Anguthimri. In R.M.W. Dixon and B.J. Blake (eds), *Handbook of Australian Languages Volume 2* (pp. 146–94). Canberra: Australian National University Press. doi.org/10.1075/z.hal2.07cro

Crowley, Terry 1983. Uradhi. In R.M.W. Dixon and B.J. Blake (eds), *Handbook of Australian Languages Volume 3* (pp. 306–428). Canberra: Australian National University Press.

Cruickshank, Joanna and Patricia Grimshaw 2015. 'I had gone to teach but stayed to learn': Geraldine MacKenzie at Aurukun Mission, 1925–1965. *Journal of Australian Studies* 39:54–65. doi.org/10.1080/14443058.2014.988636

Dances at Aurukun, 1964. Film. Director: Ian Dunlop. Sydney: Film Australia.

Dixon, Robert M.W. 1972. *The Dyirbal Language of North Queensland*. Cambridge: Cambridge University Press.

Dixon, Robert M.W. 1980. *The Languages of Australia*. Cambridge: Cambridge University Press.

Dixon, Robert M.W. 2002. *Australian Languages: Their Nature and Development*. Cambridge: Cambridge University Press.

Dozier, Edward 1966. *Hano: A Tewa Indian Community in Arizona*. New York: Holt, Rinehart and Winston. doi.org/10.1525/aa.1966.68.5.02a00500

Dozier, Edward and Ken Hale 1965. Santa Clara Tewa Notes. Unpublished manuscript. University of Arizona.

Elkin, Adolphus P. 1938. *The Australian Aborigines: How to Understand Them*. Sydney: Angus & Robertson.

Everett, Daniel 1996. *Why there are no Clitics: An Alternative Perspective on Pronominal Allomorphy*. Dallas, Texas: University of Texas at Arlington and Summer Institute of Linguistics Publication. doi.org/10.1017/s0022226700228260

Familiar Places: A Film about Aboriginal Ties to Land. 1980. Director: David MacDougall. 53 minutes. Colour. Canberra: Australian Institute of Aboriginal and Torres Strait Islander Studies.

Gaby, Alice R. 2017. *A Grammar of Kuuk Thaayorre*. Berlin: De Gruyter Mouton.

Gilbert, Kevin 1977. *Living Black: Blacks Talk to Kevin Gilbert*. Ringwood, Victoria: Penguin Books.

Godman, Irene 1993. A sketch grammar of Rimanggudinhma: A language of the Princess Charlotte Bay region of Cape York Peninsula. Honours thesis, University of Queensland. doi.org/10.14264/uql.2020.425

Gudschinsky, Sarah 1956. The ABC's of lexicostatistics (glottochronology). *Word* 12:175–210. doi.org/10.1080/00437956.1956.11659599

Gunnerson, Dolores 1974. *The Jicarilla Apaches: A Study in Survival*. DeKalb: Northern Illinois University Press.

Gunnerson, James H. 1979. Southern Athabaskan archeology. In A. Ortiz (ed.), *Handbook of North American Indians, Vol 9, Southwest* (pp. 162–9). Washington: Smithsonian Institution.

Gunnerson, James H., and Dolores A. Gunnerson 1971. Apachean culture: A study in unity and diversity. In K. Basso and M. Opler (eds), *Apachean Culture History and Ethnology* (pp. 7–27). Tucson: University of Arizona.

Hale, Ken 1960. Unpublished field notes, Cape York Peninsula, Queensland.

Hale, Ken. 1964. Classification of the Northern Paman languages, Cape York Peninsula, Australia: A research report. *Oceanic Linguistics* 3:248–265. doi.org/10.2307/3622881

Hale, Ken 1966. Appendix to XXIX: The Paman group of the Pama-Nyungan phylic family. In G.N. O'Grady and C.F. and F.M. Voegelin (eds), *Languages of the World: Indo-Pacific Fascicle 6. Anthropological Linguistics* 8(2):162–97.

Hale, Ken 1976a. Phonological developments in particular Northern Paman languages. In P. Sutton (ed.), *Languages of Cape York* (pp. 7–40). Canberra: Australian Institute of Aboriginal Studies.

Hale, Ken 1976b. Phonological developments in a Northern Paman language: *Uradhi*. In P. Sutton (ed.), *Languages of Cape York* (pp. 41–49). Canberra: Australian Institute of Aboriginal Studies.

Hale, Ken 1976c. Wik reflections of middle Paman phonology. In P. Sutton (ed.), *Languages of Cape York* (pp. 50–60). Canberra: Australian Institute of Aboriginal Studies.

Hale, Ken 1976d. Tya:pukay (Djaabugay). In P. Sutton (ed.), *Languages of Cape York* (pp. 236–42). Canberra: Australian Institute of Aboriginal Studies.

Hale, Ken 1997a. A Linngithigh vocabulary. In D. Tryon and M. Walsh (eds), *Boundary Rider: Essays in Honour of Geoffrey O'Grady* (pp. 209–46). Canberra: Pacific Linguistics.

Hale, Ken 1997b. Linguistic evidence for long-term residence of the Wik-speaking peoples in their present location in Cape York Peninsula: Part I, lexical diversity; Part II, morphosyntax. Appendix 7 to Wik Native Title: Anthropological Overview (by Peter Sutton), submission for The Wik Peoples – Native Title Determination Application QC94/3.

Hale, Ken, Thomas Cox, et al. 1977. Breve Vocabulario del Idioma Pima de Ónavas, University of Arizona. Unpublished manuscript.

Hale, Ken, and Abanel Lacayo 1988. Vocabulario Preliminar del Ulwa (Sumu Meridional), Centro de Investigaciones y Documentación de la Costa Atlántica, y Centro de Ciencia Cognitiva del MIT.

Hale, Ken, and Aquilino Melendez 1994. Materiales para un diccionario del twahka, MIT and Centro de Investigaciones y Documentación de la Costa Atlántica ms.

Hall, Allen 1976a. Methods of negation in Kuuk Thaayorre. In P. Sutton (ed.), *Languages of Cape York* (pp. 299–307). Canberra: Australian Institute of Aboriginal Studies.

Hall, Allen 1976b. Morphological categories of nouns in Kuuk Thaayorre. In P. Sutton (ed.), *Languages of Cape York* (pp. 308–14). Canberra: Australian Institute of Aboriginal Studies.

Halpern, Aaron 1992. Topics in the Placement and Morphology of Clitics. Doctoral dissertation, Stanford University.

Halpern, Aaron, and Arnold M. Zwicky 1996. *Approaching Second: Second Position Clitics and Related Phenomena*. Stanford: CSLI Publications.

Hamilton, Philip, and Lofty Yam 1994. Pakanh Vocabulary, Kowanyama, Qld. Unpublished manuscript.

Harris, Barbara, and Geoffrey N. O'Grady 1976. An analysis of the progressive morpheme in Umpila verbs: a revision of a former attempt. In P. Sutton (ed.), *Languages of Cape York* (pp. 165–212). Canberra: Australian Institute of Aboriginal Studies.

Hattori, Shiro 1953. On the method of glottochronology and the time-depth of proto-Japanese. *Gengo Kenkyu (Journal of the Linguistic Society of Japan)* 22/23:29–77.

Heeres, Jan E. 1899. *The Part Borne by the Dutch in the Discovery of Australia 1606–1765*. London: Luzac.

Helms, Mary 1971. *Asang: Adapations to Culture Contact in a Miskito Community*. Gainesville, Florida: University of Florida Press.

Henderson, John, and David Nash (eds) 2002. *Language in Native Title*. Canberra: Aboriginal Studies Press.

Hiatt, Lester R. 1962. Local organisation among the Australian Aborigines. *Oceania* 32:267–86. doi.org/10.1002/j.1834-4461.1962.tb01782.x

Hiatt, Lester R. 1965. *Kinship and Conflict: A Study of an Aboriginal Community in Northern Arnhem Land*. Canberra: The Australian National University.

Hiatt, Lester R. 1966. The lost horde. *Oceania* 37:81–92. doi.org/10.1002/j.1834-4461.1966.tb01789.x

Hiatt, Lester R. 1968. The magic numbers '25' and '500': determinants of group size in modern and Pleistocene hunters. In R.B. Lee and I. DeVore (eds), *Man the Hunter* (pp. 245–46). Chicago: Aldine Publishing Company.

Hinton, Peter 1963. Report by Mr. P.D. Hinton from Weipa. PMS 815. Australian Institute of Aboriginal and Torres Strait Islander Studies, Canberra.

Hinton, Peter 1964. Outline of Study following Field Work at Weipa, North Queensland. PMS 813. Australian Institute of Aboriginal and Torres Strait Islander Studies, Canberra.

Hodge, Carleton 1970. The linguistic cycle. *Language Sciences* 13:1–7.

Hoijer, Harry 1956. The chronology of the Athapaskan languages. *International Journal of American Linguistics* 22:219–232. doi.org/10.1086/464374

House-opening, The, 1980. Colour film 42 minutes. Directed by Judith Macdougall. Canberra: AIATSIS.

Hymes, Dell 1960. Lexicostatistics so far. *Current Anthropology* 1:3–44. doi.org/10.1086/200074

Izvorski, Roumyana 1995. The syntax of clitics in the history of Bulgarian. Proceedings of *Diachronic Syntax 4, Université du Québec à Montréal, 31 October 1995*.

Jaeggli, Osvaldo 1982. *Topics in Romance Syntax*. Dordrecht: Foris.

Johnson, Steve 1989. Glossary Nganhcara-English (10pp), English-Nganhcara (11pp). Unpublished manuscript.

Jolly, Lesley 1989. *Aghu Tharrnggala*. Honours thesis, University of Queensland.

Keen, Ian 1978. One ceremony, one song: An economy of religious knowledge among the Yolngu of North-East Arnhem Land. PhD thesis, The Australian National University.

Keen, Ian 1994. *Knowledge and Secrecy in an Aboriginal Religion*. Oxford: Clarendon Press.

Keen, Ian 1995. Metaphor and the metalanguage: Groups in Northeast Arnhem Land. *American Ethnologist* 22:502–27. doi.org/10.1525/ae.1995.22.3.02a00030

Keen, Ian 1997. The Western Desert vs the rest: Rethinking the contrast. In F. Merlan, J. Morton and A. Rumsey (eds), *Scholar and Sceptic: Australian Aboriginal Studies in Honour of L.R. Hiatt* (pp. 65–93, 257–66). Canberra: Aboriginal Studies Press.

Kenstowicz, Michael (ed.) 2001. *Ken Hale: A Life in Language*. Cambridge, Massachusetts: The MIT Press.

Kilham, Christine, Mabel Pamulkan, Jennifer Pootchemunka and Topsy Wolmby 1986. *Dictionary and Source-book of the Wik-Mungkan Language*. Darwin: Summer Institute of Linguistics.

Klavans, Judith 1995. *On Clitics and Cliticization*. New York: Garland.

Krzywicki, Ludwik 1934. *Primitive Society and its Vital Statistics*. London: Macmillan.

Lees, Robert 1953. The basis of glottochronology. *Language* 29:113–127.

Loprieno, Antonio 1995. *Ancient Egyptian: A Linguistic Introduction*. Cambridge: Cambridge University Press.

Lourandos, Harry 1997. *Continent of Hunter-Gatherers: New Perspectives in Australian Prehistory*. Cambridge: Cambridge University Press.

MacKenzie, Geraldine 1981. *Aurukun Diary*. Melbourne: The Aldersgate Press.

Martin, David F. 1993. Autonomy and relatedness: an ethnography of Wik people of Aurukun, western Cape York Peninsula. PhD thesis, The Australian National University.

Martin, David F. n.d. Approximate Locations of Clan Estates and Languages Between the Archer and Embley Rivers. Unpublished maps.

Martin, David F., and Bruce F. Martin 2016. Challenging simplistic notions of outstations as manifestations of Aboriginal self-determination: Wik strategic engagement and disengagement over the past four decades. In N. Peterson and F. Myers (eds), *Experiments in Self-determination: Histories of the Outstation Movement in Australia* (pp. 201–28). Canberra: ANU Press. doi.org/10.22459/esd.01.2016.11

Mathews, R.H. 1900. Marriage and descent among the Australian Aborigines. *Journal of the Royal Society of New South Wales* 34:120–35.

McConnel, Ursula H. 1928. Correspondence, Aurukun, to Professor Radcliffe-Brown, Department of Anthropology, University of Sydney. Elkin Papers, University of Sydney.

McConnel, Ursula H. 1930a. The Wik-munkan tribe of Cape York Peninsula, Parts I & II. *Oceania* 1:97–104, 181–205. doi.org/10.1002/j.1834-4461.1930.tb00005.x

McConnel, Ursula H. 1930b. List of local groups of the Wik-munkan tribe. Unpublished manuscript, Elkin Papers, University of Sydney Archives.

McConnel, Ursula H. 1935. Myths of the Wikmunkan and Wiknatara tribes. Bonefish and Bullroarer totems. *Oceania* 6:66–93. doi.org/10.1002/j.1834-4461.1935.tb01686.x

McConnel, Ursula H. 1936. Totemic hero-cults in Cape York Peninsula, Parts I & II. *Oceania* 6:452–77; 7:69–105, 217–19. doi.org/10.1002/j.1834-4461.1936.tb00205.x

McConnel, Ursula H. 1939–40. Social organization of the tribes of Cape York Peninsula, north Queensland, Parts I & II. *Oceania* 10:54–72, 434–55. doi.org/10.1002/j.1834-4461.1939.tb00256.x

McConnel, Ursula H. 1957. *Myths of the Mungkan*. Melbourne: Melbourne University Press.

Meggitt, Mervyn J. 1962. *Desert People: A Study of the Walbiri Aborigines of Central Australia*. Sydney: Angus & Robertson.

Merlan, Francesca 1981. Land, language and social identity in Aboriginal Australia. *Mankind* 13:133–48. doi.org/10.1111/j.1835-9310.1981.tb00716.x

Nash, David 1990. Patrilects of the Warumungu and Warlmanpa and their neighbours. In P. Austin, R.M.W. Dixon, T. Dutton and I. White (eds), *Language and History: Essays in Honour of Luise A. Hercus* (pp. 209–20). Canberra: Pacific Linguistics.

Ngakulmungan Kangka Leman (Language Projects Steering Committee) 1997. *Lardil Dictionary. A Vocabulary of the Language of the Lardil People, Mornington Island, Gulf of Carpentaria, Queensland, with English-Lardil Finder List. Grammatical Preface by Ken Hale*. Gununa (Queensland): Mornington Shire Council.

Nishida, Chiyo 1996. Second position clitic pronouns in Old Spanish and Categorial Grammar. In A. Halpern and A. Zwicky (eds), *Approaching Second: Second Position Clitics and Related Phenomena*. Stanford: CSLI Publications.

O'Grady, Geoffrey 1959–1960. Umpila field notes. Unpublished manuscript.

O'Grady, Geoffrey 1961. Arizona Tewa Notes, Museum of Northern Arizona. Unpublished manuscript.

O'Grady, Geoffrey 1976. Umpila historical phonology. In P. Sutton (ed.), *Languages of Cape York* (pp. 61–7). Canberra: Australian Institute of Aboriginal Studies.

Otero, Carlos-Peregrín 1976. *Evolución y Revolución en Romance II: Mínima Introducción a la Diacronía*. Barcelona; Caracas; México: Seix Barral, Biblioteca Breve.

Peterson, Nicolas, with Jeremy Long 1986. *Australian Territorial Organization: A Band Perspective*. Sydney: Oceania Monographs.

Radcliffe-Brown, Alfred R. 1930. Former numbers and distribution of the Australian Aborigines. In J. Stoneham (ed.), *Official Year Book of the Commonwealth of Australia* (pp. 687–96). Melbourne: Government Printer.

Radcliffe-Brown, Alfred R. 1930–31. The social organization of Australian tribes, Parts I–IV. *Oceania* 1:34–63, 206–46, 322–41, 426–56. doi.org/10.1002/j.1834-4461.1930.tb00003.x

Richter, Arthur 1910. Aurukun Mission Annual Report for 1910, to Bishop La Trobe, Moravian Mission Board, Germany. (Microfilm, Australian Institute of Aboriginal and Torres Strait Islander Studies Canberra.)[1]

Rigsby, Bruce and Diane Hafner 1994. *Lakefield National Park Land Claim, Claim Book*. Cairns: Cape York Land Council.

Rigsby, Bruce and Peter Sutton 1980–82. Speech communities in Aboriginal Australia. *Anthropological Forum* 5:8–23. doi.org/10.1080/00664677.1980.9967332

Rivero, María-Luisa 1983. Parameters in the typology of clitics in Romance, and Old Spanish. University of Ottawa. Unpublished manuscript.

Rizzi, Luigi 1986. On the status of subject clitics in Romance. In O. Jaeggli and C. Silva-Corvalan (eds), *Studies in Romance Linguistics*. Dordrecht: Foris. doi.org/10.1515/9783110878516-025

Roth, Walter E. 1900. A Report to the Under-Secretary, Home Dept., on the Aboriginals of the Pennefather (Coen) River District, and Other Coastal Tribes Occupying the Country between the Batavia & Embley Rivers. Cooktown. Unpublished manuscript. Brisbane: Queensland State Archives, Series 7328 Item 271657.

Roth, Walter E. 1905. Chief Protector of Aborigines Annual Report for 1904. *Queensland Parliamentary Papers, 1905*. Brisbane: Government Printer.

Roth, Walter E. 1910. Social and individual nomenclature. *North Queensland Ethnography Bulletin 18* (*Records of the Australian Museum* 8(1)), Sydney. doi.org/10.3853/j.0067-1975.8.1910.936

---

1   I thank Regina Ganter for providing this translation from the German.

Rumsey, Alan 1993. Language and territoriality in Aboriginal Australia. In Michael Walsh and Colin Yallop (eds), *Language and Culture in Aboriginal Australia* (pp. 191–206). Canberra: Aboriginal Studies Press.

Sapir, Edward 1916. *Time Perspective in Aboriginal American Culture: A Study in Method.* Ottawa: Geological Survey of Canada, Memoir 90 (Anthropological Series, No. 13).

Satterthwaite, Arnold 1960. Rate of morpheme decay in Meccan Arabic, *International Journal of American Linguistics* 26:256–60.

Saxton, Dean, Lucille Saxton and Susie Enos 1983. *Papago/Pima Dictionary.* Tucson, Arizona: University of Arizona Press.

Schebeck, Bernhard (ed. R.M.W. Dixon) 2001. *Dialect and Social Grouping in North East Anheim [i.e. Arnhem] Land.* Munich: Lincom Europa.

Sharp, R. Lauriston 1939. Tribes and totemism in north-east Australia, Parts I & II. *Oceania* 9:254–75,439–461. doi.org/10.1002/j.1834-4461.1939.tb00248.x

[Sheehan, Colin] 2002. Wik Native Title Determination Application QG6001/98. Native Title Connection Unit Review Report on Applicants' Connection Documentation. Unpublished report. Brisbane.

Simmons, Roy T., John J. Graydon and D. Carleton Gajdusek 1958. A blood group genetical survey of Australian Aboriginal children of the Cape York Peninsula. *American Journal of Physical Anthropology* 16:59–77. doi.org/10.1002/ajpa.1330160105

Simpson, Jane, David Nash, Mary Laughren, Peter Austin and Barry Alpher (eds) 2001. *Forty Years On: Ken Hale and Australian Languages.* Canberra: Pacific Linguistics.

Smith, Barry 1989. The Concept 'Community' in Aboriginal Policy and Service Delivery. NADU Occasional Paper 1, North Australia Development Unit. Darwin: Department of Social Security.

Smith, Ian 1986. Language contact and the life or death of Kugu Muminh. In J. Fishman et al. (eds), *The Fergusonian Impact, Vol. 2: Sociolinguistics and the Sociology of Language.* Berlin: Mouton de Gruyter.

Smith, Ian, and Steve Johnson 1985. The syntax of clitic cross-referencing pronouns in Kugu Nganhcara. *Anthropological Linguistics.* Spring:102–11.

Smith, Ian, and Steve Johnson 1986. Sociolinguistic patterns in an unstratified society: The patrilects of Kugu Nganhcara. *Journal of the Atlantic Provinces Linguistic Association* 8:29–43.

Smith, Ian, and Steve Johnson 2000. Kugu Nganhcara. In R.M.W. Dixon and B.J. Blake (eds), *Handbook of Australian Languages, Volume 5* (pp. 355–489). Melbourne: Oxford University Press.

Sommer, Bruce A. 1972. *Kunjen Syntax*. Canberra: Australian Institute of Aboriginal Studies.

Stanner, William E.H. 1965. Aboriginal territorial organization: estate, range, domain and regime. *Oceania* 36:1–25. doi.org/10.1002/j.1834-4461.1965.tb00275.x

Sutton, Peter (ed.) 1976. *Languages of Cape York*. Canberra: Australian Institute of Aboriginal Studies.

Sutton, Peter 1978. Wik: Aboriginal society, territory and language at Cape Keerweer, Cape York Peninsula, Australia. PhD thesis, University of Queensland.

Sutton, Peter 1980. Cause, origin and possession in the Flinders Island language. In B. Rigsby and P. Sutton (eds), *Papers in Australian Linguistics No. 13: Contributions to Australian Linguistics* (pp. 119–43). Canberra: Pacific Linguistics.

Sutton, Peter 1990. The pulsating heart: large scale cultural and demographic processes in Aboriginal Australia. In B. Meehan and N. White (eds), *Hunter-gatherer Demography Past and Present* (pp. 71–80). Sydney: Oceania Monographs.

Sutton, Peter 1991. Language in Aboriginal Australia: social dialects in a geographic idiom. In S. Romaine (ed.) *Language in Australia* (pp. 49–66). Cambridge: Cambridge University Press. doi.org/10.1017/cbo9780511620881.004

Sutton, Peter 1995a. *Wik-Ngathan Dictionary*. Adelaide: Caitlin Press.

Sutton, Peter 1995b. *Country. Aboriginal Boundaries and Land Ownership in Australia*. Canberra: Aboriginal History Monographs.

Sutton, Peter 1995c. Atomism versus collectivism: the problem of group definition in native title cases. In J. Fingleton and J. Finlayson (eds), *Anthropology in the Native Title Era: Proceedings of a Workshop* (pp. 1–10). Canberra: Australian Institute of Aboriginal and Torres Strait Islander Studies.

Sutton, Peter 1996. The robustness of Aboriginal land tenure systems: underlying and proximate customary titles. *Oceania* 67:7–29. doi.org/10.1002/j.1834-4461.1996.tb02569.x

Sutton, Peter 1997a. Wik Native Title: anthropological overview. Affidavit in the Wik Native Title Case, FCA QUD 6001/1998, filed in 2012.

Sutton, Peter 1997b. Materialism, sacred myth and pluralism: competing theories of the origin of Australian languages. In F. Merlan, J. Morton and A. Rumsey (eds), *Scholar and Sceptic: Australian Aboriginal Studies in Honour of L.R. Hiatt* (pp. 211–42, 297–309). Canberra: Aboriginal Studies Press.

Sutton, Peter 2001. Talking language. In J. Simpson, D. Nash, M. Laughren, P. Austin and B. Alpher (eds), *Forty Years On: Ken Hale and Australian Languages* (pp. 453–64). Canberra: Pacific Linguistics.

Sutton, Peter 2003. *Native Title in Australia: An Ethnographic Perspective*. Cambridge: Cambridge University Press.

Sutton, Peter 2010. The logic of Wik camping, north Australia. In Karen Hardy (ed.), *Archaeological Invisibility and Forgotten Knowledge. Conference Proceedings, Łódź, Poland, 5th–7th September 2007* (pp. 91–107). Oxford: Archaeopress (British Archaeological Reports International Series 2183). doi.org/10.30861/9781407307336

Sutton, Peter 2013a. Comment on Denham's *Beyond fictions of closure in Australian Aboriginal Kinship*. *Mathematical Anthropology and Cultural Theory: an International Journal* 5(5):1–5. mathematicalanthropology.org/Pdf/Sutton_MACT0513.pdf

Sutton, Peter 2013b. Cross-comment on Denham's *Beyond fictions of closure in Australian Aboriginal Kinship*. *Mathematical Anthropology and Cultural Theory: an International Journal* 5(6):1–6. mathematicalanthropology.org/Pdf/Sutton2_MACT0513.pdf

Sutton, Peter 2016a. Exploring Australia in the age of the four wheel drive vehicle. In Peter Austin, Harold Koch and Jane Simpson (eds), *Language, Land and Story in Australia: Studies in Honour of Luise Hercus* (pp. 80–101). London: EL Publishing. www.elpublishing.org/PID/2007

Sutton, Peter 2016b. Peret: A Cape York Peninsula outstation 1976–78. In N. Peterson and F. Myers (eds), *Experiments in Self-determination: Histories of the Outstation Movement in Australia* (pp. 229–50). Canberra: ANU Press. doi.org/10.22459/esd.01.2016.12

Sutton, Peter 2017. Records of births and deaths, Aurukun, Cape York Peninsula. Unpublished database.

Sutton, Peter 2019. Unofficial explorers: from Aurukun to Kendall River in 1927. In Gillian Dooley and Danielle Clode (eds), *The First Wave: Exploring Early Coastal Contact History in Australia* (pp. 243–70). Adelaide: Wakefield Press. doi.org/10.1080/1031461x.2020.1784524

Sutton, Peter 2020. Small language survival and large language expansion on a hunter-gatherer continent. In Tom Güldemann, Patrick McConvell and Richard A. Rhodes (eds), *The Language of Hunter-Gatherers* (pp. 356–91). Cambridge: Cambridge University Press. doi.org/10.1017/9781139026208.015

Sutton, Peter, Marcia Langton and John von Sturmer 1991. Kendall River Holding: Report on Aboriginal interests. Unpublished report. For Aurukun Community Incorporated.

Sutton, Peter, David Martin and John von Sturmer 1997. Supplementary site report. Appendix 3 of The Wik Peoples Native Title Determination Application QC94/3. Unpublished report, detailing sites in 37 Wik estates.

Sutton, Peter, David Martin, John von Sturmer, Roger Cribb and Athol Chase 1990. *Aak: Aboriginal Estates and Clans between the Embley and Edward Rivers, Cape York Peninsula*. Unpublished report. Adelaide: South Australian Museum.

Sutton, Peter, and Arthur B. Palmer 1980. *Daly River (Malak Malak) Land Claim*. Darwin: Northern Land Council.

Sutton, Peter and Bruce Rigsby 1982. People with 'politicks': management of land and personnel on Australia's Cape York Peninsula. In N. Williams and E. Hunn (eds), *Resource Managers: North American and Australian Hunter-gatherers* (pp. 155–71). Boulder, Colorado: Westview Press for AAAS. doi.org/10.4324/9780429304569-8

Sutton, Peter, Bruce Rigsby and Athol Chase 1993. Traditional groups of the Princess Charlotte Bay region. Appendix 2. In P. Sutton, Flinders Islands & Melville National Parks Land Claim. Unpublished report. Cairns: Cape York Land Council.

Swadesh, Morris 1954. Perspectives and problems of Amerindian comparative linguistics. *Word* 10:306–32. doi.org/10.1080/00437956.1954.11659530

Taylor, John C. 1984. Of acts and axes. An ethnography of socio- cultural change in an Aboriginal community, Cape York Peninsula. PhD thesis, James Cook University of North Queensland.

Thompson, David A. 1976. A phonology of Kuuku-Ya'u. In P. Sutton (ed.), *Languages of Cape York* (pp. 213–35). Canberra: Australian Institute of Aboriginal Studies.

Thomson, Donald F. 1933. Field Notes, Museum of Victoria, Donald Thomson Collection.

Thomson, Donald F. 1936. Fatherhood in the Wik Monkan tribe. *American Anthropologist* 38:374–93. doi.org/10.1525/aa.1936.38.3.02a00030

Thomson, Donald F. 1939. The seasonal factor in human culture. *Proceedings of the Prehistoric Society* 5:209–21.

Thomson, Donald F. 1946. Names and naming in the Wik Mongkan tribe. *Journal of the Royal Anthropological Institute* 76:157–67.

Thomson, Donald F. 1972. *Kinship and Behaviour in North Queensland* (ed. H.W. Scheffler), Canberra: Australian Institute of Aboriginal Studies.

Tindale, Norman B. 1940. Distribution of Australian aboriginal tribes: A field survey. *Transactions of the Royal Society of South Australia* 64:140–231 and map.

Tindale, Norman B. 1941. Survey of the half-caste problem in South Australia. *Proceedings of the Royal Geographical Society of Australasia, South Australia Branch* 42:66–161.

Tindale, Norman B. 1963. MS. Journal of a Visit to the Gulf of Carpentaria. Adelaide: South Australian Museum Anthropology Archives.

Tindale, Norman B. 1974. *Aboriginal Tribes of Australia. Their Terrain, Environmental Controls, Distribution, Limits, and Proper Names*. Berkeley: University of California Press.

Verstraete, Jean-Christophe, and Bruce Rigsby 2015. *A Grammar and Lexicon of Yintyingka*. Berlin: De Gruyter Mouton.

von Sturmer [Smith], Diane 1980. Rights in nurturing: The social relations of child-bearing and rearing amongst the *Kugu-Nganychara*, western Cape York Peninsula, Australia. MA thesis, The Australian National University.

von Sturmer, John R. 1978 (submitted 1979). The Wik region: Economy, territoriality and totemism in western Cape York Peninsula, north Queensland. PhD thesis, University of Queensland.

Walsh, Michael (comp.) 1981–83. Map 23: Northern Australia. In S.A. Wurm and S. Hattori (and T. Baumann, cartography), *Language Atlas of the Pacific Area. Part 1: New Guinea area, Oceania, Australia*. Canberra: Pacific Linguistics for the Australian Academy of the Humanities in collaboration with the Japan Academy.

Warner, W. Lloyd 1937 [1958]. *A Black Civilization. A Study of an Australian Tribe*. Chicago: Harper & Brothers.

Wharton, Geoff 2000. MacKenzie, William Frederick (Bill) (1897–1972). In J. Ritchie and D. Langmore (eds), *Australian Dictionary of Biography Volume 15, 1940–1980, Kem–Pie*. Melbourne: Melbourne University Press.

Wik vs Queensland. Documentary film directed by Dean Gibson, Bacon Factory Films, Sydney.

Zwicky, Arnold 1977. *On Clitics*. Bloomington, Indiana: Indiana University Linguistics Club.

Zwicky, Arnold, and Geoffrey Pullum 1983. Cliticization vs. inflection: English n't. *Language* 59:502–13. doi.org/10.2307/413900

Indexes

Topic index

Aak Puul Ngantam, 14
Aak report, 6–7, 34
Aayk estate, 13
Aboriginal and Torres Strait Islander Heritage Protection Act 1984, 7
adoption, 33, 37, 66–67
apical ancestor. *See* descent systems

bands. *See* camps
'Big Names'. *See* clan totems
bilaterality. *See* descent systems
'bottomside' / 'topside'. *See* coast/hinterland division
boundaries, 44, 80
    lack of, 222
British sovereignty, 3, 9, 10
burial. *See* death
'bush names'. *See* language, naming practices

camps, 29–36
    bands, 29–36
    fluid nature of, 29, 30
    foraging groups, 30, 33
    outstations, 29, 33, 34, 35, 50
ceremonies, 35, 46, 49
    initiation, 49
clans, 25–29
    and 'hordes', 89
    and language, 5, 29, 43, 51, 57, 59, 63, 101, 102

clan estates, 26, 43, 44, 102
clan extinction, 42, 44, 61, 86, 87
clan membership/structure, 27, 29, 34, 41, 45, 46, 48, 60, 61, 67, 69
clan names, 28, 79
clan size, 29, 45, 65, 86, 90–91
clan totemic names, 25, 37
clan totems, 25, 27, 28, 49, 59
core land holders, 27, 35
    enduring nature of, 33, 35
    See also land tenure system
classical period
    classical estates, 43
    classical system, 4, 25–76
    classical times, 25, 69, 90
coast/hinterland division, 49, 50, 80, 81, 82, 84, 85, 98, 99,
cognates. *See* lexical structure, lexical sharing
common ancestor. *See* descent systems
communal vs individual ownership, 39
community, 50–51
company land, 39, 40
'country', 4, 9, 23, 25, 28, 33, 36, 61, 103
    and inheritance, 66, 67, 68
    and language, 38, 39–41, 91, 221–222
    country-holding unit, 25, 28
    'full country', 39, 40

cremation. *See* death
cremation ceremonies. *See* ceremonies
custodial relationship, 38, 44, 66, 78, 118, 125
customary law, 39, 59, 61

de facto partnerships. *See* marriage
death, 33, 35, 40, 44, 45, 46, 47, 65, 87, 97
depopulation. *See* death
descent systems
    apical ancestors, 27
    bilaterality, 95
    cognatic descent, 5, 67, 71
    common ancestor, 27, 147, 151
    filiative descent, 5
    matrilineality, 71
    patriclans, 26, 28, 65, 66
    patrifiliation, 26, 67
    patrilineality, 25, 26, 29, 37, 40, 59, 68, 86, 95
    serial patrifiliation, 26
    unilineal descent, 67
dialect
    dialect chain, 78, 129, 155
    dialect naming, 28, 59, 60, 78, 97, 111, 139
    dialectal differences, 3, 4, 59, 60, 91
    'dialectal tribes'. *See* tribes
discontinuous distribution (of people/languages), 178
diversity, linguistic, 97–99, 134–152, 154, 177–180, 200, 215, 218–220
dogs, 25, 68

early population structure, 50, 77, 86–92, 97–103, 144, 147, 154
endonyms. *See* language, naming practices
English names. *See* language, naming practices
ergativity, 183, 192, 195, 200

estates
    descent-based claims, 27, 28, 29, 35, 37, 44
    estate-holding descent group, 4–5, 22, 61
    estate membership, 25, 26, 36, 41–46, 62, 87, 97
    extinction of an estate-owning clan, 65
exogamy, linguistic, 94
exogenous naming. *See* language, naming practices
exonyms, *See* language, naming practices
extinction
    of clans, 42, 44, 65, 90, 121, 125, 127
    of languages, 119, 214
    of patrilines, 42, 61–62

Familiar Places (film), 6, 32
financial independence, 71
foraging groups. *See* camps
'full country'. *See* 'country'

gerontocracy, 75
Gove land claim case, 7, 8
grammatical irregularities, 189, 193

'having the same name'. *See* language, naming practices
Holocene, 80, 81, 98
'horde', 29, 37, 86
households. *See* camps
House-Opening (film), 49

initiation. *See* ceremonies

lack of autogenous name. *See* language, naming practices
land tenure system, 33, 34, 36, 38–41, 59, 222
    tenurial rights, 35, 51, 67, 76
    tenurial units, 51

language
- change, 133, 141, 142, 150, 156, 180, 210, 215
- diversity, 81, 97–99, 134–157, 177–220
- group. *See* tribes
- identity, 4, 5, 6, 59, 90
- in situ language development, 13, 134, 142, 152, 164, 177, 180, 219
- mutual intelligibility, 3, 82, 89, 91, 99, 129
- naming practices, 5, 21, 22, 23, 28, 57, 59, 60, 62, 68, 94
- ownership, 4–6, 22, 86
- patrilects, 60, 174
- shift, 3, 64, 90, 97, 134
- stability, 128, 134, 144–148, 151–152

'Language Eat'. *See* language, naming practices
'Language Go'. *See* language, naming practices
lexical structure,
- lexical change, 150, 156
- lexical diversity, 134, 140, 150, 153, 154, 156
- lexical features, 28
- lexical replacement, 133, 136–138, 142, 148–151, 154, 156
- lexical sharing, 78, 99, 129, 134, 138–176

lingua franca, 23, 26, 59, 62, 64, 90, 98
linguistic areas (*Sprachbünde*), 98

Mabo v Queensland (No 2), 7
marriage, 43, 48, 64, 68, 71, 74–76, 97, 98
- marriage restrictions, 41
matrilineality. *See* descent systems
migration, 134, 146, 147, 154, 157, 220

Milirrpum v Nabalco, 7
- *See also* Gove land claim case
multilingualism, 77, 82, 97, 142
mutual intelligibility. *See* language, mutual intelligibility

Native Title Act 1993, 6, 61

outstations, 29, 33, 34, 35, 39, 45, 46
ownership of a language variety. *See* language, ownership

pastoral leases, 7
patriclans. *See* descent systems
patriclan country, 66
patrilineal descent groups. *See* descent systems
patrilineality. *See* descent systems
Pleistocene, 80, 81, 98
population
- density, 44
- distribution, 50
- estimates, 88, 90, 91, 94
- reconstruction, 85, 86, 87, 89–92, 95

possession (linguistic), 36, 38, 40
- *See also* language, ownership
post-colonial development, 4, 67

rainfall, 34, 96
respect forms and respect relationships, 40, 149

'saltwater'/'freshwater'. *See* coast/hinterland division
sedentisation, 77, 95, 96
serial patrifiliation. *See* descent systems
siblings, 25, 27, 40, 41, 68
spelling principles, 104, 109, 181
spirit-images, 45, 46
split ergative pronouns. *See* ergativity
subgrouping (linguistic), 78, 111, 126, 145, 153, 177, 219
surnames (and descent), 41, 68–76

'talking language', 22
time depth (of linguistic groupings), 128, 137, 148–157, 188–189, 215–220
totems
    totemic ancestors, 37
    totemic centres, 37, 39, 103
    totemic clans, 25–29, 49
    totemic names, 25, 35, 37
Traditional Owners, 5, 41

tribes, 8, 28, 51–60, 111
    'dialectal tribes', 4, 28
    'tribal land', 39

vocabulary change. *See* lexical structure, lexical change

Wik Peoples v The State of Queensland, 7

Languages Index

Bold entries indicate map references

Adithinngithigh, 78, 79, 120, 128
Aghu Tharrnggala, 206, 207, 209, 210, 213
Alngith, 19, 43, **58**, 65, 69 78. 105, 107, 108, 109, 110, 115, 117, 122
Anathangayth, 79, 106, 115, 116, 127
Andjingith, 57, **58**, 79, 105, 107, 109, 110, 122–123, 124
Arrithinngithigh, 78, 104, 108, 119, 120, 128
Awngthim, **58**, 79, 108, 113, 114, 117, 121
Aya-Pakanh. *See* Pakanh(u)
Ayapathu. *See* Pakanh(u)
Aya-Pathu. *See* Pakanh(u)

Barkendji, 95

Cape York Creole, 3, 109
Cape York Peninsula English, 39

Dyirbal, **146**, 146–147

English, 3, 22, 33, 38, 39, 42, 454, 47, 73

Flinders Island Language, 208

Guugu-Yimidhirr, 3, 26

Kaanju, 142, 180, 203, 211
Kaanju-Umpila-Ya'u/Kaanju-Ya'u-Umpila, 135, 179, 211
Kamilaroi, 95
Kugu Muminh [Hale], 17, 57, **58**, 83, 84, 128–129, 179, 200
Kugu Mu'inh, 28, **58**, 83, 84, 99, 129
Kugu Ngancharra, 4, 40, 59, 82–87, 99, 135, 140, 178
Kugu Nganhcara [Hale], **58**, 174–176, 199–202, 205, 214, 219
Kugu Nganhcarra. *See* Kugu Ngancharra
Kug-Uwanh, 45, 128, 129
Kuku-Warra, 62
Kuku-Yalanji, 26
Kunjen, 135, 206, 207, 209, 210, 213
Kuuk Thaayorre, 98, 137, 157, 179, 180, 203, 204–205, 206, 211
Kuuku-Ya'u, 180, 203
Kuuk-Yala, 125–126

INDEXES

Lamalama, 62, 103
Latumngith, 79, 105, 107, 109, 110, 118
Linngithigh, 17, 43, **58**, 78, 106, 108, 121–122, 205, 213

Malak Malak, 5
Mamangathi. *See* Awngthim
Mamngayth. *See* Awngthim
Mbiywom, 19, 57, **58**, 63, 78, 89, 102, 104–108, 111, 126–127

Ndra'ngith, 105, 107, 108, 109, 110, 121–122
Ndrrangith, 78, 79, 114
Ndrwa'angathi, 107, 108, 1110, 113–114
Ndwa'ngith, **56**, 79, 110, 114
Nggoth, 63, 118, 130
Ngkoth, 19, **58**, 78, 79, 102, 106–110, 115, 118–119
Nguungk Chiiynchiiyn ('Bushrat Clan Dialect'), 28, 60
Nguungk Piith ('Grassbird Clan Dialect'), 28
Ngwathangathi, 115

Pakanh(u), 80, 90, 103, 129, 136, 138, 173–174
Pakanha. *See* Pakanh(u)
Pama-Nyungan, 10, 210, 219
proto-Paman, 26, 137, 138, 209

Rimanggudinhma, 209, 210, 213

Southern Paman, 136, 143–145, 210, 213

Thanikwithi, 105, 106, 107, 108, 110, 113
Thyanngayth, **58**, 778, 105, 106, 108, 113
Trotj, **58**, 78. 106, 109, 119, 126, 127

Umpila, **58**, 135, 142, 171–172, 179, 180, 203, 211
Uuku Umpithamu, 80

Wik-Alken/Wik-Elkenh, **58**, 81, 82, 84, 99, 124, 128, 129,
Wik Chiiynchiiyn, 60
Wik-Elken, 39, 42, **58**, 81, 84, 123, 125, 128, 129
Wik-Elkenh, 81, 82, 84, 99
Wik-Ep, 17, **58**, 82, 84, 128, 129
Wik Ep [Hale], 135, 178
Wik-Iiyanh, 28, 45, **58**, 60, 90, 128, 129
Wik-Iyanh, 80, 81, 83, 84, 89, 90, 91, 99
Wik Korr', 60
Wik-Me'enh, 17, 28, 57, 72, 77, 84, 128, 129, 135, 178
Wik-Me'nh, **58**, 181–194, 214, 219
Wik-Mungkan, 3, 26, 62, 65, 84–103, 128–129, 181–182, 191–199, 213, 219
Wik-Ngathan, 27, 38–40, **58**, 81–84, 128–129, 194–199, 209–214, 219
Wik-Ngatharr, **58**, 81, 128, 194–199, 212, 214, 219
Wik-Ngencherr, *See* Kugu Ngancharra
Wik-Ompom. *See* Mbiywom
Wik-Paach, 124
Wik Paach [Hale], 79
Wik-Thint, 124
Wik-Way, 44, 47, 63–65, 77–79, 97–98, 102, 104–111
Winda-Winda, 64, 96, 106, 109–111, 117
Wiradjuri, 95
Wongaibon, 95

Yidiny, 210
Yiithuwarra, 62
Yintyingka, 26
Yir-Yoront, 143, 208, 209, 211, 213

Persons/Institutions/Groups Index

Adams, John, 6, 14
AIATSIS, 10
Ampeybegan (surname), 43, 407
Apelech (ceremony name), 48, 49
Aurukun Presbyterian Mission, 9, 11, 13, 17–19, 30–31, 63–64, 90, 102
Ayapathu people, 80, 103, 129, 299

Berndt, R.M. and C.H. Berndt, 92
Birdsell, Joseph, 92–96, 111
Blowhard family, 19, 69, 114, 118, 122
Bowenda (surname), 27, 43, 67, 116

Cape York Land Council, 9, 14
Carnie, 8
Chase, Athol Kennedy, 6, 11
Comalco, 7
Cribb, Roger Llewellyn Dunmore, 6, 11

Dead Body Language (clan name), 44
Dick, Arthur, 19, 117
Dixon, R.M.W., 58, 92

Ebsworth Lawyers, 9
Edward (clan name), 69
Eundatumweakin, Bob-Wallace, 68–69

Fitzgerald, James, 9
Fruit family, 69, 116, 127

Gajdusek, Daniel Carleton, 107, 112–115, 118–121, 122–124, 126
George family, 69, 116, 117, 119, 127

Gothachalkenin, Eembinpawn (Betty), 69
Gothachalkenin family, 68, 69
Gothachalkenin, Rupert, 69

Hall, Robert, 19
Hector, 12, 19
Henry, Jim, 17
Hercus, Luise, 9
Hiatt, L.R., 51, 93
Hunter, Philip, 6, 14

Jingle family, 69, 113
John family, 69, 116, 127

Kaantju people, 98, 106
Karntin, Jack Spear, 32
Keepas, 19
Kepple (clan name), 69, 127
Kerindun, Fred, 17, 117, 123
Kerindun, Sam, 17, 19, 20, 122
Key-elp (ceremony name). *See* Puch
Koonutta (clan name), 69
Koowarta, John, 48
Koowartas (clan name), 42, 48
Kugu people, 4, 14
Kuuchenm (environmental nickname of people), 45

Lamalama people, 62
Landis (surname), 68, 69

MacKenzie, Geraldine, 68
MacKenzie, William, 18, 20, 31, 32, 68, 71–72, 74, 75–76
Marbendinar, Joe, 17
Mark, Alice, 115, 116
Mark, Andrew, 19
Martin, David Fernandes, 6, 11, 34

Matthew family, 69, 122
Maymangkem (environmental nickname of people), 30, 31
McCarthy, Frederick, 18
McConnel, Ursula Hope, 11, 18, 20, 26, 37, 42, 45, 78, 87–91, 106, 109, 110
Merlan, Francesca, 6
Mimpanja (surname), 44
Moreton, Frank, 19
Motton (surname), 19, 119, 127
Mumpithamu (clan name), 80
Murngin, 95

Ngakapoorgum (surname), 12, 17, 44
Ngakyunkwokka (surname), 41
Ngallametta (surname), 44
Ngallapoorgum (surname), 44

Owokran (surname), 66, 69, 123, 125. *See also* Walmbeng family

Pearson, Noel, 14
Peemuggina (surname), (cover photograph), 20, 22, 28, 69
Peinkinna (surname), 66, 123, 125
Pootchemunka (surname), 41, 69
Porter, Frank, 69
Presbyterian Church. *See* Uniting Church
Puch (ceremony name), 48, 49

Radcliffe-Brown, A.R., 37, 89, 92
Rumsey, Alan, 6

Sapir, Edward, 148
Sheehan, Colin, 10
Shivirri (clan name), 48
Shortjoe family, 69
Smith, Barry, 50

Taylor, John Charles, 6, 11, 14

Thaayorre people, 59, 63
Thomson, Donald, 18, 20, 26, 36–37, 68, 72, 104–106
Tictic, 19
Tindale, Norman, 4–5, 92–93, 95–96, 110–111

Uniting Church, 74

von Sturmer, John Richard, 6, 11, 14, 26, 40

Walmbeng family, 66, 123
Wanam (ceremony name), 48, 49
Weipa Mission, 63, 102, 109, 115, 116, 118, 122
Wikmunea (surname), 28
Wildfellow (surname) 68, 69
Willie, 19
Winchanam (ceremony name), 48, 49
Winda-Winda people, 96, 109, 110, 111, 117
Wolmby, Morrison, (cover photograph)
Wolmby (surname), 20, 60, 66, 123
Woolla (surname), 69, 123
Wunchum (surname), 44

Yankunytjatjara people, 74
Yantumba (surname), 44, 69
Yunkaporta (surname), 60, 69

Places Index

Albatross Bay, 44, 101, 102, 105, 107, 108, 113, 117, 119
Archer River, 42, 47–49, 63, 77, 98, 112
Arnhem Land, 51, 93, 95, 221

Balurga Creek. *See* Christmas Creek
Beagle Camp, 44
Bentinck Island, 34, 67
Big Lake, 30, 42, 123
Boulia, 95
Breakfast Creek, 48

Cape Keerweer, 11, 13, 30, 31, 47, 66, 124
Central Australia, 74
Christmas Creek, 48, 49
Coen, 4, 59, 72

Daly River, 95, 96, 111
Darwin, 111

Edward River, 1, 4, 28, 48, 59, 63, 80, 87, 88, 90, 98, 101, 128
Eeremangk, 31, 38, 47
Embley River, 43, 47, 48, 59, 63, 64, 102, 106, 107, 114, 116, 118, 120, 122, 126
Errimangk. *See* Eeremangk

Great Dividing Range, 81, 103
Groote Eylandt, 34
Gulf of Carpentaria, 81

Hersey Creek. *See* Thuuk (Snake) River
Hey River, 102, 110, 115, 118, 120, 121, 122
Holroyd River, 31, 33, 48, 49, 103, 128

Iincheng Creek. *See* Punth Iincheng
Ikeleth, 63, 66, 102, 123

Jackin Creek, 63

Kencherrang, 30, 31, 47
Kendall River, 14, 42, 48, 99, 128
Kirke River, 41, 42, 47, 64, 97
Knox River ['Errimunka'], 31, 38, 46, 47, 48, 49, 128
Kokialah Creek, 63, 102, 105, 125, 126

Lake Eyre, 88, 93
Love River, 45, 47, 64, 97, 128

Mapoon, 63, 96, 101, 102, 106, 109, 122
Meripah, 102
Mission River, 96, 104–111, 112–127
Moonkan Creek, 102
Myall Creek, 63, 102, 115, 119, 126

New South Wales, 95
Nicholson River, 67
Norman River, 47, 121, 122, 123

Old Mapoon, 101
Oony-aw, 30, 38, 47
Ornyawa Lagoons, 38
Oyenten, 102

Palm Island, 69, 121
Peret Outstation, 11
Pilbara, 89
Pormpuraaw, 4, 34, 50, 59, 63, 101
Port Stewart, 59, 103
Princess Charlotte Bay, 80, 102, 103
Punth Iincheng, 47

Rokeby, 63, 87, 102
Running Creek, 42, 103

Small Lake, 42, 123

Thoekel, 47, 66
Thukali. *See* Thoekel
Thuuk (Snake) River, 44, 48, 49
Ti Tree, 30, 31, 32, 33, 47
Tompaten Creek, 47, 48, 125
Townsville, 69

Uthuk Aweyn, 30, 42, 67
Uthuk Eelen, 42, 67, 123

Ward River, 47, 63, 66, 102, 109, 122, 123
Watha-nhiin Outstation. *See* Uthuk Eelen
Watson River, 47, 63, 102
Weipa, 4, 64, 65
Weipa Peninsula, 43, 77, 116
Western Desert, 5, 21, 51
Wik-Way area, 44, 47, 63, 77, 80, 96, 98, 102, 118

Yonka River. *See* Yu'engk
Yu'engk, 30, 31, 38, 47

www.ingramcontent.com/pod-product-compliance
Lightning Source LLC
Chambersburg PA
CBHW040338300426
44113CB00028B/2733